Constitutional Reform in California

Constitutional Reform in California:
Making State Government More Effective and Responsive

Bruce E. Cain and Roger G. Noll
Editors

1995
Institute of Governmental Studies Press
University of California, Berkeley

©1995 by the Regents of the University of California. All rights reserved.
Printed in the United States of America.

Library of Congress Cataloging-In-Publication Data

Constitutional reform in California : making state government more effective and responsive / edited by Bruce E. Cain and Roger G. Noll.
p. cm.
Includes bibliographical references.
ISBN 0-87772-365-6
1. California--Politics and government--1951- 2. California--Constitutional history.
I. Cain, Bruce E. II. Noll, Roger G.
JK8716.C65 1995
328.794'07042—dc20 95-38514
CIP

CONTENTS

Introduction 1
Bruce E. Cain and Roger G. Noll

I. OVERVIEW

Principles of State Constitutional Design 9
Bruce E. Cain and Roger G. Noll

The Role of State Constitutions in a Federal System 31
Joseph R. Grodin

The Challenge of State Constitutions 45
Robert C. Post

II. EXECUTIVE AND JUDICIAL ORGANIZATION

Executive Organization: Responsiveness vs. Expertise and Flexibility 57
Roger G . Noll

Administrative Law and the California Constitution 87
Michael Asimow

An Effective California Judicial System for the 21st Century 107
Harry N. Scheiber and Charles Ruhlin

III. LEGISLATIVE ORGANIZATION

Reforming Representation in California: Checks and Balances without Gridlock 129
Kathleen Bawn

Creating an Accountable Legislature: The Parliamentary Option for California Government 163
Bruce E. Cain and Nathaniel Persily

A House Discarded? Evaluating the Case for a Unicameral California Legislature 195
David W. Brady and Brian J. Gaines

Terms of Office, Legislative Structure, and Collective Incentives 239
Linda R. Cohen

IV. INITIATIVE REFORM

Constitutional Change: Is It Too Easy to Amend our State Constitution? 265
Bruce E. Cain, Sara Ferejohn, Margarita Najar, and Mary Walther

Reforming the California Initiative Process: A Proposal to Increase Flexibility and Legislative Accountability 291
Elisabeth R. Gerber

Reforming the Initiative Process 313
John Ferejohn

V. FISCAL ORGANIZATION

Options for Reforming the California State Budget Process 329
John W. Ellwood and Mary Sprague

Putting the State Back into State Government: The Constitution and the Budget 353
Mathew D. McCubbins

Constitutional Limitations on Indebtedness: The Case of California 377
D. Roderick Kiewiet

VI. LOCAL GOVERNMENT

State Supremacy, Local Sovereignty: Reconstructing State/Local Relations Under the California Constitution — 401
Daniel B. Rodriguez

California Fiscal Federalism: A School Finance Perspective — 431
Daniel L. Rubinfeld

VII. RESOURCE MANAGEMENT

Real Property and Direct Democracy in California — 457
Margaret Jane Radin and Brendan P. Cullen

Environmental Policy and the State Constitution: The Role for Substantive Policy Guidance — 473
Barton H. Thompson, Jr.

Appendix — 497

About the Authors — 507

Introduction

Bruce E. Cain
Roger G. Noll

In 1994, the governor of California and the state legislature created a commission to propose revisions to the California state constitution. This action was the culmination of a long period of growing dissatisfaction with the system of governance in California. For many years prior to the appointment of the commission, Californians resorted to the ballot initiative to enact a string of reforms in the structure and process of government. Important examples are the limitations on local government taxing powers (1978), restrictions on state government spending (1979), creation of an elected insurance commissioner (1988), and term limits for state legislative offices combined with reductions in legislative agencies and staff (1990).

The effect of these and other initiatives has been to reduce dramatically the power of elected officials to make policy and to allocate fiscal resources. Citizens, unhappy with the performance of state government, have increasingly made these decisions themselves through the initiative process. But reform through initiative created its own problems, and in some cases the cure arguably has been as bad as the disease.

In 1993, a group of public policy scholars in California universities formed an informal group to investigate the relationship between the structure of the state constitution and the performance of state and local government. The group was selected on the basis of the expertise of the members, not on the basis of partisanship nor ideology. Among the group are conservatives and liberals, Democrats and Republicans. The objective has been to determine whether research in economics, law, and political science could provide useful insights about revising the constitution that would have some chance of winning widespread public support. Unexpectedly and fortuitously, the Constitution Revision Commission was created roughly in the middle of this project, giving us the opportunity to engage in much productive conversation with the members of the commission and public figures in the state who are interested in the commission's progress. The highlight of this interaction was a three-day conference in June 1995, when the research team, several members of the Commission, and nearly 100 other scholars, members of citizens groups, and media representatives met to discuss a broad spectrum of issues pertaining to the California constitution.

This book is the product of our two-year research project. Although we have enjoyed considerable productive exchange with the commission and its staff, and have deliberately timed the publication of the book to coincide with the release of the commission's report and recommendations, our project is completely independent. Collectively, the research team defined the issues to be addressed, and the authors are individually responsible for the analysis and policy proposals in their essays.

Although the essays cover a broad range of topics (far broader than the scope of public debate to date), several common themes emerge from them. The first is that the overriding problem in contemporary American government, whether at the local, state, or federal level, is the perception that government is unresponsive to citizens. The extensive use of the initiative in California reflects this frustration. Citizens are willing to support sometimes quite radical and often poorly crafted initiative proposals simply because they perceive the existing system to be so far from the ideal. Thus, many of the chapters deal with why the existing system is, or gives the appearance of being, unresponsive, and how matters could be changed through constitutional reform.

Alongside the theme of responsiveness is the parallel notion that most of us seek aims other than immediate responsiveness in government, and that these have probably received insufficient attention in the debate about the unresponsiveness of government. Among these other objectives are the desire to place limits on the extent to which electoral winners can inflict costs on the losers, the desire to give public officials enough flexibility in day-to-day decisions to respond to crises and to improve the management of the government, and the desire to allow government decisions to be informed by relevant expertise.

Much of the content of this book is addressed to identifying ways to make government more responsive without sacrificing its efficiency, equity, and flexibility. The primary means by which Californians have sought to assure responsiveness is direct democracy: enhancing the role of citizen votes on policies (initiative and referendum) and regulating the election of candidates for office (recalls, term limits, numerous elective offices). But there are good reasons to believe that the existing system does not really produce responsiveness and that it makes government far less flexible and efficient than it otherwise would be.

The objective of efficient, flexible government requires giving considerable authority to government officials. The problem of designing a governmental system is how to induce these officials to exercise their authority in a responsive manner. Stripping them of the authority by resorting to direct democracy to make important policy decisions obviously is not a solution to this problem but simply an alternative way to ensure responsiveness. Moreover, it is a costly way, for citizens cannot run the government on a day-to-day basis, cannot be expected to have expertise in management and finance issues that are a crucial part of effective governance, and cannot sensibly make informed decisions about numerous, frequent ballot measures.

Some of the ideas that emerge in this book about how to make elected officials more responsive are obvious, but others are flatly counterintuitive. On the obvious side is the notion that if the present state legislature is to be retained, the number of legislators should be larger so that citizens are more likely at least to know who represents them, and probably should be unicameral to maximize the representativeness arising from a given total number of state legislators. On the inobvious side is the observation that a very long list of separate elective executive offices, such as in California, actually makes the executive branch less responsive because it fragments responsibility, diffuses accountability, and places some policy matters in the hands of officials who are elected in almost invisible campaigns in which most citizens have no idea who they are or what they stand for.

Whereas not all participants in this project subscribe to every reform proposal that is contained in the book, we find it informative to amalgamate some of the reform proposals in various chapters to present a coherent picture of a new structure of California governance.

The new system would not eliminate the initiative and referendum, but it would change it dramatically. Constitutional changes would require a supermajority vote of the electorate in two consecutive elections. Initiative and referendum statutes would be secure only for a sufficient number of years to gain experience with them. After a few years, they would have to be reenacted by either the legislators or the voters. And, the legislature would have the power to amend initiative statutes before they appear on the ballot with the consent of the proposer, or in any case a few years after they are passed.

The state legislature would be unicameral, with 120 members elected from geographic districts and 120 additional members elected from party lists by proportional representation, 30 each from four large, geographic regions in the state. Any slate of candidates that could obtain five percent of the vote in any of the four regions would be given at least one seat, thereby assuring the representation of affinity groups that now regard themselves as excluded from the system. Half of the legislature would be elected every two years for four-year terms, with a term limit of 12 years. Supermajority requirements for budget bills in the legislature would be eliminated to facilitate the development of budgets on time. Changes in tax laws that caused more than a trivial change in total revenues and changes in total state debt ceilings would require approval in a referendum.

The only statewide elective offices would be a governor-lt. governor slate, the controller acting as the watchdog auditor for financial management of both state and local governments, and the attorney general acting as a similar watchdog for law enforcement. All other elective offices would be abolished and merged into existing executive agencies, or converted to appointive offices in the governor's cabinet.

The new system would not eliminate direct democracy, but it is designed to cause citizens to want to use it less frequently. The executive changes would make the governor responsible for the implementation of all policies, and clarify responsibilities, especially in education, where the present structure is far too complex to be workable.

Local government relations with the state would be more sharply defined. The state would be responsible for setting minimum service standards for core public services, but would have to pay for this level of service from state funds.

These reform proposals attempt to produce responsiveness in more appropriate ways than the present system. First, citizens would regularly vote on large, general issues, such as the size of state government. Second, citizens would have two avenues for representation: geographic representatives in districts that are less than half the size of congressional districts, and regional representation through proportional representation for groups of citizens whose commonality is not geographical. Presumably this would balance the actions that would increase the discretionary authority of the legislature with respect to ballot measures. Third, citizens would know more clearly who is responsible for implementing state policy by clarifying and strengthening the role of governor.

This structure provides an interesting combination of many past reforms and pending proposals from all parts of the political spectrum. We believe that it represents at least an interesting point of departure for debate about the future course of governance in California.

I. OVERVIEW

Principles of State Constitutional Design

Bruce E. Cain
Roger G. Noll

The role of state constitutions in a federal system is ambiguous. Indeed, conventional wisdom holds that truly federal systems are inherently unstable, fated either to centralize into a nation in which the highest level of government possesses all authority or to fragment into a weak confederation of largely autonomous lower governments. In practice, the U.S. federal system, while swinging back and forth in the relative powers of federal, state, and local governments, has not exhibited either convergence. A plausible explanation for this phenomenon is the presence of constitutional democracies at both the state and federal level, and of a judicial system that manages to induce elected political branches to adhere to its decisions regarding the separation of authority.

The purpose of this chapter is to provide some general observations about the proper role and scope of state constitutions in the U.S. dual constitutional system, and its implications for redesigning the California Constitution. The first section deals with several core principles that have been advanced for designing constitutions, including the relationships between the federal and state constitutions, highlighting how the problem of constitutional design is affected by the hierarchical relationship between states and the federal government. The second section deals with the organization of the state government. The third section discusses the problem of separating constitutional from statutory issues. The last section offers our conclusions about what should and should not be contained in the California Constitution.

PRINCIPLES OF CONSTITUTIONAL DESIGN

At minimum, a constitution is supposed to accomplish a few reasonably well-defined (and well-known) tasks. The first is to define the role of government, the rights of citizens, and the relationship between the two.

The second task is organizational: to define the political institutions and offices that sit at the top of the organization chart of government; to describe the method for deciding who shall hold these positions; and to allocate powers and duties among these institutions and office. The third task is to set forth procedures for changing the constitution.

Beside these general tasks lie a host of detailed issues, many of which deal with policy and are discussed at length in the other chapter that are part of this volume. Our task here is to examine some of the debates and controversies about the principles that either implicitly or explicitly guide constitutional design with respect to individual rights, government organization, and public policy.

Individual Rights and the Democratic Dilemma

By far the most important issue in constructing a democratic government is the extent to which those who control the government should be able to do what they want. The "democratic dilemma" refers to the tensions that arise in all democracies between granting power to the victors in an election versus protecting the rights of the losers and ensuring against manipulation or capture of the democratic process by a clever or well-financed elite. These concerns are well known.

First, if a group of citizens constitutes a durable majority of voters and all issues are decided solely on the basis of majority-rule votes without rules that constrain these decisions, the majority can—and probably will—exploit the minority. Of course, the voting majority is itself a minority, because not all residents of a nation or even citizens of a nation are qualified to vote, and not all of those who are qualified to vote actually cast a ballot. Consequently, the practical reality of democratic elections is that the winners typically constitute a relatively small fraction—between 10 and 20 percent—of the population.

Second, all majoritarian systems are susceptible to manipulation by someone in a position to take advantage of differences in policy preferences and incomplete information about alternative candidates and policies among voters. If citizens have significant differences in policy priorities, no proposal is likely to be preferred by a majority to all other alternatives.[1] Hence, whoever controls which alternatives are placed before the voters can manipulate the process to a selfish end. Likewise, if a policy proposal is complex, with numerous nonobvious ramifications, voters are unlikely to invest the time and effort necessary to understand it completely, and so may again be manipulated into voting for something that, if fully informed, they would not prefer. In constitutional democracies, representatives of the voting majority are given, and are expected to take, control over the normal, day-to-day politics of deciding about current policy questions and candidates for office. Some systems encourage a very strong majoritarianism in policymaking (e.g., the British form of parliamentary democracy), while others hedge the majority will with institutional decentralization (e.g., American federalism) and separation of power (e.g., separate elections for legislative representatives and executive offices).

Some electoral systems tilt the balance toward parties that represent large political coalitions, which must then solve the problem of internal differences and protections against manipulation and tyrannical majorities within the party. For example, the American system of single-member national and state legislative districts and a nationwide election for a chief

---

[1]This circumstance is called the Condorcet Paradox, after an 18th century mathematician, and is easily demonstrated by a simple example. Imagine three friends—Harry, Mary, and Terry—are going out for dinner. They are considering whether to have hamburgers, tacos, or pizza and have agreed to decide by a majority-rule vote. The rank-ordering of these options are:

Harry: hamburgers, tacos, pizza
Mary: tacos, pizza, hamburgers
Terry: pizza, hamburgers, tacos.

Note that these preferences result in the following pairwise votes: hamburgers beat tacos (2-1); tacos beat pizza (2-1); pizza beats hamburgers (2-1). Hence, a majority-rule decision process that allows reconsideration of a defeated option never ends: there is no majority-rule winner. Manipulation occurs when someone gets control of the order in which options are considered and uses that control for their own benefit. For example, if Harry is allowed to establish the rules for deciding where to eat, he can propose that the three first decide between tacos and pizza, and then pair the winner against hamburgers. In the first stage, tacos win, and in the second stage hamburgers beat tacos and Harry gets his first choice. But if Mary controls the agenda, she will pair hamburgers against pizza in the first round, then observe the winner (pizza) lose to her favorite (tacos).

executive, both decided on the basis of which candidate gets the most votes, stacks the deck in favor of a system with two large, heterogeneous political parties. Other nations have electoral systems, such as proportional representation (many smaller European nations) or multimember districts (Italy and Japan before recent reforms), that encourage division of the electorate into a large number of small but more homogeneous political parties. And some countries combine both types of representation (Germany and, in its next election, Japan). Sometimes other political institutions, such as supermajority voting rules in the legislature, force an elected majority to give consideration to minority preferences, but sometimes they do not.

Regardless of these differences, all systems that have genuinely democratic constitutions define some basic individual rights that are protected from potentially tyrannical decisions by an elected majority. In most cases, these constitutional protections are written into a constitutional document, but not always. The British "constitution," for instance, largely consists of unwritten customs and expectations. In essence, the British system is founded on commitment to tradition as opposed to a commitment by an explicit act of constitutional contract.

A premise of democratic constitutionalism is that the voting majority, when considering fundamental questions about government design, will forego the temptation to put in place rules and institutions that would establish a system of majoritarian tyranny without basic minority rights. Why this is so is more a hopeful assumption than a firm conclusion based on political theory, for it is not clear why the same majority that is willing to exploit a minority on day-to-day policy issues would be willing to behave more altruistically when designing the institutions and defining the limits of government. The hope is that a majority, when faced with fundamental issues of governance that are stripped of direct application to specific policy questions, will be more deliberative in considering alternatives. Constitutional scholar Bruce Ackerman has defined these circumstances as "constitutional moments," when interest in public affairs—usually because of a great crisis—is heightened, causing citizens to pay more attention to questions of governance and to consider public affairs in a deeper, more deliberative manner than is typical of everyday politics.[2]

Another explanation is that citizens can foresee the problems that will arise if majorities are both tyrannical and temporary, and electoral systems are susceptible to manipulation. Whereas on a single policy issue their personal preferences will outweigh their concerns for the stability and equity of the overall government, when considering questions of institutional design these same voters, knowing that most are likely to be in the minority some significant fraction of the time and that in any event they may be victimized by manipulation of the voting process, will opt for a structure that has important antimajoritarian features in everyday policy-making. These citizens are, in essence, opting for stability and protection of their rights when they are in the minority over the advantages they would gain when they are in the position to be part of a tyrannical majority.

The American constitutional system attacks the problems of tyrannical majorities and political manipulation in two ways. First, it formally specifies limits to the actions that government can take, such as in the federal Bill of Rights. Second, it goes beyond the basic democratic requirements of protecting individual rights from tyranny, and creates institutional roadblocks to the implementation of the majority will in the form of multiple decision points that must be coordinated in order to change policy. Federalism, the division of power between the state and the federal government, is one of the most important elements of this roadblock system. The separation of powers doctrine is obviously another: both state and federal constitutions create a chief executive, an independent judiciary, and bicameralism (in all states but Nebraska), and, except for the rare circumstance of a veto override by the legislative branches, require that all four of these institutions agree before a controversial policy can be changed.

The "democratic dilemma" arises because these protections against majoritarian tyranny also reduce the democratic responsiveness of government and create a formidable inertial force behind the status quo. Whereas separation of powers and constitutional limits on government authority prevent majoritarian tyranny, they also can prevent the adoption

---

[2]Bruce Ackerman, *We The People: Foundations* (Cambridge: Harvard University Press, 1991).

of policies that are widely popular and not tyrannical. For example, a recent U.S. Supreme Court ruling in *Turner v. FCC* held that the constitutional guarantee of freedom of the press might prevent the federal government from requiring cable television systems to carry the signals of local broadcasting stations.[3] Whereas the "must-carry rule" for local stations may or may not be good public policy, it can hardly be regarded as representing majoritarian tyranny.

Likewise, the separation of powers and constitutional guarantees of due process of law inevitably delay the implementation of policies that are widely popular. This delay is simply regarded as the price to be paid for also assuring that radical policy changes are not easily enacted in response to a single election. For example, in a two-party system, a corruption scandal may cause a majority of legislators to be removed from office with little popular sentiment for the policies of the new ruling party. A system in which policy is difficult and slow to change enables the electorate to enjoy the luxury of ridding itself of corrupt politicians without risking the quick, wholesale adoption of undesirable policies.

Finally, a complex system of checks and balances protects against changes advocated by a temporary tyrannical majority or a manipulative faction that has managed to seize control, but it also makes it easier for a small, dedicated interest to block change. To prevent a change in policy, a group need not gain control of the entire government. It must control only one of the many veto points along the path of policy change, perhaps a single important committee in one branch of the legislature. Thus, the American system reduces the ability of factions to make changes that benefit themselves, but enhances their ability to block changes that are favored by a majority.

In the debate at the American constitutional convention, great emphasis was placed on avoiding policy changes in response to the political passions of the moment. To some degree, this view reflected an eighteenth century fear of democracy, then a very radical and rare institution.[4] But a government in which policy is resistant to change is not necessarily

---

[3]*Turner Broadcasting System, Inc. v. Federal Communications Commission*, 114 S. Ct. 2445 (1994).

[4]The magnitude of the departure of the American Constitution from prior systems of government is generally not sufficiently appreciated. See Gordon S. Wood, *The Radicalism of the American Revolution* (New York: A.A. Knopf, 1992).

antidemocratic. Stable, predictable policy is valuable, because it enables citizens to make plans for the future in an environment in which the risks imposed on them by government through radical policy changes are limited. Likewise, risk-averse citizens may prefer a government in which change is slow and limited (even if it means sacrificing the chance of occasionally having a government that adopts their ideal policy). In this circumstance, the more responsive policy can be to respond to a preference for stability rather than to the momentary policy preferences of a majority. But in any case, neither majoritarian responsiveness nor security against temporary control by a tyrannical majority or a clever, manipulative faction can be acquired without cost, because more of one requires less of the other.

Implications for State Constitutions in a Federal System

The preceding arguments clearly apply to the federal Constitution, but their application to the state is less readily apparent. State constitutions also offer protections for individual rights. Almost all of them include provisions for the right of assembly, freedom of religion, due process, the right of petition, and freedom of speech and press (see the sample of constitutional provisions in Appendix A). Many also include equal protection and the right to bear arms. A few contain rights that are unique to state constitutions, such as rights of noncitizens and victims of violent crime.

Given that the federal Constitution already limits the possibility of state majoritarian tyrannies, what justifies the substantial overlap between federal and state rights? In particular, the federal Constitution requires that states adopt representative democracy, respect private contractual rights, and refrain from interfering in interstate commerce. The Civil War amendments to the Constitution require that states honor the Bill of Rights and grant full state citizenship rights to anyone who possesses federal citizenship. Consequently, a tyrannized minority can turn to the federal courts to undo a state action that violates basic rights. Moreover, because state judges are elected and federal judges are not, one could argue that the federal courts are in a position to be more sympathetic to such complaints and to do a better job of protecting minorities than the state courts. Bearing in mind the breadth and solidity of these federal protections, what role remains for the state constitution in dampening the effects of majority tyranny?

Three such roles seem to apply. First, states can add to, but not diminish, a federally defined right. If a state constitution does nothing more than replicate the language of the federal Constitution with respect to the powers and limits of government, differences may still emerge between federal and state courts in how these terms are interpreted. In this case, the more expansive interpretation—the one according more protections to individuals—will apply. The federal Constitution, then, sets the minimum standards for protecting individual rights and requiring due process for policies to change; the state can require more if citizens indicate that this is what they want in elections for state officials, including the state supreme court, and in votes on constitutional amendments.

Second, the state may establish individual rights and protections that are not contained in the federal Constitution. For example, Arizona, California, Illinois, Michigan, Texas, and Vermont all have provisions for so-called victims rights. These state-created constraints on state and local government action are binding unless they conflict with federal law on matters in which the federal government is judged to have the power to assert jurisdiction. As in the case of more expansive readings of federal protections, additional protections in kind (as opposed to in degree) accorded by a state have the presumption of democratic responsiveness, i.e., the majority has accorded greater or special rights to a specific group such as victims of crime, noncitizens, potential litigants, etc.

Third, state constitutional law serves to put a break on the rate and extent to which the federal government can change individual rights in a state through court interpretation. The details of federal constitutional law, including even the jurisdictional boundary between federal and state authority, are neither well-defined nor stable. The federal Constitution can be amended (with considerable political difficulty), but the far more likely source for a change in the definition of individual rights in federal constitutional doctrine is a shift in interpretation by the Supreme Court. For example, the Supreme Court recognized a constitutional right to privacy in individual decisions about sexuality and child birth in *Griswold*[5] (allowing

---

[5]*Griswold v. Connecticut*, 381 U.S. 479 (1965).

individuals to have access to birth control regardless of state law) and *Roe*[6] (creating a constitutional right for pregnant women to decide whether to have an abortion), even though the legal argument is rooted in original constitutional language. Likewise, only beginning in the 1960s was the "equal protection" requirement for states created by the Civil War amendments interpreted to require that all state and local representatives to multimember bodies be elected in equally populated districts.[7]

More recently, the 1995 decision in *Lopez* indicates that at least four Supreme Court judges, and some believe five, want to reverse 60 years of legal precedent regarding the legitimate constitutional scope of federal legislation.[8] Since the New Deal, the Court has allowed Congress to justify almost any federal law on the ground that the federal government has jurisdiction over interstate commerce as long as there is any connection at all between the object of the law and interstate business.

The extent to which *Lopez* reverses this doctrine is not yet clear, but the important point is that even identically worded state definitions of government power and individuals rights can provide a hedge against a contraction of those rights due to dramatic changes in federal Court interpretation. For example, a California right of privacy that parallels *Griswold* and *Roe* would cause rights of access to birth control and abortion to remain in force even if the Supreme Court reversed its position on these issues. The general point is that for the federal government to reduce individual protections in California on constitutional issues, two events would have to transpire: a change in federal constitutional doctrine, and federal assertion of jurisdiction on the same issue (commonly through a statute).

By contrast, an expansion of federal definitions of individual rights normally requires only a change in Supreme Court doctrine. Judicial federalism gives individual rights additional protections.

---

[6]*Roe v. Wade*, 410 U.S. 113 (1973).

[7]*Reynolds v. Sims*, 377 U.S. 533 (1964) and *Wesberry v. Sanders*, 376 U.S. 1 (1964).

[8]*United States v. Lopez*, 115 S. Ct. 1624 (1995), upholding 2 F3d 1341 (5th Circuit, 1993), which ruled that Congress lacked authority under the commerce clause to enact a statute barring the knowing possession of firearms within 1,000 feet of a primary or secondary school.

STATE CONSTITUTIONS AND GOVERNMENT ORGANIZATION

The federal Constitution requires that California adopt a system of representative democracy, so it follows that California must have a document that defines the basic political institutions of the state (including elections). This document need not be a constitution; however, all U.S. states have constitutions, and all but the original 13 gained admission to the union by presenting Congress with a constitutional document that set up democratic political institutions. In fact, it is not at all clear how a state could satisfy Congress and the Supreme Court that it had a constitutionally acceptable governmental structure without having a constitution.

Likewise, it seems unexceptional that every state will go beyond describing the institutions of governance to include the powers of state government. These provisions serve partly to limit government in the sense described previously (i.e., the protection of individual rights), but their purposes are broader, since without defining the powers and duties of elected officials, the enforceable scope of their authority is unclear.

For these reasons, then, all state constitutions contain provisions describing the organization of the state executive, judiciary, legislature, and usually, local governments. They also routinely cover aspects of elections such as voting qualifications, the timing and method of elections, the organization of the civil service and the militia, and the rules governing state statutes. Lastly, of course, state constitutions provide for their amendment and revision.

The Parallel between State and Federal Government Structures

The treatment of government organization in state constitutions is remarkably similar to the structure of the federal government. Despite the wide latitude the federal Constitution gives the states in organizing their governments, despite the autonomy states have when they invoke their procedures for constitutional revision, and despite the wide variation in state conditions and circumstances, state constitutions have almost uniformly chosen to adopt the federal model: the separation of power between three branches, an independently elected executive, a bicameral legislature, and legislative elections based on simple-plurality, single-member districts. To be sure, some states depart from certain organizational features of the federal model, such as by requiring elections or reconfirmation votes for state judges, establishing a biennial legislature, and creating multiple elected executive offices, but none of these undermines the basic antimajoritarian conservatism of state governments. Like the federal government, state governments provide multiple access points for interest groups into the policymaking process and require cooperation from many different actors in order for major legislative action to be taken. As discussed in the previous section, this is "conservative" in the sense that it gives inertial force to the status quo (what Cain and Persily call the tyranny of the status quo) and requires a higher effort and consensus for legislative change.

The desirability for replicating the federal model at the state level is far from obvious. Given that the federal constitution provides many barriers to hasty and tyrannical majority-preferred change, what are the purposes and implications of erecting more barriers at the state level? One possible explanation is that this is simply a matter of imitation and the prevalence of suspicion towards government tyranny that characterized eighteenth century political thought, i.e., people at the state level were influenced by the same ideas that persuaded the founders (and vice versa), and hence both adopted the same model. In the sense that federal ideas about constitutions still persist in American political thought, this explanation probably contains some truth, but in a specific historical sense, it is not true: most current state constitutions were adopted well after the eighteenth century. Only three [Massachusetts (1780), New Hampshire (1784) and Vermont (1793)] date to the Revolutionary period, and only one other [Maine (1819)] was written before 1820. Eight states have constitutions dating from 1840-1860, 24 states have constitutions from 1865-1915, and 14 have constitutions from the contemporary post-World War II period (all but four of which were adopted in or after 1965).

The similarity between federal and state constitutions also is not due to a lack of opportunity on the part of the states to modernize their constitutional design. States may be reluctant to depart from the conservative premises of the federal model, but they have not been hesitant to abandon their old constitutions in favor of new ones. Only 19 states still have their original constitution, and the average number of constitutions per state is three. Some remarkable outliers are Louisiana (11 different constitutions) and Georgia (10). If states had wanted to depart from the federal model, most have had several opportunities to do so.

If the prevalence of the federal model is not an historical relic and was not caused by a lack of opportunity, then it would seem that it is probably an expression of at least an implicit preference by a majority of citizens for an additional layer of antimajoritarian protection at the state level. Indeed, some of the so-called innovations in state constitutions have amplified the features of the federal model, such as splitting executive power into multiple offices as a means of extending the separation of power. As a consequence, the problems of power dispersion, divided government, and special interest vetoes are at least as substantial at the state level as they are at the federal.

Majoritarian Pressures on the States

Perhaps because of the antimajoritarian structure of the system copied from the federal government, a curious feature of state governments is that they are under constant siege from majoritarian pressures. Some of this pressure finds expression in state constitutions. If the central problem for the eighteenth century federal Constitution was preventing the concentration of power and the tyranny of one faction (particularly the majority) over another, the thrust of much state constitutional reform since the mid-nineteenth century has been to limit and constrain the power of elected state representatives altogether because of their perceived undue responsiveness to special interests. In other words, the antimajoritarian qualities of presumed policy inertia, dispersion of power over many nodes, and the multiplication of veto points have given rise to majoritarian reform measures, bestowing on state constitutions a persistent unresolved tension.

Some examples of majoritarian reforms are: (1) the initiative, recall and referendum; (2) limitations on the fiscal powers of representatives (e.g., balanced budget requirements, debt ceilings, earmarked and mandated expenditures,); and (3) term limits. Almost half of the states have some form of direct democracy, and most of these provisions were adopted as part of Progressive Era reforms that were designed to free governments that had been captured by special interests and ethnic party machines. Limitations on legislative power reflect the public's mistrust that elected representatives will spend money and tax at the level and in the manner that the majority would like. Term limits became popular because a majority of the public came to believe that the longer elected officials spent in office, the less responsive they became to the majority's electoral mandate.

In effect, what many states have done is try to "correct" the antimajoritarian bias of state governments of the federal constitutional model with "majoritarian" reforms that have constrained elected officials and imposed majority preferences in fiscal and policymaking matters. The advantage of this blend may be that it has saved the basic structure from serious crises of legitimacy and instability that arise when an electoral majority feels systematically stifled. The costs of this mixture of constitutional philosophies include a shift from deliberative to nondeliberative mechanisms, substantial inflexibility in dealing with changing circumstances and crises, and, ironically, even higher barriers to policy change because majoritarian constitutional constraints, such as balanced budget requirements, mandated expenditures and earmarked funds, are added to the already formidable requirements for changing policy in a highly dispersed political power structure. These problems will be considered in more detail in the next section.

POLICY MAKING AND STATE CONSTITUTIONS

The third domain of potential constitutional activity is the adoption of policies and the means for implementing them as constitutional provisions. In a sense, the step from constitutionally protecting rights to constitutionally protecting policy decisions is not as great as it might initially seem. The boundary between defining the scope of individual rights versus government power, and establishing a policy, can be very blurry. In philosophical terms, this transition is from so-called "negative" to "positive" rights: the right to be free from tyrannical action versus the right to basic opportunities and resources. Many policy issues contain potential rights issues of the second sort.

For example, the Delaney Amendment to the federal Food and Drug Act prohibits adding known carcinogens to any food product, regardless of how small the carcinogenic effect or how large the benefits of the additive. Thus, a substance that caused a type of cancer in one person in 10 million but immunized consumers against another, more common and deadlier form of cancer, would be prohibited. This statute amounts to the establishment of an individual right against consuming food containing a carcinogenic additive, but it does not take the form of a constitutional amendment.

Because this "right" can be taken away by an amendment to a statute, or even by a Supreme Court that became convinced that the law violates a constitutional principle, it is a "policy" despite its uncompromising character.

The important point about constitutional as opposed to statutory rights is their status in the legal hierarchy. Were the Delaney Amendment to achieve constitutional status, it could not be trumped by any subsequent federal statute, and it would be accorded equal status with other constitutional rights.

California's constitution contains "rights" that at the federal level would be found in statutes. For example, the California state constitution establishes a "right to fish" in all waters on public lands within the state, subject to regulations set forth by the constitutionally created Fish and Game Commission. There is no comparable right to camp, to hunt, or to walk in the woods; hence, California's state statutes and local ordinances in managing fish have a constitutionally restricted status compared to similar laws and regulations that manage other recreational activities.

These examples raise an important issue: What principles, if any, ought to guide whether a policy is written into the constitution, adopted by a vote of the electorate (and thereby put off bounds for elected representatives to amend by themselves), or merely adopted as a statute (whether by the legislature or through the initiative)? To answer this question requires examining the meaning and implications of the various routes to policymaking that states have adopted.

The Hierarchy of Laws

Legislative statutes, the most common way to make policy, are in essence the product of majority or supermajority decisions of the legislature and, in those states that allow the governor to veto statutes, the executive. Statutes can be overturned and amended by the same rule when political or other circumstances dictate. For reasons already given, the structural model of government in the federal Constitution presents a more substantial hurdle for making new statutes than do many other political systems.

The second route of policymaking is constitutional, and it can happen in three ways: (1) policy can be incorporated into the constitution at the time of ratification; (2) policy can be formulated in a legislative constitutional amendment that is subsequently ratified by the voters; and (3) policy can be placed into the constitution by a popular initiative in states that provide that opportunity. Methods 1 and 2 involve two or three stages of approval: by a constitutional commission or convention, the legislature, and the voters. In 41 states, amendments that pass through the legislature (LCA) require either a supermajority vote in the legislature (28 states, including California), sometimes in successive sessions of the legislature (nine states), or ratification in two successive elections. In other words, the political hurdle for a successful LCA is higher than for normal statutory measures.

Policy made in this way is a commitment by a more stable and/or larger majorities that bind potentially less stable and smaller future legislative majorities in a given policy area. Reversing this policy means creating a new stable and large majority that is willing to put forth the effort to pass another amendment. The higher political requirements of the LCA process and the higher legal status of constitutional provisions in effect produce a stronger policy commitment and lower the probability of future backtracking and policy reversals.

In states that have the initiative process, a third method for getting policy into the constitution is the initiative constitutional amendment (ICA). The third method differs from the others in that it involves only one level of approval (the popular vote) and usually does not have to meet a consecutive session or supermajority vote requirement, as in California. An ICA that gets enough signatures is placed on either a primary or general election ballot. Then, the ICA needs only to win that election by obtaining a majority of those voting on the measure. This requirement is typically far less than a majority of those voting on anything in the same election, which in turn is fewer than a majority of those eligible to vote. In essence, a policy placed in the constitution through the ICA process amounts to a constraint on the representatives of another majority (the legislature and executive) by a majority of those voting for that measure.

Usually the argument for a policy initiative constitutional amendment is aimed at elected political officials. Proponents of etching policy into the state constitution correctly state that in so doing they are preventing elected politicians from undoing the will of the majority. But constitutional policy statements do more than this. Citizens may vote on constitutional amendments, but only a very tiny fraction of the electorate ever becomes involved in drafting an amendment, working to put it on the ballot, and helping to finance the campaign for its passage. Most constitutional issues simply do not matter enough to most citizens to cause truly grass-roots constitutional movements to materialize. In the vast majority of cases, for a constitutional provision to be enacted, a necessary condition is that a well-organized, well-financed interest must have a direct stake in its passage. Hence, ICA policies do more than protect the majority from unresponsive politicians. They also prevent future legislative majorities from reversing the policy without the prior approval of the electorate in the form of a new amendment.

In effect, the ICA policy option places the policy preferences of the electoral majority ahead of the less majoritarian preferences of the representative system expressed through normal statutory means. The representative system is less purely majoritarian in several ways. First, the dispersion of power and higher levels of consensus needed in a separation of power system can frustrate the pure electoral majority. Second, the legislature's electoral mandate is formulated by districts and will in many instances differ from the statewide median voter because of differences among legislative districts in voter turnout. Third, the influences of party, contributors, lobbyists, and personal ideology can cause legislators and governors to act differently from the pure electoral mandate. Assuming that the outcome of the initiative is the expression of the pure majority will (which is a huge leap of faith given that initiatives are constructed and financed by organized interests), allowing policy to be made by ICA amounts to binding the less majoritarian representative government system with the policy preferences of an electoral majority.

Even if the initial majority is not the temporary passionate band that caused the founders to fear democracy, elevating a policy to constitutional status prevents the same sober majority from easily adapting policy to changed circumstances. Returning to the example of the Food and Drug Act, since the passage of the 1962 amendments, the Food and Drug Administration must be satisfied that a drug is safe before allowing it on to the market. But if a drug were discovered that cured AIDS while also, say, causing a heart attack in five percent of the patients who took it, Congress would almost certainly amend the statute to allow the drug to be licensed. By contrast, if the 1962 amendments were amendments to the federal Constitution, the new drug could not be licensed without two-thirds majorities in both houses of Congress and ratification by three-quarters of the states. No doubt the latter process would greatly delay, if not prevent, the licensing of the drug, at the cost of a great many lives. If the 1962 amendments were part of the state constitution, changing them would require a two-thirds majority in the legislature and subsequent popular ratification, or alternatively, building the electoral coalition to pass an ICA (with all the money and time that requires).

The preceding discussion makes quite obvious the primary disadvantage of making policy in a constitution. In a world of rapid technological progress, freezing policies in the concrete of constitutional language is very likely to cause costly policy inflexibility. If the legislative process is unresponsive, then change may not be reflected in new state law; however, because the constitutional revision process is slow, expensive, and even more unresponsive, change will not be reflected in governing law until some organized interest finds a private reason to bear the costs of amending the constitution, or the same unresponsive legislature places a legislative amendment on the ballot.

A parallel argument applies when the source of change is a change in the policy preferences of citizens. Constitutional provisions bind future generations to the policy decisions of the present generation. Thomas Jefferson noted this feature of the U.S. Constitution, and argued that the U.S. ought to be required to call a constitutional convention for each generation (every 25 years) to make certain that antiquated provisions were revised or eliminated.

Application to California

Unlike the federal system and most other states, California has a complex hierarchy of law beyond the federal distinction between the constitution and statutes. The state constitution can be changed in four distinct ways: a constitutional convention or commission, a revision, a legislative constitutional amendment, and an initiative constitutional amendment. A constitutional convention can be called by a two-step process: first a two-thirds vote of each house in the legislature to submit the question to the voters and then a simple majority approval by the voters. Citizens then elect delegates to the convention, who can then propose an entirely new constitution for the state, subject to majority approval by the voters. A revision pertains to any alteration of the basic structure of the state government or complex, multidimensional alteration of the constitution. It requires a two-thirds vote of each house of the legislature and a majority vote of the electorate. A revision cannot be proposed through initiative, nor can it be altered by any lesser form of constitutional change. Next down in the hierarchy is a constitutional amendment, which must deal with a single issue and does not propose a fundamental change in the structure of state government. A legislative constitutional amendment (LCA) requires a two-thirds vote in each legislative branch and majority approval by the electorate. An initiative constitutional amendment (ICA) requires supporting signatures by registered voters totalling eight percent of the most recent vote for governor, plus a majority vote in the subsequent election. An ICA and an LCA have equal status, in that one can revise or repeal another, and neither can be altered or repealed by statutes unless they explicitly contain a provision that allows such changes.

Still another level in the legislative hierarchy is occupied by initiative statutes (IS) and legislative initiative amendments (LIA). An IS requires valid signatures from voters that total five percent of the last vote for governor. An LIA requires a two-thirds vote in both branches of the legislature and applies to attempts by the legislature to amend initiative statutes. Notice that it is as difficult for the state legislature to amend an IS as an ICA, although the latter is more difficult to qualify for the ballot. Both would then require a majority vote by the electorate. Both can be amended by subsequent IS or LIA, or by an ICA or LCA. Finally, California has still another level in the legal hierarchy: a legislative referendum statute (LRS) and a legislative statute amendment (LSA), which amends an LRS. Each requires a majority vote in each branch of the legislature, plus a majority vote by the electorate. Neither can be amended by the legislature acting alone unless it contains a provision permitting it, but both can be amended by an LSA, IS, ICA, LCA, or LSA.

The flaw in the existing arrangement is that the most fundamental distinction lies not between revisions and amendments per se, i.e., between two types of constitutional change, but between according constitutional (or superior), as compared to statutory (ordinary), status to any change in policy or structure that makes the ballot and receives majority support from voters in a single election. Constitutional amendments, initiative statutes, and referendum statutes are too sweeping in the inflexibilities they create in writing future statutes. They are too likely to be adopted by voters outside the context of the deliberative process we normally associate with constitutional change, and too difficult to amend unless a private interest can be found to bankroll another initiative process. Hence, we return to the earlier question: What principles, if any, should guide whether a policy is written into a constitution or merely adopted as a statute? For many, the ideal answer would be the total prohibition of policy provisions in a constitution and severe restrictions on, if not prohibition of, statutory initiatives and referendums, but this is not feasible. The cat has long been let out of the bag, so to speak, in terms of policy provisions in state constitutions and citizen expressions of policy preferences through direct democracy. Most state constitutions contain many such provisions, and it would be impossible to change this even if it were for the better. Moreover, the fact is that some policies may indeed have what amounts to an important "rights" component to them, and there is a strong case for giving them special protection from legislators, elected executives, and bureaucrats.

A second approach would be to attempt to distinguish between policies that deserve protection against legislative or executive change and those that do not, based on the costs of inflexibility or the strength of the "rights" component in the policy. Unfortunately, the prospects of devising such clear guidelines and expecting them to be widely accepted either in principle or practice are not very good. Rather than add still more arbitrariness to the system by trying to develop a sharper boundary between rights and policy, between revisions and amendments, or between amendments and initiative/referendum statutes, our preferred alternative is to make all constitutional change more difficult by imposing either supermajority and/or consecutive election requirements. It settles for presuming against putting policy in the constitution or otherwise beyond the reach of the legislature, and accepts such provisions only when they embody the will of a large, stable majority. This remedy would not prevent initiatives from arising when there was a strong consensus that a certain policy was a right or should receive priority. Instead, it would simply redirect more of these efforts towards producing statutory measures that could be more easily adapted and changed in the future if circumstances required.

CONCLUSIONS: THE NATURE OF STATE CONSTITUTIONS

Most state constitutions, including California's, exhibit an underlying tension between the antimajoritarian consequences of adopting the system of separation of powers from the federal model and the majoritarian thrust of constitutional provisions for direct democracy. The California Constitution, like many others, represents a balance between these two different pressures: it combines antimajoritarian features like bicameralism and an independently elected and fractured executive with majoritarian features like the initiative, referendum, and recall. The balance is an uneasy one in the sense that the antimajoritarian features of the government can, under certain political conditions, lead to divided government, legislative stalemate, electoral impatience, and majoritarian demands for further reform.

A number of proposals for constitutional reform have been suggested, including those by authors in this volume: proportional representation; a unicameral legislature or even a parliamentary form of government; longer term limits to permit more institutional memory and expertise; stronger home rule for cities; a simpler state budget that is easier to pass; initiative reform; Proposition 13 reform; and consolidation of the state executive. Are these reforms majoritarian or antimajoritarian? The answer is both. Does it matter that they are not of one type? Does reform have to be consistently in one direction of the other? The answer, we think, is no. In fact, in order to maintain balance it probably will require that reform measures take both forms. Why?

The biggest change in California since the last major constitutional revision has been the dramatic increase in size and diversity of the state's population. California is now both a larger and more complex state, with many more constituencies, than it was 30 years ago. The political implications of these demographic shifts include: increasing numbers of minorities and women in the state legislature; shifting demands for state services due to population shifts in class composition, educational needs, language abilities, cultural expectations and the like; new expectations that majoritarian institutions, especially local governments, be modified to permit better representation of new groups; and greater heterogeneity in citizen preferences about government functions.

Changes in the population and the electorate have highlighted the conflicts between the majoritarian and antimajoritarian features of the state constitution. At the local level, this conflict can take the form of controversies about at-large (majoritarian) vs. district (minority protection) elections for local government bodies. Another manifestation is the controversy over whether boundaries for state and federal legislative districts should respect or ignore the racial and ethnic composition of the population. At the same time, the heterogeneity that has made it through the electoral filter and is reflected in who represents the people in Sacramento has increased partisanship and disagreement in the legislature.

The constitutional separation of powers is purposely designed to preserve the status quo when the level of consensus for policy change falls below the critical level needed to pull together and coordinate the many and dispersed decision points in the system (both houses, the governor, powerful interest groups, the parties, etc.). Stalemate can produce frustration when there is an electoral majority but not a legislative majority for policy change. This structural inertia accounts for the desire to make government more effective by increasing its majoritarian features (e.g., unicameralism, unified executive).

The reform proposals that are discussed in this volume are neither exclusively majoritarian nor antimajoritarian, but they follow a broad pattern. The electoral measures are for the most part antimajoritarian (proportional representation, initiative reform), because a sensible way to accommodate diversity is to give it representation and to limit the majority's power to impose its will on others. The governance measures (e.g., unicameral legislature, longer term limits, a simpler budget process, consolidation of the executive) are majoritarian, because they would make it easier for a majority to govern once elected. In other words, if adopted as a whole, the new balance proposes greater diversity in representation but easier requirements for governance once in office.

Each proposal deserves consideration on its own merits, but there is also a need to ask whether the new balance will work. A move towards majoritarianism in governance without concessions in representation could achieve greater efficacy of governance at the expense of heightening the crisis of legitimacy among minorities in California institutions. Conversely, an antimajoritarian electoral reform could lead to even further stalemate and greater majority discontent. When the final tally of proposed reforms is taken, a necessary part of their evaluation is whether, as a system, they make sense, beyond their individual merits.

The Role of State Constitutions in a Federal System

Joseph R. Grodin

When I ask students in my constitutional law class, as I do each year, how many constitutions there are in the United States, the students are generally mystified. Of course, most are inclined to say, there is only one. And if a student is quick enough to come up with the correct answer it is likely to be offered in a patronizing way, as if to say—sure, there must be fifty-one, but besides our nutty professor who cares?

The facts are, of course, that there were state constitutions before the federal Constitution even existed, and that in the everyday lives of most citizens they are likely to be of substantially greater significance. It is the state constitutions that describe the structure of state and local government, and it is the state constitutions that provide protection for individual rights and liberties beyond the scope of protection afforded by the federal charter. Some state constitutions do more than that; some, indeed, contain provisions that are more appropriately matters of statute rather than constitution, but that is another topic.

States do not have complete autonomy with respect to either the structural or the rights-protecting provisions of their state constitutions. The federal Constitution has something, though not a great deal, to say about both. Article IV, section 4 guarantees to every state a "Republican Form of Government," though what that means, in light of the United States Supreme Court's insistence that claims under the Guarantee Clause are "nonjusticiable,"[1] remains undetermined. We do know (though at the time it came as a surprise to many) that states may not structure their governments in a manner inconsistent with the federal principle of one person-one vote,[2] and, we know that states may not allocate the franchise in a manner

[1]*Pacific States Tel. & Tel. Co. v. Oregon*, 223 U.S. 118 (1911).
[2]*Reynolds v. Sims*, 377 U.S. 533 (1964).

that conflicts with federal equal protection guarantees.[3] State constitutions, as well as state statutes, are of course subject to those federal principles that protect interstate commerce against undue state interference, and citizens of one state against discrimination by another state. But subject to these limitations, the power of state governments to structure the conduct of their own affairs in their own ways is very broad.

The rights-protecting provisions of state constitutions are of course subject to the overriding principle of federal supremacy. A state could not, for example, allow prayers in public schools on the basis of a state constitutional provision protecting religious liberty if doing so violated the federal constitutional prohibition against establishment of religion, nor could a state in the name of its own constitution give to individuals the right to infringe upon federally protected rights of others.[4] But subject to these limitations, the power of state governments, through their own constitutions, to provide protection for individual rights beyond the scope of protection afforded by the federal Constitution is, likewise, very broad.

It is, indeed, the rights-protecting provisions of state constitutions that have been the principal focus of the relatively recent revival in state constitutionalism. That this revival occurred at a time when the justices of the Warren Court were being replaced by justices who were more conservative in their approach, and as a consequence protection for individual rights under the federal Constitution was on the wane, is surely no coincidence. Indeed, Justice William Brennan in his well-known article advocating greater attention to state constitutional protections made that relationship explicit.[5]

It would be a serious mistake, however, to view the recent scholarly and judicial attention to state constitutions as simply a liberal rationalization for protecting the decisions of the Warren Court against erosion. The prospect of that erosion no doubt served to stimulate interest in state constitutions, but it is an interest that was long overdue; and, once aroused,

---

[3]*Kramer v. Union Free School District*, 395 U.S. 621 (1969).

[4]Cf. *Pruneyard Shopping Center v. Robins*, 447 U.S. 74 (1980) (considering and rejecting claim by shopping center owner that a state court rule allowing handbilling on center property constituted an unconstitutional "taking" of that property.)

[5]Brennan, "State Constitutions and the Protection of Individual Rights," *Harv. L. Rev.* 90 (1977): 489.

that interest has taken on a life of its own. Scholars, judges, and at long last lawyers have begun to recognize that a principled approach to decision making not only permits but requires (1) that state constitutions be regarded as independent sources of constitutional rights; and (2) that courts confront and decide state constitutional issues before undertaking to decide potential federal constitutional claims.

The proposition that state constitutions deserve to be regarded as independent sources of constitutional rights is by now well accepted, at least in principle if not always in practice. State constitutions, after all, preceded the federal Constitution, and state Declarations of Rights date from the revolutionary era or before.[6] The federal Bill of Rights was based in large measure on the then existing provisions of state constitutions,[7] and drafters of state constitutions adopted after 1791 looked mainly to other state constitutions, rather than to the federal Constitution, for guidance.[8]

The history of Article I of the California Constitution ("Declaration of Rights") is illustrative. In 1849, when the delegates to the first California Constitutional convention gathered in Monterey, the provisions of the federal Bill of Rights were not considered applicable to the states. Except for Article I, section 10[9] there was nothing in the federal Constitution that could be relied upon to protect citizens against invasions of liberty by state, as distinguished from federal, government. That may explain why Declaration of Rights became the first Article of the new constitution and why the delegates considered it their first order of business.[10]

The drafters of Article I used the constitutions of New York and Ohio (not the federal Constitution) as their guides. Article I, even in its 1849

---

[6]B. Schwartz, The Bill of Rights: A Documentary History (1971).

[7]See Williams, "'Experience Must be Our Only Guide': The State Constitution Experience of the Framers of the Federal Constitution," *Hastings Const. L.Q.* 15 (1988): 403.

[8]See, generally, Linde, "First Things First: Rediscovering the States' Bills of Rights," *U. Balt. L. Rev.* 9 (1977): 297.

[9]Article 1, Section 10 provides, in part: "No state shall . . . pass any Bill of Attainder, *ex post facto* Law, or Law impairing the Obligation of Contracts . . . "

[10]A more detailed account of the 1849 Convention, and its consideration of Article I, may be found in Grodin, Massey and Cunningham, *The California State Constitution: A Reference Guide* (Greenwood Press, 1993).

form, contain provisions nowhere to be found in the federal Constitution,[11] as well as provisions with federal analogues but different language.[12] When delegates debated what language should be used to express protection for religious liberty, they relied upon competing state constitutional provisions, with no mention of the federal First Amendment.[13]

Article I survived the 1878-79 Constitutional Convention virtually intact.[14] By that time, the Fourteenth Amendment to the federal Constitution had been adopted, but the notion that it served to make applicable to the states various provisions of the Bill of Rights was still many years off. Thus, when California courts encountered claims of violation of constitutional rights during the latter part of the nineteenth century, they did so almost exclusively within the context of the state constitution.

An example in the area of freedom of speech is *Dailey v. Superior Court*, 112 Cal. 94 (1896). Prior to the trial of a celebrated murder case, a creative entrepreneur by the name of Dailey sought to capitalize on the publicity by producing a dramatic rendition, based on the "facts" of the case, in a San Francisco theater. The defendant sued to enjoin the production, on the ground that it would deprive him of a fair trial. The trial court granted the injunction, but the Supreme Court reversed, holding it in violation of the state constitutional provision protecting speech. At the time there were no decisions interpreting the federal First Amendment. The

---

[11]E.g., Article I, Section 1: "All men are by nature free and independent and have inalienable rights. Among these are enjoying and defining life and liberty, acquiring, possessing and protecting property, and pursuing and obtaining safety and happiness." In 1972 the provision was amended to substitute "people" for "men," and to add "privacy" to the list of inalienable rights.

[12]E.g., Article 1, Section 2: "Every person may freely speak, write and publish his or her sentiments on all subjects, being responsible for the abuse of this right. A law may not restrain or abridge liberty of speech or press."

[13]Section 4 of the 1849 constitution, based on the New York Constitution, protected "free exercise and enjoyment of religion without discrimination," but provided that "this liberty of conscience does not excuse acts that are licentious or inconsistent with the peace or safety of the state." Delegate Charles Botts argued, unsuccessfully, for the "most eloquent and beautiful" language of the Virginia Constitution.

[14]Provisions were added prohibiting the legislature from granting unrevokable or preferential "privileges or immunities," prohibiting property qualifications for voting, and stating a rule of constitutional construction.

court made reference to that provision and noted that its language differed from that of the California Constitution, but concluded that the difference "works no harm to this petitioner, for the provision here considered is the broader, and gives him greater liberty in the exercise of the right granted."

Claims based on property and contract rights have a checkered history under the California Constitution. Initially, the California Supreme Court declined to regard the language of Article I, section 1, and its protection for "liberty" and "property," as a basis for attacking regulation of business,[15] but in 1890 the court held that an ordinance prohibiting the employment of any person to work more than eight hours a day (as well as, incidentally, the employment of Chinese labor) on city contracts interfered impermissibly with the right to contract embraced within the term "liberty."[16] This was followed by other similarly based decisions invalidating a provision of the state's mechanic lien law requiring liens to be paid in money rather than in kind[17] and a statute prohibiting the "scalping" of theater tickets for more than the original price.[18] By 1909, the court had become so enamored of the libertarian principles it found in section 1 that it held the legislature could not even prohibit a person from building a fire on his own property without a permit.[19]

In these opinions the California court anticipated the U.S. Supreme Court's infamous *Lochner v. New York*; but beginning in 1925 the court began to anticipate the federal rejection of that line of reasoning, holding in *Miller v. Public Works*[20] that the police power was broad enough to sustain a residential zoning ordinance as against section 1 property and liberty claims, and by the mid-1930s the court returned to its former posture of deference to legislative judgments.

One provision peculiar to the California Constitution, added in 1879, is provided here in its original form: "No person shall on account of sex be disqualified from entering upon or pursuing any lawful business, vocation,

---

[15]*Ex parte* Andrews, 18 Cal. 678 (1903).
[16]*Ex parte* Kuback, 85 Cal. 274 (1890).
[17]*Stimson Mill Company v. Braun*, 136 Cal. 122 (1902).
[18]*Ex parte* Quarg, 149 Cal. 79 (1906).
[19]In re McCapes, 157 Cal. 26 (1909).
[20]195 Cal. 477 (1925).

or profession."[21] On the basis of that provision the California Supreme Court initially held, in 1881, that San Francisco could not prohibit the employment of waitresses in places that serve alcoholic drinks, but 11 years later the court upheld a city licensing scheme that imposed a $150 license fee on bars that employed women in any capacity (as compared to $30 per quarter on bars that did not), and in 1893 the court reversed itself completely. It was not until 1971 that the court returned to its earlier understanding.[22]

In other constitutional areas, too, the California courts branched out on their own, without benefit of federal precedent. In 1859 and 1861 the Supreme Court first struck down, then upheld the constituitonality of Sunday closing laws. [23] At the turn of the century the California Supreme Court struck down the then recently adopted primary election law, which prohibited the election of delegates to a convention of any political party not representing three percent of the votes cast at the previous election, as a violation of state constitutional provisions protecting privileges and immunities and the right to assemble and petition, and requiring laws of a general nature to have uniform application. [24]

One of the reasons why the California courts felt free, during this early period, to base decisions on the state constitution without reference to the federal Constitution is, no doubt, that until this century there was scarcely any federal precedent interpreting the Bill of Rights. That situation began to change when the U.S. Supreme Court decided *Lochner v. New York* in 1908; it changed some more as the high court began to decide free speech cases in 1919; it changed a great deal in later decades as the court came to apply various provisions of the Bill of Rights to the states; and by the Warren Court era it had changed completely: there were federal precedents on almost every issue.

Predictably, that change in the pattern and frequency of federal decision making was reflected in decisions of state courts. With respect to

---

[21]Originally Article XX, Section 18. In 1974 the section was moved to Article I, Section 8, and amended to read, "A person may not be disqualified from entering upon or pursuing a business, profession, vocation, or employment because of sex, race, creed, color, or national or ethnic origin."

[22]*Sail'er Inn v. Kirby*, 5 Cal. 3d 1 (1971).

[23]*Ex parte* Andrews, 18 Cal. 678 (1961).

[24]*Britton v. Board of Election Commissioners*, 129 Cal. 337 (1900).

issues on which the United States Supreme Court had spoken, it was natural and easier for state courts to analyze constitutional questions in terms of federal law than to reason on their own. And particularly in areas where the U.S. Supreme Court had taken an "activist" lead, there seemed to be little need for state courts to worry about the provisions of their state constitutions.

But this deferential mode of constitutional decision making brought with it serious drawbacks. It tended to marginalize state constitutions; it tended to shrivel the development of state constitutional theory; and it put the cart before the horse. As Justice Hans Linde pointed out in his early piece "First Things First," state constitutions are not only historically prior to the federal Constitution, they are logically prior as well. If the state action under attack—the statute, or the administrative decision, for example—is invalid under the state constitution, then there is simply no need to consider any federal constitutional issue.

A state cannot be said to have deprived a person of any federal constitutional right to life, liberty, or property without due process of law, or of the equal protection of the laws if the highest law of the state, i.e., its constitution, acknowledges the merits of the constitutional claim. Just as courts decline to reach a constitutional issue when the matter can be resolved through statutory interpretation, so both logic and principles of judicial constraint dictate that courts should not reach federal constitutional issues when the case can be disposed of on state constitutional grounds.

Indeed, a state court's decision on federal constitutional grounds without first deciding the state constitutional issues that are implicated is premature in a very practical sense, as well as in a theoretical sense. Such a decision runs the risk that the U.S. Supreme Court will grant review, decide the case differently as a matter of the federal constitution, and then return the case to the state court for consideration of the state constitutional issue—something the state court should have done in the first place. That has happened to state courts with some frequency, and as a former state supreme court justice I can tell you it is embarrassing when it occurs.

The California Supreme Court began to take a different tack as early as 1955, principally in criminal cases. In *People v. Cahan*[25] it held—anticipating the U.S. Supreme Court by six years—that evidence

[25]44 Cal. 2d 434 (1955).

seized in violation of the search and seizure provisions of the California Constitution was inadmissible in a criminal proceeding. In 1961, rejecting federal constitutional law to the contrary, it held that the state constitution's ban on double jeopardy precluded retrial of a criminal defendant after a mistrial granted on the court's own motion. And in 1972 the court, relying upon the distinctive language of the state constitution, held that California's death penalty statute violated the state ban on "cruel or unusual punishment."

In 1974 California's independent course received express constitutional sanction; in that year the state constitution was amended to provide, unnecessarily but importantly, "Rights guaranteed by this constitution are not dependent on those guaranteed by the United States Constitution."[26] And, in the succeeding years the California courts have acted in accordance with that sanction in a variety of contexts.

One area of independent development has occurred with respect to the right of "privacy" added to Article I, section 1 by initiative in 1972. While the federal Constitution has been interpreted to include a right of privacy as an unenumerated right, the fact that the California Constitution contains an express privacy provision has been recognized as support for a broader definition—to include, for example, protection for the confidentiality of personal information, and for personal autonomy, such as the right to make choices in matters involving living arrangements, in matters relating to medical treatment, and in matters relating to abortion in particular. Contrary to federal principles, the California right of privacy protects the right of poor people to funding for abortions under a system in which the state funds other medical procedures, and the right of unrelated persons to live together in a household unit.[27] And, on the basis of the constitutional language and the ballot arguments that led to its passage, the California Supreme Court has concluded that the privacy provision is applicable to private entities, without regard to the sort of state action that is required for application of the federal Constitution.

Free speech is another significant area in which California has developed an independent jurisprudence. In *Robins v. Pruneyard Shopping*

---

[26]Article I, Section 24.

[27]See *Committee to Defend Reproductive Rights v. Meyers*, 29 Cal. 3d 252 (1981) and cases cited therein.

Center, the California Supreme Court held, contrary to federal precedent, that a shopping center owner must allow persons to distribute handbills within the center so long as they do not interfere with the business conducted there.[28] And the California Court of Appeal has relied upon the state constitution to extend the concept of "public forum" beyond federal constitutional limits.[29]

There are, however, certain aspects of state constitutional jurisprudence in California that are somewhat problematic, and these will be the subject in the remainder of this chapter.

First, California courts have been inconsistent with respect to the "first things first" principle. Sometimes they undertake to confront the state constitution before deciding a federal constitutional issue, as that principle requires; but sometimes they ignore that principle, basing their decision on the federal Constitution without consideration of the state constitution—or, what is equally confusing, positing their decision upon *both* constitutions without separate analysis. In either event, the court runs the risk described above—i.e., that the U.S. Supreme Court will disagree, and send the case back for consideration of the state constitutional issue that might have been determinative in the first place. And in both events, the integrity of the state constitution and of state constitutionalism is compromised.

A prime example of this sort of confusion is *Sands v. Morongo Unified School District*, 53 Cal. 3rd 863 (1991), in which five justices concluded that a religious invocation at a public high school graduation ceremony violated *some* constitution, but could not agree on which. Three justices were of the view that *both* state and federal constitutions were violated, while the remaining two were prepared to hazard an opinion only with respect to the *federal* constitution, contending that it was "unnecessary" to reach state constitutional questions.

Second, California courts have yet to develop a consistent jurisprudence with respect to the role of U.S. Supreme Court decisions in state constitutional analysis. When the U.S. Supreme Court has rendered decisions in a cognate constitutional arena—in the arena of free speech, for example, or privacy, or search and seizure—what weight, if any, should those decisions have in a state court that is considering a claim under the

---

[28]23 Cal. 3d 899 (1979).

[29]*Prisoners Union v. Department of Corrections* 135 Cal. App. 3d 930 (1982).

state constitution? No one could seriously maintain that the state court is *obligated* to follow the federal decisions; such an argument would undermine the principle of state constitutional independence. And no one could seriously maintain that the state court should ignore such decisions entirely; obviously, to the extent that the decisions contain arguments worthy of consideration they ought to be considered.

The serious question is: are there policy reasons that should lead a state court to *defer* to federal decisions, beyond the persuasive power those decisions might have? Or, to put the matter differently, should a state court require some *justification* for departing from federal precedent—justification, for example, based on differences in language between the two texts, or differences in the context leading to their adoption, or in their subsequent development?

One can find in decisions of the California Supreme Court support for almost any view. There are opinions that appear to assume, without analysis, that U.S. Supreme Court decisions provide an authoritative guide to the meaning of the California Constitution; there are opinions in which the California court suggests that some justification for departing from federal precedent is required; and there are opinions in which the California Court adopts a different view simply because it disagrees with the reasoning or the values reflected in the controlling opinions of the high court. As the author of one of the latter opinions, let me try and defend that position.

The case involved an individual who was being interrogated in a police station about a crime. He had been given a Miranda warning, and he had waived his right to counsel. Unknown to him, his family had retained a lawyer, and that lawyer showed up at the police station and asked to see his client. The police had the lawyer wait while the interrogation was concluded and a confession obtained from the suspect, who was not aware that a lawyer was waiting to advise him. The question was whether that confession was admissible in evidence.

While the case was pending before the California Supreme Court, the United States Supreme Court decided a case involving almost identical facts, and it held, 6-3, that so far as the federal Constitution was concerned the confession was admissible. On the basis of the California Constitution our court reached the opposite conclusion. There was no relevant difference in constitutional language or history, but our court was persuaded by the reasoning of the dissenting justices in the U.S. Supreme Court, and by the reasoning of several state supreme courts that found in similar cases, based on *their* state constitutions, that continued interrogation violated the right to counsel.

Should we have deferred to the decision of the United States Supreme Court? And, if so, why? Some would argue that there is a value in uniformity of decision with respect to basic constitutional rights—that variations in interpretation of such rights from state to state detracts from the notion of their "fundamentality." I take this, without deprecation, to be a public relations rationale: even if there is in fact disagreement over how basic rights should be viewed in particular contexts it is important that the disagreement be concealed so as to minimize elements of subjectivity inherent in the decisional process.

A similar argument underlies the practice of constitutional courts in some European countries to issue apparently unanimous decisions no matter what the vote. But in our country the expression of different views through dissenting and concurring opinions has been the custom for nearly the full course of our constitutional history. Our citizens are not unaware that judges with different perspectives are likely to view the same constitutional provisions differently; indeed, that proposition is deeply engrained in our political culture. If the phenomenon of separate opinions within the same court expressing different interpretations of a single text does not undercut belief in the fundamentality of certain rights, it seems hardly likely that differing opinions among different courts with respect to the meaning of different texts will do so.

Apart from pragmatic considerations, the uniformity argument reflects a constrained and static view of constitutional adjudication that is not widely shared. It assumes that the meaning to be attributed to constitutional provisions is fixed by language, at least in the absence of countervailing data, that the same words must have the same meaning in whatever context they appear, and that the meaning is unchanged over time. That is not now and has not in recent times been the view of the majority of the United States Supreme Court; indeed, the very process that stimulated the growth of state constitutionalism was one in which that court gave a different and narrower meaning to certain provisions of the constitution protective of individual rights. If a state court, in interpreting its state constitution, defers to an interpretation of the federal Constitution by the United States Supreme Court, what is it supposed to do when that interpretation changes? The answer belies the premise.

Indeed, the uniformity argument is fundamentally at odds with the principle of federalism, of which state constitutionalism is an important component. Federalism assumes diversity, not uniformity. It assumes that, subject to federal constitutional constraints, states are free to fashion their protections for individual rights in any way they choose, and that this freedom is likely to enhance, rather than detract from, those interests that a constitution serves. It assumes a dialogue between federal and state governments, which cannot exist in an atmosphere of lockstep uniformity. There is an important value in state courts bringing their own independent judgment to the provisions of state declarations of rights, even when those rights are phrased in identical terms with the federal Constitution; even the United States Supreme Court can learn from the process.[30]

Finally, there are two structural differences between state governments and federal government that support independence of interpretation. First, the U.S. Supreme Court is limited, in its application of the federal Constitution, by its recognition that it is prescribing a floor applicable to all 50 states, and that recognition may lead it to a more "conservative" reading of federally protected rights than would otherwise be warranted. State courts do not operate within that constraint.

In addition, the U.S. Supreme Court is limited by its recognition that the federal Constitution can be amended only with exceeding difficulty. This is not true of most state constitutions, and certainly not in California. Indeed, there is an excellent argument to be made that the California Constitution can be amended too readily with respected rights—that there is something anomalous about permitting a simple majority of the voting electorate on a single occasion to override the decision of a court with respect to a provision that is designed to protect individuals and minorities against majority control. But that is the subject for another paper. The fact is that when the California electorate is unhappy with the way the California Supreme Court had adjudicated, they have not hesitated to use the initiative process to say so; from court-ordered busing of school children as a remedy for segregation to the admission of evidence obtained in violation of the state constitution, state Supreme Court decisions have

---

[30]Following the divergent opinions of the U.S. Supreme Court and the California Supreme Court with respect to the exclusion of evidence obtained from a suspect while his lawyer is waiting to speak with him, several other state supreme courts have chosen to follow California's lead.

been overturned at the ballot. The U.S. Supreme Court operates within a quite dissimilar political framework, and to that extent as well the argument of deference loses force.

It might well be thought that the California Revision Commission and the electorate resolved the issue between deference and independence in 1974, by adding to the state constitution the explicit proposition that the rights that it guarantees "are not dependent on those guaranteed by the United States Constitution." An argument might be made that to the extent any doubt remains it should be resolved by yet another amendment, making the decision in favor of independence even clearer. I would not make that argument, however, or at least not for the present, for the simple reason that the California Supreme Court has yet to declare itself definitively on this issue. The problem is one that the court itself can, and should, confront and resolve.

The Challenge of State Constitutions

Robert C. Post

Constitutions establish "the fundamental and paramount law" of a state.[1] Constitutional law is fundamental because it reflects and embodies the essential political ethos that makes governance possible within a particular culture.[2] Thus John Marshall writes that the federal Constitution sets forth the "principles" upon "which the whole American fabric has been erected."[3] These principles are meant to define who we are as citizens of the United States.

These principles are of course supreme within the nation. The federal Constitution displaces or preempts all inconsistent law, including the provisions of the constitutions of the separate states. This poses a sharp difficulty for state constitutions. The very premise of our federalism is that states are not merely administrative organs of the national government, useful only for facilitating the efficient management of a large and geographically heterogeneous population. States are instead conceived as independent loci of governance and authority. State government is said to rest on a "binding tie of cohesive sentiment"[4] that establishes a true and real polity, reflecting the "special relations between a State and its

---

[1]*Marbury v. Madison*, 5 U.S. (1 Cranch) 137, 176 (1803).

[2]See, e.g., Hanna Fenichel Pitkin, "The Idea of a Constitution," *J. Leg. Ed.*, 37 (1987): 167; Robert C. Post, "Theories of Constitutional Interpretation," *Representations,* no. 30 (1990): 13-41.

[3]*Marbury v. Madison*, 5 U.S. 137 at 175.

[4]*Minersville Dist. v. Gobitis*, 310 U.S. 586, 596 (1940).

citizens."[5] The function of a state constitution is to reflect and embody these special "relations."

State constitutions, therefore, face a fundamental challenge: They must constitute a polity within a polity. They must establish a distinctive political culture within the confines of the encompassing and transcendent political culture of the nation. Whether this ambition is coherent and realizable, or whether it is under modern conditions merely a vestigial solecism, is the question that must lie at the core of any serious contemporary assessment of state constitutionalism.

Constitutions are primarily visible in the United States through the medium of judicial interpretation. Courts read constitutions as sources of rights that constrain all subordinate forms of lawmaking. These rights express fundamental constitutional "principles," or, to put it more bluntly, they function as legal directions for the achievement of constitutional policies.

There is sometimes a tendency to conceptualize state constitutions as primarily repositories of judicially cognizable rights. This tendency is reflected in Justice Joseph Grodin's illuminating paper for this symposium. Grodin views the California Constitution chiefly as a source of legally enforceable rights, and he argues that these rights ought to be interpreted independently of similar federal rights.

Grodin's argument assumes that state constitutional rights are analogous to federal constitutional rights. Just as the latter are paramount because they reflect the "principles . . . on which the whole American fabric has been erected,"[6] so Grodin must argue that state constitutional rights are supreme within the state because they reflect the fundamental principles upon which the state's political culture has been established. Any such argument, however, necessarily presupposes that the state is in fact a true polity, united by a commitment to unique and distinctive principles.

---

[5]*Toomer v. Witsell*, 334 U.S. 385, 408 (1948) (Frankfurter, J., concurring). See Robert C. Post, "Cultural Heterogeneity and Law: Pornography, Blasphemy, and the First Amendment," 76 *Calif. L. Rev.* 297, 302 (1988). For a remarkable contemporary statement of this position, see *U.S. Term Limits, Inc. v. Thornton*, 115 S.Ct. 1842, 1875-1884 (1995) (Thomas, J., dissenting).

[6]*Marbury v. Madison*, 5 U.S. 137 at 175.

This presupposition recalls the fundamental challenge we have already identified, which is whether states can now meaningfully be said to constitute polities within a polity. This is not an issue that can be analyzed merely at the level of judicial interpretation. The willingness of state courts to develop special state constitutional rights may be one indication of a state's unique political culture, but it is by no means definitive. It could, for example, merely signify that state constitutionalism has become a refuge for legal professionals who have lost the national battle for the definition of federal constitutional rights.[7]

A deeper evaluation of Grodin's article, therefore, will require us to explore whether California in fact comprises a polity, capable of sustaining the articulation of its own unique constitution. One way to pursue this inquiry is to address the process of constitutional formation within California.

All agree that a constitution must reflect the sovereign will of the population. But contemporary circumstances in California force us to distinguish between, on the one hand, a popular sovereignty that expresses itself in the ordinary politics of democratic lawmaking, and, on the other, a popular sovereignty that coalesces into a will that is distinctly *constitutional* in that it expresses and establishes a polity. Grodin assumes that the latter form of popular sovereignty is manifest in contemporary California. But this assumption is questioned by Bruce Cain and Roger Noll in their excellent article on the "Principles of State Constitutional Design" in this volume.

In California today the process of constitutional formation occurs almost exclusively through constitutional amendments. Constitutional amendments are often enacted by popular initiative. They can be approved by a mere majority of those voting in the relevant election. Cain and Noll correctly note that these circumstances threaten to collapse the distinction between ordinary politics and constitutional formation. They therefore ask the penetrating question: "What principles, if any, should guide whether a policy is written into a constitution or merely adopted as a statute?"[8]

---

[7]See, e.g., William J. Brennan, "State Constitutions and the Protection of Individual Rights," 90 *Harv. L. Rev.* 489 (1977).

[8]Bruce E. Cain and Roger G. Noll, "Principles of State Constitutional Design," in this volume.

This is a question well worth exploring.[9] Cain and Noll argue that the difference between constitutional and statutory policies are that the former are far more inflexible and hence costly. In the absence of any clear guidelines as to the desirability of inflexibility, Cain and Noll prefer "to make all constitutional change more difficult by imposing either supermajority and/or consecutive election requirements on all future initiative constitutional amendments."[10]

Cain and Noll's reasoning is incomplete and untheorized. They accept the necessity for some constitutional inflexibility, yet they decline to offer an account of the circumstances that justify this inflexibility. Hence they necessarily deprive themselves of criteria by which to evaluate the antimajoritarian measures they seek to impose on the process of constitutional amendment.

Such criteria must flow from a conceptual understanding of the relationship between a popular will that is constitutional, and a popular will that is simply majoritarian. Any such understanding will be essentially normative, because it will reflect for us the meaning of establishing a polity.

We can begin to explore the characteristics of a distinctively constitutional will by examining constitutional language. The federal Constitution famously begins with the words "We the People." The Constitution does not invoke the authority of the majority of the people, but it instead speaks with the voice of the people whole and entire.

This is in fact typical constitutional usage. The California Constitution begins with the same language:

> We the People of the State of California, grateful to Almighty God for our freedom, in order to secure and perpetuate its blessings, do establish this Constitution.

Constitutions establish a polity in the name of the whole people who will inhabit and comprise that polity. They do not speak in the name of a majority of people who may make up merely a faction within that polity.

---

[9]I agree with Cain and Noll that the question cannot be answered by reference to a distinction between rights and policies, because rights effectuate and give legal expression to policies.

[10]Cain and Noll, in this volume.

This notion of the whole people has a long and distinguished history within political theory. It is clearly related to the concept of the "general will" most famously theorized by Jean-Jacques Rousseau.[11] A constitution seeks to embody the general will of a polity, as distinct from the particular wills that make up the everyday politics of the polity. This difference is recognized in most versions of modern American constitutional jurisprudence. Perhaps the clearest contemporary account may be found in Bruce Ackerman's distinction between constitutional decisions, which are "made by the People," and ordinary political decisions, which are made "by their government."[12]

For Americans this distinction between a general constitutional will and a particular majoritarian will does not require any fancy theoretical construction. It is pervasive in our political self-understanding. Take, for example, the writings of that most prosaic and untheoretical figure, William Howard Taft.

As you may remember, Taft was strongly opposed to the kinds of progressive majoritarian reform measures that Cain and Noll now condemn. Indeed, Taft vetoed the congressional joint resolution admitting Arizona to statehood, on the ground that the proposed Arizona constitution contained a provision for recalling judges. In his statement justifying his veto Taft offered a precise and clear formulation of the distinction between the will of the whole people and the will of a majority of them:

> Now, as the government is for all the people, and is not solely for a majority of them, the majority in exercising control either directly or through its agents is bound to exercise the power for the benefit of the minority as well as the majority. But all have recognized that the majority of a people, unrestrained by law, when aroused and without the sobering effect of deliberation and discussion, may do injustice to the minority or to the individual when the selfish interest of the majority prompts. Hence arises the necessity for a constitution by which the will of the majority shall be permitted to guide the course of the government only under

---

[11]Jean-Jacques Rousseau, *The Social Contract*, Maurice Cranston, trans. (Harmondsworth: Penguin, 1968).

[12]Bruce Ackerman, *We the People: Foundations* 6-7 (Cambridge, Mass.: Belknap Press of Harvard University Press, 1991).

> controlling checks that experience has shown to be necessary to secure for the minority its share of the benefit to the whole people that a popular government is established to bestow. A *popular government is not a government of a majority, by a majority, for a majority of the people. It is a government of the whole people, by a majority of the whole people under such rules and checks as will secure a wise, just, and beneficent government for all the people.*[13]

A constitution, says Taft, no doubt expressing what he viewed to be merely the most obvious of premises, speaks for the people as a whole, and in the name of that people it frames the arena within which particular majorities may conduct normal politics.

If the theoretical distinction between a majoritarian and a constitutional will is an American commonplace, the operationalization of this distinction is not. One important question is how the content of the people's constitutional will may actually be determined. Rousseau advanced the logic that citizens could unproblematically be compelled to obey the general will because by doing so they were merely being "forced to be free," which is to say to obey their own more general will.[14] In the twentieth century we have witnessed unspeakable horrors flowing from the abstract and unproblematic application of this logic. In the American constitutional tradition, by contrast, we have always been exceedingly cautious in attributing determinate content to the general constitutional will. We have tended to do so primarily through mechanisms like judicial review that fully recognize the place of dissent and difference in the ascertainment of constitutional meaning.

Cain and Noll's paper, however, raises a different and more pointed question of operationalization. Their paper forces us to ask how we can actually know whether a particular effort to amend the California Constitution reflects an exercise of a constitutional will, as distinct from a majoritarian will. It is pertinent to note that this question almost never arises within the context of the federal Constitution, where we have

---

[13]William Howard Taft, "Special Message of the President of the United States Returning Without Approval House Joint Resolution No. 14, 62nd Cong., 1st Sess., H.R. Doc. 106, p. 3 (August 15, 1911) (emphasis added).

[14]Rousseau, *supra* note 11, at 64. ("Obedience to a law one prescribes to oneself is freedom." *Id.* at 65.)

entrusted this distinction to the positive mechanisms of Article V. We tend simply to accept enactments that meet the criteria of Article V as genuine expressions of a constitutional will.

This positivist solution is denied to us within the context of the California Constitution, because Cain and Noll claim, most plausibly in my view, that current amendment procedures authorize enactments that sometimes express merely a majoritarian will. This claim cannot be understood as empirical; it can not be reduced to the assertion that in California Constitutional amendments are sometimes in fact adopted by a majority vote. The claim is instead interpretative and normative. Cain and Noll's indictment is that in California the process of constitutional formation has collapsed into the ordinary politics of majoritarian power.

To evaluate this indictment we must explore how the American constitutional tradition has operationalized the distinction between a constitutional and a majoritarian will.

In practice, this distinction has crystalized along two metaphoric dimensions, which we might call the spatial and the temporal. The spatial dimension references the aspiration of a constitutional will to be general, to be the will of all. Of course actual unanimity is impossible in any modern heterogeneous state. But unanimity nevertheless remains as a kind of regulatory ideal. The force of that ideal is expressed in the supermajoritarian requirements that typically attach to processes of constitutional formation. We do not require that constitutional amendments be approved by everyone, but we generally set stringent requirements that force such amendments to reflect a large proportion or broad consensus of the electorate.

The temporal dimension refers not to the percentage of the electorate that agrees with a proposed constitutional provision, but rather to the quality of popular assent. William Howard Taft once again perfectly expresses the received wisdom with respect to this dimension:

> To protect against the momentary impulse of a temporary majority of the electorate to change the fundamental law and deprive the individual or the voting minority or the non-voting majority of inalienable rights, the Constitution provided a number of checks and balances whereby every amendment to the Constitution must be adopted under forms and with delays that are intended to secure

> much deliberation on the part of the electorate in adopting such amendments.[15]

A constitutional will, says Taft, is not momentary. It is not impulsive or "hasty."[16] It is instead considered, thoughtful, a product of "deliberation." It reflects the judgment of Philip sober, rather than Philip drunk. Hence we create mechanisms of "delay" that serve to test the stability and durability of a popular will that claims to be constitutional.

A popular will that endures is interpreted to be a will that is deliberate and considered. In popular characterization the metaphor of temporal duration slides into and fuses with the metaphor of rationality. This is because both rationality and endurance are rooted in a common notion of integrity, of a will that reflects an agent that is complete and whole.

Suppose, for example, that an instant computer poll of the California population discovers that 75 percent of the population favors a particular constitutional amendment. The temporal dimension suggests that we would not comfortably recognize this expression of popular will as constitutional unless we could also feel some assurance that the poll reflects a judgment that will endure over time. A history of deliberate consideration might well constitute this evidence. Just as we conceive of reason as the faculty that ensures the temporal coherence of individual personality, transcending the momentary gusts of passion that shake us all, so we conceive rationality as the guarantor also of the long-term coherence and integrity of the people, conceived as a collective political agent.

Article V of the federal Constitution functions in both spatial and temporal dimensions to isolate and define a distinctively constitutional will. Article V decrees supermajoritarian requirements for constitutional amendments. It also establishes a process that is likely to take a long time and hence to resist impulsive decision making. The California Constitution, by contrast, enables constitutional amendments to occur by simple majority vote in a single election.

---

[15]William Howard Taft, "The Judiciary and Progress," Senate Document No. 408, 62nd Cong., 2d Sess., p. 4 (1912).

[16]Taft, *supra* note 13, at 4.

We might conclude, therefore, that the California Constitution has simply misunderstood the normative requirements for ascertaining a constitutional will. Cain and Noll are correct in their indictment.

The deeper question, however, is why California has designed its processes of constitutional amendment to conflate constitutional and ordinary politics.

One dark possibility is that California's procedures reflect the truth of its condition. It may be that in California today there is no meaningful distinction between these two forms of politics. It maybe that contemporary California is not a polity within a polity, but merely a local center for the administration of a national legal order.

In such circumstances Grodin's plea for a special California Constitutional law would be quite beside the point, for California would not be the locus of any distinctive set of political principles defining a unique political culture. Hence any attempt to "constitutionalize" majoritarian decisions, and thereby render them inflexible and entrenched, would be presumptively illegitimate, or at the very most justifiable only by reference to the purely instrumental logic of managerial efficiency.

Many of us would be inclined to repudiate this dark possibility and to seek to preserve a legitimate role for constitutionalism within California government. The temptation, however, would be to do so merely by tinkering with procedural mechanisms. It would of course be easy enough to change the mechanisms of constitutional amendment so as to require them to contain the "supermajority and/or consecutive election requirements" recommended by Cain and Noll.

But merely altering these procedures will not summon a true polity into being. Focusing on amendment procedures is merely a distraction if the real issue facing California Constitutionalism is whether an authentic state polity can exist under modern conditions of national centralization and burgeoning local diversity.

Those of us who continue to care about the California Constitution must instead assume a different and more fundamental task: We must articulate a convincing vision of the California polity. Without some such vision, without a re-animated sense of California's distinctive political culture, no state constitution will mean much, despite the best intentions of judges of good will or political scientists of extraordinary brilliance.

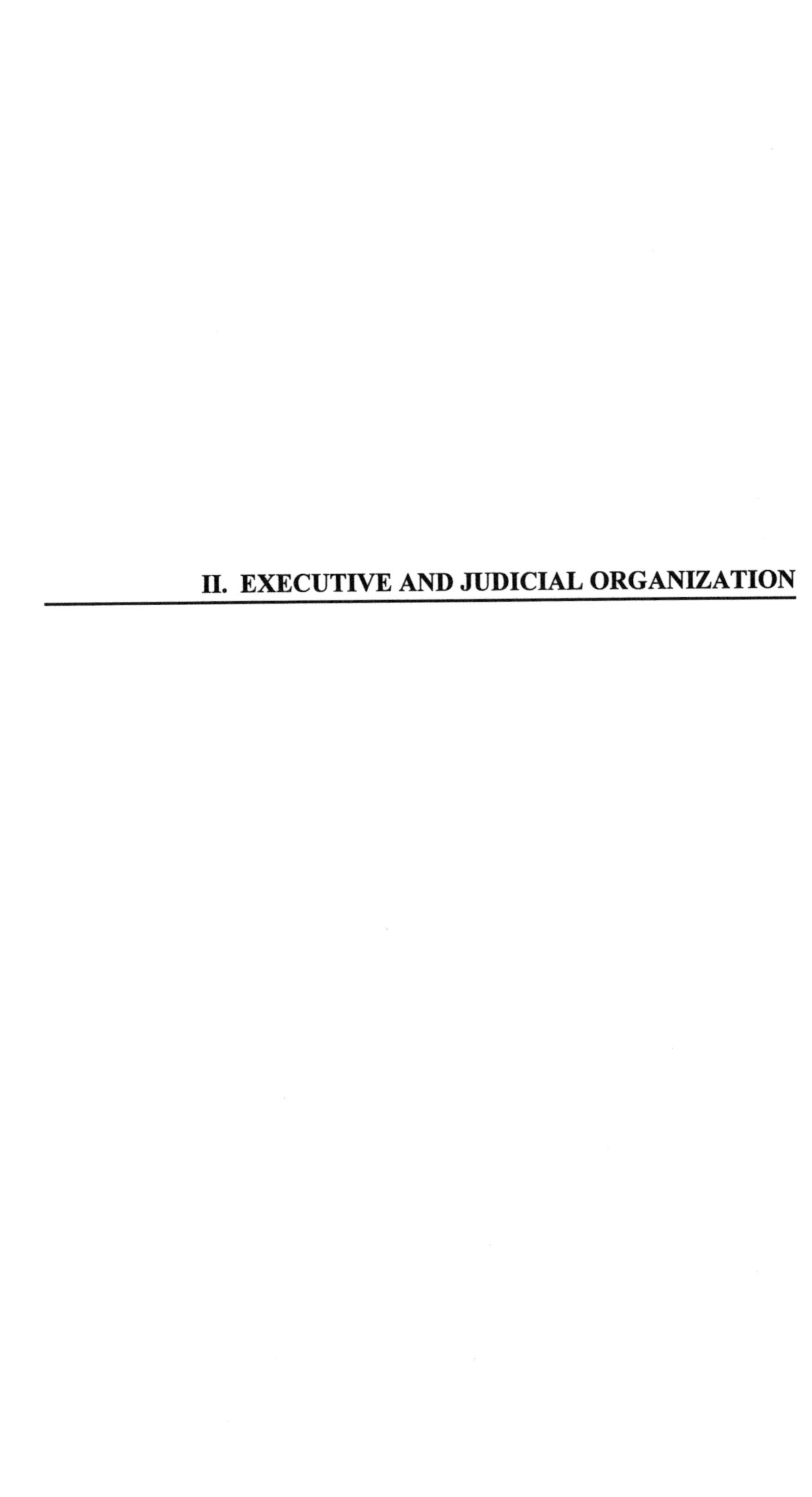

II. EXECUTIVE AND JUDICIAL ORGANIZATION

Executive Organization: Responsiveness vs. Expertise and Flexibility

Roger G. Noll

All state constitutions contain provisions that create executive branch offices and agencies and that specify which executive officials are to be selected by election. California is no exception. The state constitution and various initiative and referendum statutes[1] specify that eight executives plus the Board of Equalization are to be elected and create a long list of agencies and boards to be led by appointed officials. Usually the governor appoints these agency heads and commissioners, but in some cases state legislative leaders and other elected officials also make appointments to constitutional offices.

The purpose of this chapter is to provide some background information and analysis concerning the scope of constitutional specification of executive organization in California. The term "executive organization" is broadly construed to include various independent agencies and boards. All that is being excluded are legislative offices, the judicial system, and local government entities.

The primary messages of this essay are as follows. First, California is substantially more prone than other states to create executive organizations and elective offices by constitutional methods. Second, this method of organizing the executive branch creates inflexibility, fragments responsibility, and reduces accountability, so that a plausible case can be made that

---

Research assistance by James Ho and Scott Wallsten and financial support from the James Irvine Foundation is gratefully acknowledged.

[1]Statutory initiatives and referendums can not be repealed or amended without approval of the electorate and so are functionally much more like constitutional amendments than like legislative statutes. Hence, in the ensuing discussion all ballot measures that establish offices and agencies are considered to be constitutional in nature.

policy would be more responsive to voters if more agencies were brought into the governor's administration and the governor and legislature were given more authority to reorganize the executive branch. In particular, this chapter proposes that the California Constitution should be amended to eliminate the direct election of the Board of Equalization, the commissioner of insurance, the treasurer, the superintendent of public instruction, and the secretary of state, and that the election for lieutenant governor should be combined on a single ticket with the office of governor. This proposal would leave three statewide elections: a governor/lt. governor pair, attorney general, and controller.

PRINCIPLES OF EXECUTIVE ORGANIZATION

The primary objective of the organization of executive functions is to promote efficiency and responsiveness in the implementation of state policy. Efficiency refers to the provision of public services at low cost and high quality, with freedom from corruption. In addition, because part of the job of the executive is to detect aspects of policies that are incomplete or outdated, efficiency also means possessing the capability to evaluate policies and to propose ways to improve them. And, efficiency also has a time dimension: the ability to change policies quickly when they are outmoded or simply not working.

Responsiveness means that the policy preferences of a majority of voters, within limits to protect against exploitation of those who lose elections, are reflected in the way policy is implemented. To some degree, efficiency and responsiveness can be in conflict. Efficiency requires expertise and experience; responsiveness requires accountability to voters. To citizens, the most easily recognizable form of this conflict is that a policy may have the purpose of redirecting or constraining the actions of a professional group, whose members also possess the greatest expertise about how different policies are likely to effect the efficiency with which the professional group provides its services. Hence, citizens face a dilemma: place a fox in charge of the henhouse, or rely on a guardian who is less expert in fox behavior but more likely to protect the hens.

Means for Achieving Efficiency and Responsiveness

The standard tradeoff between efficiency and responsiveness cannot explain why the state constitution establishes so many executive agencies, insists that so many officials be elected, and for other offices specifies who has appointment powers. The alternative means for assuring responsiveness is to vest authority for executive management in a single elected official, such as the president in the U.S. federal government or the prime minister in a parliamentary system like Britain's.

Some states follow this practice: Maine and New Jersey elect only a governor; Alaska and New Hampshire elect only one official other than the governor; and Hawaii, Tennessee, and Virginia elect only two officials other than the governor. In these systems, a chief executive is held accountable for the performance of the executive branch and has the authority to hire and fire subsidiary executives and to propose to the legislature reorganization of the executive branch to improve the efficiency of policy implementation. When the constitution states that some positions are to be elected, others are to be appointed for fixed terms, and an agency is to be organized in a particular way and to carry out specific functions, the governor cannot reorganize the executive to respond to changing citizen preferences and other external circumstances. Because changing a law that has constitutional status is difficult and time consuming, the seemingly politically responsive act of creating an agency or elected position by initiative or referendum becomes a significant barrier to the responsiveness of policy to the preferences of future voters.

Parliamentary systems provide an interesting example for highlighting the subtlety of the responsiveness issue. Standard practice in parliamentary systems is for parties to be highly disciplined and for the ruling party or coalition to be held accountable for both legislative policymaking and its effective implementation in the executive. Responsiveness is achieved because the electoral system forces parties to adhere to clear, coherent policies and holds legislators accountable for the effective implementation of the laws that they pass.

A parliamentary system goes to the opposite extreme of the California system, which exhibits the separation of powers that is shared by all states and the federal government and which has the added feature of numerous elective executive offices. In a purely technical sense, neither system can be said to be more or less democratic: both select policymakers by majority-rule elections. But the parliamentary system holds the ruling party (or coalition) accountable for both policy and implementation; the California system fragments responsibility and in a sense makes officials less accountable to the electorate because the ultimate responsibility for the performance of government cannot be as clearly identified.

The Case for a Strong Governor

The most powerful argument in favor of centralizing appointment and organization power in the chief executive is that it makes the governor accountable and responsible for the effectiveness of the government. Accountability and responsibility require that the governor has the power to make executive decisions and to force executive branch officials to speak with a single voice. Decentralization has two inevitable consequences: fragmentation of responsibility and an increase in the relative power of the legislature compared to the executive.

An example of a policy arena in which the governor does have reasonably strong authority is the maintenance of the state highway system, which is managed by the secretary of the California Department of Transportation (Caltrans), a gubernatorial appointee. After the 1994 Northridge earthquake, Governor Pete Wilson immediately took actions to assure speedy, effective repair of the Los Angeles freeway system. By contrast, Governor George Dukmejian had not taken such action after the 1989 Loma Prieta earthquake, and many of the freeways in the Bay Area remained unrepaired after the Los Angeles freeways were back in full operation. Wilson's unprecedented and effective response to the Northridge disaster is widely regarded as an important factor causing the dramatic increase in his political popularity that led to his reelection later that year.

Fragmentation arises when two or more elected officials bear overlapping responsibilities. A clear example to contrast with the transportation case is state education policy. The players include the elected superintendent of public instruction, who as the head of the state Department of Education is appointed by the governor, and various boards for each level of education, with some members *ex officio* and others appointed. Fragmentation such as this enables each official to blame others for failure and to claim credit for success. The structure undermines the ability of the superintendent or the governor to design and to adopt new policies that would improve the schools, and encourages the governor to give low priority to education. Because the executive organization for education does not speak with a single voice, inevitably its internal policy disputes are resolved in the legislature, placing legislators in the position of having to make decisions about organization and administration, which the state legislature is not designed to do effectively.

California's complex administrative structure for educational administration surely cannot be given very high marks for effectiveness. Education is politically popular in California, usually succeeding in gaining majority support in bond, tax, and expenditure initiatives. Yet the system of educational administration has been unable to prevent the steady deterioration of California's public education system in comparison with other states. A plausible explanation is that no one has the authority to implement reforms, and so nobody is held responsible for the system's performance.

Because the governor is responsible for preparing the state budget, and because the performance of an organization depends upon its budget, some fragmentation of authority and responsibility is present in every area of policy in which the administrative head of an agency is either elected separately or is appointed by someone other than the governor. In California, the governor's line-item veto guarantees a blurring of accountability between the governor and literally every executive body that is not run by a gubernatorial appointee and that does not have its budget, both the total and the allocation across programs, determined by initiative.

Centralization of executive authority in the governor has another advantage: it allows policy implementation to be more flexible by letting the governor, perhaps with consent of the legislature, decide how to implement a policy. If the organizational structure and operating procedures of an agency are constitutionally specified, adjusting policy implementation to either changes in voter tastes or new information about the performance of the agency is protracted and difficult.

Arguments Against Centralization of Executive Power

The arguments against a strong governor fall into three categories: on-the-job training, representativeness, and protection from mistakes.

Training

The training argument is that having many elective offices enables officials to gain minor executive experience running a small part of the government before moving on to a major office, such as governor. Recently, another version of this argument has emerged in the context of legislative term limits: multiple elective offices provide a career hierarchy outside the legislature for the most able elected officials.

This set of arguments suffers from two serious problems. The first is that statewide elected offices constitute a tiny proportion of important elected positions in the state when one takes into account county commissions, mayors, school boards, and congress. A change in the number of statewide elected offices, therefore, will have a tiny effect on the opportunities for executive training in government or the availability of career options for politicians. The second problem is that most of these offices have not proven to be training grounds for governors. Whereas holders of lesser statewide offices frequently run for governor, the only offices that consistently produce viable candidates for governor are lt. governor and attorney general. Thus, these offices simply are not an important training ground for higher office nor an important career track for term-limited legislators.

Representation

The representation issue is a more serious argument. One representation argument is partisan. Governors and other statewide officials are elected by statewide popular vote. The legislature is apportioned on the basis of total population. Because turnout rates vary dramatically across socio-economic and ethnic groups, groups with low turnout are much more influential in the state legislature than in statewide votes. For example, consider three legislative districts with the same population, and with turnouts of 70 percent, 30 percent, and 10 percent. If the first district votes 60 percent Republican and the other two vote 60 percent Democratic, the three will send a two-thirds majority of Democrats to the state legislature. But the vote for governor will be 58-42 for the Republican, and Republican policies will obtain the same majority in initiative and referendum elections. Obviously, in this example, Democrats might fear a proposal to give the governor more power compared to the legislature, and Republicans might be wary of curtailing the scope of the initiative and referendum. There really is no effective response to this argument, other than to appeal to the inefficiency of the present system. A weak governor and outdated constitutional language that was adopted in a ballot measure some time in the distant past reduce the efficiency of executive management, perhaps sufficiently so that these effects offset the partisan consequences enjoyed by those who benefit from the status quo.

Another representation argument stems from the observation that the governor cannot possibly represent all voters on all issues, and on some issues may not even represent a majority. A single elected official is evaluated on the basis of a long list of attributes: policy positions, management skills, personal integrity, reliability, and leadership. Voters are likely to find every candidate for governor to have both strengths and weaknesses, and, in particular, to espouse some policy positions that are regarded as distinctly inferior to positions of other candidates. Hence, voters might prefer to elect different officials to deal with different kinds of issues: a separate executive to run the schools, the health care system, the system for regulating business, etc. The partisan election system can contribute to this phenomenon, for a majority of voters may prefer Republican positions on some issues and Democratic positions on others. A long list of separate elected executives enables them to emphasize different attributes for different offices.

The difficulty with this argument is that it depends on a view of elections that is too idealistic. Because individual voters have essentially no effect on who wins elections, the election system has two serious problems: rational ignorance, and interest-group bias.

The first problem derives from the low individual payoff to casting an informed ballot. Because an individual vote is extremely unlikely to effect the outcome of an election, a voter has no incentive to spend the time and effort necessary to learn all relevant facts about all candidates for office. Consequently, most voters do not make much of an investment in evaluating candidates for most offices. For the most part, they will act passively in response to media coverage and campaign information.

If the ballot contains numerous offices and propositions, the media will tend to focus only on the few that it deems most important. Consequently, if voters are called upon to cast a large number of separate votes, they will cast most of them based on very little information. (As a mental exercise, readers are encouraged to write down from memory the positions advocated in the last election by the major-party candidates for secretary of state, their district representative on the Board of Equalization, and the controller.) Hence, direct election of numerous officials does not mean that the policies advanced by these officials are in any meaningful sense responsive to voter preferences.

The second problem with multi-office elections is that voters will tend to focus on issues that are most important to organized interests. Voters play a passive role with respect to most of the information about elections that they receive. Some information is provided at the expense of specific organized interests, or by candidates who are financed by these interests. Other information is provided through organizations to which voters belong, such as citizen organizations (like the Sierra Club), occupational organizations (like unions and trade associations), or sociocultural organizations (like churches). Again, this information will reflect the priorities of the organization that delivers it: how does the candidate stand on the environment, minimum wage, or school prayer? Consequently, voting decisions are likely to be based on selective information shared by affinity groups, and election outcomes are stacked in favor of well-organized groups, especially those reflecting a common means of earning income or an unusually intense policy preference.

The importance of these problems varies according to the number of elected offices, and the type of office in question. The problem with a system in which voters cast a large number of votes is that some votes will deal with candidates for offices about which most voters care very little and are not informed. California, with numerous propositions on every ballot, with numerous special districts, with significant authority vested in both counties and cities, with elected judgeships at all levels, and with numerous statewide elected offices, simply places unreasonable and unrealistic demands on voters.

Malfeasance

The last argument for not centralizing power in the governor is the fear that a governor will misbehave. Obviously, with respect to public policy, fragmentation of authority limits the degree to which any official can adopt bad policies; however, fragmentation does not do anything about policy neglect arising from a lack of accountability and unclear responsibility, and it does create opportunities for chaos and finger-pointing.

The paralyzing effect of fragmentation is most apparent in multimember boards and commissions in which members are appointed by different officials who have antagonistic objectives. The argument in favor of such bodies is that everyone has a "seat at the table"; the working hypothesis is that such bodies can serve as mirrors of the electorate to hammer out some policy compromise. In practice, fragmented bodies face great difficulty in resolving issues—and, especially, in implementing a policy. Because every management decision has a policy effect, each brings an occasion for reopening settled policy debates.

Originally, multimember bodies with long, fixed terms were created precisely for the purpose of slowing down policy change. The classic example is the United States Supreme Court, which the Founders designed to reflect the political values of previous elections and so to cast skeptical looks at innovations by newly elected officials. Later, this approach was copied in creating economic regulatory commissions, which by being distanced from elected political officials theoretically would be more able to withstand short-term pressures from the right to use regulation to form cartels and from the left to use regulation to expropriate capital. To ensure against undesirable short-term political influences, entities were created that had built-in inflexibility, with the loss of flexibility and accountability being judged worthwhile to protect against arguably worse consequences.

A more clear-cut argument in favor of fragmentation is that it provides some insurance against corrupt practices. The most likely places where corruption will emerge is in financial affairs (favoritism in contracts and taxation) and in criminal prosecution (persecution of enemies, and ineffective prosecution of friends or corrupt political allies). The standard protection against the former is an independent auditor/inspector general (a federal example is the Government Accounting Office), and against the latter is an independent legal authority (at the federal level, a special prosecutor).

In the federal government, watchdog activities are usually organized by Congress as part of its oversight function. In the states, a common approach is to have elected officials perform these functions: typically the attorney general and some audit office (the title can be controller, comptroller, or auditor). The tendency to create a separate executive function, rather than a legislative one, has a rationale: state legislators are less likely to be professionalized (that is, they devote less time to official duties than do members of Congress), are less likely to have relevant professional skills (partly because their pay is low), and are likely to have less experience in government (they served fewer terms than federal legislators even before term limits were imposed, and the best frequently move on to higher office, including the Congress). Hence, state legislators, on balance, might be less able than members of Congress to manage an effective oversight operation.

In California, these arguments have somewhat less applicability, because the California legislature is more professionalized than most state legislatures. Nevertheless, term limits and recently enacted initiatives that limit state legislative staff make extensive legislative monitoring of executive behavior less likely. Hence, the argument for an independent attorney general and controller is reasonably strong.

An Assessment of the California System

With protection against malfeasance in office in place, the case for direct election of other state executives is weak. For some offices, like treasurer, the main criterion for office must be managerial and financial expertise, yet it is difficult to imagine exactly how voters can assess this capability in a campaign. The county treasurer who bankrupted Orange County had won several elections, the last against a candidate who had correctly predicted the debacle to follow. By contrast, a governor (like a president) has a strong incentive to appoint a treasurer who is adept at financial management in order to maximize the executive's ability to carry out other policies effectively.

For other offices, like superintendent of public instruction, the basis for election is state policy; however, fragmentation of authority attenuates the degree to which these officials can be held accountable for policies in their domain of responsibility, and to the extent that the position includes an important management function, elections are a less effective means for ascertaining professional qualifications than appointment processes.

The essence of the issue concerning executive organization is whether government works best when voters pick individual policies or elect governments that are then held accountable for all policies. Which approach to elections works best depends on whether voters, in the normal course of events, can be expected to possess enough information and expertise to make policy decisions that they later will regard as desirable and effective, or whether the low information content of elections (and the excessive influence of organized interests, especially in elections with long ballots), makes citizens better off if they vote for governments, rather than for individual policies.

PRACTICES IN OTHER STATES

California has nine statewide elected offices: governor, lieutenant governor, secretary of state, treasurer, attorney general, controller, superintendent of public instruction, insurance commissioner, and the Board of Equalization (four members elected from districts plus the controller). The duties of these officials as specified in the state constitution are shown in Table 1.

Elective Offices in Other States

The average number of elected officials in the 50 states is 7.06; nine states elect more statewide offices than California, five others elect nine, and 36 states manage with fewer.[2] The distribution of the number of statewide elected offices is shown in Table 2. As is apparent from this table, there is really no discernable trend during the past 30 years in the number of state elected officials.

Surprisingly, the states that elect more officials than California's nine tend to be relatively small. North Dakota leads the nation with 14 elected state offices. Louisiana, Mississippi, North Carolina, and Washington elect 11, and Georgia, New Mexico, Oklahoma, and South Carolina elect 10. Among the most populous states only Texas elects as many as California; Florida elects eight, Illinois elects seven, Michigan and Pennsylvania elect six, and New York five.

The specific elected offices among the states are shown in Table 3. States exhibit some broad similarities in the offices that they elect.[3] Nearly

---

[2]All data about the number of elected officials are taken from various issues of *The Book of the States*, published by The Council of State Governments.

[3]Counting the number of elected state officials for a given function is not straightforward. Some offices with the same title have different functions in different states, and some functions are performed by different officeholders in different states. Hence, the number of states that elect a particular office is not entirely clear. The most important judgments are noted in the discussion.

Table 1. ***California Elected Officials: Duties and Responsibilities***

Lieutenant Governor

* Chair, Economic Development Commission
* Member, State Lands Commission
* Regent, University of California
* Trustee, California State University
* Assumes Governorship in case of impeachment, death, resignation, removal from office, absence from state, or inability to perform duties of Governor

Attorney General

* Supervises district attorneys, sheriffs, and other law enforcement officers
* May prosecute any law in Superior Court jurisdiction if law not being properly enforced
* May assist district attorneys

Secretary of State

* Chief Election Officer
* Commissions notaries public
* Charters corporations
* Maintains records: Uniform Commercial Code, financing statements, tax liens, certificates of limited partnerships, campaign and lobbyist disclosures
* Oversees state archives
* Member, California World Trade Commission
* Appoints one member to Fair Political Practices Commission

Treasurer

* Manages state investment portfolios and bank accounts
* Administers sale of bonds and notes
* Administers state payments and receipts system
* Monitors fiscal affairs of special districts
* Periodically reports on fiscal conditions of state andlocal governments

Table 1. ***Continued***

Controller

- Provides fiscal controls for receipts and payments
- Monitors equity and efficiency of tax collections
- Administers unclaimed property and property taxpostponement programs
- Fiscal adviser for local governments
- Member, Board of Equalization

Board of Equalization

- Appellate body for Franchise Tax Board, utility tax assessments, county property tax assessments, someother tax assessments
- Issues rules and regulations on state taxes
- Sets property values of utilities for tax purposes
- Sets some tax rates
- Guides and evaluates county assessors

Superintendent of Public Instruction

- Administers state role in public schools
- Secretary and executive office, State Board of Education
- Chair, Curriculum Commission and Teacher Credentialing Commission
- Member, Board of Governors, California Maritime Academy
- Regent, University of California

Insurance Commissioner

- Licenses, examines and regulates insurance companies
- Licenses and regulates insurance producers, solicitors, and surplus line brokers
- Approves policy forms
- Furnishes policy services to the public
- Approves Workers compensation rates
- Handles conservation and liquidation of insurers
- Collects insurance taxes

Table 2. ***Number of Elected Offices: All States***

Number of Elected Offices	Year 1992/93	1980/81	1970/71	1960/61
16	0	0	0	1
14	1	0	0	1
13	0	0	3	0
12	0	2	1	1
11	4	1	0	3
10	4	1	3	4
9	6	8	10	9
8	5	6	6	6
7	11	11	7	7
6	9	9	8	8
5	3	3	2	3
4	0	2	2	1
3	3	2	3	2
2	2	3	3	4
1	2	2	2	2
11+	5	3	4	6
6-10	3	35	34	32
1-5	10	12	12	12
mean	7.06	6.66	7.02	7.28

Source: Council of State Governments, *The Book of the States*, various issues.

Table 3. *Constitutional Offices in the States*[1]

Type	Agency or Office Title[2]	# Elected	#Appointed
General Government	*Secretary of State[3]	37	11
	*Government Employees/ Civil Service	1	7
	*Political Practices	0	4
	Reapportionment	0	15
	Constitution	0	3
	*Salaries of Elected Officials	0	5
Justice and Courts	*Attorney General	39	5
	Prisons	0	5
	Parole and Pardons	0	11
	# of Judicial Boards		
	One	0	16
	Two	0	11
	*Three	0	4
Regulatory	*Alcohol	0	3
	*Utilities/Transport	5	4
	*Fish and Game	0	7
	Water	0	4
	Land	4	9
	Mines	0	6
	*Coastal Zone	0	1
	*Insurance	7	2
	Agriculture	7	6

Table 3. *Continued*

Type	Agency or Office Title[2]	# Elected	#Appointed
Public Finance	*Treasurer	35	6
	*Controller[4]	8	2
	Auditor	27	7
	*2 or 3 of Above[5]	29	10
	*Board of Equalization[6]	3	7
	Investment Commission	0	5
Specific Policies	*Superintendent of Education	15	15
	*K-12 Board of Education	8	17
	*University Board	2	22
	Health	0	5
	Welfare	0	6
	*Gambling, Racing	0	2

Source: Council of State Governments, *The Book of the States: 1992-93.*

[1]Includes offices in California that were created by initiative statutes.

[2]Asterisk indicates that the office is contained in the California Constitution or an initiative statute. Several other offices have been created and then repealed by initiative.

[3]Sometimes called the Commissioner of Elections. In two states this function is performed by a constitutionally established appointive board.

[4]Sometimes called comptroller.

[5]The first column is the number of states electing at least two of auditor, controller and treasurer. The second column is the number of states that elect none of these offices. The remaining 11 states elect one of these positions.

[6]Among the 10 states that have separate constitutional tax administration offices, the function is sometimes narrower than California's Board of Equalization, focusing only on standardizing property taxes, and sometimes the scope of authority is broader, covering all taxes. In two states this function is performed by a single tax commissioner (one is elected, one is appointed).

all states elect a lieutenant governor (42 states) and an attorney general (39), and about three-quarters elect the treasurer (35) and the secretary of state (37). Most also elect someone like the California controller, although the most common name is the state auditor. For other offices, two trends emerge. First, few other offices are elected. Second, states are getting out of the business of electing regulators and chief education officers. The former is down from 15 to five states since 1960, and the latter has fallen from 24 to 15.

The unusual elected offices in California are the superintendent of public instruction (a counterpart in 15 states), the insurance commissioner (seven states), and the Board of Equalization (only three states elect any tax official of any kind). California is also unique in that it has four constitutional agencies with some responsibilities for taxes. No other state has more than three, and the median number is two, with most states having an agency for motor vehicle taxes plus another agency for everything else.

Elections in Large and Neighboring States

Probably the most useful comparisons for California are either other populous states[4] or the most populous western states.[5] These states are most likely to face governance problems that are similar to California's.

Among the eight large states and the four largest western neighbors all but Oregon elect the attorney general, 10 elect the lt. governor, and nine elect the secretary of state and the treasurer. Eight states elect something like the controller. None of the comparison states elects anything like the Board of Equalization, and only two state constitutions—Arizona and Colorado—create an entity resembling this board, but in both cases it is appointive. Likewise, none of the comparison states elects an insurance commissioner, although Colorado has an appointive one in its constitution.

Florida, Arizona, and Washington elect the head of the state education system; Michigan and Colorado elect a state Board of Education. In the other seven states, state education officials are appointed, and in all states

---

[4]Florida, Illinois, Massachusetts, Michigan, New York, Ohio, Pennsylvania, and Texas.

[5]The most populous western states are Arizona, Colorado, Oregon, and Washington, each of which contains one major metropolitan area and a diverse economic base.

other than Massachusetts and Oregon the duties of the state educational administration (chief executive, board, or both) are defined in the state constitution. Hence, using the constitution to specify the state role in education is far more common than making these positions elective.

Executive Organization by Constitutional Means

California is more likely than other states to establish agencies and boards in the constitution. Among the large comparison states, in only five does the state university system have constitutional status (Arizona, Colorado, Michigan, New York, and Texas). Among all states, 24 have a constitutional university governance structure. California also has three constitutionally established entities for overseeing the state judiciary: the Commission of Judicial Appointments, the Commission of Judicial Performance, and the Judicial Council. Among the large comparison states, only Arizona and Pennsylvania have three separate entities for judicial oversight; the median number among these 12 states is one. Among all 50 states, the average number of such entities is two and the median is one.

The California Public Utilities Commission was created by a constitutional amendment; only Arizona, Colorado, and Texas among the large states use the constitution, rather than statutes, to establish a state economic regulatory agency. Among all states, only 12 have constitutional regulatory institutions of utilities and/or transportation, and nine have constitutional entities for regulating insurance.

California's constitution is unique in making provisions for a Citizen Compensation Commission and in creating two bodies to execute policy regarding alcohol (the Alcoholic Beverages Control Board and the ABC Appeals Board); only Michigan has a constitutional alcoholic beverages agency, and it manages to make do with one. Among the comparison states, only Colorado and Michigan join California in using the constitution to establish an entity for governing the state civil service, and only Illinois and Michigan used constitutional amendments to set up entities to regulate fair political practices.

In resource policy, California has one unique entity: the Coastal Commission; however, Washington has a constitutional Harbor Commission, and several other state constitutions establish a land commission, including Colorado, Oregon, Texas, and Washington. Among the comparison states, only Florida is like California in having a constitutionally established Fish and Game Commission.

By contrast, there is no important government function that appears in many other state constitutions but not California's. A significant number of states (not a majority and five of 12 in the comparison group) set up a reapportionment process in the constitution. Quite a few state constitutions set up entities for governing land use, mining, and agriculture, all of which California lacks. Overall, it is unusual to find a constitutional agency, function, or elective office that exists in several other states but not California, yet quite common to find California by itself, or with only a handful of others, in using the constitution to established boards, agencies, and executive offices.

REFORMING CALIFORNIA'S EXECUTIVE STRUCTURE

Among California's elected offices, few seem clearly to be well served by being elective rather than appointive. In addition, many other agencies have constitutional status in that, although the agency head is not elected, the position is defined by constitutional amendments or other ballot measures that are hard to change. This section reviews the elected offices and other constitutional positions.

Elective Offices

The problem arising from California's many elective offices is not that the functions that they perform are unimportant, but that their status as independently elected positions actually undermines their effectiveness and the overall efficiency and responsiveness of state government. This section reviews each of these elective offices and recommends that most of them be redefined as appointive positions in the governor's administration.

Lieutenant Governor

The problem arising from a separately elected lieutenant governor is apparent. The lieutenant governor has only two significant functions: to break tie votes in the state senate and to serve as governor when the governor is out of the state or incapacitated. The lieutenant governor is also a member of various boards and commissions and has various assignments that lack direct policy responsibility for state economic development, but hardly serves a unique or irreplaceable function in these capacities. Frequently the governor and lieutenant governor are of different political parties, causing the governor to want to avoid letting the lieutenant governor do anything. Whereas this keeps the governor in the state, it also serves to make the lieutenant governor almost completely useless and functionless. In the contemporary world of extensive, instantaneous electronic communication and fast, reliable transportation, the point of requiring the governor to abdicate office upon leaving the state is obscure at best.

The two alternatives to the present system are to force the governor and lieutenant governor to run as a team (thereby making the office effectively appointive) or to abolish the office altogether, placing succession rights elsewhere.[6]

Historically, lieutenant governors, like vice presidents, usually have been unused, but at least they were part of the chief executive's administration and so able to continue executive policies when the need for succession arose. Continuity of succession makes sense from the standpoint of both managerial effectiveness and political legitimacy, so succession is better placed in a member of the chief executive's inner circle.

To argue that this should be a lieutenant governor (or vice president) is more difficult. The argument in favor of electing lt. governors is that the identity of the successor is known to the electorate before the votes are cast for governor, but because neither voters nor candidates usually pay much attention to running mates this argument is not very persuasive. For the most important cabinet positions, one can make the case that the chief executive probably uses something besides political expediency to make appointments. Thus, no strong conclusions are offered about how to arrange succession to the governor, but surely the separately elected lieutenant governor should be eliminated.

---

[6]In three states, the first in line of succession is the secretary of state, and in five states it is the president of the state senate.

Secretary of State

The job of the secretary of state is primarily to keep records, to oversee registration, elections, and ballot propositions, and to register corporations, notaries public, and trade marks. There is simply no good reason to make this position elective. Most of these duties have relatively little policy content and are classically of the standard bureaucratic management task that primarily requires expertise and systematic, reliable implementation. Citizens want votes to be counted quickly and correctly, petition signatures to be authenticated with accuracy and dispatch, and historical archives to be well maintained; however, partisan political campaigns are not very informative about whether candidates have these skills, and the attributes that partisan campaigns reveal—ideology, values, policy positions—are largely irrelevant to the tasks. Only the tiny fraction of citizens that must deal with the record-keeping operation are likely to have information about how the secretary of state performs them; others are unlikely to know or to care.

Most likely, these functions will be performed with greater care and reliability if the governor is held accountable for them and so has an incentive to find a competent appointee. One could accomplish these tasks through an appointive secretary of state (as is done in 11 states) or by distributing these tasks among other agencies. For example, registration and elections are already managed primarily by county registrars; coordinating this activity and checking the validity of ballot petitions could be assigned to the office of attorney general. Likewise, the attorney general or the secretary of consumer affairs could handle business record keeping and notaries public.

The duties with respect to collecting information about lobbying and campaign activities and appointing one of the members of the Fair Political Practices Commission have greater political content and arguably call for some independence from other elected officials to protect against favoritism and corruption. To retain this protection, the activities related to monitoring the fairness of elections could be reassigned to the independent Fair Political Practices Commission (FPPC). Instead of giving the secretary of state the power to appoint a member, one could have all members appointed to long terms by the governor subject to confirmation by the legislature and requirements with respect to partisan mixture.

Multimember bodies with long-term appointments are designed to minimize the chance of partisanship in their decisions, and nothing requires insulation from partisan politics more than the body that regulates campaigns. Moreover, giving the FPPC the responsibility to collect relevant information about campaigns, elections, and lobbying enables it to prioritize resources for information gathering in accordance with the most important issues in regulating politics.

Treasurer

As noted above, most states elect the treasurer, but it is far from clear why they do so. The principal job of the treasurer is to manage state debt and investments. This job, as much as any other, requires expertise, not political responsiveness: all citizens can agree that the state should pay as little as possible for debt, earn as much as possible on its financial investments, write and mail checks when payment is due, and time capital expenditures so as to minimize their costs. In addition, in most other states and in the federal government the treasurer also is responsible for implementing tax laws. All of these functions are classic executive duties that should be integrated with other executive responsibilities, such as making purchase commitments, planning investments, and developing the budget. Erecting a political barrier against integration of these functions while creating the possibility for partisan conflict between the treasurer and other executive agencies with similar and overlapping responsibilities makes no sense.

If concern for corruption motivates this separation, citizens can protect themselves against a corrupt administration by electing a state auditor (the controller) with mandatory access to all financial records. As the citizens of Orange County have learned recently, the right to elect a treasurer really offers no protection against corruption because the tasks of the job are simply too arcane and professionally specialized for direct scrutiny by voters. Hence, there is something to gain and nothing to lose by moving the state treasurer into the governor's administration as an appointive office, subject to confirmation by the legislature.

Controller

The controller manages a watchdog agency for state expenditures, although other duties are policymaking in character (such as administering unclaimed property and implementing certain tax policies) or advisory (financial guidance to local governments). The policy and advisory functions do not have any necessary relation to the watchdog function, and could be integrated with similar activities that are carried out in other executive agencies. In particular, if the state constitution creates an appointed treasurer with broad policies in managing tax collections, state debt, and expenditures, these functions of the controller would fit naturally into this new office.

The watchdog activities, including monitoring the adequacy and integrity of financial controls in local governments, do provide citizens with the assurance of an independent auditor of government activity. In principle, campaigns for this office give citizens the opportunity to evaluate the integrity of candidates and to use votes to pass judgment on the effectiveness of an incumbent. As a practical matter, the office of the controller is also not very visible politically, and the effectiveness of the controller in carrying out the audit function is quite difficult to ascertain. Consequently, the case for the controller must be like the case for buying insurance: the presence of an independent auditor encourages elected and appointed officials to maintain good financial practice.

Board of Equalization

Essentially, the board acts as a regulatory body for tax policy. It is quasi-judicial in that it hears appeals against decisions by taxing authorities (including itself), and it is quasi-legislative in that it issues regulations regarding tax procedures and sets some taxes. Finally, it is also executive in that it assesses some types of property and coordinates assessment practices by local governments.

The existence of the board raises two separate issues. The first is whether such a body should exist, and the second is whether it should be elected. Certainly the functions of the board cannot be avoided: tax disputes must be adjudicated, regulations spelling out in detail how to calculate tax liability must be written, property must be assessed, and tax rates must be set. The issue is who should perform these functions. In the federal government and most state governments, a treasury department performs the function of defining and assessing tax liability, and the courts resolve disputes, usually after some formal internal review process.

This division of responsibility makes sense. Implementing the tax code by developing appropriate forms, record-keeping requirements, and regulations and definitions regarding sources of taxable income, allowable deductions, and valuations of capital assets is a highly technical field that requires the expertise of accountants, economists, and lawyers. Likewise, reviewing tax enforcement is a classic judicial responsibility that should be as free as possible from political interference. Neither task should have much policy and partisan content.

In California, the existence of a separately elected board serves mainly to absolve elected officials of responsibility for the equity and efficiency of the tax collection system. The governor, treasurer and state legislature can rightfully claim that implementation of tax policy is largely out of their hands. And, because Board of Equalization elections are almost completely invisible—in part because the members are elected from districts, and in part because the office is so specialized—the effect of the system is to remove tax implementation as an election issue for the governor and members of the legislature.

Because board members are invisible and have very large constituencies, their campaign success is highly dependent on raising campaign contributions to finance activities that give them name recognition. Not surprisingly, interests with much at stake in the narrow details of the interpretation of the tax laws contribute substantially to these campaigns. One cannot imagine a worse method for selecting officials to enforce tax laws than running beauty contests in very large districts. The problem is not just the opportunity for corruption—the explicit purchase of a favorable tax ruling in return for campaign contributions. The problem is far deeper. Suppose in a primary election for a vacant seat on the board, several candidates are running, one of whom believes sincerely that a particular industry or type of investment simply should not be taxed. People whose self-interest accords with these beliefs will certainly have a strong reason to make completely noncontingent, even anonymous, donations to that candidate. And, because the election is mostly invisible and the candidates mostly unknown, these contributions will enable the favored candidate to buy name recognition and so have a higher probability of winning the election. The net effect is that the system produces a corrupt outcome without any single person behaving in a corrupt fashion.

Because the existence of an elected Board of Equalization fragments responsibility and allocates great power to a nearly invisible, untouchable body, the board should be abolished. Its regulatory and executive functions should be assigned to the treasurer, and its adjudication functions should be assigned to either the superior courts or a state tax court.

Commissioner of Insurance

The insurance commissioner is California's most recently created elected official. In general, states are rapidly moving away from electing regulators. Regulatory issues are rarely at the forefront of the voter's attention; the circumstance a few years ago when Californians decided to directly elect the insurance commissioner, which previously had been an appointed position.

Like the Board of Equalization, the invisibility of the insurance commissioner, combined with the necessity to run for office in a statewide election that receives almost no media attention, intensifies the likely influence of organized interests that finance campaigns. Most states have gotten out of the business of electing regulators because of the tendency of election to cause regulators to manage regulation as a gigantic scheme to tax political enemies and reward political friends, rather than to try to make regulated industries more efficient. This fate is almost certain to be the eventual state to which this position will sink.

The argument against electing this office is not an argument about the wisdom of regulatory policy in general. Californians can write insurance legislation through statutes or the initiative regardless of how the legislation is implemented and enforced. Many other regulatory bodies have been established by ballot propositions: the Public Utilities Commission, the Fish and Game Commission, the Coastal Zone Commission, etc. The issue is whether it makes sense to elect such officials, given the fact that voters are likely to pay almost no attention to the campaign for the office.

Superintendent of Public Instruction

The argument for abolishing the superintendent of public instruction is not that the job is unimportant, but that it is organizationally untenable.

Education is an important issue, and for several reasons (especially the role of the state as dictated by court decisions that require comparable expenditures per pupil across school districts) the state must play an important role in public education. Moreover, the debates about educational policy are intensely political in the best sense: arguments about values and the appropriateness of different basic philosophies of education. Hence, it makes sense to organize the political components of state government in a way that facilitates bringing education high on the public agenda during political campaigns. The problem is that one cannot effectively focus educational policy in a single elected executive (or an elected board) if that office lacks fiscal and managerial control.

In California, the balance of power on all of these issues lies with someone other than the superintendent: personnel and practice decisions lie with local boards; overall budget control lies with the governor and the legislature to the extent it is not controlled by initiatives; and overall policy for textbooks, testing and standards rests in the appointed board, of which the superintendent is but one member.

One approach would be to strengthen the position by granting far more power to the superintendent: eliminate the state Board of Education, make the superintendent the executive head of the state Department of Education, give the superintendent responsibility for proposing the education budget and transfer the governor's line-item veto on the education budget to the superintendent. The other alternative is to eliminate the superintendent, and place all of the responsibilities of the superintendent in the governor's appointee to head the Department of Education.

The latter is organizationally superior for two reasons. First, educational policy should not be separated from matters of educational finance, and the latter cannot be separated from overall state budget policy. Separation of educational policy from responsibility for the budget cannot avoid fragmentation, and creates distorted incentives for the superintendent (who can be an unabashed advocate for education without directly bearing responsibility for its costs) and the governor (who can be an unabashed advocate for tax reductions and for other programs, without bearing direct responsibility for the performance of the educational system). Expanding the role of the cabinet official responsible for education forces the more visible and powerful office of the governor to take responsibility for education and to make trade-offs between education and other programs.

This approach would force public education on the governor's agenda by holding the governor clearly accountable for it.

Attorney General

The case for an independent attorney general is a very close call. The advantage of independence is that the attorney general is better positioned to deal with corruption of the criminal and civil justice systems, and so to serve the watchdog function. The disadvantage is that independent political status interferes with the role of the attorney general as the chief lawyer for the executive branch of the state government. Often the governor and attorney general are of different parties, so that the latter may oppose the actions under the law that are carried out by the governor's administration. In most areas of law statutory language does not unambiguously define the boundary between legal and illegal action, so that considerable discretion is available to executive officials to decide how to resolve the close cases. If the governor and attorney general disagree, two effects will emerge: the beneficial one of making ambiguities and conflicts visible and so more easily resolved politically, but a detrimental effect of creating confusion in the enforcement and implementation of the law.

Regardless of one's conclusions about whether an independent legal watchdog is more or less valuable than the greater coordination that would arise from making the attorney general part of the governor's administration, the issues here are far less clear than in the other cases. Hence, retaining the status quo, at least until experience is gained with the other reforms, is most likely to be perceived as the prudent strategy.

Other Constitutional Positions and Agencies

The California Constitution contains provisions that create and define the duties of numerous state agencies, commissions, and offices. The propensity to make policy in the constitution through the initiative and referendum process is the subject of several other chapters of this book, so a discussion of this problem is unnecessary here. Suffice to say that all of the ballot measures that have established the organizational structure, procedures, and specific duties of these positions should be converted to statutes that can be amended by the legislative process. This issue is separable from the policy content of these ballot measures. Whereas other chapters of this book argue that policy initiatives and referendums should also be easier to amend, one can easily separate the organizational issues—which offices will implement a policy, and how officials will be selected—from the questions of policy.

The argument in favor of this proposal is that it serves both efficiency and responsiveness objectives to make government more flexible. For example, consider the issues of water resource management and regulation of fisheries. When the state agencies for water regulation (a referendum statute in 1914) and fish and game control (a legislative constitutional amendment in 1940) were established, water pollution and diversion were not as extensive as they have become. In recent years, the relationship between water management and the maintenance of high-quality fisheries has become far more important, partly because the public has demanded greater conservation efforts and partly because in drought years the state's demands on the water system are so extensive that water diversion threatens many important fisheries. Recent issues that would not have been anticipated early in this century when the state's resource agencies were established are the controversy over diversions from Mono Lake (and the success of the Mono Lake Committee in forcing reestablishment of trout fisheries in the Mono Lake tributaries as a means to stop the decline of Mono Lake), the decline of striped bass fisheries in the Sacramento delta and San Francisco Bay, and the near extinction of the salmon runs in the Sacramento River system.

As an illustration of this problem, an important cause of the decline of the striped bass fishery in the Sacramento delta and San Francisco Bay is that large numbers of recently hatched juvenile fish have been trapped in the intake valves that pump water into the state aqueduct system. In 1994, the state water project developed a method for trapping striped bass fry at the intake tunnels of the California Aqueduct, and implemented the plan by catching and raising several hundred thousand fish. But raising and releasing fish are the responsibilities of Fish and Game, and initially Fish and Game opposed the plan to release the fish back into the waterways after they had matured. Eventually the conflict was resolved, and the first fish were released into San Francisco Bay in the summer of 1995, but even this action is only an experiment.[7] The delay, discussion, and possibility for unresolved conflict in the program was created purely by the organizational structure of government.

The creation of the existing set of water and fisheries agencies arguably was politically responsive to the policy preferences of citizens in the early decades of the twentieth century, but the organizational and policy inflexibility in the system of water rights and regulations and fisheries management now inhibits flexible response to new problems and citizen preferences. Making these agencies and policies easier to change, therefore, would increase both responsiveness and efficiency.[8]

Assuredly, ballot measures that eliminate agencies that were created by previous ballot measures occasionally do pass. For example, the California Horse Racing Board was created by a legislative constitutional amendment (LCA) in 1933, but eliminated by another LCA in 1962, and in 1960 an LCA reduced the size of the Board of Equalization from an unmanageably large one per congressional district—today, this would be a regulatory commission with over 50 members—to five. Likewise, an initiative constitutional amendment (ICA) created the position of an elective director of the Department of Social Welfare in 1948, then another ICA repealed it one year later.

These and other examples of reorganization of positions and agencies created by the ballot are unusual. The reason is clear: to undertake the task of crafting and qualifying a ballot initiative to reorganize government requires considerable effort on the part of the legislature or considerable cost on the part of a private group seeking a change, and then to mobilize electoral support requires still more expenditures. For the most part, neither the legislature nor private organizations are likely to bear these

---

[7]The federal Department of Interior also must approve, and also has not authorized anything more than a trial.

[8]The 1940 amendment that created the Fish and Game Commission does not specify its duties, but only empowers the legislature to delegate to the commission the responsibility for managing fisheries. The implication is that the state legislature could make Fish and Game an empty shell by stripping its powers; however, it is far from clear whether the courts would enable the state to delegate fisheries management to any body other than the commission, such as a comprehensive water resource management commission, without approval from a ballot measure.

costs unless the stakes are immense and a substantial proportion of the electorate perceives a problem and wants to fix it. By contrast, reorganizations by statute or executive order are easier, quicker, and cheaper, and so require a far lower threshold of public importance and support to be worth the effort of the legislature or the governor.

CONCLUSIONS

As other chapters in this book maintain, California is too prone to solve policy problems and organizational management issues by the relatively inflexible process of constitutional change. As a result, the state has too many elected offices that citizens do not care about or understand, and too many agencies, boards, and executives inflexibly specified in constitutional language.

This chapter offers two principal proposals. The first is to cut the number of elected statewide offices. The highest priority should be to end the election of the Board of Equalization and the superintendent of public instruction, and to have the governor and lt. governor run as a team, with the lt. governor selected by either the governor or the governor's party at a state convention. Second priority is to end the election of the state treasurer and secretary of state, with the latter's duties for managing the political system reassigned to the Fair Political Practices Commission. Second, all constitutional provisions (including statutory initiatives and referendums) establishing the organizational structure of the government other than the offices of elected officials should have their status converted to that of legislative statutes. In addition, to protect against erosion of these changes, the state constitution should contain supermajority requirements for ballot measures that establish new elected offices or create an executive or regulatory organization.

Administrative Law and the California Constitution

Michael Asimow

This chapter criticizes a judicial doctrine grafted by the California Supreme Court on the due process provision of the California Constitution. It also criticizes the constitutional status of certain California administrative agencies.

PROCEDURAL DUE PROCESS

California's Unique Due Process Doctrine

Both the federal and California Constitutions guarantee "procedural due process," meaning that no person shall be deprived of "life, liberty, or property without due process of law."[1] Normally procedural due process[2] assures appropriate procedural protection before government acts against an individual. The process typically includes notice, a fair hearing (which usually includes confrontation of adverse witnesses), an exclusive record,

---

Thanks to Daniel Asimow, LeAnn Bischoff, Evan Caminker, Gary Schwartz, and Dan Lowenstein for help and advice.

[1]The Fifth and Fourteenth Amendments protect persons from such deprivations by the federal and state governments respectively. California's due process clause, Art. I, §7(a), provides: "A person may not be deprived of life, liberty, or property without due process of law. . . ." Thus the language of Art. I §7 is the same as that of the federal Constitution except that the California provision arguably does not contain a state action requirement. I have not researched the state action issue, but constitutional revisers should consider this question. Art. 1, §15 calls for due process protection in criminal cases.

[2]This comment does not discuss substantive due process, according to which people have certain rights of liberty and property of which they cannot be deprived regardless of procedure without sufficient justification.

and an unbiased decisionmaker.[3] The problem to be addressed here is which interactions between government and persons outside government trigger procedural due process protection.

This chapter cannot discuss the federal law of procedural due process in any detail.[4] Federal due process protections are triggered only by governmental deprivation of liberty or property; the words "liberty" and "property" have far broader meanings than the uninitiated might expect.[5] Thus the word "property" includes not only traditional forms of property but also entitlements provided by state law or custom.[6] The word "liberty" similarly covers a great range of interests, some but not all of them based on positive law entitlements.[7]

For this purpose, an entitlement means a protected status or benefit that the state cannot deny or take away absent a nondiscretionary reason for doing so. But if the interest can be taken away or denied in the discretion of an official, it is not an entitlement and does not qualify as property and, in some situations, not as liberty either.

---

[3]In certain circumstances, due process has been held to require only a conference with the decision maker, not an adversarial hearing before a neutral arbiter. See, e.g., *Goss v. Lopez*, 419 U.S. 565 (1975).

[4]See Laurence Tribe, *American Constitutional Law,* 2d ed. (Mineola, N.Y.: Foundation Press, 1988), 663-768; Jerry Mashaw, *Due Process in the Administrative State* (New Haven: Yale University Press, 1985). For an excellent critical discussion, see Cynthia R. Farina, "Conceiving Due Process," *Yale J. of Law & Feminism* 3 (1991): 189.

[5]See Edward L. Rubin, "Due Process and the Administrative State," *Calif. L. Rev.* 72 (1984): 1044.

[6]See *Board of Regents v. Roth*, 408 U.S. 564 (1972); *Perry v. Sindermann*, 408 U.S. 593 (1972), distinguishing between tenured and untenured teachers. Professional licenses are "property" under this definition. *Barry v. Barchi*, 443 U.S. 55 (1979). A whole range of less significant entitlements are also treated as property. See *Goss v. Lopez*, 419 U.S. 565 (1975) (10-day suspension from public school); *Memphis Light, Gas & Water Div. v. Craft*, 436 U.S. 1 (1978) (right to continued service from municipal utility); *Logan v. Zimmerman Brush Co.*, 455 U.S. 422 (1982) (right to sue under antidiscrimination law).

[7]Liberty interests go far beyond freedom from bodily restraint and include "those privileges long recognized as essential to the orderly pursuit of happiness by free men." *Board of Regents v. Roth*, 408 U.S. 564 (1972), quoting *Meyer v. Nebraska*, 262 U.S. 390 (1923).

In adopting this positivistic liberty/property methodology, the Supreme Court consciously turned away from earlier precedents that used more amorphous tests and appeared to provide due process in a much broader range of cases.[8] Of course, determining whether a particular interest is actually liberty or property requires resorting to a vast and confusing body of constitutional law. This law is constantly being remade and litigation is incessant. Nevertheless, the liberty/property methodology is stable and reasonably workable. Once a particular interest is identified as liberty or property, there is a second stage: a court must determine the precise elements of the process that is due and when it must be provided. These issues are resolved by application of a balancing test that weighs the strength of the plaintiff's interest, the utility of the procedure being used and of the procedure that the plaintiff wants in terms of avoiding error, and the strength of the government's interest in resisting the proposed procedure.[9] Again, this three-factor balancing gives rise to numerous disputes, but most of the big questions have been answered.

California Has Rejected the Federal Approach

Procedural due process under the California Constitution covers a vastly greater universe of deprivations than does federal due process *and* provides for more process than is due under federal balancing. In the leading *Ramirez* decision,[10] the California Supreme Court veered sharply

---

[8]*Board of Regents v. Roth*, 408 U.S. 564 (1972), involved a sharp narrowing of the broader and more amorphous tests articulated by the Court in *Goldberg v. Kelly*, 397 U.S. 254 (1970). *Goldberg* seemed not to hinge the applicability of due process on a deprivation of liberty or property but instead on "whether the recipient's interest in avoiding [the] loss outweighs the governmental interest in summary adjudication." *Id.* at 263.

[9]*Mathews v. Eldridge*, 424 U.S. 319 (1976).

[10]*People v. Ramirez*, 25 Cal. 3d 260, 158 Cal. Rptr. 316, 599 P.2d 622 (1979). Two concurring justices expressed reservations about extending California due process protection past the limits set by federal law. See the sharp criticism of *Ramirez* in Stephen F. Williams, "Liberty and Property: The Problem of Government Benefits," *J. Leg. Stud.* 12 (January 1983): 3, 17-19. Williams argues that *Ramirez* cuts loose from the linguistic moorings of the due process clause and is ahistorical.

from the federal entitlement-based approach. In *Ramirez*, the director of corrections excluded a convict from in-patient status in the California Rehabilitation Center (CRC), a drug diversion program. The decision to admit a convict to CRC was, to a degree, controlled by some standards but it was also discretionary.[11]

The court stated that the federal approach is misconceived because it encourages statutemakers to empower officials to act in their unfettered discretion.[12] Moreover, the federal standard undervalues the dignity and worth of the individual—treating one as a nonperson, an object, rather than a respected participating citizen.[13] *Ramirez* is worth quoting:

> Thus, even in cases in which the decision-making procedure *will not alter the outcome* of governmental action, due process may nevertheless require that certain procedural protections be granted the individual in order to protect *important dignitary values*, or, in other words, "to ensure that the method of interaction itself is fair in terms of what are perceived as minimum standards of political accountability—of modes of interaction which express a collective judgment that human beings are important in their own right, and that they must be treated with *understanding, respect, and even compassion*. . . ." We therefore hold that the due process safeguards required for protection of an individual's *statutory interests* must be analyzed in the context of the principle that freedom from *arbitrary adjudicative procedures* is a substantive element of one's liberty. This approach presumes that when an individual is subjected to deprivatory governmental action, he *always* has a due

---

[11]The director may exclude a person from CRC if he concludes "that the person, because of excessive criminality or for other relevant reason, is not a fit subject for confinement or treatment. . . . " Welf. & Inst. C. §3053. Since the director's decision is, to some extent, controlled by a standard, the Court suggested that due process might apply even under the federal standard.

[12]*Ramirez*, 266-67. This argument has little merit. Even when statutes articulate standards for decision makers to follow, they are so broadly stated that they give little more guidance than a statute conferring pure discretion. See, for example, the statute governing the CRC quoted in note 11.

[13]*Id.* at 267-68.

process liberty interest both in fair and unprejudiced decision-making and in being treated with respect and dignity.[14]

Thus, under *Ramirez*, California due process protections always apply in the case of "deprivatory governmental action" because liberty includes freedom from "arbitrary adjudicative procedure." The purpose of due process is to protect an individual's "statutory interests," regardless of whether the procedures might "alter the outcome." Due process is designed to protect "important dignitary values," meaning an individual's right to "understanding, respect and even compassion."[15]

Once it is established that due process applies under this approach or under the standard federal liberty/property approach, the court reaches the next question: what process is due? The precise contours of what must be provided and when it must be provided can be ascertained only by balancing four factors—the individual's interest, the risk of error in the given procedure and the value of substituted procedure, the dignitary interests in providing notice and hearing to the individual, and the government's interests (including fiscal and administrative burdens).[16] The

---

[14]*Ramirez*, 25 Cal. 3d at 268 (emphasis added and footnotes deleted).

[15]The Court came up with this pastiche of theories by combining the work of several scholars who criticized *Roth*. The idea that freedom from "arbitrary administrative procedure" is "liberty" comes from William Van Alstyne, "Cracks in 'The New Property:' Adjudicative Due Process in the Administrative State," *Cornell L. Rev.* 62 (1977): 445. The idea that due process protects a person's dignitary interest belongs to Frank Michelman, "Formal and Associational Aims in Procedural Due Process," *Nomos* 18 (1977): 126, and has been echoed by numerous other authors. The work of Richard Saphire was particularly influential. Saphire, "Specifying Due Process Values: Toward a More Responsive Approach to Procedural Protection," *U. Pa. L. Rev.* 127 (1978): 111 (U. S. Supreme Court's due process jurisprudence fails to protect dignitary values).

[16]*Ramirez* at 269. This has led to numerous judicial balancing acts. See, e.g., In re Malinda S., 51 Cal. 3d 368, 383-85, 272 Cal. Rptr. 787, 795 P.2d 1244 (1990) (in child dependency proceeding county is not required to call as witnesses all persons whose statements are contained in social study); In re Jackson, 43 Cal. 3d 501, 510-16, 233 Cal. Rptr. 911 (1987) (prison disciplinary board need not interview confidential informants); *Van Atta v. Scott*, 27 Cal. 3d 424, 166 Cal. Rptr. 149 (1980) (judge need not give reasons for refusing own recognizance application); *Smith v. Bd. of Med. Qual. Assur.*, 202 Cal. App. 3d 316, 248 Cal. Rptr. 704

federal balancing approach has only three factors and omits dignitary interest as a factor.

Because *Ramirez* indicated that its result might have been the same under federal due process, the decision could be considered *dictum*. Also, *Ramirez* might be limited to disputes about confinement or similar deprivations of physical liberty. But in *Saleeby v. State Bar*,[17] *dictum* became holding and California due process was applied to a clearly noncriminal interaction between an individual and the state.

Saleeby involved the bar's decision to deny a defrauded client's application for reimbursement from the Client Security Fund. The statute explicitly leaves this decision to the discretion of the bar; consequently, federal due process would not require a hearing. But in an opinion by then-Justice Lucas (hardly a flaming liberal and now the chief justice), the court followed *Ramirez* and held that California procedural due process applied. Balancing the four *Ramirez* factors, the court required an informal hearing at which an applicant could present information in support of his claim. The court also required written findings of fact sufficient to apprise the parties and the courts of the basis of the action taken by the bar.

Bottom line—any unpleasant interaction between person and government might trigger California procedural due process but most of them would not trigger federal due process. Some examples:

- A nonstigmatic decision to discharge a probationary employee who, according to law, can be discharged without cause;[18]

(1988) (board's investigatory procedures pass muster); *People v. Davis*, 160 Cal. App. 3d 970, 981-84, 207 Cal. Rptr. 18 (1984) (second opinion required before convict denied admission to CRC).

[17]39 Cal. 3d 547, 562-68, 216 Cal. Rptr. 367, 702 P.2d 525 (1985).

[18]See Comment, Chris Scott Graham, "The California Dignitary Interest: Procedural Due Process and the Probationary Employee," *Pac. L. J.* 15 (January 1984): 321-48. But see *Schultz v. Regents of Univ. of Calif.*, 160 Cal. App. 3d 768, 780-87, 206 Cal. Rptr. 910 (1984) (nondisciplinary decision to alter employee's classification does not trigger due process protections). The somewhat dubious holding in *Schultz* is that the employee had no "statutory interest" in his job classification so *Ramirez* does not apply.

Schultz, however, is really based on policy disagreement with *Ramirez* and its implications. The court noted: "Public employees are adversely affected by countless daily decisions—from reassignment of job responsibilities to relocation

- A decision to transfer a prisoner from one prison to another;[19]
- A discretionary decision to deny a concealed gun permit;[20]
- A decision refusing an applicant admission to a graduate program at a state university;[21]
- A government decision to stop purchasing paper clips from vendor A and start buying from vendor B;[22]
- Allowing A rather than B to purchase choice season tickets behind the bench for UCLA basketball games.

I am not saying that the California courts would demand a hearing in each of these cases or would call for procedures more protective than federal procedures. I am only saying that they might, depending on the tastes of the judge and the equities presented by the specific case. And that

---

of a soft drink machine—made by their public employers. . . . If in the adjudication of disputes involving relations between public employees and employers, we abandon the prerequisite property interest, and require the courts in each instance to fashion suitable procedures by applying the *Ramirez* balancing test of private and governmental interests, we believe the courts could well end up attempting to manage the bureaucracy of the State of California. . . . " *Id.* at 786.

[19]Federal due process does not apply to most decisions concerning prisoners. See, *Sandin v. Conner*, 63 U.S.L.W. 4601 (1995.) Because such decisions implicate dignitary interests, however, California due process may require hearings in such cases. See, e.g., *Inmates of Sybil Brand Inst. for Women v. County of Los Angeles*, 130 Cal. App. 3d 89, 106-08, 181 Cal. Rptr. 599 (1982).

[20]See *San Jose Police Officers Ass'n v. City of San Jose*, 199 Cal. App. 3d 1471, 1478-86, 245 Cal. Rptr. 728 (1988). After a careful four-factor *Ramirez* balancing, including serious treatment of the dignitary interest, the court upheld the city's informal procedures. But *Nichols v. County of Santa Clara*, 223 Cal. App. 3d 1236, 273 Cal. Rptr. 84 (1990), held that no process was due upon the revocation of a concealed gun permit, even under *Ramirez*. *Nichols* is an example of a decision that simply ignores *Ramirez*.

[21]Under federal law, procedural due process does not apply to academic decisions of graduate programs. See *Univ. of Missouri v. Horowitz*, 435 U.S. 78 (1978) (no hearing for student dismissed from medical school for academic deficiencies). Under *Saleeby*, who knows?

[22]Federal courts hold that the interest of one contracting with the government is not "property" so government need not provide a hearing before breaching or not renewing a contract. *Mid-American Waste Systems, Inc. v. City of Gary*, 49 F. 3d 286 (7th Cir. 1995).

creates serious problems of overproceduralization and indeterminacy that I will address in the next section.

California Should Follow Federal Due Process Law

When should state courts expand constitutional rights beyond federal levels?

Should state courts construe state constitutions more broadly than the federal constitution? Many scholars, led by Justice William Brennan,[23] argue that state courts should be aggressive in interpreting state constitutions.[24] Others urge uniformity of the two regimes.[25] I believe that state courts should sometimes interpret state constitutions broadly. For example, different interpretations might arise from federalism concerns.[26] Or a state constitutional provision's legislative history might justify a unique reading. Or the U.S. Supreme Court's decision might be unclear or might lack the support of a majority of the justices. Or—and this is the tricky one—state judges may sincerely believe that a federal decision is so poorly reasoned or unprincipled that they feel compelled to depart from it.[27]

---

[23]William J. Brennan, Jr., "State Constitutions and the Protection of Individual Rights," *Harv. L. Rev.* 90 (1977): 489.

[24]See, e.g., Joseph R. Grodin, "The Role of State Constitutions in a Federal System," in this book; Lawrence Gene Sager, "Foreword: State Courts and the Strategic Space Between the Norms and Rules of Constitutional Law," *Tex. L. Rev.* 63 (1985): 959; "Developments in the Law—The Interpretation of State Constitutional Rights," *Harv. L. Rev.* 95 (1982): 1324; Hans A Linde, "First Things First: Rediscovering the States' Bill of Rights," *U. Balt. L. Rev.* 9 (1980): 379.

[25]See, e.g., James A. Gardner, "The Failed Discourse of State Constitutionalism," *Mich. L. Rev.* 90 (1992): 761; Earl M. Maltz, "The Dark Side of State Court Activism," *Tex. L. Rev.* 63 (1985): 995.

[26]For example, the U.S. Supreme Court may hesitate to impose a national standard with respect to such matters as school funding or Medicaid abortions. Yet individual states legitimately may decide to assume greater responsibilities. Procedural due process may be an example; the U.S. Supreme Court hesitates to impose excessive procedural burdens on every state or local government in the land, but nothing prevents individual states from assuming such burdens.

[27]I need not take a position on an earlier and related dispute: Proposition 8 was a 1982 initiative that conformed federal and California due process with respect to

A state court should require some substantial justification before departing from the U.S. Supreme Court's interpretation of identical constitutional language.[28] Most people believe that the U.S. Supreme Court plays a leadership role in defining constitutional language. Its decisions are carefully considered; the justices are aided by staffs of law clerks and by thorough briefing. This role is worthy of respect on the part of state supreme court judges. Even though a state court is empowered to define the identical constitutional language differently, it should hesitate before introducing disuniformity in the law. There are many instances in which Court A defers to a precedent from Court B, even though it is not required to follow that precedent, out of respect for Court B and for the sake of avoiding disuniformity.[29] Similarly, the Supreme Court hesitates before

---

confessions and search and seizure. Art. I, §28(d). It washed out numerous decisions of the California Supreme Court. See J. Clark Kelso and Brigitte A. Bass, "The Victims' Bill of Rights: Where Did It Come From and How Much Did It Do?" *Pac. L. J.* 23 (April 1992): 843, 852-56. One might have opposed Proposition 8 on the ground that the U.S. Supreme Court decisions decimated constitutional protections for the accused.

[28]Justice Grodin would not require any justification at all before the California Supreme Court strikes off on its own. Grodin, note 24. At the California Constitutional Reform Conference, Grodin stated that a decision of the U.S. Supreme Court should have no more weight than a decision of the Kansas Supreme Court. This theory is based on the fact that the state constitution is state law and there is no basis for deferring to any other body with respect to state law. See also Jennifer Friesen, *State Constitutional Law* (New York: M. Bender, 1992) ¶1.04.

As the text indicates, I do not agree with this view. Nobody thinks the Kansas Supreme Court plays a national leadership role in constitutional law, but most people think the U.S. Supreme Court does play such a role. Similarly, many people are troubled by court decisions that construe identical constitutional language differently, so that, for example, "due process" means one thing in one state and something quite different in another.

[29]See, e.g., Thomas W. Merrill, "Judicial Deference to Executive Precedent," *Yale L. J.* 101 (1992): 969. Merrill defends "weak deference," in which courts often defer to administrative agency statutory interpretation even though the court is empowered to decide the question independently. Similarly, a federal court of appeals for one circuit or a California Court of Appeal for one district need not follow the precedent of a sister circuit or district. Nevertheless, the court hesitates before creating a conflict. In these situations, the court puts a thumb on the scale

overruling one of its own precedents; it has the power to do it but it does not do so lightly.

The dispute about whether the California Supreme Court owes any deference to the U.S. Supreme Court, however, is not central to this chapter. In my view, California's *Ramirez-Saleeby* approach to defining the parameters of procedural due process is bad policy. It should be disapproved by the California Supreme Court or changed by constitutional amendment even if one believes that the California courts owe no deference at all to the U.S. Supreme Court's interpretation of the same language.[30]

California's Procedural Due Process Methodology Is Unjustified

For two reasons, California's procedural due process clause should not protect a broader class of interests, or require different procedures, than federal due process. First, the California standard overproceduralizes government action. Second, the California standard is radically indeterminate.

Overproceduralization. Society cannot afford to provide due process procedures in every single case in which an interaction between government and a person outside government produces an outcome that the person dislikes. Procedural due process is costly; society must allocate substantial resources to conduct hearings. These costs generally come from the budget of the governmental unit in question, thus decreasing the resources available to solve social problems.[31] Due process also causes delay; absent

---

in favor of following the precedent in question, but other factors can outweigh the precedent.

[30]See *San Jose Police Officers Ass'n v. City of San Jose*, 199 Cal. App. 3d 1471, 1486-88, 245 Cal. Rptr. 728 (1988) (dissenting opinion) (severe criticism of *Ramirez*—no justification to depart from federal due process standard).

To achieve the recommended goal of disapproving *Ramirez-Saleeby*, Art. 1, §7(a) could be amended to require California courts to follow federal precedents in applying the due process clause. Compare Art. 1, §28(d), the effect of which is to require California courts to follow federal precedents concerning coerced confessions and search and seizure.

[31]See Henry J. Friendly, "'Some Kind of Hearing,'" *U. Pa. L. Rev.* 123 (1975): 1267, 1276: "It should be realized that procedural requirements entail the

exigent circumstances, government action must stop until the hearing is concluded. Therefore, due process must be rationed, so that it will apply only to cases in which a person is likely to face a highly detrimental outcome or suffer serious disappointment of a reliant interest. California's due process methodology fails to provide a defensible rationing scheme, because it appears to apply to every unpleasant interaction with the government.

The objections to *Ramirez-Saleeby* go beyond cost and delay. Overproceduralization paralyzes government action. For example, let us examine a discretionary decision, like a manager's decision to let a probationary employee go rather than make her permanent. If due process applies, the official who makes the choice will be required to state the reasons why; hunches will not do. And if you have to give reasons, and build a file in support of those reasons, and suffer through a hearing where you get cross-examined about whether these reasons were mere pretexts, you will probably decide that it is not worth it. It is far easier to just grant what an individual wants (a benefit, a license, a permanent job, admission to a program) than to be bothered with due process.[32] Anyone who has tried to terminate a mediocre employee protected by civil service or by a collective bargaining agreement will immediately understand the dimensions of the problem.

Giving decisionmakers discretion to run their programs as best they can is not always a bad thing. Government without discretion tends to be rulebound, inflexible, sluggish. Discretionary decision making should not be neutered by overproceduralization. Administrators can be held accountable for how well they run their program without having each of

---

expenditure of limited resources, that at some point the benefit to individuals from an additional safeguard is substantially outweighed by the cost of providing such protection, and that the expense of protecting those likely to be found undeserving will probably come out of the pockets of the deserving."

[32]I have argued that procedures that raise the cost to an official of taking a particular action will cause the official to substitute some other (and often suboptimal) regulatory outcome for the more costly action. See Michael Asimow, "On Pressing McNollgast to the Limit: The Problem of Regulatory Costs," *Law & Contemp. Probs.* 57 (Winter/Spring 1994): 127, 135-37. I cite evidence that bureaucratic supply curves are quite elastic in the sense they are highly responsive to cost increases.

their decisions scrutinized by neutral arbiters and then by courts whenever a disappointed individual chooses to challenge them.[33]

Indeterminacy. The trigger for due process protection must be defined in a way that does not leave courts with a virtually unconstrained choice about whether hearings are required or what they should look like. Due process standards that narrow indeterminacy should be favored. California's standard is radically indeterminate.

Nobody can explain what the dignitary interest protected by California due process might mean. You know it when you see it. The "dignity" standard is an open invitation for courts to indulge their own predispositions about what interests seem important to them and what procedures seem important in protecting those interests. Note that *Ramirez-Saleeby* applies not only to the question of what interests are protected; it also applies to the question of what procedure is due. Therefore, take an interest (e.g., a tenured job) that is clearly protected by federal due process. One cannot just follow federal precedents, because the dignitary interest has to be considered in figuring out what procedures are due *and* when they're due. This greatly increases the field of indeterminate results.

California courts have struggled mightily with the *Ramirez-Saleeby* standard. Sometimes, it is benignly ignored;[34] the court does not know what to do with it or implies that the Supreme Court could not have really meant it. Sometimes, counsel seems to have overlooked it entirely. Sometimes, the court engages in a four-factor balancing and comes up with a result that seems hopelessly *ad hoc*. And sometimes, as in *Saleeby*, it is outcome-determinative

Indeterminacy of procedure stimulates lengthy and costly litigation; such litigation imposes deadweight loss on society as well as on the litigants. Standardless jurisprudence does a discredit to the judicial system; it is bad when judges are viewed as simply imposing their own policy preferences without constraints. To the extent possible, the procedure by

---

[33]See Peter N. Simon, "Liberty and Property in the Supreme Court: A Defense of *Roth* and *Perry*," *Calif. L. Rev.* 71 (1983): 146, 156-71.

[34]See, e.g., *Tyler v. County of Alameda*, 34 Cal. App. 4th 777, 40 Cal. Rptr. 2d 643 (1995). *Tyler* holds that due process is not violated by making you pay a parking ticket before administratively challenging it. Only federal due process authorities are discussed; the court ignores the applicability of the higher California standards.

which government must act should be knowable in advance, not discoverable only by protracted litigation in appellate courts.

Indeterminacy in this area has a particularly pernicious result: knowing that a court may find *post hoc* that a particular procedure was inadequate, a risk-minimizing administrator will provide all possible protections *ex ante*.[35] That is smart administration, because reversal on judicial review is often quite costly to an agency[36] and involves a considerable loss of face. But it is also bad government. In an era of government austerity, we should provide incentives for government decisionmakers to minimize costs, not the contrary. Grant Gilmore once wrote that "in Hell there will be nothing but law, and due process will be meticulously observed."[37] California due process illustrates this aphorism well.

AGENCIES IN THE CONSTITUTION

While most California agencies are created by statute, the California Constitution creates or authorizes a number of them. For example, the constitution creates or authorizes the following:

- Public Utilities Commission[38]
- Workers' Compensation Appeals Board[39]
- Department of Alcoholic Beverage Control and Alcoholic Beverage Control Appeals Board[40]

---

[35]In *Vermont Yankee Nuclear Power Corp. v. Natural Resources Defense Council*, Inc., 435 U.S. 519 (1978), the Supreme Court stripped lower courts of the ability to require rulemaking procedure beyond that provided in the Administrative Procedure Act. One of the reasons—persuasive to me—was that an agency would provide any procedure *ex ante* that a court might ultimately require in order to minimize the risk that a rule would be judicially overturned. As a result, the advantages of streamlined rulemaking procedure would be lost and all rulemaking would be transformed into adjudication.

[36]For example, the agency might be stuck with backpay obligations and, often, required to pay part or all of the appellant's attorney's fees.

[37]"The Ages of American Law" 111 (1977).

[38]Art 12, §§1-9.

[39]Art. 14, §4.

[40]Art. 20, §22.

- State Personnel Board[41]
- State Board of Equalization[42]
- Fish and Game Commission[43]
- Commission on Judicial Appointments[44]
- Commission on Judicial Performance[45]

These agencies enjoy their constitutional status as the result of some titanic political struggle of years past, such as the fight to regulate the railroads,[46] to install workers' compensation in place of traditional tort rules,[47] to install civil service instead of the spoils system,[48] or to wrest alcocoholic beverage licensing away from the Board of Equalization.

But these skirmishes are ancient history; there is no current need for constitutional protection for any of these agencies.[49] Instead, the placement of agencies in the constitution rigidifies the law and makes it difficult for the legislature to modify their jurisdiction, structure,[50] or procedure or to abolish them completely when conditions change.

Space does not permit a comprehensive examination of the degree to which constitutional status of certain agencies precludes the legislature

---

[41]Art 7, §§1-11.

[42]Art. 13, §17.

[43]Art. 4, §20(b).

[44]Art. 6, §7.

[45]Art. 6, §§8, 18.

[46]See Peter E. Mitchell, "The History and Scope of Public Utilities Regulation in California," *So. Calif. L. Rev.* 30 (1957): 118, 119-21.

[47]See *Western Indem. Co. v. Pillsbury*, 170 Cal. 686, 151 Pac. 398 (1915).

[48]*Pacific Legal Foundation v. Brown*, 29 Cal. 3d 168, 181-84, 172 Cal. Rptr. 487, 624 P.2d 1215 (1981).

[49]For example, you don't need to put the PUC into the constitution. Under the police power, the legislature can adopt systems of administrative rate regulation for public utilities when it believes that such action is required because of market failures. Under Art. 20, §5, the state reserves power to pass laws regulating existing corporations. Corporations thus cannot claim any vested right to be free of regulation.

[50]The PUC has five members that serve for staggered six-year terms. Art. 12, §1. Therefore, the legislature cannot shrink the membership to three if, *mirabile dictu*, deregulation of the energy and transportation sectors lessens the PUC's workload. Similarly, the State Personnel Board must have five members, appointed for 10-year terms. Art. 7, §2.

from making desirable changes to the agency or to their regulatory programs or disables courts from applying normal doctrines of administrative law to these agencies. I offer some illustrative examples here.

1. Independence of Agency

Whether there should be independent regulatory agencies is a leading and perennially debated topic of administrative law. Independence, for this purpose, means that the agency heads cannot be removed by the governor except for good cause. Proponents of independence say that certain functions of agencies are so important that they should be taken out of politics; the governor should not be able to discharge commissioners in order to implement some political agenda. Opponents of independence speak of accountability; a popularly elected governor should be able to bring the entire bureaucracy in line with the governor's political program. I need not take a position on this issue here. My position is more modest. The legislature should be able to decide whether an agency should be independent of executive control.

The Public Utilities Commission appears to be constitutionally independent. The constitution provides for legislative impeachment of a member of the PUC.[51] A member can be removed for incompetence, neglect of duty, or corruption by a vote of two-thirds vote of each house. It would appear that this provision prohibits the governor from removing a member of the PUC for any reason, including gross corruption. Only the legislature can remove the commissioner, and only by a two-thirds vote.

This provision seems anomalous. Legislative impeachment should be reserved for elected officials or judges, not for officials appointed by the governor who are executing the laws. Under federal law, it would be improper for the legislature to reserve to itself the power to remove an official who carries out executive functions.[52] At the very least, the

[51]Art. 12, §12. The same is true of the State Personnel Board, Art. 7, §2, but this provision contains no standard for legislative action. A member of the Fish and Game Commission may be removed by majority vote of the legislature. Art. 4, §20(b).

[52]See, e.g., *Bowsher v. Synar*, 478 U.S. 714 (1986), which invalidated the Gramm-Rudman Act because it gave an executive function to the comptroller general, an official who could be removed by Congress.

legislature should have the power to decide whether or not the governor should be able to remove the members of the PUC and whether that power should be restricted to for-cause removals.

2. Rigidity of Substantive Law

The constitution sometimes freezes into place principles of substantive or procedural law. A good example is rate regulation. Under the constitution, "a transportation company may not raise a rate or incidental charge except after a showing to and a decision by the commission that the increase is justified, and this decision shall not be subject to judicial review except as to whether confiscation of property will result."[53]

Now whether the rates of transportation companies should be regulated, and how this should be done, are hotly debated subjects. It would be fair to say that views on this issue have changed; many people now think that the market is a better regulator of transportation rates and charges than a regulatory commission. Yet this ancient provision of the constitution lingers on, creating doubts about whether the legislature could deregulate transportation.[54]

Another example is California's rickety structure for the regulation of alcoholic beverages.[55] There is the Department of Alcoholic Beverage Control. It denies or revokes liquor licenses. If you do not like its decision, you get a hearing before an independent ALJ, then another decision from the director of the department. If you are still not happy, you travel to the Alcoholic Beverage Control Appeals Board, a specialized and independent administrative court in business only to review decisions of the department. Still not happy? Either the licensee or the director can seek judicial review of decisions of the appeals board. The constitution contains detailed language spelling out the domains of these sister agencies

---

[53]Art. 12, §4.

[54]See *People v. Western Air Lines*, 42 Cal. 2d 621, 637, 268 P.2d 723 (1954) (rates set by PUC not subject to legislative control); *Western Assn of Short Line RRs v. RR Comm'n*, 173 Cal. 802, 162 Pac. 391 (1916) (PUC must regulate truckers even though legislature failed to include trucking in the statute).

[55]Art. 20, §22.

but they seem to engage in frequent turf wars.[56] Just in case the legislature would like to simplify this baroque structure, it cannot. Nor can a new judicial review statute apply to the ABC agencies since the precise nature of the appeals board's procedures and jurisdiction is frozen into the constitution.[57]

Another example is state civil service. The constitution creates the State Personnel Board and provides ground rules and exemptions from civil service in great detail. But numerous other agencies are also involved in administering civil service and turf problems are constant. If the legislature wanted to modernize and simplify this system, the constitutional status of the board would be a serious impediment.[58]

3. Immunity of Constitutional Agencies from State

Constitutional Law

Because of its constitutional status, the PUC is exempt from all constraints imposed by the state constitution on other agencies.[59] As a

---

[56]See Michael Asimow, "Toward a New California Administrative Procedure Act: Adjudication Fundamentals," *UCLA L. Rev.* 39 (1992): 1067, 1163; *Department of Alcoholic Beverage Control v. Alcoholic Beverage Control Appeals Bd.*, 195 Cal. App. 3d 812, 240 Cal. Rptr. 915 (1987).

[57]The California Law Revision Commission is currently working on a statute to modernize California's byzantine law relating to judicial review. Its draft statute exempts the ABC agencies, however, since so much of the review structure is constitutional.

[58]The Little Hoover Commission recently recommended abolition of the board. "Too Many Agencies, Too Many Rules: Reforming California's Civil Service" 27-38 (April 1995). Of course, this would require a constitutional amendment. Isn't that silly?

[59]*Pacific Tel. & Tel. Co. v. Eshleman*, 166 Cal. 640, 658, 137 Pac. 1119 (1913): "The constitution of this state has in unmistakable language created a commission having control of the public utilities of the state, and has authorized the legislature to confer upon that commission such powers as it may see fit, even to the destruction of the safeguards, privileges, and immunities guaranteed by the constitution to all other kinds of property and its owners. And while, under our republican form of government . . . it is perhaps the first instance where a constitution itself has declared that a legislative enactment shall be supreme over

result, this one agency is free from all of the provisions of the state constitution in respect to separation of powers or protection of individual rights. Thus it appears that the legislature could abolish all judicial review of PUC decisions.[60] It seems implausible that the problem of the regulation of public utilities is so unique that the PUC should not be encumbered by any provision of the state constitution.

4. Judicial Review of Agency Findings of Fact

In California (but nowhere else), a court reviews agency findings of fact under an independent judgment test when the agency action deprives an individual of a fundamental vested right. This means that the findings of an administrative law judge and of the agency heads count for nothing. The superior court judge substitutes his or her own view of the facts, even on questions of credibility. In federal administrative law and in every other state, the court must affirm the agency if its findings are supported by substantial evidence, meaning that a reasonable fact finder could come to the same conclusion as the agency. This is not the place to debate the merits of independent judgment.[61]

---

all constitutional provisions, nevertheless this is but a reversion to the English form of government which makes an act of parliament the supreme law of the land. . . . So, here, the state of California has decreed that in all matters touching public utilities the voice of the legislature shall be the supreme law of the land." The same thing is true of the Workers' Compensation agencies. Art. 14, §4.

[60]The normal rule is that delegation of judicial power to an agency is permitted only if this is reasonably appropriate to the agency's regulatory mission and the principle of judicial check is preserved. *McHugh v. Santa Monica Rent Control Bd.*, 49 Cal. 3d 348, 261 Cal. Rptr. 318, 777 P.2d 91 (1989). Evidently, however, this principle of check does not restrain delegations to the PUC. Art. 12, §5; *Pacific Tel. & Tel. Co. v. Superior Court*, 60 Cal. 2d 426, 34 Cal. Rptr. 673, 386 P.2d 233 (1963); *Pacific Tel. & Tel. Co. v. Eshleman*, note 59 at 660. I don't explore here the extent to which such a provision would offend federal due process. That is a difficult issue and many elements of it are unresolved.

[61]I have attacked independent judgment at great length in a forthcoming article. Michael Asimow, "The Scope of Judicial Review of Decisions of California Administrative Agencies," *UCLA L. Rev.* 42 (1995): 1157, 1161-92 . It is unlikely that the California Constitution still mandates independent judgment, but the constitution should be clarified to make clear that the legislature can set up any

What is relevant here is that it makes a big difference whether the agency in question is lodged in the constitution. The independent judgment rule applies only to nonconstitutional agencies. As a result, personnel decisions of the State Personnel Board and of the Regents of the University of California are reviewed under substantial evidence since these agencies are constitutional. In contrast, personnel decisions of local government or of the California State University and College system are reviewed under independent judgment.[62] Similarly, decisions of the Workers' Compensation Appeals Board as to whether an employee is disabled are reviewed under substantial evidence, but disability decisions of the Board of Administration of the Public Employees' Retirement System are reviewed under independent judgment.[63] These absurd results flow directly from the random inclusion of some but not all agencies in the constitution.

CONCLUSION

The process of constitutional revision requires that every provision of the constitution, and every court decision interpreting the constitution, be weighed and evaluated in light of contemporary realities. There is no persuasive justification for lodging certain California administrative agencies in the constitution and thus placing them beyond majoritarian control. Similarly, the California Supreme Court's *Ramirez-Saleeby* doctrine is poorly considered and has created problems of overproceduralization and indeterminacy. Revision of the constitution presents a rare opportunity to correct these problems.

---

scheme of judicial review and call for any appropriate scope of review. The constitutional issue is discussed in the UCLA article. *Id.* At 1169-70.

[62]*Skelly v. State Personnel Bd.*, 15 Cal. 3d 194, 217 n.31, 124 Cal. Rptr. 14 (1975); *Webster v. Trustees of Calif. State Univ.*, 19 Cal. App. 4th 1456, 24 Cal. Rptr. 2d 150 (1993); *Richardson v. Bd. of Supervisors of Merced County*, 203 Cal. App. 3d 486, 493, 250 Cal. Rptr. 1 (1988).

[63]*Quintana v. Board of Administration*, 54 Cal. App. 3d 1018, 127 Cal. Rptr. 11 (1976).

An Effective California Judicial System for the 21st Century

Harry N. Scheiber
Charles Ruhlin

The structure of the state judicial system is prescribed in the spare prose of only a few terse paragraphs of the California Constitution, Article VI. There are some detailed rules of jurisdiction set forth in Article VI, and also a few other references to judicial authority elsewhere in the document. The text scarcely serves, however, to capture the reality of what California's courts actually do—let alone to describe the functioning of the larger system, or set of interrelated systems, for resolution of disputes in which the public courts play the central but not the exclusive role. For in both the courts and these other forums are brought issues reflecting every aspect of the institutional mandates and behavioral norms embodied in every other aspect of this state's long and detailed constitutional document, as well as the entire range of issues brought forth by ordinary legislation and administrative decision making in a complex modern government. From livestock fencing to toxic waste siting, from control of DNA experimentation to the subsidizing of technology transfer, from celebrity criminal trials to neighborhood noise disputes, the public courts and other dispute-resolution forums are continuously involved in the process of legal ordering for modern California society.

As with many other institutions in both the public and private sectors, the California judicial systems thus are required to serve the needs of a society vastly more populous, vastly more complex in its organization and activities, and by many orders of magnitude more demanding of its government that was California society in 1849 or 1879, when the basic elements of today's constitutional design were put in place.

Let us consider, then, the adequacy of the constitutionally prescribed structure and functional roles of the California judiciary. How well they can be expected to respond to modern needs has long been a subject of urgent inquiry, a variety of reform initiatives, and intense frustration for many would-be innovators. Whatever their differences of opinion as to the direction in which change ought to be attempted, however, observers of the court system have agreed that the public values properly associated with a justice system in a constitutional democracy are being severely challenged.

The challenges have appeared in various forms. Much attention has been given to the dramatic pressures on the courts that derive from case loads, both criminal and civil, affecting both trial courts and the appellate courts. The caseload "crisis"—one that has had its counterpart in earlier periods of California history—is itself the result of multiple forces.[1] Among its important sources are the rise in crime rates and criminal prosecutions; the trend of recent years to assert individual or group rights (the "rights consciousness revolution") that broadened from its original civil liberties and civil rights base to include consumers, workers, environmentalists, the aged population, and many other groups; and the extension since the 1950s of new procedural rights to criminal suspects and defendants—resulting from both federal decisions and California state courts' decisions based on independent state constitutional grounds. Innovative strategies in litigation, including mass tort actions, organized citizens' class-action suits against public agencies and developers, and an expanding range of public-interest litigation has further complicated the courts' efforts keep up with docket caseloads and reduce the notorious problems of delay. An underlying issue is the impact of local "legal culture"—a phrase that is used to describe the unique bundles of attitudes, expectations, and style of litigating that characterize the work of lawyers and judicial bureaucracies in particular localities. In urban areas of California, the legal culture has generally worked in favor of accommodating elaborate, time-consuming procedures for discovery in civil litigation, tactics of delay, and forcing of manifold litigative expenses upon opposing disputants as a technique for discouraging the pursuit of claims. More generally, California juries continue to be clearly sympathetic to the notion that harms of many sorts, accidental and otherwise across a broad spectrum, deserve—and indeed require—full redress and compensation

---

[1]See, for example, Molly Selvin and Patricia A. Ebener, *Managing the Unmanageable: A History of Civil Delay in the Los Angeles Superior Court* (The Rand Corporation, Report R-3165-ICJ, 1984). The annual reports of the Judicial Council of California provide data and analysis on caseloads.

through resort to law, as a reflection of what has been termed a demand for "total justice."[2]

Other pressures on California's courts have come from the political arena. The threat from this source is to the traditional role that courts have played in the scheme of separation of powers, which provides for courts to be insulated from sudden waves of majoritarian demands (or "passions," as Madisonian rhetoric always had it) and hence to be secured from the toils of partisan combativeness. The political challenges have appeared in various forms. One is contested judicial retention elections, especially the traumatic campaign in 1986 that was the culmination of protracted criticism for more than a decade, directed against the California Supreme Court's decisions relating to the death penalty, environmental regulation, natural resources and the public trust, racial segregation, and church-state separation. On several occasions since the 1960s, moreover, direct-ballot measures have produced overnight, and often fundamental, revisions of substantive law—most lately in the realm of criminal procedure through Proposition 8 in 1982 and Proposition 115 in 1990. These measures produced fundamental changes in the balance of influence between prosecutors and judges in the criminal courts and represented a backlash against the California Supreme Court's attempt to establish a constitutional jurisprudence holding state officials to a higher standard of behavior than federal law required. Liberal as well as conservative elements in state politics have effected substantive reforms of law through initiatives and referendums, witness the success achieved by an environmentalist coalition in the 1972 Proposition 20 campaign to mandate the comprehensive state control of coastal zone development. In yet another important way have direct ballots impinged on the courts: the restrictive tax and spending measures that began with the success of Proposition 13 in 1978 have adversely affected the judiciary by placing stringent limits upon the fiscal support available for support of the public justice system. At an operational level, moreover, courtrooms have been strained in their ability to

---

[2]Lawrence M. Friedman, *Total Justice* (New York: Russell Sage Foundation, 1985). See also Robert Kagan, "Adversarial Legalism and American Government," *Journal of Policy Analysis and Management* 10 (1991): 369; and, *inter alia*, essays in a forthcoming book, *Legal Cultures and the Legal Profession*, ed. Lawrence M. Friedman and Harry N. Scheiber (Denver: Westview Press, expected publication 1995).

process caseloads because of the indirect effects of substantive changes in law, both statutory (e.g., the impact of sentencing appeals law on appellate loads, the toughening of drug laws, and the three strikes legislation) and constitutional in form.[3]

None of the foregoing is meant to suggest that the causes of court congestion and delay are exclusively external in origin. In trial court organization, for example, there has been a continuing campaign for decades to achieve unification of superior, municipal, and justice courts as a means to achieve simple administrative efficiency. There also have been numerous proposals over the years championing a new intermediate "court of review," above the existing appellate courts, that would separate the more "routine" cases from those of serious constitutional import, thereby limiting the caseload of the state supreme court. Reformers have also advanced numerous ideas for reducing the appellate docket of the high court in other ways, especially with respect to death penalty appeals and special appeals privileges that are constitutionally mandated, e.g., legal challenges to Public Utilities Commission rulings. One major burden of the high court has been reduced significantly already, it should be noted, with the reform of procedures for the disciplining of members of the bar.[4]

The ideologies and policy preferences that have motivated judicial reform efforts over the years are by no means uniform. With respect to the demands for more activist "case management" in the regular courts' operations, for example, some reformers are principally interested in creating mechanisms that will encourage litigants to find grounds for compromise, settlement, and adjustment without going to trial. This is what Professor Marc Galanter has called the "warm" theme in case

---

[3]See, e.g., the symposium on criminal justice procedures reformed through direct popular ballot, in "Victim Rights Symposium," *Pacific Law Journal* 23 (1992): 815. On financing, see John Hudzik, "Financing and Managing the Finances of the California Court System: Alternative Futures," *Southern California Law Review* 66 (1993): 1813.

[4]See Harry N. Scheiber, "Innovation, Resistance, and Change: A History of Judicial Reform and the California Courts, 1960-1990," *Southern California Law Review* 66 (1993): 2049; J. Clark Kelso, "A Report on the Independence of the Judiciary," *Southern California Law Review* 66 (1993): 2209; William Gallagher, "Ideologies of Professionalism and the Politics of Self-Regulation in the California State Bar," *Pepperdine Law Review* 22 (1995): 485.

management debates. There is also a "cool" theme in these debates, however, as other, more technocratic, reformers emphasize removing bottlenecks and clearing the dockets.[5]

Similarly, in the Alternative Dispute Resolution (ADR) reform movement, there are sometimes intersecting, yet distinctive, factions and themes: the "warm" concern with reasonableness, conflict-reduction, neighborliness, and the preservation of "community," at the one pole; and at the other pole, the "cold" element of concern with reduction of time, costs, and complexity in reaching settlements and avoiding resort to the courts, without much concern about psyches or bruises. The problem is that ADR procedures too often seem to sell short the importance of articulating public values traditionally associated with the norm-setting function expected of public courts. (We return to this last issue in later parts of this chapter.)

The specific agendas that various reform groups have sought to advance have come in part from the judiciary itself, especially the Judicial Council, but also in part from academics, the California bar and its specialized segments and political factions, national bar and law reform groups, coalitions of local officials and others concerned with their own prerogatives, and partisan or *ad hoc* groupings of California legislators and state political leaders. A great variety of specific reform proposals has been put forward, many of them falling on one end or the other of the spectrum of concerns suggested by the "warm" to "cold" polarities already described with respect to case management and ADR proposals. It is important to note, however, that reform concerns once associated only with the "populistic" proponents of ADR—concerns about transparency in procedure, greater assurance of access, and gender and ethnic representativeness on the part of those who decide cases—in recent years have also become part of the agenda even in the more conservative and efficiency-oriented rhetoric and platforms of the professionally oriented reformers on the "cool" side.

An inventory of the specific types of reform that have gained the most attention in California in the last 50 years brings to the surface another

---

[5]Marc Galanter, "The Emergence of the Judge as Mediator in Civil Cases," *Judicature* 69 (1986): 257; See also Judith Resnik, "Managerial Judges," *Harvard Law Review* 96 (1982): 376; and *id.*, "From Cases to Litigation," *Law and Contemporary Problems* 54 (1991): 5.

question of importance to the present study: the issue of multiple pathways to reform. Some reforms have been sought or achieved through judicial rules-making innovations, a few through constitutional amendment, but most of them through ordinary legislation.[6] Innovations and reforms have been classified to include, first, professionalization and coordination, mainly through the Judicial Council—established through constitutional revision, with its subsequent history of expanded functions and staffing achieved by legislative decisions. Second, unification and consolidation of courts, also the result of both constitutional revision and ordinary legislation but still, in the view of many critics, incomplete and wanting further innovation. Third, procedural reform, including demands for placing full control of judicial rules in the hands of the judiciary—a continuing quest of the chief justices since the 1940s, one that has been largely resisted by the legislature—and for reform of appellate procedures, abandonment or modification of the practice of depublication of decisions, and other issues.

This element of the reform agendas has been directed entirely at the operations of the regular courts, but there are parallel concerns aimed at administrative agencies' procedures and, at least potentially, on similar grounds with respect to ADR forums.

The recent developments in so-called "court-annexed" settlement procedures (overseen by judges in the regular court system)—reforms achieved both through new legislation and also Judicial Council initiatives—reflect the intermingling of concerns about "case-processing" efficiency with concerns that express very different values. Illustrating this point, in an analysis of proposals for court-annexed alternative procedures and structures, Deborah Hensler has written that some legislatures have viewed such innovations

> primarily as a means of reducing judicial workload, and hence, reducing the demand for new judgeships. Judges and court administrators frequently view them as components of a differenti-

---

[6]For a full discussion of the trends in reform proposals and also analysis of the multiple pathways to reform, see Scheiber, *supra* note 4 and Edward F. Sherman, "A Process Model and Agenda for Civil Justice Reforms in the States," *Stanford Law Review* 46 (1994): 1553. The ensuing subsection of this paper draws heavily from this earlier work.

> ated strategy for caseload management, in which specific categories of cases are assigned to different treatments. Lawyers may view the alternatives as a means of clearing the trial calendar for "more important" litigation. Public and private interest groups may regard ADR procedures as a means of saving litigants' time and money, while perhaps providing a better quality of justice [however defined!][7]

Fourth, there have been continuing efforts—again, with only mixed success to date, though they include proposals dating in their origins from the Progressive Era—to develop separate, specialized courts in areas such as family law and juvenile justice, and to supply them with more adequate physical facilities and associated social services than they enjoy at present.

Fifth, there is the ever-present money issue. As with other elements of the public sector in California, since the passage of Proposition 13 in 1978 the justice system has suffered severe financial pressure, with manifest effects on its quality of performance. Buildings and other facilities are in many localities in the state outmoded, overcrowded, and sometimes simply squalid. Staff levels have lagged badly behind the pace of growing caseloads, and the average numbers of cases handled by individual judges and appellate justices has been growing in nearly all respects, beyond what is generally accepted as the proper professional standard. Meanwhile, state funding of public defenders and of appellate litigation costs for indigents has been consistently below what even the most ungenerous view of needs might postulate.[8] Other interests in the public sector, for example, the K-12 public schools, have obtained through the direct ballot or by other means significant formulaic claims upon the state fisc. Thus many reformers are asking whether the courts, too, deserve constitutionally protected revenue sources if the quality and efficiency of justice are not to be further eroded.

The impact of initiatives and referendums is of special significance in any discussion of constitutional reform goals and strategies in California. As noted earlier, in the field of criminal justice there has been overnight revision of key elements of the criminal procedure code through the

---

[7]Deborah R. Hensler, "What We Know and Don't Know about Court-Administered Arbitration," *Judicature* 69 (1986): 270.

[8]See, e.g., the family court proposal in California legislature, senate, *Task Force on Family Relations Court*, Final Report, November 1990.

popular ballot (as with Prop. 8 and Prop. 115). Apart from the burdens of interpretation and adjustment that such changes can place upon the courts, many commentators would question whether substantive legal matters of such importance as a criminal code and basic procedure in the criminal courts ought to be subject to this sort of majoritarian decision making.[9]

TOWARD DEFINING CRITERIA OF "EFFECTIVENESS"

Because varying goals work into the equation in every effort to address the crisis in the courts and in the larger system of dispute resolution in California, we must necessarily concern ourselves with the proper balance among those goals. The criteria that ought to apply must be relevant, moreover, not only to the state courts but also to the larger justice system, existing or proposed, that serves the society. Some commentators have set out the goals of the judicial system in rather elaborate classifications. Professor Kelso, for example, has offered as the "minimum" list some 17 items ranging from "Improve fairness in the courts" to "Improve the function of juvenile law, family law, and other proceedings involving children and families," to "Recognize and honor contributions to the administration of justice."[10]

Taking a broader perspective, we suggest that there are three criteria, each of a general nature, to be considered in the analysis of effectiveness:

(1) *Considerations of "processing" efficiency*: This is a category that embodies all the traditional goals of reform with respect to reaching settlements in a timely manner and clearing out docket backlogs without risking loss of confidence in the quality of justice—as has been attempted in such recent California legislation as the Delay Reduction Act.

(2) *Considerations of appropriate forum "fit" as an element of fairness*: The several dimensions of "fit" or "appropriateness" of forum become potentially controversial when gatekeeper functions are performed in a multi-option system, in which public values, the private preferences of disputants, and concerns of processing efficiency have to be weighed

---

[9]The Judicial Council has undertaken new research on the effects of Proposition 115 on caseload composition and volume, so the results of the innovation in narrow management terms are not yet amenable to full evaluation (Judicial Council special report 1995).

[10]Kelso, 1994, *supra* note 4.

against one another. What has been termed "process pluralism"—the rational matching of disputes with appropriate resolution or decision processes—and how it bears on the analysis of the comprehensive justice system is a subject to which we return in the following section.

(3) *Considerations of public norm creation and value articulation*: Recognizing that the "provision of dispute resolution . . . [as] a central function of the state . . . [is] closely linked with such important public responsibilities as maintaining order and establishing norms of behavior,"[11] a soundly functioning justice system must provide articulation of legal and behavioral norms and values, not merely process cases.

Against these broad criteria, we seek in the following section to analyze the merits of the case for redrawing the traditional boundaries between the courts and other institutions of dispute settlement in California society—reserving to the end the question of whether it is wise to pursue any or all of the reforms implied in new model through the process of constitutional revision.

A MULTIDIMENSIONAL JUSTICE SYSTEM FOR CALIFORNIA

In its recent report *Justice in the Balance 2020*, the Commission on the Future of California Courts seems to have fully embraced a pluralistic vision of institutional reform, implicitly acknowledging that rapidly changing socio-economic conditions warrant a wide array of "appropriate" (as opposed to "alternative") dispute-resolution mechanisms involving both public and private institutions. Decrying the inefficiencies and injustices of a loosely organized "system" of courts and administrative agencies with little communication and coordination among the component parts, the commission has called for the creation of a multidimensional, multi-option

---

[11]Elizabeth Rolph, Erik Moller, and Laura Petersen, "Escaping the Courthouse: Private Alternative Dispute Resolution in Los Angeles" (Santa Monica: Rand Institute for Civil Justice, 1994); see also studies by Resnik *supra* note 5; and Richard L. Abel, "The Contradictions of Informal Justice," in *The Politics of Informal Justice, ed. Richard L. Abel* (New York: Academic Press, 1982); and Owen Fiss, "Against Settlement," *Yale Law Journal* 93 (1984): 1073, for process-focused normative critiques.

justice system.[12] The hope is that such an approach would enhance courts' effectiveness, and though the Judicial Council has declined to endorse its implementation, it undoubtedly will be part of the agenda for court reform in California in the coming years.

This multidimensional system counts both a fully integrated public justice system and private dispute resolution services as part of its structure, recognizing the disappearing boundaries between public and private domains (see Figure 1). The public justice system would include multi-option justice centers that provide a varied menu of dispute-resolution processes including mediation, minitrials, arbitration, early neutral evaluation, expedited proceedings, referee-panel adjudication, administrative law forums, and traditional bench and jury trials. These centers would be related to the multidoor courthouses conceived in the 1970s and with which several jurisdictions across the country are currently experimenting.

Like its multidoor courthouse counterparts, the proposed multidimensional justice system would pull together various dispute-resolution options into one "court," or multi-option justice center. Some centers would involve simple, understandable mechanisms well-suited to parties unrepresented by counsel. Other, larger regional centers could offer specialized services to disputants in large, complex cases involving advanced technology, mass tort litigation, and certain commercial disputes.

Judges would develop, monitor, review, and periodically update assessment and referral guidelines, which skilled assessment officers would use to counsel parties about resources and processes available to them both within and outside the justice system, and to match their dispute with an appropriate resolution mechanism. These assessment officers, termed "gatekeepers," would play a central role in this process, actively managing cases so as to increase both the efficiency of the dispute-resolution process and disputants' satisfaction with the process. Multidoor courthouses in fact have successfully used nonjudicial personnel for this assessment function, prompting the commission to recommend a similar move.[13] To enhance the

---

[12] *Justice in the Balance: 2020 Vision for the California Courts*, Commission on the Future of the California Courts, 1993.

[13] *Id.*

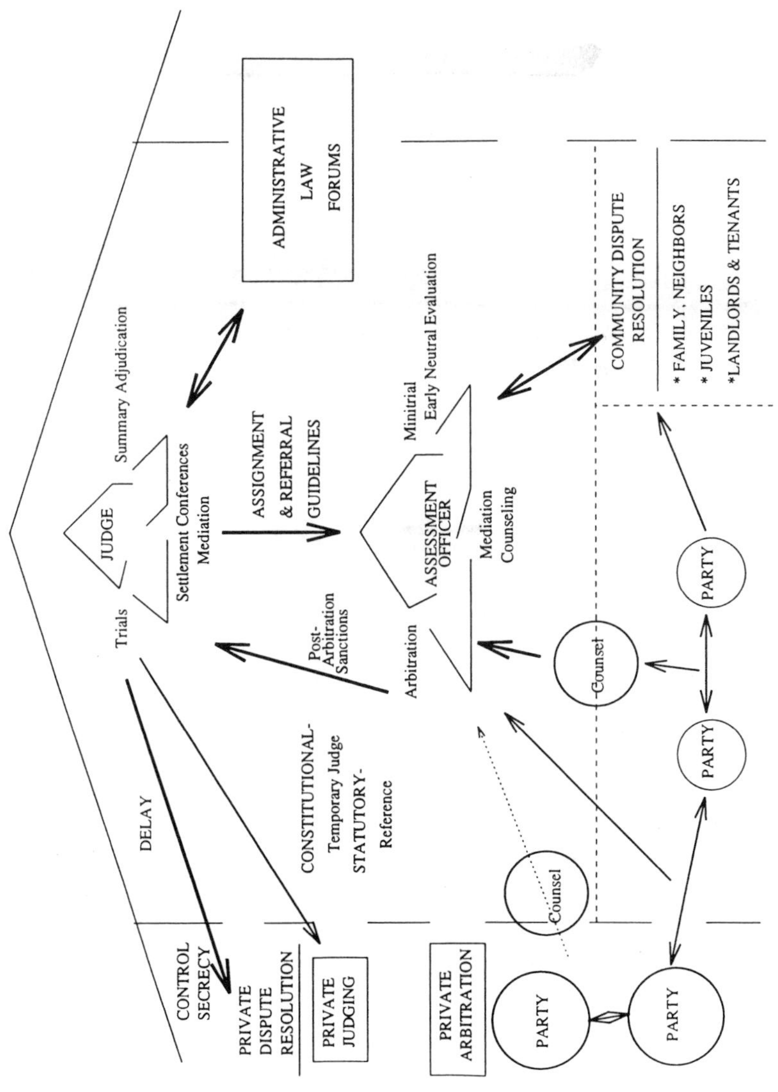

Figure 1. *Multi-Option Justice Center*

effectiveness of this gatekeeping function, multimedia kiosks in public locations could be developed as well to allow parties to communicate with gatekeepers.[14]

To maximize processing efficiency in dispute processing, the commission argues that parties should not have the right to appeal a gatekeeper's decision as to the appropriate forum for their case. Furthermore, the commission believes that incentives should be put in place to increase the probability that parties will make good-faith efforts to resolve their disputes through the appropriate resolution process chosen by the gatekeeper. If disputes are not resolved in a nontrial forum, then parties would bear some of the costs of taking their case to court, with the judge to determine the relative share of these costs according to the reasonableness of the parties' conduct in the nontrial process. User fees based on ability to pay would be assessed in all cases, for assessment, referral, and utilization of processes, whether trial or nontrial.

Parallel to public multi-option justice centers' development would be the continued evolution of private-sector and community-based dispute-resolution mechanisms. "Community dispute-resolution centers," would be similar to multi-option justice centers, but would be smaller and rely more on local connections, norms, and cultures to resolve disputes. These centers, analogous to neighborhood justice centers of today, would be publicly funded yet locally managed. They could serve as an entry point for the larger justice centers, with a gatekeeper to counsel the parties on the appropriate process, and with multi-media systems giving them instant access as well to the larger center's options. These centers might handle disputes between neighbors, families, juveniles, and landlords and tenants, among others.

At the same time, in the commission's view, continued use of private judging and arbitration is to be encouraged. On one hand, allowing contracting parties more control over the tailoring of specific types of dispute-resolution processes for specific types of conflicts can permit a richer set of norms and institutional arrangements to develop in society. Multi-option "justice centers" could then adapt some of these practices for

---

[14]*Id.* These kiosks currently exist in Long Beach and other areas. Future advances in information technology might allow expert systems to perform the screening functions otherwise carried out by assessment officers.

their own use, and even perhaps develop new procedures of their own that could be used privately. On the other hand, there is concern that increased reliance on private dispute resolution erodes the public norm-creating function of the courts. Either way, the effectiveness of private mechanisms will depend on courts' (or justice centers') continuing enforcement of their decisions without which they would not be binding.

ASSESSING THE MULTIDIMENSIONAL JUSTICE SYSTEM

Can this multidimensional justice approach improve upon the present system as it has been evolving until now? In terms of processing efficiency, it seems that important features of the proposed system—consolidating court administration and unifying the provision of traditional adjudicative, ADR, and administrative law services—are occurring already either due to legislative mandate (i.e., Trial Court Realignment and Efficiency Act of 1991, Trial Court Delay Reduction Act of 1986) or else because judges in different jurisdictions are experimenting with different mechanisms in response to pressures that vary across regions. Indeed, there is evidence from various jurisdictions that demand for private judging depends on courts' inability to effectively manage caseloads, with private judging either failing or not taking root where courts resolve disputes in timely fashion.[15] Viewed in this light, simply improving case management practices may obviate the need for deeper reforms, especially if trial court unification finally becomes reality.

Even with court unification, however, it is an open question whether courts will assign cases to the most appropriate fora absent deeper reforms. Judges now routinely refer disputants to court-annexed arbitration, early neutral evaluation, or minitrials, but objective criteria for the timing and appropriateness of such assignments seems lacking. Judges, as neutral authorities, are less likely than attorneys to suffer conflicts of interest when recommending an appropriate forum for disputants.[16] They also are much

---

[15]Gordon M. Giller and Michael D. Planet, "Rent-A-Judge Programs: A Sign of Failure to Move Cases in the Courts or Just an Alternative Dispute Resolution Technique?" *The Court Manager* (Summer 1989): 4-6.

[16]A disputant's attorney on one hand is a trusted representative, but on the other hand is unlikely to be immune from financial incentives to eschew ADR in favor of a more profitable litigation strategy. For instance, contingency fee lawyers

less likely than attorneys to meet with clients sufficiently early in the process for ADR to be effective (even under fast-track judges do not meet with parties until well after initial pleadings). Also, because they have limited knowledge and experience with ADR,[17] and can spend little time with the parties to learn more about their dispute, judges probably are not in the best position to match disputants with the most appropriate forum.

Gatekeepers, on the other hand, can help disputants learn about ADR earlier in the process. Like judges, they are neutral, yet it is presumed that they would be more knowledgeable of ADR and that their time would be much less of a scarce resource (indeed, their entire job would be to fully inform themselves of the pros and cons of all available options and to spend time with parties to guide them most appropriately). By educating parties about ADR and litigation options, the gatekeeper helps correct any information asymmetries, allowing the dispute-resolution market to function more effectively. The caveat, however, is that the gatekeeper does not simply increase the flow of information to parties so that they may voluntarily choose their preferred dispute resolution mechanism. Besides counseling and guiding parties, the gatekeeper, in the end, mandates which dispute-resolution mechanism parties will employ to resolve their conflict. Though it seems unlikely that this function poses any serious constitutional question,[18] it may threaten disputants' satisfaction with the process if the

---

would have stronger incentives to promote ADR. See Lisa Bernstein, "Understanding the Limits of Court-Connected ADR: A Critique of Federal Court-Annexed Arbitration Programs," *University of Pennsylvania Law Review* 141 (1993): 2169.

[17]Though many attorneys do provide as much information about ADR as they can to clients to assist them in making appropriate litigation decisions, it seems that they often have as little information about ADR as judges. Calls have been made for the Judicial Council to provide information pamphlets and checklists for attorneys to use to help increase the information flow. See Jay Folberg, Joshua Rosenberg, and Robert Barrett, "Use of ADR in California Courts: Findings and Proposals," *University of San Francisco Law Review* 26 (Spring 1992): 343.

[18]On a constitutional level, one may ask if such a subordinate judicial officer should have the authority to assume case management responsibilities traditionally handled by judges. Article VI, Section 22 of the California Constitution states that "the Legislature may provide for the appointment by trial courts of record of officers such as commissioners to perform subordinate judicial duties." To the extent that gatekeepers simply follow assessment and referral guidelines handed

gatekeeper fails to lead parties to the point where, with more complete information, they would come to agree with the assessment.

It is unclear how the commission's approach would affect parties' satisfaction with the process; or, if it would diminish levels of satisfaction sufficiently to push even more of them to resort to private dispute resolution, increasing confidentiality and enhancing private control over the process,[19] but leaving the courts with even fewer cases from which new precedent could be developed. Preliminary evaluations of one of the nation's first multi-option justice centers, the Middlesex MultiDoor Courthouse in Cambridge, Massachusetts, show high client satisfaction with the process. In large part, this may have to do with the fact that, unlike in the commission's proposal, the final choice of dispute resolution process is left to the parties and their counsel. Comparing multidoor courthouse participants' experience with that of a control group involved in traditional adjudication, the evaluation noted that while both groups expressed satisfaction with their respective processes, the multidoor courthouse group expressed consistently higher levels of satisfaction with the manner in which legal as well as nonlegal matters were addressed, with the broad opportunities to participate in structuring the outcome of the case, and with the fairness of the process.[20]

---

down by a judge, then there seems little doubt that their work would qualify as a subordinate judicial duty within the scope of Section 22. However, problems may arise where gatekeepers exceed their authority or even have to exercise discretion in cases that are not covered clearly in the guidelines. Some mechanism could be established in such cases where a gatekeeper can consult with judges in deciding which dispute resolution service is most appropriate for the parties. Of course, such consulting takes up judges' precious time and reduces the potential time and cost savings anticipated under the new system. In addition, as discussed above, judges may not be in the best position to decide what dispute resolution mechanism is most appropriate in a given case. It seems the important issue here is that the gatekeeper be highly skilled and that she or he have up-to-date information on what processes are most effective in given cases.

[19]*The Report and Recommendations of the Judicial Council Advisory Committee on Private Judges,* Judicial Council of California, Administrative Office of the Courts, 1990, 15.

[20]National Center for State Courts, *Middlesex MultiDoor Courthouse Evaluation Project Final Report*, 1992; Commission on the Future of the California Courts, *supra* note 13, 48-49.

The extent to which the problem of perceived satisfaction would exist in a multi-option justice context depends in part on the relative position of parties and the degree to which they rely on the public system to resolve their disputes. Larger, wealthier parties such as corporations already resolve many disputes via private mechanisms such as arbitration, most often involving contractual matters between themselves or even with more risk-averse parties such as workers or consumers (see lower left corner of Figure 1). It is uncertain how the presence of a gatekeeper would affect the incentives of parties to participate in the public system in these circumstances, but it seems likely that private dispute resolution will become increasingly popular in these types of cases.

Though large organizations are attempting to minimize the extent to which they have to deal with litigation by writing arbitration clauses into more and more contracts, they will undoubtedly continue to face the threat of litigation from smaller parties with whom they have no contractual relationship. But even when they are forced to litigate, these larger parties often still possess a strategic advantage insofar as they are often able to bear the costs of delay and hence can credibly threaten to go to trial, using the discovery process to grind down an opponent with fewer resources or by participating in ADR but concealing information and true intentions.

Hence, having a gatekeeper order parties to resolve a dispute under court-annexed arbitration may do nothing to prevent the more powerful party better able to bear the costs of delay from requesting a trial, provided the arbitration is nonbinding (as it is in California). Postarbitration user fees and cost-shifting sanctions, as called for by the commission, do little to change this scenario. The party with the strategic advantage can simply change its presentation at the arbitration hearing to reduce the probability of being penalized when requesting a trial.[21]

A large organization cannot only afford to delay but is less sensitive than more risk-averse opponents to any sanctions that might be imposed because of these tactics (unless sanctions are higher for wealthier disputants). Postarbitration fees and sanctions seem more likely to harm risk-averse individual disputants (typically plaintiffs) at a bargaining disadvantage. Professor Lisa Bernstein has pointed out that these plaintiffs would have to bear more risk to obtain information through postarbitration

---

[21]See Bernstein, *supra* note 16.

discovery than they would to obtain the same information through pretrial discovery if arbitration was not ordered.[22] Assuming the wealthier defendant is more likely to strategically reject the arbitration award and seek to string this plaintiff along, the decision for the plaintiff then becomes one between abandoning the case to avoid these additional postarbitration discovery costs or swallowing them in the hope that eventually a trial will result. It seems that in these types of cases, forcing arbitration can only benefit the stronger party, unless the more risk-averse party can somehow overcome this bargaining disadvantage in some way (say, by joining with others similarly situated in a class-action suit).

An area of concern, then, is how the gatekeeper might best deal with these cases where parties have incentives to distort the justice process to their own ends. For instance, the assessment and referral guidelines might specify that the gatekeeper look to see if there are significant disparities in wealth and power between the parties and if theirs is a relationship involving little, if any, repeat interaction. The existence of the factors might suggest that the far wealthier party might have more incentives and ability to resort to delaying tactics. If such a case, say, involving product liability, were to come to the gatekeeper, she should be able to spot quickly that the wealthier party would have superior bargaining strength in this respect and could simply wait it out, forcing the plaintiffs to pile up huge legal costs, and, in all likelihood, bow out of the case. So in this case, the gatekeeper should not mandate court-annexed arbitration, but should instead move the case to trial as expeditiously as possible, using all possible techniques to reduce the defendant's delaying tactics.

Taking control of the case in such a way may be necessary when large disparities in bargaining power exist, but where smaller, more risk-averse parties are in conflict with each other, the concern that such control by the gatekeeper will cause disputants to become more dissatisfied with the process becomes more important. Parties with fewer resources to commit to dispute resolution have far less ability to hire private judges or engage

[22]This is because when calculating the cost of requesting a trial and of postarbitration discovery, a risk-averse plaintiff must take into account the possibility that the arbitration award was relatively advantageous to him, which would render less favorable to him the expected trial judgment. This prospect increases the expected cost of postarbitration discovery and makes the plaintiff more willing to accept the arbitration award. See *Id.*

in private arbitration. In circumstances where both disputants are positioned in this way (see bottom center portion of Figure 1), it seems that gatekeepers would do well to emphasize counseling and facilitating skills, spending time with parties to make them understand that regardless of whether all of their perceptions as to what is an appropriate forum coincide, the forum chosen will nonetheless provide each side with a fair hearing from a neutral, third party. This will most likely help allay any dissatisfaction parties may feel from not being able to have the final say over the choice of forum.

Guaranteeing the most neutral third party to hear each side's claims is important in all cases, but even more care should be exercised in cases with smaller parties, where, because of the smaller absolute amount at stake, or because of an ongoing relationship between the parties, it is automatically assumed that mediation or another form of ADR is the appropriate mechanism. Take, for instance, family law cases, where many times in recent years mediation has been prescribed as the most appropriate forum, despite the potential for bias in this approach favoring male parties.[23] Gatekeepers should be trained to be aware of the potential for such biases in different dispute- resolution processes, and ongoing research should provide them with updated information as to what are the most unbiased approaches.

CONCLUSIONS AND RECOMMENDATIONS

If these concerns have merit, as we believe, then it is important to consider whether constitutional rules should be formulated as to both operating procedures and institutional boundaries that will keep control of the system of justice within the public domain. This difficult issue needs to be confronted along with other questions that are appropriately raised in the context of the present efforts at constitutional revision, some of which need to center on improvements in the traditional system of public courts.

Our first specific proposal addresses a primary—and, we think, undeniable—need of the courts for adequate funding that will relieve the

---

[23]Penelope E. Bryan, "Killing Us Softly: Divorce Mediation and the Politics of Power," *Buffalo Law Review* 40 (1992): 441; Andree G. Gagnon, "Ending Mandatory Divorce Mediation for Battered Women," *Harvard Women's Law Journal* 15 (1992): 272.

public judicial system's present condition of chronic stress and shortfall. Until a decent level of funding is achieved, the public courts cannot serve society properly in the realms in which it performs best—measured by the criterion of effectiveness that we presented above. And until this happens, private alternatives will have a seductive appeal simply because the public courts are inadequate to do the job; and so, debate of how to effect dispute resolution will continue to be driven on the basis of what is the least of evils, rather than on the basis of what works best. The solution that is required for the courts is the same as is necessary for revitalization of state government as a whole: it is constitutional reform of the tax system which, since passage of Proposition 13 in 1978, has reduced the state fisc to its present woeful condition. The arguments for fiscal reform and for reform of the initiative/referendum processes are made by other writers in this volume; it is enough here to underline that serious reform in this direction is essential if the courts are to be placed on a sound fiscal foundation.

Second, we propose that a revised constitution should contain provision for the full consolidation of all trial courts into district courts as called for by Senate Constitutional Amendment 4 (SCA 4) currently pending in the state assembly. This move, supported almost universally by court administration professionals, would enhance courts' efficiency and put in place a unified structure that could more readily accommodate multi-option justice centers with gatekeepers. Like the Judicial Council itself, we do not recommend immediate structural reforms to create multi-option justice centers as envisoned by the commission model; but we do anticipate that continuing experimentations will probably lead to efforts to bring this model before the public in the not-too-distant future.

Third, we propose that attention be given to whether the constitution as it now stands provides sufficient safeguards against the practical erosion of the norm-setting functions of the justice system. It is no easy matter to find the right balance of civil litigants' right to privacy in consensual dispute settlements against the desirability of the public's having information—such as would routinely have been reported in the media, had the dispute been taken to open court—of the facts in cases, of the trend of decisions in important areas of policy, and of the interpretations of law that were being argued and either upheld or rejected in decision making. Consider, for example, whether the terms of settlements should be permitted to be sealed, as now happens routinely, in civil cases; and whether courts should be permitted to sanction settlements in which a losing party in effect buys a “win” through a post hoc settlement, after having failed to carry its view in a trial. Even if one decides that such issues ought to be addressed in the course of the current revision effort, there will remain for a future time, if the commission’s model should be instituted, the much more comprehensive issue of how to sustain the vitality of traditional procedural guarantees for litigants—and how to sustain the role of California’s judicial system as a curator and nurturer of public values.

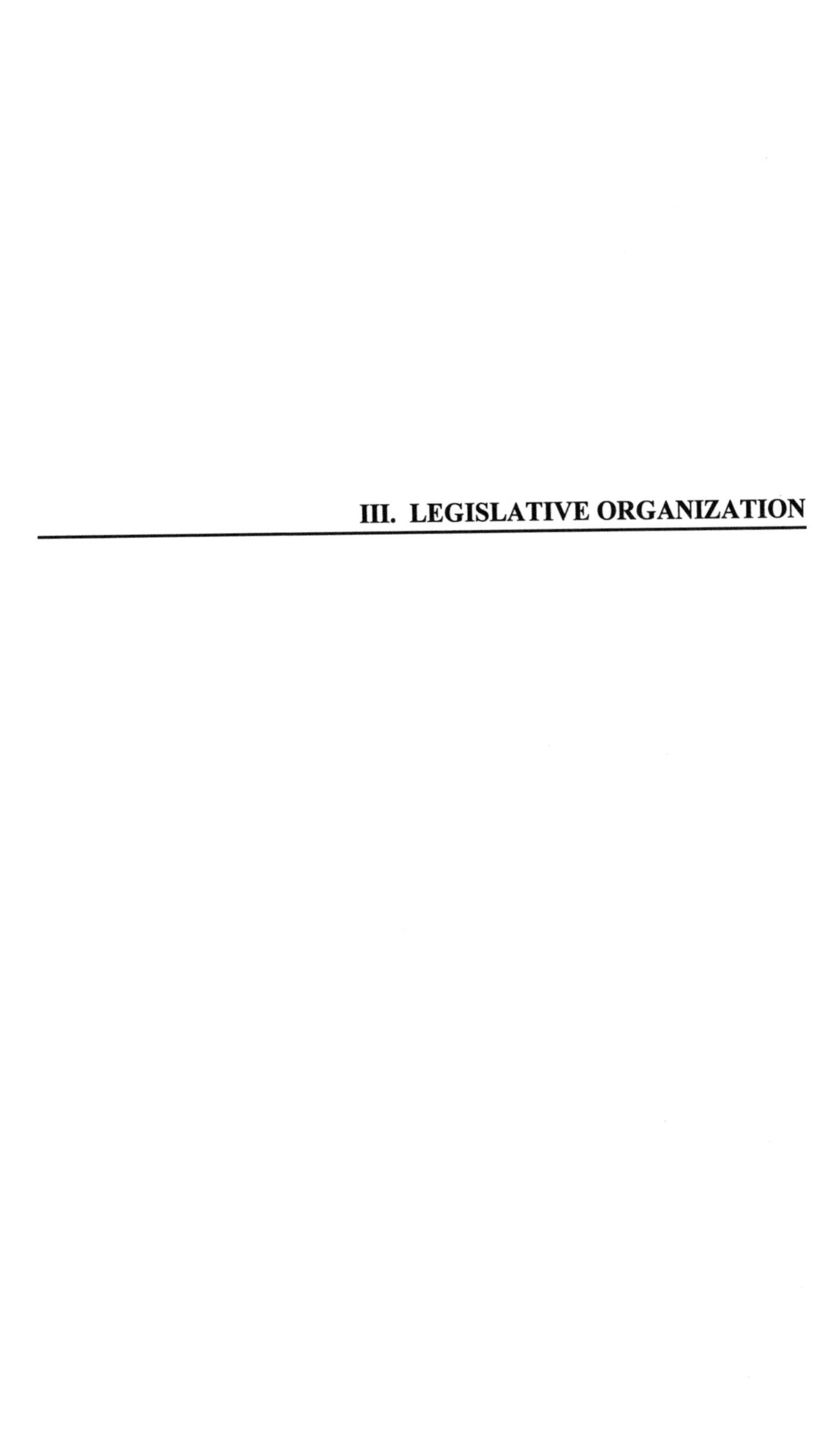

III. LEGISLATIVE ORGANIZATION

Reforming Representation in California: Checks and Balances without Gridlock

Kathleen Bawn

Designing political institutions inevitably requires making trade-offs between competing goals. We would like government to be sensitive to minority rights without being captured by special interests, to adapt to changing needs without being manipulated for short-term political advantage. The problem is that reforms designed to solve one problem in the implementation of democracy typically exacerbate others.

These trade-offs can be particularly difficult in designing representation systems. For the purposes of this chapter "representation system" means a set of rules for electing a legislature. Specifically, will representatives be elected in winner-take-all elections in single-member districts, or will there be proportional representation of parties? Will the legislature have one or two chambers? Will all legislators be elected by the same rules, or will there be differences in, for example, the definition of districts? How many legislators will there be? Although the relative merits of alternative systems have been debated for centuries, there is no clear consensus about what is optimal. Indeed, a notable feature of representative democracies worldwide is how diverse they are in their institutional arrangements (Lijphart 1984).

The existence of trade-offs does not mean that reform is inherently futile. Rather, evaluation of reforms requires comparing the relative advantages and disadvantages of different systems. In this chapter, I evaluate the advantages and disadvantages of alternative representation

---

I would like to thank Roger Noll and the other participants in the California Constitution Project for feedback on early drafts, as well as Jeff Frieden, Leroy Graymer, Dan Lowenstein, Mike Thies, and Barry Weingast for helpful comments and conversations. Research support was provided by the Institute of Governmental Studies at the University of California, Berkeley.

systems for the state of California. I focus on two key features: the incentives created for legislators and the information provided to voters.

I begin by discussing the goals that should motivate design of a representation system. First, I argue that the primary goal should be to limit bias. Second, I discuss sources of bias in California's current system, those peculiar to California and those common to all state governments. Finally, I argue that bias is exacerbated by the exclusive reliance on single-member districts and propose a system that mixes single-member districts with proportional representation.

STANDARDS FOR EVALUATING REPRESENTATION SYSTEMS

Political institutions create systems for making policy decisions. In principal, the goal in designing institutions should be to produce policy decisions that are good for society. There are two problems, however, in using this goal as the basis for reform. One is that disagreement about what is good policy prevents consensus about what are good institutions (Riker 1980). The second problem is that it is extremely difficult to separate the electoral system's influence on policy from the influence of other institutions. In particular, the policy consequences of representation systems are contingent upon the organization of the legislature, the scope of the initiative process, and policy roles of the executive and judicial branches.

I deal with the first problem by judging policies on a utilitarian basis: adopting policy X is a good choice if the total benefits (to everyone in society) exceed the total costs. While utilitarianism is not without its critics, it is the implicit basis for most policy debate in the U.S. I deal with the second problem by focusing on the most direct effects of electoral systems: the incentives created for elected policymakers and the information provided to voters.[1]

---

[1]Presumably, higher-order effects exist. Electoral systems contribute, in conjunction with other political institutions, to the nature of specific policy decisions, such as economic policies that will have long-run impact on growth and income distribution (Rogowski 1989). Attempting to account for higher-order effects in a paper at this level of generality would be necessarily incomplete, highly contingent, and would make the problem intractable.

These decisions bring me to a workable normative goal: representation systems should minimize bias, either bias in favor of particular groups, or bias in favor of particular alternatives. If policy choices should maximize net social benefits (utilitarianism), then the system for making policy choices should treat all people equally (my utility is as good as yours) and all choices equally (utility from one policy choice is as good as utility from another). Unbiased institutions are necessary but not sufficient for maximizing net social benefits.

Moreover, bias is a natural framework in which to discuss the direct effects of electoral systems. Electoral systems affect bias by creating incentives for legislators to be more responsive to some groups than others, and by providing information about incumbent performance more easily to some groups.

Other normative goals can be subsumed in the unbiasedness criterion. For example, we would also hope that representation systems make elected leaders accountable to the public, and that they promote the feeling that government institutions are fair and legitimate. Both accountability and legitimacy can be thought of as ways of achieving unbiasedness. The more accountable a representation system is, the easier it is for citizens to associate policy choices with elected officials and to remove the officials for bad choices. In this sense, greater accountability is one way of reducing bias toward organized interests. Promoting legitimacy does the same. When citizens perceive government institutions to be illegitimate or unjust, their alienation leads to decreased participation and increased bias toward organized groups. There are two important sources of bias in electoral institutions: (1) bias for or against minorities, and (2) bias for or against the status quo.

Bias For or Against Minorities

The framers of the United States constitution worried about bias created by institutions that are too majoritarian. To see how majoritarian institutions can create bias against minorities, consider the following example. Suppose citizens are to vote directly on policy A. Policy A provides a net benefit of $5 each to 60 percent of people in society, but costs the remaining 40 percent $500 each. If people vote on the basis of their personal stake, policy A will be adopted, despite the fact that society as a whole is worse off.[2] Majoritarian decision making is biased because it ignores costs imposed on minority groups. ("Minority" in this case means minority interest, not necessarily an ethnic minority.) Although this example does not involve representation, if the representation system creates a legislature responsive to the majority, it will enact the biased policy.

If we are worried about bias against minority interests, we can reduce it by requiring supermajorities or by establishing multiple veto points through separation of powers. Most modern political scientists would argue, however, that we need to worry at least as much about bias in favor of minorities. The reason is that participation in democratic decision making requires time and effort. Effort is required to go to the polls, to express opinions to elected officials, and, most important, to learn enough about policy decisions (or candidates) to have a meaningful opinion. The benefits of informing oneself about political decisions are small because the likelihood of being the pivotal voter in a large election is tiny. For this reason, the typical citizen is "rationally ignorant about" about and unlikely to participate in political decisions (Downs 1957).

In effect, individuals in large societies are disenfranchised by the fact that the extremely low probability that their vote (or other political activity) will have an effect. A group of people with similar interests, however, can affect outcomes if the group can organize itself to act collectively. Organized groups can inform members about policies and candidates, and can use opportunities for political participation to their best advantage.

Informed political participation is one example of a *collective action problem,* that is, a situation in which individual interest conflicts with group interest. Some groups overcome collective action problems and organize effectively for political participation and others do not. Groups are more likely to be organized if they are relatively small, homogeneous, and if the individual members each have a large stake (Olson 1965). For this reason, producers are usually more organized than consumers, and beneficiaries of targeted government programs are more organized than taxpayers.

---

[2]The net loss to society in this example is $197 times the number of people in society.

Returning to the example of Policy A, suppose the $5 gain is insufficient to cause the 60 percent majority to organize for effective participation. Members of the 60 percent majority may not bother to vote, or may vote contrary to their interests because they are not aware of the consequences of Policy A. Suppose further that the $500 loss is big enough that the minority group does organize for participation. In this case, the socially efficient decision, rather than the biased one, will be made. But now consider policy B, which imposes costs of $1,000 per person on one percent of the population, and gives benefits of $15 each to 99 percent of the population. Policy B is socially efficient. But here, if the one percent minority is organized effectively to participate and the 99 percent is not, the decision (against policy B) will be biased in favor of the minority group. (In the real world imposing a pollution regulation or removing a subsidy for a particular industry often has the basic profile of hypothetical policy B.)

Representation systems can be biased either because they fail to protect minority rights, or because they are overly responsive to organized groups. Figure 1 depicts the two dimensions of this first source of bias and illustrates a problem in comparing representation systems. System X does a better job than System Y of protecting minority rights, but is more prone to favor organized groups. Choosing between X and Y will be difficult unless we have a clear consensus on which problem is more important. This sort of choice occurs quite often: institutions that are designed to protect minority rights can be easily exploited by organized groups.

On the other hand, choosing between System X and Z is straightforward. System X is no worse than Z on protecting minority rights, and it is less prone to overrespond to organized interests. System X is clearly a better choice. Of course, a system like System W is better than any of the other alternatives, but may not be available. The goal of this chapter is to identify where clear improvements can be made (as in the choice between X and W) and to discuss details of the trade-offs when choices are not clear-cut (as between X and Y). I will not be able to suggest a system that removes all sources of bias.

Figure 1. ***Bias For and Against Minority Groups***

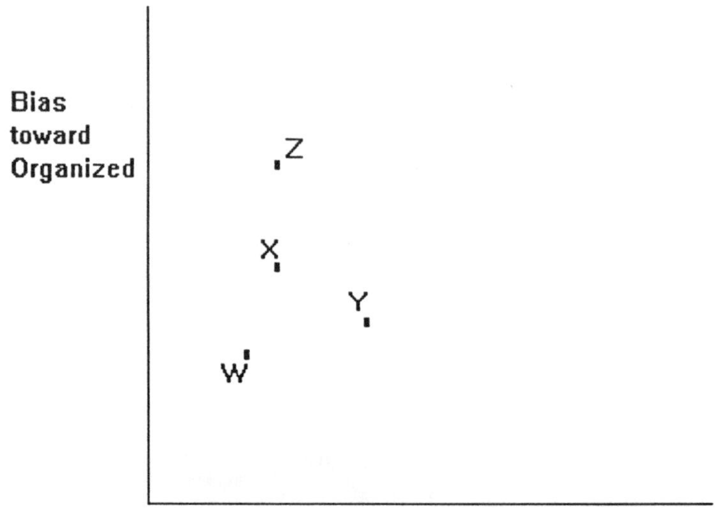

Bias For or Against the Status Quo

Political institutions can be biased toward particular policies as well as toward particular groups. In particular, institutions can be biased toward or against the status quo. When representation systems are biased toward the status quo, we get gridlock.[3] In general, the more people whose official approval is required to change policy (the more "veto players" there are), and the more different the goals of the veto players, the harder it will be to change the status quo.

Gridlock is a problem when it prevents government from responding to crises and to changes in the preferences of citizens. However, institutions that make the status quo easy to change present problems as well. First, constant changes in policy impose costs on society, as people have

---

[3]While I discuss bias for or against minority groups and bias for or against the status quo as separate issues, in practice they are often related. In particular, institutional choices made to protect minority rights frequently increase gridlock.

difficulty adjusting their behavior to changing legal requirements. *Overresponsiveness* can be a problem that arises when the status quo is too easy to change. Overresponsiveness is essentially the opposite of gridlock. It occurs when political institutions respond too quickly and too drastically to short-term political change.

Overresponsiveness is particularly troublesome when it permits manipulation, that is when a group currently in control can use the power of office not to promote any notion of the public good, but to directly increase its chances of remaining in power. Governments not only design policies, they must also design institutions as new problems require new decision-making processes and old processes become obsolete. In making institutional choices, politicians often try to "stack the deck" to the advantage of themselves and the groups that they represent (McCubbins, Noll, and Weingast 1987, 1989; Bawn 1992).

Manipulation is particularly problematic in district-based representation systems. Such systems require periodic reapportionment, when those currently in office redraw the district lines for future elections. Reapportionment decisions are particularly vulnerable to both real and perceived manipulation.

Figure 2 depicts trade-offs between gridlock and overresponsiveness. As with bias for and against minorities, institutions that improve one dimension (gridlock) often make the other dimension (overresponsiveness) worse. Bicameralism and a directly elected governor will reduce overresponsiveness, for example, but also promote gridlock. Again, choices about representation systems will frequently involve trade-offs between the two dimensions, as in the choice between X and Y, with clearly superior points like W unavailable. When possible, however, we want to rule out clearly dominated points like Z.

Making Trade-Offs in California in the 1990s

Because choosing a representation system involves trade-offs, evaluating different representation systems requires judging which types of bias are most serious. My proposals are based on two judgments. First, the problem of bias toward the organized is more serious than the tyranny of the majority. In part, this is because minority rights are protected by the national constitution (McCubbins, this volume). Moreover, representation systems function via legislatures. Legislatures are particularly susceptible

Figure 2. ***Bias For and Against the Status Quo***

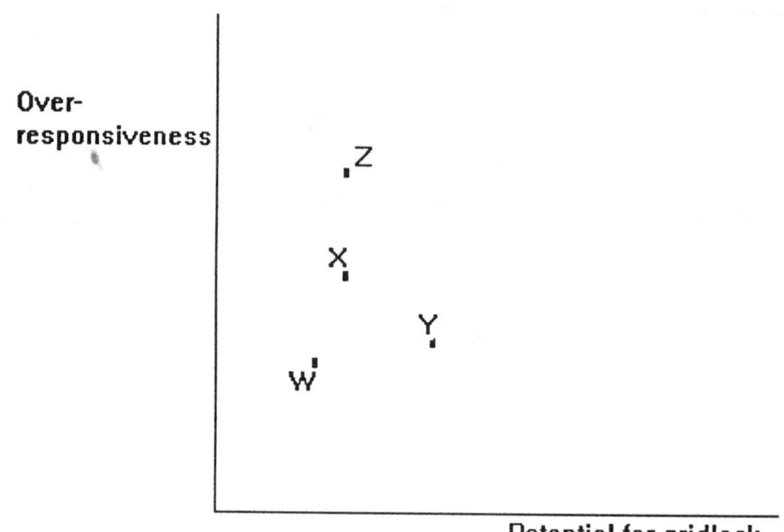

to organized interests because there is always difficulty in associating collective policy choices with individual legislators.

Second, with respect to California's current representation system, overresponsiveness is a more serious problem than gridlock. While there may seem to be gridlock in the government as a whole, this is not due to the representation system, but to other features of the policy process—notably the two-thirds rule and other limitations on legislative decision making. It is reasonable to think that the institutions that promote gridlock were adopted specifically to counter the overresponsiveness of the electoral system. Other participants in this project (Brady and Gaines, Cain and Persily, Ellwood, McCubbins) argue that many of the nonelectoral ways of reducing overresponsiveness create problems as bad as those they were intended to solve. If these authors' recommendations are adopted (the two-thirds rule is abolished, along with bicameralism and an independently elected executive), some guard against the dangers of overresponsiveness can, and probably should, be reintroduced through the electoral system.

CALIFORNIA'S CURRENT REPRESENTATION SYSTEM

Choosing a representation system for a state is not identical to choosing a representation system for a nation. For one thing, some options are not available to California because they do not conform to federal law. Most notably, California could not adopt the system used at the national level in the U.S. In a series of decisions in the 1960s, the Supreme Court ruled that state legislatures cannot give some citizens' votes more weight than others. These decisions preclude electing one chamber from districts of differing population, as is done in the U.S. Senate.

The fact that California is a state and not a sovereign nation not only rules out some alternatives, it also affects how electoral systems work. At the national level, electoral systems influence the number and type of political parties. Parties in California are imbedded in a national party system, and many California politicians aspire to national office. We cannot expect parties to react to changes in California's representation system as fully as they would to changes in national institutions.

Like every other state except Nebraska, California has a bicameral legislature. As in other states, both chambers are elected from geographic districts in which the single candidate with the most votes wins. This type of electoral system is referred to as "plurality" or "single-member districts" (SMD). California's current representation system stands out, however, in two respects. First, each of California's state legislators represents an unusually large number of citizens. Second, the two chambers are not very different from each other.

California is the largest state, yet it has one of the smallest state legislatures. Tables 1 and 2 show the number of legislators in each chamber of each state's legislature, and the number of people represented by each legislator. California has more citizens per legislator than any other state. Indeed, members of California's assembly (the lower chamber) represent almost three times as many people as those of the state with the second largest districts (New York). Moreover, state senators represent more citizens than California's delegates to the U.S. House of Representatives.

Small districts have both advantages and disadvantages. Weingast, Shepsle, and Johnsen (1981) have argued that a small number of large districts are preferable to a large number of small ones because the amount of pork barrel spending is proportional to the number of people who must

Table 1. *District Population of Lower Chambers*

	State	District Population[1]	State Population (thousands)	Number of Districts
1.	New Hampshire	2,778	1,111	400
2.	Vermont	3,800	570	150
3.	North Dakota	6,000	636	106
4.	Wyoming	7,281	466	64
5.	Maine	8,179	1,235	151
6.	Montana	8,240	824	100
7.	Rhode Island	10,050	1,005	100
8.	South Dakota	10,157	711	70
9.	Idaho	12,702	1,067	84
10.	Alaska	14,675	587	40
11.	Delaware	16,805	689	41
12.	West Virginia	18,120	1,812	100
13.	Kansas	20,184	2,523	125
14.	Mississippi	21,426	2,614	122
15.	Connecticut	21,728	3,281	151
16.	New Mexico	22,586	1,581	70
17.	Hawaii	22,745	1,160	51
18.	Arkansas	23,990	2,399	100
19.	Utah	24,173	1,813	75
20.	Iowa	28,120	2,812	100
21.	South Carolina	29,056	3,603	124
22.	Nevada	31,595	1,327	42
23.	Oklahoma	31,802	3,212	101
24.	Missouri	31,859	5,193	163
25.	Minnesota	33,433	4,480	134
26.	Maryland	34,809	4,908	141
27.	Massachusetts	37,488	5,998	160
28.	Georgia	37,506	6,751	180
29.	Kentucky	37,550	3,755	100
30.	Alabama	39,390	4,136	105

Table 1. ***Continued***

	State	District Population[1]	State Population (thousands)	Number of Districts
31.	Louisiana	40,829	4,287	105
32.	Oregon	49,617	2,977	60
33.	Wisconsin	50,576	5,007	99
34.	Tennessee	50,747	5,024	99
35.	Washington	52,408	5,136	98
36.	Colorado	53,385	3,470	65
37.	Indiana	56,220	5,622	100
38.	North Carolina	57,025	6,843	120
39.	Pennsylvania	59,158	12,000	203
40.	Virginia	63,770	6,377	100
41.	Arizona	63,867	3,832	60
42.	Michigan	85,791	9,437	110
43.	New Jersey	97,363	7,789	80
44.	Illinois	98,568	11,600	118
45.	Ohio	111,273	11,000	99
46.	Florida	112,400	13,500	120
47.	Texas	117,707	17,700	150
48.	New York	120,793	18,100	150
49.	California	385,838	30,900	80

[1]1992 population.

Table 2. ***District Population of Upper Chambers***

	State	District Population	State Population (thousands)	Number of Districts
1.	North Dakota	12,000	636	53
2.	Wyoming	15,533	466	30
3.	Montana	16,480	824	50
4.	Vermont	19.000	570	30
5.	Rhode Island	20,100	1,005	50
6.	South Dakota	20,314	711	35
7.	Idaho	25,405	1,067	42
8.	Alaska	29,350	587	20
9.	Nebraska	32,776	1,606	49
10.	Delaware	32,810	689	21
11.	Maine	35,286	1,235	35
12.	New Mexico	37,643	1,581	42
13.	New Hampshire	46,292	1,111	24
14.	Hawaii	46,400	1,160	25
15.	Mississippi	50,269	2,614	52
16.	West Virginia	53,294	1,812	34
17.	Iowa	56,240	2,812	50
18.	Utah	62,517	1,813	29
19.	Kansas	63,075	2,523	40
20.	Nevada	63,190	1,327	21
21.	Minnesota	66,866	4,480	67
22.	Oklahoma	66,917	3,212	48
23.	Arkansas	68,543	2,399	35
24.	South Carolina	78,326	3,603	46
25.	Connecticut	91,139	3,281	36
26.	Kentucky	98,816	3,755	38
27.	Colorado	99,143	3,470	35
28.	Oregon	99,233	2,977	30
29.	Maryland	104,426	4,908	47
30.	Washington	104,816	5,136	49

Table 2. ***Continued***

	State	District Population	State Population (thousands)	Number of Districts
31.	Louisiana	109,923	4,287	39
32.	Indiana	112,440	5,622	50
33.	Alabama	118,171	4,136	35
34.	Georgia	120,554	6,751	56
35.	Arizona	127,733	3,832	30
36.	North Carolina	136,860	6,843	50
37.	Massachusetts	149,950	5,998	40
38.	Wisconsin	151,727	5,007	33
39.	Tennessee	152,242	5,024	33
40.	Missouri	152,735	5,193	34
41.	Virginia	159,425	6,377	40
42.	New Jersey	194,725	7,789	40
43.	Illinois	197,136	11,600	59
44.	Pennsylvania	240,180	12,000	50
45.	Michigan	248,342	9,437	38
46.	New York	297,033	18,100	61
47.	Ohio	333,818	11,000	33
48.	Florida	337,200	13,500	40
49.	Texas	569,548	17,700	31
50.	California	771,675	30,900	40

be included in a majority coalition. The logic is that coalition-builders in the legislature gain support for legislation by including pet projects for individual members' districts. The more votes needed to build a majority coalition, the more projects must be included. Gilligan and Matsusaka (1994) examined spending in the 50 states over time and found that states with more seats in the upper chamber do in fact spend more.[4]

The size of districts also affects who runs for the state legislature and the amount of low-cost information that voters receive from campaigns and the news media. Other things equal, it is more expensive to conduct a successful campaign in a large district than a small one. The smaller the district, the more candidates can rely on personal contact with voters, as opposed to mass advertising. Because challengers have more trouble raising money than incumbents, we might expect smaller districts to make elections more competitive. Qualified challengers would be more likely to run if the costs of conducting a campaign were lower, and they would be more likely to win if they could cheaply make contact with voters (Jacobson 1983). Moreover, candidates are less likely to use attack strategies and negative campaigns when they rely on making personal contact with voters than when they rely on media campaigns. Ansolabehere et al. (1994) have shown that the cumulative effect of negative campaigns is to alienate voters and depress turnout.[5]

While smaller districts could lead to more balanced and positive campaigns, they could also lead to an electorate that is worse informed overall about state legislative elections. A large number of state legislative districts creates more competition for press coverage, and makes it harder for voters to get any information about the candidates from noncampaign sources (Jewell 1982). Even if candidates are better able to walk precincts in small districts, the net effect of less free media coverage makes it harder for voters to obtain information about incumbent behavior and candidate

---

[4]The fact that Gilligan and Matsusaka found an effect for upper houses rather than lower houses is surprising. Upper houses generally have fewer seats than lower houses, and the logic of Weingast, Shepsle, and Johnson's argument implies that total spending should be sensitive to the number of seats in the house that requires more votes to make a majority.

[5]While both Ansolabehere et al. and Jacobson studied national congressional elections, the logic should apply to state elections as well.

positions. Raising the costs of information for voters increases the rational ignorance and leads to greater influence by organized interest groups.

Finally, smaller districts are more likely to correspond to demographically homogeneous areas. This has the advantage of preventing some mechanical suppression of minorities. In Figure 3 the squares represent groups of voters; each square is a group of equal size. The shaded areas represent Group A, which has different political interests from Group B (unshaded). If the area is divided into four compact districts of equal size, there is no way that Group A will have any representation in the legislature. If there are 16 districts, Group A will elect three members to the legislature.[6] Of course, it is possible to draw 16 districts so that Group A remains excluded. Smaller districts do not guarantee minority representation, but they do make it easier to achieve them, given the political will to do so.[7]

Determining the number of voters per district simultaneously determines the number of legislators in each chamber. Increasing the number of legislators creates greater opportunities for division of labor and specialization by policy area.[8] At the same time, it makes each individual less accountable for the decisions of the entire body and may promote irresponsible behavior (*Federalist* 55). It is not clear when the costs of greater numbers outweigh the benefits of greater specialization. However, specialization becomes more important as the social and economic policy problems faced by the legislature become more complex. This implies that the optimal size of California's legislature is smaller than that of the U.S., but larger than that of a smaller more homogeneous state.[9]

---

[6]Representation in the legislature, of course, does not guarantee inclusion in policymaking (Guinier 1991), but it certainly improves the odds. Even though Group A in this example gets only 18.75 percent of the seats, its representatives may be able to form coalitions with other legislators in order to pursue policy goals.

[7]Homogeneous districts are not without problems. In particular, they are much more likely to lead to "safe seats" where high quality challengers decide not to run because of the low odds of defeating an incumbent.

[8]On the general topic of specialization in legislatures, see Krehbiel 1990.

[9]Of course, we have no compelling reason to believe that the actual sizes of the U.S. and other state legislatures are optimal.

Figure 3. ***Minorities Can Be Mechanically Excluded If Districts Are Too Large.***

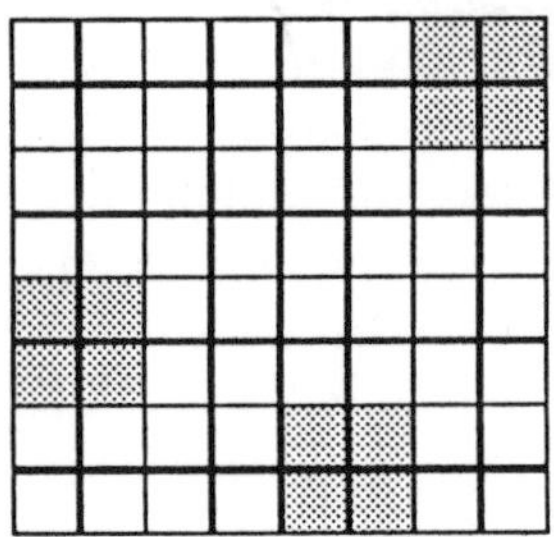

In summary, the net effect of decreasing district size is not clear. Smaller districts could lead to more pork barrel spending and lower-profile elections more dominated by organized interests—outcomes worse than the status quo. Or they could lead to more competitive elections with more direct personal contact between candidates and voters and greater representation of minority interests. In this light, the problem with California's state legislature is not that either chamber tops the national lists of people per district, but that *both* do. Indeed, California's lower chamber has larger districts than the upper chamber of every other state except New York, Ohio, and Texas.[10] Neither chamber allows the possible advantages of small districts to emerge.

This brings me to the second striking feature of the California state legislature. The two chambers are not very different. Both are elected from single-member geographic districts drawn on the basis of population. Both have large districts, with lines drawn at the same time by the same process. If the districting process for one chamber is manipulated to favor some group, the other chamber will likely reflect this same bias.

The similarity between the two chambers undermines the logic of bicameralism. Bicameralism should decrease overresponsiveness by creating an additional hurdle for new legislation. A second chamber means that

[10]In most states, the chambers of the legislature have the same powers, so the labels "upper house" and "lower house" are somewhat arbitrary. The primary distinction is that the "lower house" is the one with more seats (and often shorter terms of office.)

control of the assembly is not sufficient to dictate state policy. As Madison observed, however, "the improbability of sinister combinations will be in proportion to the dissimilarity of the two chambers" (*Federalist* 62). Other justifications for bicameralism also depend on the two chambers being systematically different. For example, groups that end up disenfranchised because they end up as district minorities in one chamber (whether by design or by accident) could gain representation in the other chamber if the electoral systems were sufficiently different.

As with decreasing district size, increasing the difference between the chambers would have mixed effects. The primary advantage is a decrease in overresponsiveness through representation of a wider range of interests. The primary disadvantage is an increase in the probability of gridlock. Making it harder for one narrow group to change policy makes it easier for another narrow group to maintain the status quo.

As mentioned above, the effectiveness of state bicameralism is limited by national policy. In *Baker v. Carr* and *Reynolds v. Simms,* the Supreme Court decreed that state legislatures must adhere to the principle of "one person-one vote." California could not, for example, elect assembly members from population-based districts and state senators from counties because doing so would give extra weight to voters in sparsely populated counties.

One person-one vote leaves two ways to increase bicameral differences when both chambers use single-member districts. First, one chamber could be made much larger. This option has the added advantage of implementing the previously discussed advantages of small districts. Practical problems exist however. If the number of seats in the assembly were increased to 400 (the current maximum among the 50 states), district population would still be 77,250 (in the top 20 percent among lower houses among the states). In order to obtain an "average" lower house district size, the California assembly would have to have 900 seats!

The advantages of small districts thus may not occur for any feasible size in a state as populous as California. Even drastic increases in the number of seats in the lower house would result in districts too large to effectively permit low-cost campaigns based on personal contact.

A second alternative is to use different processes for drawing district lines for the two chambers. For example, the executive branch could be given the authority to district the upper houses, and the assembly could be allowed to district itself. Both processes would have to conform to national policy regarding issues like one person-one vote, and the representation of racial minorities. Despite these constraints, the districting process nonetheless allows for considerable discretion. If this discretion were exercised by different bodies, the result would be greater bicameral differences.

Both of these methods of increasing bicameral differences would decrease the overresponsiveness in California's current electoral system. I will argue below, however, that they are dominated by another alternative. Before doing so, I need to discuss some generic problems that affect all state legislatures.

GENERIC PROBLEMS OF STATE LEGISLATURES

Two additional issues create problems for representation in all state legislatures in the U.S. They are (1) low information elections, and (2) the arbitrariness of districting decisions.

I argued above that smaller districts lead to less informed voters because each race is less likely to get media coverage. With regard to state legislative contests, the difference in voter information between large and small districts may be too small to matter. In general, state and local elections suffer from low salience and little media coverage (Jewell 1982). Voters know little about the candidates and are likely to cast uninformed votes or to abstain.[11]

The second problem is that the way in which districts are defined has a tremendous impact on electoral outcomes. No districting scheme is neutral (Lowenstein and Steinberg 1985), and normative arguments for particular districting principles (such as compactness) are weak. Any system with single-member districts will be vulnerable to gerrymandering

---

[11]One way in which reformers have dealt with the problem of low salience local elections is by scheduling them apart from national elections. The idea was that removing the distraction of national elections would permit voters and the press to focus on the local issues. This reform back-fired. The primary result was not more attention to local issues, but extremely low turn-out in elections without salient national races.

(Taagepera 1984). Moreover, systematic efforts to prevent gerrymandering themselves constrain voter choice (Guinier 1993).[12]

ALTERNATIVES TO SINGLE-MEMBER DISTRICTS

The problems of reapportionment and low-information elections both result from basing representation entirely on districts. If citizens are divided into districts, the location of district lines inevitably helps some groups and hurts others, and the creation of many small localized races diminishes the salience of each, as each district race competes with the others for media attention.

District-based elections are the norm in Britain, the U.S., and other countries that were once British colonies. They are less common in other parts of the world. Most of Europe uses some form of party list-based proportional representation (PR). In these systems, voters vote for parties, rather than candidates. After votes are counted, each party is assigned a share of seats in the legislature approximately equal to its share of votes in the election. The particular people who fill the party's seats are usually taken from lists published in advance by the party.

To the extent that PR is discussed at all in the U.S., the feature normally emphasized is that it permits more parties to gain representation. Imagine a party whose candidates get 20 percent of the vote in 20 of California's senate 40 districts. This party received 10 percent of the vote overall—that is, the number of people who voted for the party is roughly equal to the entire voting population of four senate districts. Yet, because 20 percent is almost certainly not a plurality in any district, the party would get no seats under California's current electoral system. Under PR, the party would receive 10 percent of the seats in the legislature (four seats in a 40-person senate).

---

[12]In California, the ability of one party or group to dominate the districting process is limited by the possibility of divided control of government (e.g., a Democratic legislature and a Republican governor). Increasing bicameral differences would make it even more unlikely that a single group could capture the districting process. However, even when the degree of systematic bias introduced by districting is small, the public's perception that districting involves political manipulation is harmful in and of itself.

PR systems generally involve districts—a party establishes a list for each district, and the district's seats are divided proportionally based on district voter shares. However, because district results are proportional, rather than winner-take-all, the overall election results are not very sensitive to the way in which districts are defined. As the number of seats per district (the "district magnitude") increases, seat shares become closer to vote shares and the impact of district boundaries lessens. Groups cannot capture future elections by gaining control of the districting process, and the perceived manipulation of election results via districting will not contribute to voter alienation.

Because voters vote for party lists rather than individual candidates, campaigns are conducted by parties. Higher profile campaigns and less fragmented media coverage are likely to result in a better-informed electorate. Statewide campaigns in California (for governor, U.S. senator, and many ballot initiatives) receive a great deal of media coverage. It is reasonable to think that media coverage of statewide party campaigns would provide voters with better information about the choices they will be offered at the polls.

Proportional representation mitigates the two generic problems with representation in state legislatures, the impact of districting and low salience races. Before discussing PR as a serious possibility for California, I need to discuss two potential problems. In both cases, I will argue that the problems can be solved by common variants of the basic PR format.

Problem 1: PR creates splinter parties, which lead to unstable legislatures. The notion that single-member districts lead to two-party systems and PR to many parties is referred to in political science as Duverger's Law. To the extent that small parties represent groups in society who would be systematically excluded under single-member districts, this constitutes an advantage of PR. There are two problems, however.

The first is that while winner-take-all elections give all candidates the incentive to appeal to the center of the political distribution, PR rewards parties for appealing to extremes (Cox 1987). Thus, PR may intensify, rather than merely reflect, divisions in society. This tendency would be mitigated in California by the presence of a national two-party system with centrist tendencies. Any group that could potentially form a new party (extremist or otherwise) faces the alternative option of convincing an existing party to adopt its policy goals. If the group wants to participate in national politics, it faces strong incentives to ally itself with one of the two national parties. This incentive makes the alliance option more compelling at the state level as well, because most groups' policy goals involve both national and state government.

The second potential problem is that when there are many parties in the legislature, majority coalitions must often consist of members of different parties. When coalitions include splinter parties, there is a danger that extremist groups will exert undo influence and cause frequent crises in government. This problem is much more serious in parliamentary systems, where a legislative majority is necessary to sustain a government, than in systems with a separately elected executives.

Even in national parliamentary systems, where instability poses the greatest worry, the basic PR scheme can be modified to reduce the influence of small extremist parties. Most countries that use PR require parties to get a minimum share of the vote in order to be included in the legislature. The higher this "hurdle," the more difficult it is for small parties to obtain seats in the legislature.

Moreover, the extent to which PR creates centrifugal incentives is affected by how centralized the nominating process is. If there is a single district, or if all party lists are chosen by the central organization, it is easier for splinter parties to form than if lists are drawn up by independent district organizations. In the latter case, potential splinter parties with geographically concentrated support can be co-opted by the district organization of an existing party. To see this, consider a potential splinter party representing radical environmentalists, with strong support in Marin County. The Democrats could perhaps co-opt this party by including strong environmentalists on the Democratic list and running a campaign that emphasized environmental issues. The costs of this strategy would be negative reactions from anti-environmentalist voters, and the foregone votes that could have been captured by emphasizing other issues. The costs of co-opting splinter parties will be less when there are more districts because there will be more opportunities for large parties to tailor their platforms to local concerns.

Problem 2: Legislators are accountable to party organizations, not voters. Under list PR, an individual's chance of gaining a seat in the legislature is determined by position on the party list. List position is typically determined by the party leaders and activists. A legislator's direct incentive then is to be responsive to party elites, rather than voters. This incentive is problematic when party leaders are slow to respond to changes in the preferences of the electorate.

A related problem is that citizens do not have a single person officially responsible for representing their interests, whom they can contact to express opinions and seek help with problems. On the other hand, it is often argued that single-member districts lead legislators to devote *too much* effort to running errands for constituents (dealing with lost social security checks, etc.) and too little effort to policymaking (Fiorina and Noll 1977). If list PR gives legislators insufficient incentive to respond to needs to individual voters, single-member districts seem to give too strong an incentive. The problem is clearly a matter of degree.

Weak voter-legislator linkage does not derive from proportional representation, per se, but rather from the use of party lists. There are a variety of ways to make candidates directly responsible to the electorate and still achieve proportional or semiproportional results. In particular, proportional representation can incorporate single-member districts. There are two basic ways to do this. In both, some legislators are elected from single-member districts. The others are chosen from party lists either (1) in proportion to vote shares or (2) so that seats shares *in the entire legislature* match vote shares.

The first variant, adopted recently in Japan and much of Eastern Europe, does not count the legislators elected in districts as part of their party's seat share. The legislature as a whole is not proportional, and the ability to win districts increases a party's seat share over its vote share. The second variant, used in the Federal Republic of Germany since 1949, does count the district legislators toward the party's seat share, giving a proportional legislature. With this variant, a party that wins many district seats simply draws fewer party members from its list.

Both systems are often referred to as either "Additional Member Systems" (list members are added to results of district results) or "Personalized PR" (the district races allow voters to vote for individual candidates, rather than simply for parties). However, "Additional Member System" most accurately describes the first alternative, in which the list members are added to those elected from districts. A better name for the second system is "Compensatory Member System" because the list members compensate for distortions created by districts (Taagepera and Shugart 1989). In this paper, I will use "Additional Member System," or AMS, to refer only to the system that does not count district members towards a party's seat share. Compensatory Member System, or CMS, refers only to the system in which district members do count. Finally, I will use "personalized PR" to refer to both variants.[13]

Personalized PR has a number of appealing qualities. The impact of districting is significantly diminished by the AMS and virtually nullified by the CMS. The drawing of district lines may influence specific local races, but the systematic impact on the partisan composition of the legislature is small, because the list results are not affected by district lines.

In contrast to pure list PR, personalized PR creates a direct link between voters and legislators. Each voter has an individual representative to whom opinions and complaints can be expressed. District members have an incentive to respond to individual voters in their district, because failure to do so will damage their reelection chances. Not only would unresponsiveness anger the individual voter involved, it could also be effectively used in a challenger's campaign: "Representative Smith is too busy rubbing shoulders with Sacramento lobbyists to respond to the concerns of ordinary citizens." Moreover, when district opinion is strong and diverges from party position, district members have an incentive to vote against their party. In contrast, in list-only systems, an individual member's reelection chances depend largely on list position. The primary incentive of a list member is to support the policy positions of the party elite—the small group of political insiders who will participate in deciding list positions.

Personalized PR leads to higher profile elections and potentially to better informed voters. State (or regional) party organizations would have an incentive to conduct campaigns on behalf of the party lists. Parties would not experience as much difficulty conducting statewide campaigns as current state legislators do in conducting their individual campaigns. Statewide races and statewide campaign issues are more likely to receive media coverage than individual district races (Jewell 1982).[14] While the actual information content of campaigns and news media may seem quite

---

[13]Using "personalized PR" to refer to the Additional Member System is arguably as misleading as using "Additional Member System" to refer to both, because AMS does not give proportional representation. In this case, I hope that the convenience of a generic name outweighs the potential for misunderstanding.

[14]The district candidates could organize their individual campaigns to complement the statewide party campaigns, although these individual campaigns would presumably have an even lower profile than they do now.

low, Lupia (1994, 1995) has shown that voters are able to make efficient use of the limited information they receive from these sources.

Perhaps most significantly, personalized PR creates two distinctly different sets of electoral incentives. For this reason, a single chamber with personalized PR reduces overresponsiveness better than two chambers both elected from single-member districts. Because passing legislation requires support from both district and list members, policy changes must be acceptable to both district legislators, responsive to local interests, and to list legislators, responsive to the party's statewide constituency. Neither type is guaranteed to consider the good of the state as a whole, unless motivated by their own civic-mindedness (which should be hoped for but not counted on). The combination of SMD and PR, however, ensures that both types of interests will be represented.

Personalized PR creates checks and balances, not only in the legislature, but within each party. Countervailing electoral incentives discourage overresponsiveness, as two very different sets of legislators must support new legislation. The fact that these two types of legislators will be represented *within each party* discourages gridlock. When conflicting groups are represented by different parties, each faces the incentive to block compromises in order take a position or to avoid blame. When the conflicting groups are members of the same party, this strategy is less likely to be successful. Creating checks and balances within the party encourages compromise and discourages stalemate.[15]

Personalized PR is an attractive alternative for California. A unicameral chamber elected by personalized PR prevents overresponsiveness better than any bicameral legislature in which both houses are elected in districts drawn to achieve one person-one vote. It avoids some of the exclusion of groups who are too small or too dispersed to win a majority. At the same time, it diminishes bias toward organized interests, by reducing the number of legislators who must win individual reelection on the basis of perceived individual credit. Finally, it limits the impact of districting decisions. This lessens overresponsiveness because groups in control at

---

[15]It has been argued that there is too much compromise in legislative decision making in the U.S. because incumbents don't run against each other (Mayhew 1974). Note that this problem is also addressed by personalized PR because the list incumbents of different parties will in fact run against each other in the next election.

one point in time cannot use districting to increase their chances of staying in control.

OPTIONS IN IMPLEMENTING PERSONALIZED PR

The previous section argued that personalized PR would be an improvement over California's current representation system. The extent of the improvement depends on details.

Proposal

California should adopt an Additional Member System, in which 120 members are elected from single-member districts of equal population and 120 are drawn from party lists. The legislature will be unicameral. Voters will be allowed two votes, so that they can vote for the district candidate of one party and the PR list of another. There will be three PR districts, with lines to be drawn to reflect geographic and socio-economic boundaries. List seats will be divided between the three PR districts according to population, so that magnitudes may differ. However, each PR district must have at least 20 seats. In order to receive seats in the PR half of the legislature, a party must win at least five percent of the PR vote statewide.

The logic behind these choices is as follows:

AMS vs. CMS: AMS does a better job than CMS of creating checks and balances, especially within the party. Under CMS, members who win district seats do not generally contribute to the party's overall seat share. Holding PR vote share constant, the more district seats a party wins, the fewer members it takes from the list. The CMS does not give party leadership an incentive to respond to the policy demands of the district members. Indeed, leaders may have an incentive to work against the reelection chances of the district members. Fewer district seats simply means more list members, who depend directly on the leadership to maintain their positions (Bawn 1993).

With AMS, on the other hand, each district seat won by a party member is an additional seat for the party. Party leaders have greater incentive to respond to the district seat-holders, who in turn have an incentive to respond to constituent opinion. AMS thus does a better job of maintaining a balance within parties between geographically dispersed and geographically concentrated interests.[16]

The primary disadvantage of AMS relative to CMS is that the potential for district lines to influence election outcomes remains. This influence is much less, however, than under the current all-SMD system.

Numbers of SMD and PR seats: The number of SMD and PR seats should be equal. As with the choice between the AMS and the CMS, the goal is to promote an even balance between representing geographically concentrated and geographically dispersed interests.

The specific number of seats is somewhat arbitrary. Table 3 shows the total number of seats in each state legislature, both chambers combined. By doubling the current number of state legislators, California would move from being the state with the 13th smallest number of state legislators to the 3rd largest, behind New Hampshire (424) and Pennsylvania (253). This position seems more reasonable, given California's large complex economy and diverse population.

Unicameral legislature: The same mix of electoral incentives could be achieved by a bicameral legislature in which one house was elected from single-member districts and the other from party lists. The bicameral mix of PR and SMD would be even more effective at reducing over-responsiveness. Passing legislation would require approval of both a majority of district legislators and a majority of list legislators, rather than a single majority coalition that could consist of any combination of the two types of legislator. Holding the preferences of members constant, it is easier to pass legislation in a unicameral legislature (Hammond and Miller 1987, Tsebelis 1995).

The potential for gridlock could be very large with this sort of bicameralism. It would be possible for the SMD chamber to be dominated by one party, the governorship by a second, and the PR chamber by a third—

---

[16]An additional advantage of AMS over CMS is that it is easier to allow voters to cast separate votes for party list and district candidate, for example to allow a voter to vote for the Libertarian party list and the Republican district candidate. Under CMS with two votes, it is possible for a party to win more district seats than its total allocation of seats. In Germany, this problem is addressed by allowing the party to keep its extra district seats. This correction has worked without difficulty, but it creates an opportunity for manipulation, in that a group of voters could cast split tickets to obtain overrepresentation.

Table 3. ***Total Seats in State Legislatures: Both Chambers***

	State	Total Seats
1.	Nebraska	49
2.	Alaska	60
3.	Delaware	62
4.	Nevada	63
5.	Hawaii	76
6.	Oregon	90
7.	Arizona	90
8.	Wyoming	94
9.	Colorado	100
10.	Utah	104
11.	South Dakota	105
12.	New Mexico	112
13.	California	120
14.	New Jersey	120
15.	Idaho	126
16.	Tennessee	132
17.	Ohio	132
18.	Wisconsin	132
19.	West Virginia	134
20.	Arkansas	135
21.	Kentucky	138
22.	Alabama	140
23.	Virginia	140
24.	Louisiana	144
25.	Washington	147
26.	Michigan	148
27.	Oklahoma	149
28.	Iowa	150
29.	Rhode Island	150
30.	Indiana	150
31.	Montana	150
32.	North Dakota	159

Table 3. *Continued*

	State	Total Seats
33.	Florida	160
34.	Kansas	165
35.	North Carolina	170
36.	South Carolina	170
37.	Mississippi	174
38.	Illinois	177
39.	Vermont	180
40.	Texas	181
41.	Maine	186
42.	Connecticut	187
43.	Maryland	188
44.	Missouri	197
45.	Massachusetts	200
46.	Minnesota	201
47.	New York	211
48.	Georgia	236
49.	Pennsylvania	253
50.	New Hampshire	424

or by a coalition involving a third, a fourth, and a fifth party. Variants of this problem could occur with different bicameral alternatives, such as one chamber elected by the AMS and the other entirely by SMD.

One Vote Or Two: If voters have a single vote that counts toward both the party list and district candidate races, the system will be less effective in simultaneously promoting representation of geographically dispersed and geographically concentrated groups. A one-vote system works against the representation of geographically dispersed interests because parties that represent them are unlikely to win a plurality in any district. With the one-vote AMS, voters who want to support these parties must forego any influence on the district races because votes for minor parties in plurality elections are essentially wasted.[17] For this same reason, constraining voters to a single vote also increases the impact of districting. Under the one-vote AMS, district lines affect the list results as well as the district races.[18]

PR districts: The larger the PR districts, the greater the difference will be between the list and the district legislators. The goal of promoting differences in electoral incentives would be best served by a single large PR district, in which geographic concentration would provide no advantage at all. However, multiple PR districts have the advantage of discouraging splinter parties by allowing large parties to accommodate diverse groups. The idea then is to have enough PR districts to accommodate California's macro diversity without diminishing the representation of geographically dispersed interests. Three districts would accomplish this and are consistent with the common practice of thinking of California in terms of northern, central, and southern regions.

If the PR districts were required to have equal numbers of legislators, they would have to have roughly the same popula-tion—other-wise the system would violate one person-one vote. The point of multiple PR districts is to allow for differences between large geographic areas. There is no reason to expect areas defined on the basis of economics, geography, and culture to necessarily have the same number of people. For this reason, PR districts should be allowed to vary in size, subject to a minimum value, and the magnitude of each district should be adjusted based on population.

Hurdle: The point of the hurdle is to discourage the formation of extremist splinter parties. Extremist parties may have such a low stake in the system that they behave irresponsibly. A hurdle of five percent of the statewide vote is fairly high, encouraging small interests to incorporate themselves into large parties. Incorporation of potential splinter parties moderates extremism and encourages cooperation.

Personalized PR has been adopted by a variety of old and new democracies in the 1990s. The system's current popularity is presumably

---

[17]This second-order bias against small parties is what Duverger (1953) termed the "psychological effect" of SMD. For a more extensive analysis of how this effect works in personalized PR and of the question of one or two votes, see Bawn, 1993.

[18]To my knowledge, the only use of personalized PR with one vote was in 1949 in the Federal Republic of Germany, for the election of the first Bundestag. All subsequent German national elections have allowed two votes.

only partly due to its intrinsic merits—political expedience and the notable success of CMS in Germany have certainly played a role as well. Nonetheless, it is instructive to compare my proposal with versions of personalized PR recently adopted elsewhere. In the 1990s, personalized PR has generally been implemented as AMS with two votes, as proposed here, but also with more SMD than list members.[19] For example, Japan adopted AMS with 300 SMD seats and 200 PR seats (Christenson 1994). Russia uses AMS with equal numbers of SMD and PR legislators, although Yeltsin supported a greater fraction of SMD members (Remington and Smith 1995). In some cases the AMS is used for one or both chambers of a bicameral legislature, although the upper house may have weaker powers.

My proposal differs from these recent implementations of personalized PR by having equal numbers of district and list members. One reason for having excess district members is to limit the number of small parties (Remington and Smith 1995). As discussed above, the problem of splinter parties is less serious for a state legislature imbedded in a national two-party system. And it is less serious when there is a directly elected executive, rather than a parliamentary government.[20] These differences between my proposal for California and other recent electoral reforms derive from California's particular circumstances.

CONCLUSION: REDUCING OVERRESPONSIVENESS WITHOUT GRIDLOCK

The electoral system I have outlined here generally complements the nonelectoral reforms recommended by other participants in this project, correcting for potential problems and objections without undermining the

---

[19]Albania and New Zealand have recently adopted CMS, however.

[20]My argument against a bicameral version of AMS also presumed a directly elected executive. Countries with parliamentary government would be less concerned with bicameralism's potential for gridlock, because the executive branch would be controlled by the same parties as the lower house. Some details of my proposal may need to be re-evaluated if the Cain and Persily recommendation for parliamentary government is adopted. In particular, when there is parliamentary government, the electoral system should be less sensitive to gridlock (bicameralism becomes a more appealing choice) and more concerned with the splinter parties (reason to have more district than list members, or a higher hurdle).

goals. In particular, AMS offsets potential problems created by eliminating bicameralism, as Brady and Gaines and McCubbins advocate, by creating divergent electoral incentives within a single chamber. The AMS complements elimination of the two-thirds rule, advocated by Ellwood and Sprague and McCubbins, by ensuring that most simple majorities will consist of both list and district members, that is, both legislators with an incentive to respond to geographically concentrated interests and those with an incentive to respond to geographically dispersed interests. Finally, AMS complements greater integration of the legislature into the initiative process, as Gerber recommends, by increasing the variety of interests represented in the legislature.

The fundamental argument in favor of personalized PR is that it balances competing goals and minimizes overall bias better than California's current system or other reasonable alternatives. In particular, the AMS proposal dominates the preliminary suggestions made to increase bicameral differences, namely increasing the number of seats in one chamber or requiring the two chambers to be reapportioned by different bodies. Neither of these more incremental alternatives creates the difference in electoral incentives that personalized PR does, nor do they address the problems of the impact of districting or of low-profile elections.

The most important feature of personalized PR is that it offers serious variance in electoral incentives without promoting gridlock. In a diagram like Figure 2, it lies below and to the left of the current system: a clear improvement. List members will be systematically responsive to an entirely different set of interests than district members, but the fact that both types will be represented in most parties gives them a compelling reason to cooperate. Creation of checks and balances within the party gives personalized PR its unique ability to decrease one major source of bias without causing an increase in another.

REFERENCES

Ansolabehere, Steven, Shanto Iyengar, Adam Simon, and Nicholas Valentino. 1994. "Does Negative Advertising Demobilize the Electorate?" *American Political Science Review* 88(4): 829-38.

Bawn, Kathleen. 1992. "Institutional Arrangements and Legislative Behavior: The Politics of Institutional Choice." Ph.D. dissertation, Stanford University.

__________. 1993. "The Logic of Institutional Preferences: German Electoral Law as a Social Choice Outcome." *American Journal of Political Science* 37(4): 965-89.

Christenson, Raymond. 1994. "Electoral Reform in Japan." *Asian Survey* 34, no. 7 (July): 589-605.

Cox, Gary. 1987. "Centripetal and Centrifugal Forces in Electoral Systems." *American Journal of Political Science* 34: 903-35.

Downs, Anthony. 1957. *An Economic Theory of Democracy*. New York: Harper.

Duverger, Maurice. 1954. *Political Parties*. New York: J. Wiley.

Fiorina, Morris, and Roger Noll. 1979. "Majority Rule Models and Legislative Elections." *Journal of Politics* 41, no. 4 (November): 1081-1104.

Gilligan, Thomas, and John Matsusaka. 1994. "Deviations from Constituent Interests: The Role of Legislative Structure and Political Parties in the States." MS.

Guinier, Lani. 1991. "No Two Seats: The Elusive Quest for Political Equality." *Virginia Law Review* 77: 1413.

________. 1993. "Groups, Representation and Race-Conscious Districting: A Case of the Emperor's Clothes." *Texas Law Review* 71: 1589-1642.

Hammond, Thomas, and Gary Miller. 1987. "The Core of the Constitution." *American Political Science Review* 81: 1155-74.

Jacobson, Gary. 1987. "Running Scared." In *Congress: Structure and Policy*, ed. Mathew D. McCubbins and Terry Sullivan. Cambridge: Cambridge University Press.

Jewell, Malcolm. 1982. *Representation in State Legislatures*. Lexington: University of Kentucky Press.

Krehbiel, Keith. 1991. *Information and Legislative Organization*. Ann Arbor: University of Michigan Press.

Lijphart, Arend. 1984. *Democracies*. New Haven: Yale University Press.

Mayhew, David. 1974. *Congress: The Electoral Connection*. New Haven: Yale University Press.

Lowenstein, Daniel, and Jonathan Steinberg. 1985. "The Quest for Districting in the Public Interest: Elusive or Illusory?" *UCLA Law Review* 33: 1-75.

Lupia, Arthur. 1994. "Short-Cuts versus Encyclopedias: Information and Voting Behavior in California Insurance Reform Elections." *American Political Science Review* 88: 63-76.

_________. 1995. "Who Can Persuade? A Formal Theory, A Survey and Implications for Democracy." MS.

McCubbins, Mathew, Roger Noll, and Barry Weingast. 1987. "Administrative Procedures as Instruments of Political Control." *Journal of Law, Economics and Organization* 3: 243-77.

_________. 1989. "Structure and Process; Politics and Policy: Administrative Arrangements and the Political Control of Agencies." *Virginia Law Review* 75(2): 431-82.

Olson, Mancur. 1965. *The Logic of Collective Action.* Cambridge: Harvard University Press.

Remington, Thomas, and Steven Smith. 1995. "Political Goals, Uncertainty, Institutional Context, and the Choice of Electoral System: The Russian Parliamentary Election Law." MS.

Riker, William. 1980. "Implications from the Disequilibrium of Majority Rule for the Study of Institutions." *American Political Science Review* 74: 432-46

Rogowski, Ronald. 1989. *Commerce and Coalitions*. Princeton, N.J.: Princeton University Press.

Rossiter, Clinton, ed. 1961. *The Federalist.* New York: New American Library.

Taagepera, Rein. 1984. "The Effect of District Magnitude and the Properties of Two-Seat Districts." In *Choosing an Electoral System: Issues and Alternative*, ed. Arend Lijphart and Bernard Grofman. New York: Praeger Publishers.

_________, and Mathew Shugart. 1989. *Seats and Votes*. New Haven: Yale University Press.

Tsebelis, George. 1995. "Decision-Making in Political Systems: Veto Players in Presidentialism, Parliamentarism, Multicameralism and

Multipartyism." *British Journal of Political Science* 25 (July): 289-325.

Weingast, Barry, Kenneth Shepsle, and Christopher Johnsen. 1981. "The Political Economy of Costs and Benefits: A Neoclassical Approach to Distributive Politics." *Journal of Political Economy* 89 (August): 642-64.

Creating an Accountable Legislature: The Parliamentary Option for California Government

Bruce E. Cain
Nathaniel Persily

For the past decade, journalists, politicians, and pollsters have noted the antigovernment fervor of Americans in general and Californians in particular. Terms like "gridlock" and "stalemate" have integrated themselves into the regular vocabulary of those with a variety of gripes about government's inability to "do the right thing." If politicians would only represent the will of the majorities that elected them, instead of catering to special interests, the argument goes, the governor and assembly could address the serious social and economic problems that plague California. The question is: are the basic institutions of California government to blame?

The verdict from the public is unequivocal. The Field poll shows that the percentage of those giving the legislature an excellent or good rating has dropped since 1988 from just over 30 to under 10, and confidence in all executive branch officials has dropped dramatically. The data also suggest that the public's regard for the legislature is at least partially correlated with events in Sacramento. Following the difficult 64-day budget stalemate in 1992, for example, 58 percent of the Field poll respondents gave the legislature poor or very poor marks for their handling of the fiscal crisis. It should have come as no surprise, then, that in 1990, voters expressed their dissatisfaction by approving Proposition 140, a measure that places severe limits on legislators' terms of office and also cuts their budget by 40 percent.

Finally, perhaps the most revealing indication that something is wrong in Sacramento comes from the ranks of legislators themselves. In SCA 28, Senator Lucy Killea proposed the abandonment of the two-house system and the adoption of a unicameral legislature (based on the model of

Nebraska). And most recently, Senator Alfred Alquist and former Senator Barry Keene have proposed a British-style parliamentary form of government as a solution to the problem of almost constant divided government that has prevailed in California since 1961.

Clearly, some of the public's dissatisfaction with their government derives generically from the economic, social, and political difficulties California has faced in the last decade. No form of government can guarantee that policies will always be made wisely or that political rifts will permanently disappear. The issue at hand is whether the basic design of California government provides sufficient opportunity for accountable and effective policymaking, and if not, whether an alternative legislative form should be considered.

The proponents of a parliamentary system for California charge that the current system (which we will term the congressional system) is excessively prone to divided government and legislative stalemate, and that, as a consequence, it lacks sufficient accountability. Frustrated with the inability of the formal, constitutionally prescribed institutions of California government to respond to popular will, citizens turn to the least deliberative forms of policymaking by opting for government by initiative. The purposes of this essay are to explore what accountability means in this context and to consider whether a parliamentary form of government might increase accountability in California politics. If Californians seek swiftness and accountability in their government, we conclude, then a British-style parliamentary system will give it to them. For those who would prefer only to nudge the system away from situations of nearly perpetually divided government, there are other, less potent options that we will discuss.

LEGISLATIVE ACCOUNTABILITY

Accountability is one of those terms that is often used and infrequently defined. People tend to use the term when things are not going well. Hence, the legislature is not accountable when it makes "bad policy" or when it is stalemated. Such uses confuse the notion of accountability with effectiveness. *Legislative accountability* refers to the translation of changes in legislative composition into policy shifts. It has two components. *Responsiveness* is the rate at which these changes are translated into policy shifts. In other words, how quickly and dramatically do we see policy implications follow from electoral change? The other component is the *degree of bias*, which refers to the degree of skew between the electoral mandate and the final policy outcome. All democratic systems are, to some degree, "biased" in the sense we use the term here. This skew can be the product of a number of intervening forces such as the influence of special interests, caucus pressures on individual members, and trades and log-rolling between individual legislators. *Effectiveness* refers to whether the legislature can pass policy solutions in a timely way to the problems that face California.

Taking these concepts and applying them to the common complaints we hear about the California legislature, we can categorize them in the following way. A common lament about the legislature is that the two-thirds vote requirement for the state budget is a major obstacle. Examined closely, criticism of this requirement stems from both responsiveness (i.e., one aspect of accountability) and effectiveness concerns: responsiveness in the sense that the majority party cannot have its way on the budget even though it has the larger electoral mandate, and effectiveness in the sense that the two-thirds vote makes it harder to produce a budget on time. To take a second example, another common complaint about the legislature is that it is excessively influenced by large special interests such as the California Teachers Association, California Medical Association, agricultural groups, and the chambers of commerce. Once again, this can be seen as an issue of either accountability or effectiveness. In terms of the former, the problem is one of bias: is the influence of groups that lobby or make campaign contributions skewing the legislature away from its electoral mandate to an undesirable degree? But, it is also a question of effectiveness—can powerful interest groups prevent the legislature from taking the necessary policy actions in a timely manner?

But, one might ask, so what? In their wisdom, people are using one term to summarize a variety of things they do not like—what difference does it make? The problem is that an accountable system might be purposely designed to be ineffective in the short run in order to be more stable and effective in the long run. Consider again the case of the two-thirds vote. A strong argument in favor of it is that it purposely makes agreement on the budget harder to reach in order to force a higher level of bipartisan consensus. In theory, this could make for more stable policymaking over time (i.e., fewer reversals and more inclusiveness of the minority's point of view). To use the earlier language we introduced, one defense of a supermajority vote is that it lessens responsiveness in order to maximize long-term effectiveness and stability. The point is not to make the case for a supermajority vote per se, but to see that institutional design is usually a trade-off between different features and values: the short versus the long term, responsiveness versus stability, etc. This is critical to the discussion that follows. The case for legislative reform is not for the overall superiority of one system over another. Rather, it is for exchanging the trade-offs implicit in one system for those in another because it fits the needs of that polity better for the foreseeable future.

Another important point to bear in mind before we consider the case for parliamentary government in California is the distinction between electoral and legislative accountability. Electoral accountability refers to the fairness and impact of the electoral rules in California, a topic discussed at length in Kathleen Bawn's chapter in this volume. Electoral accountability can be adjusted by reforms of the rules by which we decide winners and losers in elections (through "winner-take-all" elections in single-member districts versus proportional representation from large multi-member districts) and the rules that govern the eligibility for voting, registration requirements, and the like. As we argue at the end of the paper, variations in these rules can have significant implications for governance in either parliamentary or congressional systems. While the choice between electoral systems is separate from the choice between parliamentary and congressional government, understanding how electoral rules and other "secondary" institutional characteristics interact with the constitutional form is essential for those who wish to moderate the extreme effects of either system.

CHARACTERISTICS OF PARLIAMENTARY AND CONGRESSIONAL SYSTEMS

The "parliamentary system of government," which governs the overwhelming majority of democratic nation-states, comes in a variety of forms throughout the world. At least one comprehensive compendium of parliamentary governments arrayed them on a grid with 47 major features and hundreds of secondary differences. To name just a few, parliaments vary by size, term of office, members' rights to amend legislation, the powers of the presiding officer, the recognition of groups, the types of committees, and limitations on debate. For the purpose of understanding the implications of introducing a parliamentary form of government to

California, we will focus on the British form of parliament (which also happens to be the model implicit in the Alfred Alquist-Barry Keene proposal). Also, since we are primarily interested in accountability, we will single out three features of the system that contrast most sharply with the status quo, which we have termed the congressional system: namely, the relation between the legislative and executive branches, the locus of agenda control, and the degree of member independence.

With respect to the first of these, perhaps the most important difference between the parliamentary and congressional systems is the degree of formal separation between the legislative and executive branches. In the prototypical British model, the governor of California would be chosen by the majority legislative caucus, and members of the governor's cabinet could (and probably would be) chosen from the ranks of the legislature. In short, members of the government would be simultaneously executive and legislative officers. Under the current system, the governor is elected separately from a statewide constituency, and members of the cabinet are appointed by the governor and do not sit in the assembly or senate. What would be the effect of this aspect of parliamentary government? Clearly, it would facilitate coordination between the legislature and the governor, and *ceterus paribus*, giving the governor more formal, undivided control over policymaking. Since the governor would be the choice of the majority caucus, there would be less likelihood of disagreement between the governor and the legislature than exists under the current system.

A second critical feature is who controls the policy agenda. In the current system, bills can be initiated in either house, they can be amended substantially in committees or on the floor, and the timing is controlled by the majority party leadership. In the British parliamentary model, the power of backbenchers (members without ministerial positions) to initiate legislation is severely restricted, the ability to amend the government's bill in committee or on the floor is almost nonexistent, and the timing and pace of policymaking is up to the prime minister and cabinet. The effect of this in California would be to reduce substantially not only the friction and delays that arise from disagreements between the governor and the legislature, but also the dilution of a bill's original intent through amendments in committees and on the floor. In particular, the potential weakening of committee powers closes off points of leverage for interest groups and individual members who may oppose the governor.

The last crucial feature concerns the degree of member independence. In addition to all the formal advantages the parliamentary system would bestow upon the governor, the incentives of advancement would tend to strengthen majority party discipline and diminish member independence. Within the government, the probability of advancement to the front benches (cabinet posts) would depend to a greater degree upon party loyalty. Governors would be unlikely to promote disloyal members to positions of power and trust. Ambitious members will seek to rise up the government ranks, and inevitably, the pressures to conform to party discipline (which are already substantial in the California legislature) will increase.

Assuming the adoption in California of a parliamentary system that had all of the features described above, what would be the likely implications for accountability? We will offer three predictions based on the logic of parliamentary incentives and substantiated by evidence from parliamentary systems across the world. They are as follows: (1) a parliamentary form of government would increase the level of legislative responsiveness; (2) it would change the nature of "skew" in the system (where skew is the difference between the pure electoral mandate and what the legislature produces); and (3) that many of the secondary features of a parliamentary system can be adjusted to soften or harden the first two effects. After considering the cross-national evidence for these propositions in the next section of the paper, we will return in the end to the question of whether these effects would be desirable for California in the present context.

THE RESPONSIVENESS OF PARLIAMENTARY SYSTEMS

Parliamentary systems of government tend to have a higher rate of legislative responsiveness than the congressional, because the threshold of consensus necessary for action is lower. In a Westminster-style parliamentary system, election results are definitive in determining the policy direction of the governing party. Party platforms or "manifestos" are a reasonably good predictor of the behavior of parties once in office. Without checks from separate branches, highly unified parties led by the prime minister can execute policies and follow through on electoral promises more swiftly and completely than could parties in congressional systems.

The success of parliamentary parties in following through on electoral promises is a function both of the absence of alternative veto points in the policymaking process and of parliamentary party cohesiveness. As Richard Hofferbert and Ian Budge show in their study of British party manifestos, the spending programs of governing parties can be effectively predicted by party manifestos propounded during the campaign. "British constitutional theory is simple," they write, "A government enjoying the confidence of parliament can do anything." In 17 out of the 18 cases they studied,

> government programs (were) remarkably well reflected in post-election policy priorities, measured as percentages of central government spending in major policy areas. . . . The Westminster model, which concentrates all responsibility and power in the government of the day, appears better suited than alternative democratic arrangements for translating agendas into policy.[1]

If responsiveness—the tendency of government policy to follow an electoral mandate and reflect its voters' preferences—is what constitutional revisionists want from their legislatures, parliamentary systems with their oligarchic parties and relatively hurdleless policymaking processes are more likely to give it to them.

Perhaps the most revealing (and certainly most often cited) example of this characteristic of parliamentary systems is the story of the British steel industry. After being nationalized by a Labor government in early 1951, it was denationalized by the conservatives, renationalized by Labor in 1967, and then privatized by the conservatives in the 1980s. This example speaks most of all to the opportunities (and risks) available to governing parties in parliamentary systems to push through truly massive legislative initiatives once given the chance by the voters. Parliamentary systems based on the Westminster model are not plagued by the coalition and

---

[1]Richard Hofferbert and Ian Budge, "The Party Mandate and the Westminster Model: Election Programmes and Government Spending in Britain, 1948-1985," *British Journal of Political Science* 22 (April 1992): 151-82. See also Richard Rose, "The Capacity of the President: A Comparative Analysis," *Studies in Public Policy*, Number 130, Center for the Study of Public Policy (1984): 46; and Geofrey Brennan and Alan Hamlin, "Rationalising Parliamentary Systems," *Australian Journal of Political Science,* vol. 28 (1993): 443-57.

bargaining politics exemplified, for instance, by budget battles at the federal level in the United States (let alone in California). The bargaining over the key components of the party agenda occurs before an election in Great Britain. While individual members may disagree over specific policies (as the recent battles over European Union membership attest), party leaders command discipline when they believe the stakes are high.[2]

The trade-off of the responsiveness of a parliamentary system is the risk of unstable policymaking. Such "seesaw" governance, where major policies are initiated and then repealed in parliamentary systems, is the price that is paid for streamlined policymaking. "The downside of party government systems' high innovative capacity is the risk of major policy reversals when control shifts between two parties with highly polarized views on an issue."[3] One consequence of rapid reversals in certain policy spheres, such as housing or tax policies, is that the "probability that a government of a very different ideological stripe may come to power in the near future is likely to disrupt implementation in sectors where it is important to provide clear and consistent long term signals and incentives to private sector actors."[4] In their impressive comparative study of energy policies during the 1970s, Harvey Feigenbaum, Richard Samuels, and R. Kent Weaver detail how the innovative National Energy Program (NEP) proposed by the Trudeau administration in Canada would have been improbable under a separation of powers scheme. In particular, they point out how new taxation and energy pricing measures were ushered in by the Liberal government of the early 1980s and, despite implementation

---

[2]See Hofferbert and Budge, 179. Of course, politicians break promises in parliamentary systems as they do in all systems. "The Liberal party in Canada won reelection in 1974 largely by criticizing the Conservatives' proposal for wage and price controls. The Liberals instituted wage and price controls the following year." Taken from R. Kent Weaver, "Are Parliamentary Systems Better?" *The Brookings Review* (Summer 1985): 17.

[3]R. Kent Weaver and Bert A. Rockman, "When and How Do Institutions Matter," in *Do Institutions Matter?* ed. R. Kent Weaver and Bert A. Rockman (Washington, D.C.: The Brookings Institution, 1993), 458.

[4]Harvey Feigenbaum, Richard Samuels, and R. Kent Weaver, "Innovation, Coordination, and Implementation in Energy Policy," in *Do Institutions Matter?* ed. by R. Kent Weaver and Bert A. Rockman (Washington, D.C.: The Brookings Institution, 1993), 49.

problems in the provinces, were in force until the 1984 general election. With the election of Brian Mulroney's Progressive Conservative government, however, many of the key elements of the NEP were overturned in favor of a more market oriented approach. The authors conclude that the NEP case illustrates how "party government institutions . . . increase the risk of policy reversal and . . . similarly, the absence of veto points at which interest groups can hold policy hostage enhances governmental capability to coordinate conflicting objectives."[5]

The United States' response stands in stark contrast to the Canadians'. With so many veto points in the U.S. system, American energy policy throughout the same period was characterized by "Difficulties in adopting comprehensive and loss imposing policies; repeated stalemate over energy pricing, exploration and taxation . . . and numerous nuclear plants (were) delayed or canceled."[6] As Congress formulated the Energy Policy And Conservation Act, it impeded President Gerald Ford's proposals for phased decontrol of oil prices. At the same time that Carter created the Department of Energy (DOE) in 1977, specialized and ad hoc committees and subcommittees sprung up in the Congress. Those committees tried to articulate a comprehensive program along the lines Carter had proposed, but the program was eventually defeated in the Senate. And while President Reagan's attempts to dissemble DOE did not come to fruition, budgetary conflict with the Congress produced the next best thing—debilitation in many key areas of regulation and research.[7]

This story of political indecision, conflict and gridlock is a familiar one for students of American politics. Whether exemplified in the debate over health care policy as proposed by the president or the various elements of the Contract with America as proposed by congressional Republicans, policymaking in America, as Chief Justice Burger ruled in the

---

[5]Feigenbaum, et al., in Weaver and Rockman, 74. See also James A. Desveaux, *Designing Bureaucracies: Institutional Capacity and Large Scale Problem Solving* (Stanford: Stanford University Press, 1994).

[6]Feigenbaum et al., in Weaver and Rockman, 98.

[7]See Bruce I. Oppenheimer, "Policy Effects of U.S. House Reform: Decentralization and the Capacity to Resolve Energy Issues," *Legislative Studies Quarterly*, vol. 5 (February 1980): 5-30. Cited in Weaver and Rockman, 55.

Gramm-Rudman case, "produces conflicts, confusion, and discordance."[8] By channeling "ambition to counteract ambition," as Madison willed it, the federal Constitution and the states' that emulated it force a high degree of consensus for the swift legislation, execution, and achievement of public policy goals.

THE NATURE OF BIAS IN A PARLIAMENTARY SYSTEM

Because it defines the rules of the game in which interest groups win political power, the process of constitutional design always implies a structure for how interest groups will maximize their influence under a given system. The "bias" of any system does not imply unfairness or mistreatment of a particular group. It merely refers to the strategies open to interest group leaders as they attempt to affect the governmental process. The nature of bias in a parliamentary system differs from that in a congressional system since it takes the form of large, state/nationally organized interests as opposed to smaller interests. This bias is a function of the concentration of authority between the executive and legislative branches and the degree of party discipline among members in the legislature.

In a two-party Westminster-style system, the parties have little incentive to "represent" small, potentially controversial or divisive "interests" in their party platforms or policy stances. Or conversely, "special interests" tend not to capture particular legislators, committees, or bureaucracies. Instead, parliamentary governments tend to represent those interests necessary for election—large, clearly defined, and stable interests that are active across the range of policy debates with which the governing party will concern itself.

While the size of an interest group is important under either system, the congressional system with its weaker parties and multiple points of access provides additional strategies for smaller, well-organized interest groups to win over politically powerful allies. The porousness of policymaking in congressional systems allows interest groups to concentrate on certain individuals in several branches rather than try to budge a heavy, unified

---

[8]Cited in James Q. Wilson, "Does the Separation of Powers Still Work?" *Public Interest*, no. 86 (Winter 1987): 39.

parliamentary party that will be held collectively accountable for representation of the interest group. For this reason, the Democratic party was able to maintain its contradictory affiliations with northern liberals and southern conservatives throughout most of its history, or more recently, labor leaders could find representation in the fights over the NAFTA and GATT despite the fact that the president of the party they sought to influence was staunchly against them.

There are several consequences to the difference in bias provided by the two systems. First, there is the argument that parliamentary systems are better suited to make the difficult decisions that will impose losses on interest groups. In their study of pension policies in Great Britain, Canada, West Germany, and the United States, Paul D. Pierson and R. Kent Weaver argue that party government provides opportunities for loss imposition not present in the separation of powers model.

> It is widely recognized that the diffusion of power in the U.S. system, requiring cooperation among political antagonists, is an obstacle to loss imposition. Equally important, however, individual legislators and the president usually can be held individually accountable . . . for their actions that contributed to loss imposition, if not for the final outcome. Unless there is near-unanimous agreement, accountability is neither concentrated nor diffused; instead it is divided and targeted at individual politicians through the American system of weak parties and candidate-centered politics.[9]

Of course, institutional variation does not tell the whole story. The authors argue that the fusion of power under the British system allowed the Thatcher government to make radical cuts in SERPS (State Earnings Related Pension Scheme) expenditures to levels 50 percent lower by the year 2021. But politicians in Canada, another Westminster-style government, were less successful than their British counterparts in making necessary cutbacks in pension programs. This was true despite the large

---

[9]Paul D. Pierson and R. Kent Weaver, "Imposing Losses in Pension Policy," in *Do Institutions Matter?* ed. R. Kent Weaver and Bert A. Rockman (Washington, D.C.: Brookings Institution, 1993), 144.

majority held by the Mulroney administration in the mid-1980s. Political will is independent of institutional form and the cowardice of party leaders to risk reelection for public policy ends comes in both Anglo and American forms. The difference for a congressional system is that a smaller set of cowards can stalemate the process even once the "majority" has overcome its inhibitions.

One ought not overlook the impact of secondary institutional factors on this debate over loss imposition under alternative institutional arrangements. The first concerns the timing of elections. Politicians will become less likely to take risks as elections become imminent. With frequent elections at regular two-year intervals, every other year becomes an election year when California legislators fear their actions may remain in the short-term memory of their constituents. Parliamentary governments, within certain limits, have discretion as to when elections will be held.[10] Second, party discipline in a parliamentary system provides a ready-made excuse to divest individual legislators from responsibility for controversial decisions. When John Major turns a vote on membership in the European Union into a vote of confidence for the Tories, for example, anti-Europe conservatives reluctantly vote "yes" while their constituents recognize that they are essentially "forced" to cast their vote with the government. In stark contrast, even a powerful representative, like Jack Brooks of Texas (previous chair of the House Judiciary Committee), cannot escape responsibility for his vote on the assault weapons ban with the disclaimer "my party made me do it."

All that has been said so far as to the responsiveness and bias of parliamentary systems, however, must be tempered by a recognition of the role of bureaucracies in parliamentary and congressional systems. While parliamentary supremacy is a fundamental characteristic of the British system, the functions and power of the British civil service cannot be ignored in an explanation of that country's policymaking process. British bureaucrats view their governmental role in a completely different way than do their American counterparts. As James Douglas explains:

---

[10]See Mathew Soberg Shugart, "The Electoral Cycle and Institutional Sources of Divided Presidential Government," *American Political Science Review*, vol. 89, no. 2 (June 1995): 327-43. From the data on 16 presidential systems, he concludes that the primary cause of divided government is presence of midterm legislative elections.

> The British civil servants see their role primarily as helping their ministers to develop some policy, that is to say, policy that makes sound technical sense. They are not primarily concerned with setting broad policy objectives, which is essentially the responsibility of ministers who, in turn, are accountable to parliament and, ultimately, to the electorate.[11]

The stereotype of the British civil servant is a nonpartisan expert who displays "neutral competence" as he searches for the "right" way to execute parliamentary directives. In contrast, American bureaucracies are more politicized or "captured" than their European counterparts, forcing lawmakers to enact legislation that narrowly confines bureaucratic discretion in the execution of laws. These extreme descriptions ignore the changes over time in both countries as well as the different bureaucratic cultures existing among the various departments in the British and American executive branches. Still, the key difference between the adversarial American bureaucracy and the consensual Whitehall system is the perpetuation of political conflict even after the successful enactment of a bill into law. Again, the multiple and never-vanishing points of entry into the American legislative process will check and balance the legislative will long after Congress and the president offer their consent. As Douglas concludes:

> In the British system, the adversarial electoral system creates a government which lays down the "broad public policy goals." But, thereafter, parliamentary sovereignty and party discipline mean that there is not much point in going on fighting at the electoral level—at least when no election is imminent. It is much easier to accept governmental policy and discuss its application with officials. The non-partisan character of civil servants isolates them somewhat from the adversarial character they would acquire if they were partisan political appointments. . . . By contrast, the adversarial approach (*typified by the United States*) creates the

---

[11]James Douglas, "How Actual Governments Cope with the Paradoxes of Social Choice: Some Anglo-American Comparisons," *Comparative Politics* (October 1984): 78.

need for detailed statutory regulation and, in practice, since means are inevitably controversial, statutory regulation then itself creates a further adversarial situation.[12]

The British system, therefore, places more trust in bureaucrats to carry out the will of the legislature. The congressional system, consistent with the distrust of authority that produces checks and balances throughout the policymaking phase, attempts to constrain unelected bureaucrats in a number of ways:

1. By expanding the number of appointed positions in the bureaucracy serving at the discretion of the governor and overseeing career bureaucrats.
2. By maintaining a role for the legislature in holding hearings and advising bureaucrats as part of fulfillment of its oversight responsibilities.
3. By forcing agencies to notify the public in anticipation of executive rule-making.
4. By allowing extensive recourse in the courts for interest groups or persons who feel ignored in the executive or legislative arena or who feel that the executive regulations violate the legislative intent.

As we note in the last sections of this paper, these features of congressional governance can be modified or eliminated in the interest of a more fluid policymaking process. Similarly, they could be instituted in parliamentary systems so as to slow down the enactment of the majority party's legislative program. All other things being equal, though, bureaucracies in parliamentary systems maintain a life of their own that dominates the executive phase of governance while congressional systems institutionalize a perpetual fight between mistrusted, regulated bureaucrats and partisan legislators.

To conclude this discussion of the nature of bias in the two systems, the difference boils down to a trade-off between "tyranny of the majority" and "tyranny of the status quo." Parliamentary systems seem better suited for imposing losses on particular groups, but less able to accommodate diverse viewpoints in the decision making process. The options open for intense interests held by a small number of voters without allies in the cabinet are

---

[12]Douglas, 81, italicized portions added.

few in a parliamentary system. The price of efficiency and coordination is a risk of majoritarian tyranny. In contrast, the influence of interest groups at every stage of the policymaking and implementing process increases the possibility that nothing will be done in a congressional system. The veto power, not only of the governor, but of committee chairmen, judges, and bureaucrats, forces institutional coalition building for most major policies to be enacted. What results is a majority held hostage by institutional rules that allow organized interests to delay, if not actually kill, a policy favored by the governor, a majority of legislators or sometimes, both. By opting for a system designed with a status quo bias, the framers of the California Constitution codified their fear that whimsical majorities pose a greater threat to liberty than does the frustration of inaction. As William Livingston writes of the difference between the British and American systems,

> [b]oth were designed to give representation to the people of the nation; both were designed to preserve liberty against a threat of tyranny; both were designed to afford equal justice under the law. But the techniques by which these objectives were to be achieved differed sharply.[13]

The decision over which tyranny to risk—that of the majority or that of the status quo—should be based on an evaluation of the potential consequences of capricious action versus paralysis. The decision is different for a nation, where the costs of frequent foreign policy reversals, for example, may be catastrophic, than it would be for a state. Reformers of the California constitution must decide which they fear more: a strong majority party with the powers to tax, spend, and regulate or a government that is incapable of performing any of those functions sufficiently and forces citizens to resort to the undeliberative initiative process to overcome political stalemate.

---

[13]William S. Livingston, "Britain and America: The Institutionalization of Accountability," *The Journal of Politics*, vol. 38, no. 4 (November 1976): 881.

CONSTITUTIONAL OPTIONS FOR CALIFORNIA GOVERNMENT

We have until now spoken of congressional and parliamentary systems as ideal types: the former typified by the United States Constitution and the latter by the British constitutional structure. In certain respects, this misrepresents the world of options available to constitutional framers and revisionists since most governments fall in between or outside of these two types. The nature of skew in the system as well as the responsiveness of the legislature or government to the electorate varies with the particular institutional forms that represent and organize political conflict for a state or nation. The list of constitutional options is as varied as the polities that have employed them.

The central difference between congressional and parliamentary systems is the fusion or separation of executive and legislative authority. Two features stand out in congressional systems, according to Juan Linz:

1. Both the president, who controls the executive and is elected by the people, and an elected legislature (unicameral or bicameral) enjoy democratic legitimacy. It is a system of "dual democratic legitimacy."
2. Both the president and the congress are elected for a fixed term, the president's tenure in office is independent of the legislature's, and the survival of the legislature is independent of the president. This leads to . . . the "rigidity" of the presidential system.[14]

With independent electoral bases, the system is geared for conflict and, in general, requires a higher threshold of consent in the formation of public policy. Of course, the nature of the presidential veto can differ between systems. It could be more easily overridden than in the American case, for example. But compared to a parliamentary system that normally requires only that a majority of legislators vote yes on a bill, the congressional system mandates that an independently elected governor or president also consent. As Robert Dahl explains:

---

[14]Juan Linz, "Presidential or Parliamentary Democracy," in *The Failure of Presidential Democracy: Comparative Perspectives,* ed. Juan J. Linz and Arturo Valenzuela (Baltimore: Johns Hopkins Press, 1994), 6.

> In parliamentary systems there is a single electorate. In Presidential systems there are two electorates, and they are not identical. The president is likely to be more responsive to his own electorate, and the legislators to theirs. . . . A parliamentary system provides the cabinet and leaders of the majority coalition in parliament not only with stronger incentives for resolving conflicts but also with strategic opportunities for doing so. In presidential systems the incentives are weaker—indeed, may work to sharpen the conflict—and opportunities for resolving it are much more limited.[15]

All other things being equal, then, presidential systems tend toward less coordinated policymaking than do parliamentary systems. But all other things are rarely equal when comparing the variety of different democratic forms and parliamentary governments. The following list of micro-institutional characteristics, which is by no means exhaustive, may produce dramatic effects as to the responsiveness and skew of either congressional or parliamentary systems:

The Nature of Executive-Legislative Relations

1. Whether the legislature can call new elections for the government.
2. The nature and extent of the veto power of the chief executive and how many legislators are needed to override the veto.
3. Who appoints and approves which members of the bureaucracy and whether there are separate, independent elections for certain executive officials.
4. The conditions under which the legislature can remove the chief executive.
5. The additional stringencies (e.g., supermajority requirements) required for government action on certain issues (e.g., taxation).
6. Whether members of the legislature can also serve in the executive branch.

---

[15]Robert Dahl, "Thinking about Democratic Constitutions: Conclusions from Democratic Experience," unpublished manuscript, 23-24.

Electoral Differences

1. The timing of the elections: Are elections for the governor and legislature held contemporaneously and are there "midterm" elections?
2. The terms of officeholders: Are they fixed by the constitution or does the government serve only until it loses the confidence of the parliament? And is the number of terms limited?
3. The size of each legislative district and whether districts vary in sizes.
4. How many representatives serve per district and is the number the same for all districts?
5. Whether elections are candidate-based versus party-based.
6. How easy it is for voters to split their tickets between legislative and executive officials?
7. Whether elections are staggered among members of the same house.

Centralization of Legislative Power

1. The degree of bicameralism: How similar are the two houses with regard to enumerated powers, rules, size, and length of terms?
2. Whether any individual member can introduce bills and whether there is a quota for the number of bills per member per session.
3. The powers of committees: Can they amend, delay, or in other ways obstruct or change legislation favored by the larger legislature?
4. The powers of the presiding officer to control the power and fortunes of the members of the legislature.

In addition to recognizing the variety of congressional or parliamentary institutions and choices, it is crucial to recognize how institutional forms interact. The choice between parliamentary and congressional systems may be highly affected by the division of authority between the state and the locality and certainly between what type of electoral system (proportional or plurality) should be employed for the legislature. We ought to separate in our mind the "genetic" features of these institutions and the site-specific manifestations of the institutional option. One is tempted, for example, to misrepresent "presidentialism" by merely referring to the most well-studied case, the United States, without concern for the variety of presidential forms in the countries of Latin America and in France. The danger of such an approach is to assume that the mere "congressional" character of the constitution is the decisive constitutional characteristic that produced the observed phenomena.[16]

Indeed, parliamentary systems can tend toward even greater political stalemate than an American-style congressional system. Under certain conditions or with certain alterations, a parliamentary government can institutionalize multiple vetoes and points of access. The putative maleficent characteristics of congressional systems—"gridlock" and "factionalism"—can arise by accident or design in parliamentary systems. By varying the characteristics listed above, one can design parliamentary systems to be more porous so that interest groups can penetrate the policymaking process at various points of entry. Strong bicameralism, powerful committees, supermajority requirements and significant member autonomy from party leadership will generally slow down policymaking (and give greater access) in parliamentary systems. Conversely, tying together the elections of governors and legislators by contemporaneous terms of office or the denial of split ticket voting would "parliamentarize" a congressional system, as would making vetoes easier to override, restricting committee powers or allowing assemblymen to serve in the executive branch.

Member autonomy, strong committees, or multi-partyism can, in varying degrees, put the brakes on what might otherwise be the hasty legislative responsiveness of a parliamentary system. Member independence will naturally be greater when each member's electoral base is

---

[16]Until this point, we have only stressed the formal institutions of policymaking and accountability. One ought not overlook the informal mechanisms that develop in each democracy to deal with the problems caused by gridlock and other institutional consequences. "The real techniques of accountability in Britain, and consequently the ultimate rationalization of British democracy," explains William Livingston (1976), "are found in a variety of other arrangements: through the channels of the party, especially the parliamentary party; through the procedure and spirit of the House of Commons with its elaborate provisions for the satisfactory performance by the Opposition of duties that the constitution assigns to it; through the pattern of debate and the conduct of affairs at Question Time; through the Prime Minister's relations with the senior cabinet members and the senior civil servants; through the Prime Minister's constant need to conciliate political factions within his own party; and above all through the ultimate threat of the next election which hangs over government and Opposition alike," pp. 884-85.

autonomous of the rest of his party's, as is the case in single-member district systems. Party-line voting is less frequent in such instances since party elites might not be able to coerce members with the threat that they will not be on the party list in the next election as in states governed by proportional systems. Also, systems vary in the mechanisms available to party elites to discipline their members.[17] On one extreme are American parties that rarely punish their members for voting against the party line on certain issues and more often allow for issues without clear partisan divisions to come before the respective chambers (e.g., NAFTA, GATT, the crime bill). The other extreme would be parliamentary systems in which members owe their livelihood to the party leadership and wherein prime ministers can attach a vote of confidence to any specific issue before the house. Under such a system, leaders of the majority party can "up the ante" of the bill to one where the member must decide whether a vote against the government is worth toppling it.

The other manifestation of parliamentary decentralization is the existence and power of subparliamentary groupings, such as committees.[18] Committees divide the labor of the legislature, provide small forums for information gathering and publicity, and serve as mechanisms to maintain party influence over its members in a variety of issue domains. The last consequence, partisan coordination, will become more and more difficult as committees become more numerous and autonomous. Parliaments vary

---

[17]See Richard Jankowski, "Responsible, Irresponsible and Westminster Parties: A Theoretical and Empirical Evaluation," *British Journal of Political Science*, vol. 23 (1993): 107-29.

[18]See Michael A. Jogerst, "Backbencher and Select Committees in the British House of Commons: Can Parliament Offer Useful Roles for the Frustrated?" *European Journal of Political Research* 20 (1991): 21-38; Michael M. Atkinson and Kim Richard Nossal, "Executive Power and Committee Autonomy in the Canadian House of Commons: Leadership Selection, 1968-1979," *Canadian Journal of Political Science* 13:2 (June 1980): 287-308; A. Paul Pross, "Parliamentary Influence and the Diffusion of Power," *Canadian Journal of Political Science* 138:2 (June 1985): 235-66; Grace Skogstad, "Interest Groups, Representation and Conflict Management in the Standing Committees of the House of Commons," *Canadian Journal of Political Science* 18:4 (December 1985): 739-72; and especially, Ingvar Mattson and Kaare Strom, "Parliamentary Committees," in *Parliaments and Majority Rule in Western Europe*, ed. Herbert Doring (Frankfurt: Campus, forthcoming).

in number, size and type of their committees. Also, they differ on the jurisdiction of committees and their correspondence with ministerial departments. Finally, some have subcommittees and place restrictions on multiple committee memberships for their members. Generally speaking, though, strong parliamentary committees are associated with low party control over committees.[19]

In addition to designing constitutions in order to achieve a middle ground between the congressional and parliamentary models, comparative experience suggests that under certain social conditions parliamentary governments of any sort can achieve the stalemate and skew of a congressional system. The electoral system is usually the prime determinant of how interest group conflict is translated or filtered into partisan conflict in the political realm. Therefore, a discussion of the consequences of electoral laws should accompany and moderate our description of the virtues and vices of parliamentarism. Parliamentary governments come in different forms and the nature of the underlying issue cleavages of the society as filtered through electoral institutions can determine the responsiveness and skew of the legislative system.

It is well established that plurality electoral systems, such as the U.S. House of Representatives and British House of Commons, tend to produce two-party systems while proportional systems more dominant in continental Europe tend toward multi-partyism. Since a second place finish in a congressional contest wins zero power, the argument goes, smaller interests or parties will join with each other in order to get the only prize the district can offer—its single seat in the legislature. Proportional systems with multimember districts will allow a more "accurate" representation of electoral interests since second place finishers will receive the portion of the legislative representation from that district correlated to the vote percentage they received. Underlying these "laws" of electoral systems, however, are assumptions about the geography of conflict in the political system.

As the cases of the United Kingdom and Canada reveal, plurality systems can produce multi-partyism when conditions are ripe. When

---

[19]From Mattson and Strom, 9. See also John D. Lees and Malcolm Shaw, eds., *Committees in Legislatures: A Comparative Analysis* (Durham, North Carolina: Duke University Press, 1979), ch. 10.

regional interests are unified and salient, regional parties such as the Bloc Québecois or Scottish Nationalist party can win individual districts while not being competitive across all districts. Such parties are marginal to the political system until they gain "blackmail potential" when one of the larger parties needs them to form a coalition. Such is usually the case in proportional systems when the actual formation of government is taken out of the hands of the electorate and placed in the hands of party elites who bargain in forming a coalition government. The more fragile a coalition, the more like a congressional system does the parliamentary system resemble in terms of its status quo bias and skewed representation of certain interests. Given such conditions, policy is made only after overcoming the hurdles presented by the various actors with veto potential—in one, the governor and a majority of the legislature, in the other, the coalition members representing at least a majority of the parliament.[20]

This essay has argued that institutions do matter and that the underlying political conflicts of nations or states can work their way through different institutional arrangements to produce different outcomes. Generalizations about presidential and parliamentary systems are difficult to pin down, however. While Westminster systems seem to produce strong parties that can have their way until the next election (or lose a vote of confidence), regional parties can transform plurality systems into the same bargaining game as proportional representation-style coalition governments or separation of powers systems. Similarly, a parliament with strong

---

[20]David Olson and Michael Mezey, *Legislatures in the Policy Process: The Dilemmas of Economic Policy* (New York: Cambridge University Press, 1991), 9-10, 14. The authors argue: "the policy activity of legislatures will be greater in presidential systems than in parliamentary systems" and "greater in decentralized and candidate centered electoral systems than in party-centered and centralized electoral systems" and "greater in party systems in which parties are numerous and in which no party or coalition is dominant, rather than in systems in which there are few parties and in which one party or coalition is dominant." "Activity" in this sense, might be substituted for "Innovativeness" in Weaver and Rockman's formulation noted earlier. Activity does not necessarily guarantee results, however. An active parliament, as formulated by these authors, is one where a high number of issues is potentially considered by the legislature. Naturally then, the more entry points into the legislative process, the more "active" the parliament appears.

committees and high member autonomy will not exhibit the streamlined policymaking features associated with the British system. Indeed, it is quite easy to make policymaking difficult—simply increase the number of hurdles a bill must overcome for passage. "If we want to make the system work," explains Jennifer Hochschild, "it does pretty well; if we don't, it doesn't."[21] Fearing control by a tyrannical faction, the framers of the United States and California Constitutions did not want to make policy-making easy. The policy spurts characteristic of Westminster systems can take place only after elections in a presidential system only after elections that result in governing majorities in both houses of Congress plus the presidency for one party. Even then, however, policy creation, consensus building, and implementation are not perfunctory (as unified Democratic control from 1992-1994 exemplified).

From the experience of old and new democracies we have learned much about the tendencies of certain institutions to produce certain outcomes. While institutions can organize societal conflict and structure the incentives of political elites, however, ultimately the constitutional form is only as effective as the people who operate within it. To what degree was the early success of the semi-presidential system of the French Fifth Republic, we might ask, attributable to the leadership of Charles de Gaulle? Political will, courage, and leadership are not exclusive to either the parliamentary or congressional system. Yet with each set of institutions comes a set of probabilities to guide the expectations of constitutional designers tailoring parliamentary or congressional systems to fit the needs of particular polities.

THE MEANING FOR CALIFORNIA POLITICS

Bearing in mind the differences between the British parliamentary model and the current configuration of the California legislature, the obvious questions to ask are what would this mean for policymaking in California and would it be a good thing? As mentioned earlier, proponents of parliamentary government hope that a move away from the independent

---

[21]Jennifer Hochschild, discussion following Theodore Lowi, "Presidential Democracy in America: Toward the Homogenized Regime," *Political Science Quarterly* (Special Issue, 1994): 429.

branch structure of the congressional system will diminish the prospects of divided government and policy stalemate. Critics such as Senators Alfred Alquist and Barry Keene say it is frustrating to serve in a legislature that is stacked against change: to use our earlier term, they claim that the current legislative system produces a tyranny of the status quo. As they point out, major legislative initiatives can be thwarted at many points in the process: they can be blocked in committee, amended beyond recognition in committee or on the floor, killed or altered substantially due to differences between the senate and assembly, or vetoed by the governor.

With so many constitutional hurdles, it takes only a moderate level of dissonance to produce stagnation. Senator Alfred Alquist, in his position paper supporting SCA1, lays out the indictment of the current system in three key assertions:

1. An elaborate system of separation of powers, checks and balances, supermajority requirements, and the multitude of other forms of limitations and controls that characterize the present form of representative government have led to a condition of political gridlock and unaccountability. The causes of gridlock are not rooted in specific problems such as the economy or particular social issues. The cause is the system of constitutional provisions frozen in place by cultural circumstances.
2. All these checks and balances have given political minorities of any political party an excessive ability and power to thwart the will of the majority of Californians.
3. Frustrations arising from political gridlock and the consequent unresolved societal problems are increasingly undermining the stability of society in California and leading to hastily conceived, sweeping legal measures, the loss of governmental flexibility, tax inequities, and occasional threats to individual freedoms.

The last assertion refers to the rise of statutory and constitutional initiatives as a consequence of the legislature's inability to overcome stalemate—e.g., the insurance measures, Propositions 13 and 98. In effect, Alfred Alquist and Barry Keene are arguing that when the status quo is not acceptable to the public, legislative stalemate moves the venue of policymaking from the legislature to the initiative process—i.e., from deliberative to direct democracy.

Would parliamentary government have the policymaking effects that Senators Alfred Alquist and Barry Keene suggest? Based on evidence discussed earlier, we would have to say that on balance the answer is yes. Under the initial version of SCA 1, the legislature would become a 120-member unicameral body that would elect the governor from among its membership. The governor would appoint the lieutenant governor, attorney general, secretary of state, as well as agency heads, heads of state departments, and members of boards and commissions. It would also eliminate the two-thirds vote on the budget. The bill has no provisions regarding committees and their powers, but we can assume that at the least their membership would be tightly controlled by the governor under this arrangement. What would this mean?

First, it would mean that the governor would be the most powerful figure in determining the policy agenda in California. Second, legislative-executive disagreements would be reduced by having the governor and some or all of his/her appointees come from the ranks of the legislature. Third, the fact that there would be one legislative body rather than two would eliminate another potential source of stalemate. Fourth, party loyalty would likely become a more important factor in determining a legislator's vote for reasons discussed previously. Fifth, the majority party would more easily have its way on all legislation, including the budget, and would need to court minority party votes only if it could not maintain a simple majority. Finally, interest groups would still lobby the legislature, but they would have to concentrate their efforts on the governor, creating an incentive to build wider coalitions than exist currently. Given these effects, it is likely that legislative stalemate would occur on average less frequently.

Would this be good for California? The most important thing to bear in mind when considering this question is that the choice between the current structure and some alternative parliamentary form is a matter of trade-offs between competing strengths and weaknesses, not a decision between clearly superior and inferior structures. The parliamentary system would produce a higher level of responsiveness to changes in majority control, and while that is appealing at one level (i.e., things get done more quickly), it also means that policies will be subject to more frequent reversals as the result of changing majorities after elections. The parliamentary system would strengthen parties and provide stronger incentives for groups to build wider coalitions, but lacking the introduction of proportional representation, it would also consolidate the two-party hold on

California politics (which would not be viewed favorably by some Californians).

There are proper and improper ways to think about these trade-offs. One perspective that some will be tempted to adopt is purely political: if I prefer government to be as inactive as possible, then I should prefer a form of government in which legislation is as difficult as possible to produce. Or if I prefer a pro-active government, then I want to make the legislative process as easy as possible. Clearly, there are significant dangers when constitutional designs follow political or ideological expediency: structures implemented for these reasons tend to lose legitimacy (particularly if majority sentiment is out of step with the political premises of the structure) and can become unstable over time.

The more beneficial way to think about these problems is to ask whether the deliberative system is being undermined by its vulnerability to stalemate, and whether the splintering of interests in contemporary California politics needs to be slowed down and re-aggregated into broader cooperative coalitions. In the end, democratic government is rule by the majority. If the majority is stifled, the policy agenda will flow to the initiative process instead. It is all well and good to say that bicameralism and supermajority votes lead to more careful deliberation of issues, but if public frustrations with the process leads to more policymaking by direct democracy and constitutional constraint, we are in danger of making the legislature irrelevant. This leaves us with several options. One, the Alfred Alquist-Barry Keene approach, is to make majority rule more effective in the legislature. Another, discussed in the papers on initiative reform, is to close off the avenue of policymaking by initiative, forcing interest groups and the public to do their business in the legislature. But even if the latter were possible, without some sort of legislative reform, restrictions on the majority's right to make policy through the initiative process might serve to heighten the frustrations of the majority, lessening legitimacy and confidence in the system.

As to the issue of splintering interest groups, it has never been more apparent than at this point in California's history that the two most distinctive aspects of California as a state are its size and diversity. Our state government was devised at a time when the state was much smaller and more homogeneous. Must government structures be sensitive to demographic considerations? Absolutely. Some forms of governance work well for small groups (rule by consensus, unanimity, open ballots, etc.) but not in large settings. Size matters in California because as the state becomes larger, the challenges of fair representation become more complex. Diversity—economic, social, and racial—changes the demands that are placed upon the system. The key problem is how to provide recognition for the diversity without hardening the lines of separation. A point to bear in mind is that political group identities and strategies are sensitive to the incentives that political structures offer. If it is possible for a group to do business by itself, it will (because the costs of compromise and negotiation are not negligible). The reasons to build coalitions have to be built into the political structures or coalitions will tend not to occur. Political scientists have tried for over 50 years to get journalists, "good government" groups, and activists interested in the problems of devising responsible government and to recognize that parties can play a coalition-building role and can tie electoral outcomes more closely to programmatic choices. For the most part, this advice has fallen on deaf ears. But in the meantime the power of incumbency, specialized interest groups, and independent consultants has risen.

Parliamentary government may be too potent a medicine for what ails California, but as we pointed out earlier, we do not have to adopt the prototypical British model. Features of parliamentary government such as unicameralism, majority vote on the budget, or contemporaneous terms of office for the governor and the legislature could be adopted piecemeal as smaller steps towards making California government more accountable to majority will. If policy instability is more problematic in certain areas (e.g., tax policy for businesses), supermajority votes could be kept for those policy areas. In short, legislative structural change, even if not all the way to a British system, may be necessary if we are to rescue deliberative democracy in California.

REFERENCES

Atkinson, Michael M., and Kim Richard Nossal. 1980. "Executive Power and Committee Autonomy in the Canadian House of Commons: Leadership Selection, 1968-1979." *Canadian Journal of Political Science* 13, no. 2 (June): 287-308.

Blaustein, Albert P., with Mario G. R. Oriani Ambrosini and Paul Aliferis. 1994. *Framing the Modern Constitution: A Checklist.* Littleton, Colorado: Fred B. Rothman and Co.

Brady, David. 1988. *Critical Elections and Congressional Policymaking.* Stanford: Stanford University Press.

Brennan, Geofrey, and Alan Hamlin. 1993. "Rationalising Parliamentary Systems." *Australian Journal of Political Science* 28: 443-57.

Cain, Bruce, John Ferejohn, and Morris Fiorina. 1987. *The Personal Vote.* Cambridge, Mass.: Harvard University Press.

Dahl, Robert. 1994. "Thinking about Democratic Constitutions: Conclusions from Democratic Experience." Unpublished manuscript.

Desveaux, James A. 1994. *Designing Bureaucracies: Institutional Capacity and Large Scale Problem Solving.* Stanford: Stanford University Press.

Douglas, James. 1984. "How Actual Governments Cope with the Paradoxes of Social Choice: Some Anglo-American Comparisons." *Comparative Politics* 17, no. 1 (October): 67-84.

Epstein, Leon, D. 1994. "Changing Perceptions of the British System." *Political Science Quarterly*, Conference Issue: Presidential and Parliamentary Democracies: Which Works Best? 109:3.

Fiorina, Morris. 1992. *Divided Government.* New York: Macmillan.

Goldwin, Robert A., and Art Kaufman, eds. 1986. *Separation of Powers: Does it Still Work?* Washington, D.C.: American Enterprise Institute.

Hardin, Charles M. 1974. *Presidential Power and Accountability: Toward a New Constitution.* Chicago: University of Chicago Press.

Headey, Bruce. 1978. *Housing Policy in the Developed Economy: The United Kingdom, Sweden and the United States.* London: Croom Helm.

Hofferbert, Richard, and Ian Budge. 1992. "The Party Mandate and the Westminster Model: Election Programmes and Government Spending in Britain, 1948-85." *British Journal of Political Science* 22 (April): 151-82.

The Inter-Parliamentary Union. 1986. *Parliaments of the World*, 2d ed. Aldershot, England: Gower.

Jacobson, Gary. 1990. *The Electoral Origins of Divided Government: Competitions in U.S. House Elections, 1964-1988*. San Francisco: Westview Press.

Jankowski, Richard. 1993. "Responsible, Irresponsible and Westminster Parties: A Theoretical and Empirical Evaluation." *British Journal of Political Science* 23: 107-29.

Jogerst, Michael A. 1991. "Backbencher and Select Committees in the British House of Commons: Can Parliament Offer Useful Roles for the Frustrated?" *European Journal of Political Research* 20: 21-38.

Kornberg, Allan, ed. 1973. *Legislatures in Comparative Perspective*. New York: David McKay Company, Inc.

Laver, Michael, and Kenneth A. Shepsle, eds. 1994. *Cabinet Ministers and Parliamentary Government*. New York: Cambridge University Press.

Lees, John D., and Malcolm Shaw, eds. 1979. *Committees in Legislatures: A Comparative Analysis*. Durham: Duke University Press.

Lijphart, Arend. 1984. *Democracies: Patterns of Majoritarian and Consensus Government in Twenty-One Countries*. New Haven: Yale University Press.

_________, ed. 1992. *Parliamentary versus Presidential Government*. New York: Oxford University Press.

Linz, Juan J., and Arturo Valenzuela, eds. 1994. *The Failure of Presidential Democracy: Comparative Perspectives*. Baltimore: Johns Hopkins University Press.

Livingston, William S. 1976. "Britain and America: The Institutionalization of Accountability." *The Journal of Politics* 38, no. 4 (November): 881.

Lowi, Theodore. 1994. "Presidential Democracy in America: Toward the Homogenized Regime." *Political Science Quarterly*, Special Issue.

Mackie, Thomas T., and Brian W. Hogwood, eds. 1985. *Unlocking the Cabinet: Cabinet Structures in Comparative Perspective*. London: SAGE Publications.

Mackie, Thomas T., and Richard Rose. 1991. *The International Almanac of Electoral History*, 3d ed. Washington, D.C.: Congressional Quarterly.

Mattson, Ingvar, and Kaare Strom. 1995. "Parliamentary Committees." In *Parliaments and Majority Rule in Western Europe*, ed. Herbert Doring. Frankfurt: Campus, forthcoming.

Mayhew, David R. 1991. *Divided We Govern: Party Control, Lawmaking, and Investigations 1946-1990*. New Haven: Yale University Press.

Norton, Phillip, ed. 1990. *Legislatures*. New York: Oxford University Press.

Olson, David, and Michael Mezey. 1991. *Legislatures in the Policy Process: The Dilemmas of Economic Policy*. New York: Cambridge University Press.

Pious, Richard. 1994. "Which System Works Best?" *Political Science Quarterly*, Conference Issue: Presidential and Parliamentary Democracies: Which Works Best? 109:3.

Powell, G. Bingham, Jr. 1982. *Contemporary Democracies: Participation, Stability, and Violence*. Cambridge: Harvard University Press.

Pross, A. Paul. 1985. "Parliamentary Influence and the Diffusion of Power." *Canadian Journal of Political Science* 138, no. 2 (June): 235-66.

Riker, William. 1992. "The Justification of Bicameralism." *International Political Science Review* 13, no. 1: 101-16.

Rohde, David. 1991. *Parties and Leaders in the Postreform House*. Chicago: University of Chicago Press.

Rose, Richard. 1984. "The Capacity of the President: A Comparative Analysis." *Studies in Public Policy Number 130*, Center for the Study of Public Policy.

Shugart, Mathew Soberg. 1995. "The Electoral Cycle and Institutional Sources of Divided Presidential Government." *American Political Science Review* 89, no. 2 (June): 327-43.

Skogstad, Grace. 1985. "Interest Groups, Representation and Conflict Management in the Standing Committees of the House of Commons." *Canadian Journal of Political Science* 18, no. 4 (December): 739-72.

Steinmo, Sven. 1989. "Political Institutions and Tax Policy in the United States, Sweden and Britain." *World Politics* 41 (July): 500-35.

Weaver, R. Kent. 1985. "Are Parliamentary Systems Better?" *The Brookings Review* (Summer).

_________, and Bert A. Rockman, eds. 1993. *Do Institutions Matter?* Washington, D.C.: Brookings Institution.

Wilson, Bradford P., and Peter W. Schramm, eds. 1994. *Separation of Powers and Good Government*. Lanham, Maryland: Rowman and Littlefield Publishers, Inc.

Wilson, James Q. 1987. "Does the Separation of Powers Still Work?" *Public Interest* 86 (Winter): 36-62.

A House Discarded? Evaluating the Case for a Unicameral California Legislature

David W. Brady
Brian J. Gaines

No civilized people pretend to pass laws without at least making them run the gauntlet of two houses, differently constituted.

—C. T. Botts
Delegate to California's constitutional convention, 1849[1]

I doubt that the purposes of a legislature, however they are understood, are served by any of the expensive, trivial, byzantine, and maddening convolutions that the presence of two houses creates for anyone who is trying to get an issue heard or a bill passed.

—Jess Unruh
Former Speaker of the California Assembly, 1971[2]

INTRODUCTION

In 1849, the 48 delegates to California's founding constitutional convention created a two-chamber state legislature, in imitation of the U.S. Congress. Bicameralism at the national level—the famous "Great Compromise"—was rooted in suspicion between states, and especially in the small states' fears of their larger neighbors. The idea of separating a legislature into rival bodies was not, of course, invented out of whole cloth

---

In writing this chapter, we benefited from conversations with John Ferejohn, and from comments made by other participants in the conferences.

[1]Quoted in Browne (1850), 33.

[2]Unruh, in Herzberg and Rosenthal (1971), 91.

at that constitutional convention. Indeed, 10 of the 13 state legislatures in 1787 were bicameral (Grant 1927, 28). This fact, however, represented not conscious constitutional design so much as inheritance from British colonial government, and, in turn, from the division of Parliament into Houses of Commons and Lords, as had gradually occurred over the course of the Fourteenth Century in Great Britain. By contrast, bicameralism in the U.S. Congress was very deliberately chosen, with explicit purpose.[3]

In California, however, the existence of two legislative chambers was largely an accident of mimicry, grounded neither in abstract theory nor in political exigencies.[4] In that light, it is not surprising that calls for unicameralism have periodically arisen in the frequent bouts of constitutional reform the state has since undergone. Unicameral fever raged in the 1910s, simmered in the 1920s, and made occasional appearances in California's "federal" period (1930-1966), as a means of restoring proportionate power to southern California. In the 1970s it made a bipartisan comeback, with such notables as former Governor Pat Brown and former Speaker Jesse Unruh advocating the unicameral cause. Most recently, Independent state Senator Lucy Killea has waged a publicity

---

[3]See Madison et al. (1987 [1788]): *Federalists* 62 & 63, and Madison (1987 [1840]): 155-66. Riker (1955) argues that the success of American federalism followed, ironically, from the Senate having quickly evolved *away* from its designed purpose of representing state governments towards representing instead the peoples of the states. Others contend that it was designed, from the outset, to be something more than a chamber in which states gained a national voice (e.g., Swift 1993). There is, in any case, a consensus across scholars and statesmen, of yesterday and today, on the paramount importance of the Senate to the nation's founding.

[4]Botts' comment reproduced above as the first epigraph was followed closely by a unanimous vote approving Article IV, Section I, establishing two legislative chambers. Even the matter of how the two chambers would be "differently constituted" was little discussed. Article IV, Section 6 specified that the number of senators would be no less than one-third and no more than one-half the number of assembly members. It passed with almost no debate. After fairly brief discussion, the delegates decided against the assembly and senate having different age qualifications (Browne 1850, 83-84) and against a requirement that money bills originate in the assembly (Browne 1850, 313-14). They relied entirely upon longer terms and staggered elections to "secure a more experienced and independent group in the senate" (Grant 1927, 39).

campaign for yet another plan to remodel the state legislature into a single chamber.

This essay evaluates the arguments for and against revising the California Constitution to eliminate one chamber of the legislature. The paper proceeds in four sections. The first section offers a historical review of unicameral schemes proposed for California, with the primary aim of identifying what specific arguments have been marshaled for the reform. Then we consider in detail a feature deemed central by all sides: the tendency towards inertia inherent in bicameralism. We review theoretical models of two-chamber legislatures, and find that the existence of two houses is thought to be inertial mainly to the extent that membership in the chambers differs significantly. The following section is an empirical investigation of the contemporary California assembly and senate in search of such interchamber variation. In conclusion, the final section places this discussion in a larger context by drawing all of these components together into our specific recommendations.

A HISTORY OF THE UNICAMERAL MOVEMENT IN CALIFORNIA

There have been more than a dozen serious efforts to bring unicameralism to California. While agreeing that one chamber is enough, these proposals have differed in myriad respects: the best number of legislators; the ideal length of term; whether or not terms should be staggered; what salaries to establish; how frequently the legislature should sit; whether concomitant procedural or organizational reforms (concerning the committee system or the means by which legislation is passed, for example) were required; how districts should be drawn; and, even whether or not districts should be apportioned strictly by population. Some of the purported merits of any given proposal have had less to do with unicameralism than with some other proposed change.

The 1849 constitution established a bicameral legislature that met annually. Both chambers were apportioned by population, although the districts were of only approximately equal size, because they were not permitted to cross county lines.[5] Initially, there were 36 members of the assembly and 16 senators. The chambers were allowed to grow with the state's population, with the stipulation that senators continue to be between one-third and one-half as numerous as assemblymen. The 1879 constitution set a permanent limit of 40 senators and 80 assemblymen. Since 1862, senators have been elected to four-year terms, members of the assembly to two-year terms. Biennial sessions were also established at that time, though since 1966 sessions have again been annual.

Unicameralism was first proposed against a backdrop of growing regional division. Reapportionment became a controversial issue after the 1910 census. Having been surpassed as the state's largest city, San Francisco was due to lose representatives to Los Angeles. Moreover, the growth of Los Angeles meant that for the first time three urban counties (San Francisco, Alameda, and Los Angeles) contained half of the state's population. Tensions between North and South and between city and country kept the legislature in deadlock during the regular session, as various coalitions formed and then broke apart over competing apportionment schemes.[6] San Francisco legislators finally devised a compromise to soften the reapportionment blow, trading votes on a bill to allow improvements to the Los Angeles harbor for promises to endorse a slight

---

[5]Section 6, Article IV of the constitution stipulated that, "In the formation of [electoral] districts, no county, or city and county, shall be divided unless it contains sufficient population within itself to form two or more districts, nor shall a part of any county, or of any city and county, be united with any other county, or city and county, in forming any district." The precise meaning of this passage was hotly debated in the reapportionment crisis of 1911; however, it is plain that in prior apportionments, considerable variance in district size was permitted in ostensible adherence to this principle (see Hichborn 1911, 284-96).

[6]These events foreshadowed both the "re-match" in California after the 1920 census and the coincident (first and only) failure by the U.S. Congress to reapportion itself that year. After the 1911 decision to freeze membership in the House at 435, federal apportionment (like California apportionment) became a "zero sum game"—i.e., it transparently resulted in winners and losers. The stalemate at the federal level, moreover, also had its origin in urbanization. The 1920 census was the first to reveal that a majority of Americans were urbanites, and rural representatives fought a rearguard action against their dwindling power, ironically reminiscent of the San Franciscan delegation's 1910 battle against the rural-Los Angeles cabal.

overrepresentation of San Francisco. In a special session, however, rural legislators shrewdly intervened, forming a coalition with some of the Los Angeles delegation to pass an apportionment that cost San Francisco five assemblymen and two senators, actually leaving the city underrepresented (Hichborn 1911, 284-323).

The 1913 session, not surprisingly, saw continuing regional tension, in part manifested in various plans to re-organize the legislature. That year constitutional amendments to switch to unicameralism were introduced in both chambers. Both were favored by majorities but fell short of the required two-thirds support. In both chambers, the strongest support came from Bay Area representatives, the obvious losers in the previous apportionment (see Table 1). Not that the drive to eliminate one house was solely an effort by San Franciscans to reclaim power or wreak revenge on Los Angeles, but regional jealousies were one part of the movement. Identical unicameralism amendments were proposed again in 1915 (SCA 16, ACA 38), but without reaching a vote. A separate plan calling for a "senate" of 50 members, each of whom would receive $5,000 per year (a large raise), was put to a vote in the assembly, losing 24-37 (ACA 49). Another variation on the proposal (SCA 8) was drafted in 1917, this time with fewer members (40) in the new house and a smaller pay increase for legislators. The vote in the senate was 19-17, indicating that proponents of unicameralism remained far from securing a two-thirds majority.

After the 1920 census, the legislature again proved unable to adopt a reapportionment bill. The state had, of course, become even more urban, and Los Angeles was by then very large and growing fast. This left three blocs of legislators in a classic "Mexican standoff," with rural-urban and intercity suspicions running high, and with no sustainable alliance emerging. The 1921, 1923, and 1925 sessions all failed to produce a plan that could win a majority. In each of those years some variety of unicameralism was also proposed, tacitly as a means of resolving the apportionment deadlock (SCA 18 [1921]; SCA 34 [1923]: SCA 12 [1925]). Only in 1925, however, did the unicameral plan even reach a vote, and it lost in the senate 15-17, again falling far short of the two-thirds threshold for constitutional amendments. In 1926, the California Farm Bureau broke the deadlock by sidestepping the legislature, sponsoring an initiative for a "Federal Plan" that eventually made its way onto the general election ballot. It radically

Table 1. ***Votes for Constitutional Amendments to Establish a Unicameral Legislature in 1913, By Region***

	SCA 73		ACA 91	
	For	*Against*	*For*	*Against*
Bay Area[1]	7	4	15	6
South[2]	5	5	14	11
Remainder[3]	7	6	8	13
Total	19	15	37	30

[1]Districts wholly in San Francisco, San Mateo, Santa Clara, Alameda, Contra Costa, or Marin counties.

[2]Districts wholly in Imperial, San Diego, Riverside, Orange, San Bernadino, Los Angeles, Ventura, or Santa Barbara counties.

[3]All other districts.

Source: Compiled from relevant volumes of *Assembly Journal* and *Senate Journal.*

departed from the state's tradition by apportioning senate seats (approximately) by county.[7] A competing initiative would merely have transferred re-apportionment power to an independent official in the event that the legislature did not produce a new electoral map. The "federal" approach triumphed: every county except Los Angeles (where it lost 39:61 percent) gave it a majority, and it passed with 55 percent of the total state vote. Two years later, a referendum intended to vitiate the federal plan—promoted on the claim that people had supposedly not understood the impact of the 1926 plan at the time of its passage—failed in a nearly identical vote, with only San Francisco (58:42 percent) joining Los Angeles (64:36 percent) as the counties where abandoning geographic apportionment was majority-approved (*The Legislature of California*, 57). The 1930 election was thus the first to return senators from the new, county-based districts. After 1932,

[7]"Approximately," because the smallest counties were to be combined in pairs or triples to make 40 senate districts out of the 58 counties.

the whole senate was made up of members elected from the newly established districts.

Rural interests unambiguously having gained an upper-hand, the next batch of unicameral plans was aimed, in part, at restoring power to the cities. Two fresh constitutional amendments for dissolving one legislative chamber were considered in the 1935 session (SCA 6, ACA 69). The former aimed to steer a middle ground between representation-by-population and representation-of-districts, by stipulating that seats should be apportioned amongst counties according to population, with the added condition that no county ever be permitted to return more than one-fourth of the members of the new chamber. Perhaps not surprisingly, neither of these bills, nor three more crafted in 1937 (SCA 21, ACA 28, ACA 33), was ever reported favorably from committee, and none reached a third reading.

Two more legislative attempts were made at dropping one chamber, in 1939 (ACA 24) and in 1941 (ACA 17), but neither resulted in any action. If the odds against legislators voting to abolish their own institution were slim in the 1910s, they seemed close to nil in the new era. The arrival of geographic representation had all but ensured that the stiff two-thirds threshold could not be reached in both chambers—a unicameral plan maintaining rural power would have infuriated much of the assembly, while senators could not be expected voluntarily to commit the political suicide of endorsing a population-based single-chamber. Most everyone agreed that a single chamber featuring members elected from differently constituted districts had too much the appearance of a Rube Goldberg device. Hence, the movement could hope to succeed only as had the Farm Bureau, in the realm of direct democracy.

Nationwide, interest in unicameralism peaked at about this time. Nebraska had actually started (and, as it turned out, ended) the stampede in 1934, when the public backed a constitutional amendment creating a nonpartisan one-house legislature.[8] Unicameral bills had been considered (but not passed) in 12 more states by 1936, and then in 1937 alone over 40 bills were proposed in 21 states (*The Legislature of California*, 86). In

[8]The existing Nebraska legislature had been opposed to unicameralism by about 3:1; however, the 1934 initiative passed by 60 percent: 40 percent, with only nine out of 93 counties failing to give it a majority (see *The Legislature of California*, 106).

California, however, the initiative movement was plainly inseparable from the rural-urban schism, and none of the various drafts had succeeded even in making it onto a ballot by the mid-1940s. Despite intense efforts by small minorities, there was no public clamor against the "federal" bicameral legislature as an institution. There were eventually several more unsuccessful assaults on the geographically-apportioned Senate, but none involved abrogating one of the two chambers. Between 1951 and 1957, six more constitutional amendments to revamp senate apportionment were introduced in the assembly, but none was adopted. Propositions 13 in 1948 and 15 in 1960 would also have altered the basis of senate representation, but each failed badly, the former actually losing in every county, *including* Los Angeles (Allen 1965, 16-23).

Clearly, a strong undercurrent in the first waves of unicameralism was the distribution of power by region within the state. There were, as well, other issues at play: the 1913 movement was spurred on by the desire to create a better-paid, longer-sitting, more professional legislature. Nonetheless, the recurring element of abolition of one chamber was not entirely coincidental. Proponents looked to unicameralism to improve: (1) efficiency; (2) economy, and (3) responsibility (see, e.g., *The Legislature of California*, 91-92). Moreover, the claim was often made that the legacy of Hiram Johnson's Progressive governorship was an increase in "executive control and leadership" that left the two-house legislature, "unwieldy and cumbersome" (Grant 1927, 172). When groups such the Commonwealth Club and National Municipal League endorsed a switch to unicameralism, the justification was always some variation on one of these four themes.

Moreover, when, in the late 1960s and early 1970s, unicameralism resurfaced as a popular reform, these concerns took center stage. After 1964, the basis of state legislatures' apportionment was no longer a live issue, the Supreme Court having enforced its own standard nationwide (see below). Unicameralism was, perhaps for the first time, not tangled up in other matters. Former Assembly Speaker Jesse Unruh was amongst the loudest champion of unicameralism at that time, speaking on the matter frequently and writing articles endorsing the reform (see Herzberg and Rosenthal 1971; Lee and Berg 1976).

Economy, most observers recognized, was a relatively minor issue. If a unicameral legislature were smaller than the combined size of the two houses it replaced, there could, of course, be some savings for taxpayers.

Then again, these might equally be obtained simply by making the existing chambers smaller. Direct savings, though, would undoubtedly follow from the consolidation of houses and the accompanying reduction in administrative and support structures. Even Unruh acknowledged that these savings would be tiny as a proportion of the state budget, certainly a mere fraction of one percent of the total (Unruh 1971, 93).

The central issues, instead, were efficiency and effectiveness, particularly in executive-legislative relations. For Unruh, unicameralism was overdue because state legislatures were crippled, and the efficiency of the legislature's structure was directly connected to its effectiveness in responding to the governor. Facing two houses, "governors can, and do, arrange alignments of one house against the other over pieces of legislation and programs" (93). When governors favored with a unified executive branch faced off against a fragmented legislative branch, the legislators never stood a chance.

Unruh would later be elected state treasurer, an office whose very existence undermines somewhat his portrayal of the executive as being wholly unified under the governor. There is greater irony still in his description of interbranch relations, coming as it did from the individual widely acknowledged to have been almost singly responsible for having strengthened both the legislature *vis-à-vis* the governor, and the speaker, *vis-à-vis* the assembly.[9] On the latter point, Muir comments:

> . . . importantly, bicameralism was a crucial factor in the legislators' willingness to lodge formidable disciplinary powers in the Speaker. I maintain that it would be unthinkable to concentrate authority in the Speaker if the assembly were the only legislative body . . . bicameralism reduced the risk of so much concentrated power and at the same time encouraged its use to neutralize legislative bullies and to make the process fair in other ways. Like a car that can handle a powerful engine because it has powerful

---

[9]For colorful accounts of his career, see Mills (1987) on the early years and Cannon (1969) on the later years. Unruh's rule was so notorious that even popular magazines took notice; *Time* and *Newsweek* profiled the Speaker in August of 1963. The usually less political *Life* eventually chimed in with a pictorial under the telling headline, "'Big Daddy' of California: He has the Assembly in his Pocket."

> brakes, a bicameral legislature could accommodate a strong disciplinarian because it could redress abuses (Muir 1982, 195).

In the same manner, one can turn around Unruh's argument that the existence of two houses allows a governor to play one against the other, to note that there being two houses allows groups to choose strategically the more favorable environment in which to set in motion a new policy measure, in the hope of building public support and winning over the less supportive chamber.

BICAMERAL GRIDLOCK?

Thus, when ancillary concerns are stripped away, the dominant theme in assaults on bicameralism is that having two chambers is redundant and prevents adequate legislative responsiveness. In other words, it causes undesirable inertia—in current jargon, "gridlock." In this section we assess the theoretical case for bicameralism's alleged encouragement of gridlock. Rather than trying to establish how much inertia is too much, we now concentrate on what reasons there are to believe that an increase in the number of independent chambers within a legislature does in fact make it harder to change policies.

In its emptiest usage, the term "gridlock" is merely a convenient piece of jargon for those with relatively extreme preferences, who are frustrated with moderate policy that is actually reasonably consistent with most electors' preferences. If, however, across a wide range of areas, it proves repeatedly hard to change status quo policies, one might characterize the system as being in gridlock, and presume that there is an underlying source of inertia beyond the consonance of voters' interests and current policy. In California and in the United States, government is, with increasing frequency, decried for being in a state of gridlock largely because budget constraints impose severe restrictions on policy choices. A natural question is whether this stalemate is born of voters' inconsistent demands, or is an indictment of government structure (or both). To answer such questions, it is useful to begin with a stripped-down model of governing.

Consider first a hugely simplified representation of a legislature. Figure 1 depicts a single "left-right" dimension on which (we assume) all policies, on any issue, can be placed. At various points on the line are legislators,

Figure 1. ***A Simple Representation of Preferences in a Legislature***

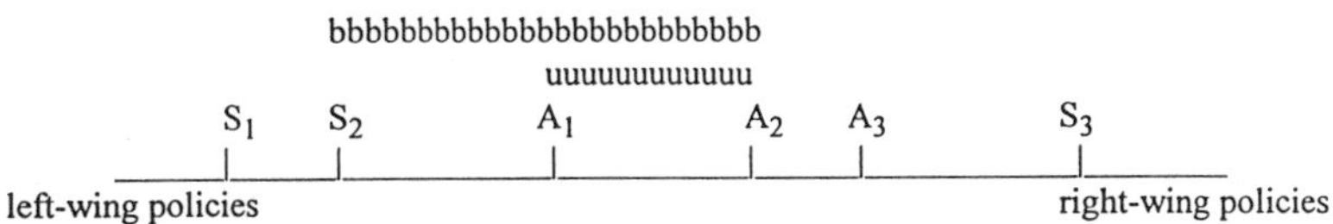

uuu = range of possible policy outcomes in a unicameral legislature
bbb = range of possible policy outcomes in a bicameral legislature

labeled with S's and A's. Each is positioned at his "ideal point," and likes policies less the further away they are from this point. If we assume that laws pass by majority rule and consider what outcomes will obtain if these policymakers consider some new issue, it seems a reasonable assumption that only policies somewhere between A_1 and A_2 will have any hope of securing four votes to pass.[10] Next, add just one institution to this barren world, and reconsider the problem if the S's sit in one chamber and the A's in another, and if policy is formed by means of some compromise between the chambers. Now the situation incorporates both majority rule (within chambers) and unanimity (between chambers). It seems equally reasonable to predict a policy that lies somewhere between S_2 and A_2, the ideals of the two median members in their respective chambers, each of whose vote is required to form a chamber majority.

Thus far, we have described the selection of a policy as a lone occurrence. The implication of the much larger set of feasible policies in the bicameral case, however, is that it will generally be harder, with two houses, to change policy once there is in place some status quo. It could be "harder," at least, in the sense that there are more policies against which a

[10]To specify more exactly what outcome would occur, we would have to model every facet of the process explicitly. For now, we are engaging in the (often perilous) exercise of using this modeling framework as a heuristic device, but not in fact solving a completely specified game. The one-dimensional example is typically invoked to demonstrate some variant on Black's median-voter results, which we do not predict here because we incorporate, in a rather vague way, uncertainty.

new alternative probably cannot command majority support. Suppose, for example, that compromise is a costly process, occupying time and energy that legislators can expend on other valuable activities. Next, consider that, following an election, this legislature is newly formed exactly as in Figure 1, and that the status quo is a policy equal to S_1 (or to A_3). Presumably, either the bi- or unicameral version of the legislature might move policy to the right, away from S_1 (or left, away from A_3). On the other hand, there will be policies positioned somewhere between S_2 and A_1 that would be revised in a one-house world, but would not necessarily be changed in a two-house world. In this rather basic sense, the existence of two chambers as against one does, indeed, seem to foster a kind of inertia.

Actually, quite apart from the artificiality of this model or the ambiguity in our depiction of compromise, we have not yet demonstrated any inherent connection between the number of chambers and the degree of legislative inertia. The example constructed above relies particularly on the fact that the two kinds of legislators are somewhat clustered. If S_2 and A_1 were to change places, the question of bi- versus unicameralism would be irrelevant. In that sense, a fragmenting of authority (in this case, division of legislative powers between chambers) is inertial only to the extent that there is significant variation in the composition of the institutions between which power is divided.

Although there is a long history of debate concerning the merits of bicameralism, deductive, systematic, and mathematical analysis of the organization of legislatures is a relatively young tradition. An early work that endeavored to inquire theoretically and logically into the ramifications of bicameralism is Buchanan and Tullock's *The Calculus of Consent* (1969 [1962]). Their conclusions are ringing, and are broadly congruent with our simple example above. The central insight in their work is that politics revolves around vote-trading ("log rolling") and that any individual's preferences over issues vary in intensity. In large part, then, politics consists of the formation of coalitions by intense minorities. When successful, such minorities can impose "external costs" on relatively inattentive and uninterested majorities. In the event of fairly even intensity of preferences, Buchanan and Tullock expect little difference to follow from a legislature being divided into separate chambers (130). However, the authors propose that control of an issue area by an intensely interested minority is far more difficult when it requires building majority coalitions in two houses. Hence, "the two-chamber legislature, by automatically distinguishing between the two cases and imposing much greater restraints on the erection of coalitions by members of intense minorities than on majorities of equal-intensity cases, can perform a very valuable function" (244). Such protection is by no means guaranteed, since "precise results will depend in each case on the overlapping of the interest-group coalitions in each house" (235), and most specifically, " . . . unless the bases for representation are significantly different in the two houses, there would seem to be little excuse for the two-house system" (236). In short, they predict bicameral inertia precisely where it should be most appreciated, as a guard against minority tyranny. They stipulate, though, that this bonus stems from interchamber difference, not the mere existence of multiple chambers.

Riker also produced a defense of bicameralism based on its power to insulate against certain kinds of undesirable policies (1992a, 1992b). In his rendition, the two classes of policy area to consider are those that are one-dimensional (as in our Figure 1) and those that span two dimensions. A now familiar property of decision making is the possibility of "cycles." The classic illustration involves three individuals making a collective choice over three options.

individual	*X*	*Y*	*Z*
most preferred alternative	**a**	**b**	**c**
second best alternative	**b**	**c**	**a**
least preferred alternative	**c**	**a**	**b**

in a vote pitting **a** against **b**, **a** beats **b** 2-1 (*X* and *Z* vote for **a**, *Y* votes for **b**)

in a vote pitting **b** against **c**, **b** beats **c** 2-1 (*X* and *Y* vote for **b**, *Z* votes for **c**)

in a vote pitting **c** against **a**, **c** beats **a** 2-1 (*Y* and *Z* vote for **c**, *Z* votes for **a**)

Since **a** can beat **b**, which can beat **c**, which can, in turn, beat **a**, it is not clear which alternative represents the proper social choice for this group: their preferences "cycle." In a given decision, the actual outcome will be determined by the order in which the alternatives are compared. Riker deems such a result "majority tyranny," since one majority is favored over rival majorities, without any obvious justification. Arrow (1951) proved that this sort of phenomenon is a general property of voting procedures: no method of aggregating preferences can meet conditions that seem, *a priori*, to be a minimal description of traditional democratic theory.

Black (1958) then demonstrated that such cycling will not occur when decisions concern issues that have only one dimension, provided that each individual voter's preferences are not themselves somewhat odd (in a special technical sense). Implicitly, we rely on his median result above in our example. However, McKelvey (1976, 1979) established that in multidimensional policy spaces the analog to the median is quite rare: under some fairly general conditions, an indefinite sequence of votes can lead to any point at all in the policy space winning majority approval. What followed was a large body of literature addressing how various institutions that modify majority rule can work against the resulting "chaos." Riker's argument is that bicameralism is unique amongst such institutional arrangements insofar as it thwarts majority tyranny in a multidimensional setting, but does not destroy natural majority rule outcomes (which are not "tyranny") in a one-dimensional setting.

Rather than track through the details of Riker's argument, we will note that he neglects a central point. In his Figures 6 and 7 (1992a) he demonstrates how the range of passable policies is reduced by imposing a supermajority requirement (6) or bicameralism (7) on a legislature choosing policy in two dimensions. His bicameral example, though, relies on legislators who are split into two houses being different. The reduction in "chaos" of which he approves occurs only when the two houses that are created have different kinds of members.

Miller and Hammond in a series of papers (1987, 1989, 1990) have established that fact very clearly. Their concern has been to analyze the degree to which the institutions established by the American Constitution have, in defiance of theories of cycles and chaos, established a stable policy environment. They quote Madison approvingly that, "the improbability of sinister combinations will be in proportion to the dissimilarity in the genius of the two bodies" (Madison, quoted in Hammond and Miller 1987, 1158). In particular, the "dissimilarity" in their models is, yet again, separation in policy space. Stability in these models is represented by a "core," a set of points that cannot be beaten in two-way votes. Their key finding is that whenever there exists a core in a unicameral setting, the bicameral equivalent will have a core at least as large. The familiar qualifier is, "the more the chambers resemble each other—the more overlapping their sets of ideal points—the less likely it is that bicameralism will create a core" (1987, 1160). Or, again, "The stability-inducing properties of bicameralism are thus dependent on the existence of distinctly different viewpoints in the two chambers" (1989, 92). Hammond and Miller analyze two-dimensional policy areas, but Brennan and Hamlin (1992) have extended their results to n-dimensional space.

Finally, Tsebelis (1993) takes yet another approach to a mathematical formulation of bicameralism's effects. His focus is on "veto players," those actors (individuals or collectivities) whose approval is required for policy to pass. Though he disputes Riker's justification of bicameralism, his broad argument has a remarkably familiar ring. Generally, stability increases with the number of veto players, their incongruence, and their internal cohesion. Hence, a two-house legislator will, in general, be more stable than its one-house counterpart, and stability will increase with the difference between the chambers, and will also increase with the homogeneity within these chambers.

In summary, there is quite a broad consensus that bicameralism can be a source of stability, in direct proportion to how different the two chambers are. In contrast to those behind the unicameral movement, the authors of the formal works we briefly reviewed have been at least agnostic, and at most enthusiastic about the net effect of this stability. The next obvious question for this paper is, how different are the California assembly and senate? Do these two chambers even fulfill the condition emphasized time and again that the two chambers must be differently constituted for bicameralism to make much difference?

REPRESENTATION IN THE ASSEMBLY AND THE SENATE

In this section we compare and contrast California's assembly and senate. Our motivating question is whether California's two kinds of state legislators differ in preferences. Does the bicameral arrangement within the state resemble theoretical models in which there is indeed policy stability as a consequence of multiple houses? James Mills, a member of the assembly from 1961 to 1966 and a senator from 1966 to 1980 contrasted the two chambers:

> In general, the Senate was guilty of drunkenness but, unlike the Assembly, was innocent of philandering. Its members were, in

> large part, old goats who did not engage in the pursuit of women because it conflicted with their favorite pastime, drinking (1987, 62).

Lacking adequate data to examine Mills's description, we pass on to other sources of variation.

Preferences cannot be directly observed, so our comparison of the two kinds of legislators must instead rely on behavior and on specific differences in the institutions that might induce different preferences. In 1964, the U.S. Supreme Court's decision in *Reynolds v. Sims* (377 U.S. 533) forced sub-national legislatures to follow strict representation-by-population in apportionment. That command, only briefly resisted, broke the rural power base in Sacramento in a way that experience seems to indicate the legislature itself could not possibly have done. Before *Reynolds*, there were excellent reasons to expect differences in the priorities of the roughly "rep-by-pop" assembly and the senate, where the ratio of largest to smallest district population was over 400:1. In the ensuing three decades, California's legislators have differed in only three *prima facie* manners: senators enjoy four-year terms, assembly members only two; only half of the senate faces re-election every two years, while the entire assembly must run; senators, being half as numerous, represent districts about twice as large as the members of the assembly. One can imagine various significant behavioral differences arising between the two classes of legislators on the basis of these fairly simple institutional differences. Senators, for example, might be more detached from public opinion, on the basis of their less frequent encounters with the polls. Or, large districts might be less homogeneous, allowing senators more freedom to select their constituencies of supporters. But is there any evidence for such effects? Our strategy will be simplicity: we will look for evidence of differences in partisan composition of the chambers and in demographic profiles of the 80 assembly districts and the 40 senate districts. Finally, we examine data on roll call voting to see whether we can detect variation in actual legislative behavior.

We can dispense rather quickly with an especially obvious comparison. Have the assembly and senate shown any marked differences in partisan composition? Often when one does hear complaints about "gridlock" these days, divided government is selected as the culprit. However, Table 2 illustrates that the legislature has not been the source of division within California government. In terms of partisan control, the two houses have moved more or less in lock-step. Divided government, infrequent until the last 30 years, is a child of separation-of-powers, not bicameralism. Moreover, from 1899 to 1959, the era in which California politics were dominated by Republicans, the senate and assembly generally looked similar. On average, over that period, the senate was 73 percent and the assembly 71 percent Republican. In the years since 1960, when Democrats have dominated the legislature, the senate has been 39 percent and the assembly 40 percent Republican, on average. Figure 2 demonstrates this congruence, and, perhaps surprisingly, reveals that California is similar to the nation as a whole in this regard. Despite the different bases of apportionment and the difference between two- and six-year terms, the U.S. House and U.S. Senate have also not offered strikingly different electoral environments for the parties. Of course, looking to differences in partisan composition as an indicator of varied preferences assumes that parties are powerful and homogeneous. To the extent that there are large differences between different members of the same party, Figure 2 is not particularly telling in regard to interchamber variations.

In Table 3, we shift our attention to the characteristics of the 80 assembly districts and the 40 senate districts in California. There is little to be gained in comparing the means of the two chambers with regard to any variable, because the court has ensured that districts are very close to identically sized. Hence, averaging across all seats in both chambers will nearly always reproduce the arithmetic mean of the state on any particular measure. What is of some interest, though, is the spread in values. There is an astronomical number of ways, for example, to split a state that is 20 percent Hispanic into 80 assembly districts and 40 senate districts. Regardless of how it is done, districts with equal populations will be, on average, 20 percent Hispanic. One extreme, though, is to make each of the 120 districts a perfect microcosm of the state, having a population that is 20 percent Hispanic. At the other end of the spectrum, one might draw 16 assembly districts and 8 senate districts that are entirely Hispanic, leaving the other 96 districts 0 percent Hispanic. With some limitations based on the geographic concentrations of types of voters and the need to make districts somewhat compact, it is possible to draft maps in which the two

Table 2. ***California Governments in the Twentieth Century***

Governor			*Assembly*		
Dates	Name	Party	Dem.	Rep.	Other
1899-1900	Henry T. Gage	Rep & UL	20	**59**	1
1901-02	Henry T. Gage	Rep & UL	20	**60**	0
1903-04	George C. Pardee	Rep	19	**60**	1
1905-06	George C. Pardee	Rep	4	**75**	0
1907-08	James N. Gillett	Rep	6	**71**	3
1909-10	James N. Gillett	Rep	20	**60**	0
1911-12	Hiram W. Johnson	Rep	11	**69**	0
1913-14	Hiram W. Johnson	Rep	25	**54**	1
1915-16	Hiram W. Johnson	Prog	15	**33**	32
1917-18	Hiram W. Johnson	Prog	9	**69**	2
1919-20	William D. Stephens	Rep & Prog	10	**70**	0
1921-22	William D. Stephens	Rep & Prog	2	**78**	0
1923-24	Friend W. Richardson	Rep	4	**76**	0
1925-26	Friend W. Richardson	Rep	5	**75**	0
1927-28	C.C. Young	Rep	6	**74**	0
1929-30	C.C. Young	Rep	7	**71**	2
1931-32	James Rolph, Jr.	Rep	7	**73**	0
1933-34	James Rolph, Jr.	Rep	25	**55**	0
1935-36	Frank F. Merriam	Rep	37	**42**	1
1937-38	Frank F. Merriam	Rep	**33**	47	0
1939-40	Culbert Olson	Dem	**44**	36	0
1941-42	Culbert Olson	Dem	**42**	38	0
1943-44	Earl Warren	Rep	36	**44**	0
1945-46	Earl Warren	Rep	37	**42**	1
1947-48	Earl Warren	Rep	32	**48**	0
1949-50	Earl Warren	Rep	34	**45**	0
1951-52	Earl Warren	Rep	33	**47**	0
1953-54	Earl Warren	Rep	27	**53**	0
1955-56	Goodwin J. Knight	Rep	32	**48**	0
1957-58	Goodwin J. Knight	Rep	38	**42**	0
1959-60	Edmund G. Brown	Dem	**48**	32	0
1961-62	Edmund G. Brown	Dem	**47**	33	0

Senate			*Legislature*	*Government*
Dem.	Rep.	Other		
14	**26**	0	unified R	unified R
6	**34**	0	unified R	unified R
5	**33**	0	unified R	unified R
4	**36**	0	unified R	unified R
7	**33**	0	unified R	unified R
10	**29**	1	unified R	unified R
8	32	0	unified R	unified R
10	**30**	0	unified R	unified R
10	**21**	9	unified R-P	unified R-P
11	**20**	9	unified R-P	unified R-P
7	**32**	1	unified R-P	unified R-P
7	**33**	0	unified R-P	unified R-P
3	**36**	1	unified R	unified R
3	**37**	0	unified R	unified R
5	**35**	0	unified R	unified R
5	**35**	0	unified R	unified R
4	**35**	0	unified R	unified R
5	**35**	0	unified R	unified R
8	**31**	1	unified R	unified R
15	**25**	0	*divided*	*divided*
18	**22**	0	*divided*	*divided*
16	**24**	0	*divided*	*divided*
16	**24**	0	unified R	unified R
13	**27**	0	unified R	unified R
14	**26**	0	unified R	unified R
14	**26**	0	unified R	unified R
12	**28**	0	unified R	unified R
11	**29**	0	unified R	unified R
16	**24**	0	unified R	unified R
20	20	0	*divided*	*divided*
27	13	0	unified D	unified D
30	10	0	unified D	unified D

Table 2. ***Continued***

Governor			Assembly		
Dates	Name	Party	Dem.	Rep.	Other
1963-64	Edmund G. Brown	Dem	**52**	28	0
1965-66	Edmund G. Brown	Dem	**49**	31	0
1967-68	Ronald W. Reagan	Rep	**42**	38	0
1969-70	Ronald W. Reagan	Rep	39	**41**	0
1971-72	Ronald W. Reagan	Rep	**43**	37	0
1973-74	Ronald W. Reagan	Rep	**50**	30	0
1975-76	Edmund G. Brown Jr.	Dem	**55**	25	0
1977-78	Edmund G. Brown Jr.	Dem	**57**	23	0
1979-80	Edmund G. Brown Jr.	Dem	**55**	25	0
1981-82	Edmund G. Brown Jr.	Dem	**47**	33	0
1983-84	George Deukmejian	Rep	**48**	32	0
1985-86	George Deukmejian	Rep	**47**	33	0
1987-88	George Deukmejian	Rep	**44**	36	0
1989-90	George Deukmejian	Rep	**47**	33	0
1991-92	Pete Wilson	Rep	**47**	33	0
1993-94	Pete Wilson	Rep	**49**	31	0
1995-96	Pete Wilson	Rep	**39**	39	1

Senate			*Legislature*	*Government*
Dem.	Rep.	Other		
27	13	0	unified D	unified D
27	13	0	unified D	unified D
21	19	0	unified D	*divided*
19	**21**	0	unified R	unified R
21	19	0	unified D	*divided*
20	20	0	unified D	*divided*
25	15	0	unified D	unified D
26	14	0	unified D	unified D
25	15	0	unified D	unified D
23	17	0	unified D	unified D
25	15	0	unified D	*divided*
25	15	0	unified D	*divided*
24	15	1	unified D	*divided*
24	15	1	unified D	*divided*
27	12	1	unified D	*divided*
23	15	2	unified D	*divided*
21	17	2	unified D	*divided*

Democrats controlled the Assembly (providing the Speaker), without constituting a majority of members in both the 1937 session and the 1995-96 session. In the latter case, they were assisted by the defection from Republican to Independent of Paul Horcher, immediately following the election. They also controlled the senate with exactly half the members of the 1957 session.

Figures for the early part of the century, and the Progressive Era, should not be taken too literally. In the 1915 session, for example, a count of Republicans can vary between 24, the number of members elected with only the Republican nomination, and 52, the total number who had Republican nominations, including those with other parties' nominations as well. One member was actually nominated by five parties (Republican, Democratic, Progressive, Prohibitionist, and Socialist). See Hichborn (1916) for details on the partisan tangle of that period.

Sources: *1899-1989 Almanac of California Government and Politics*, 7th ed., 87-88; *California Political Alamanac 1995-96* (4th ed.).

Figure 2. ***Partisan Composition of the California Legislature and the US Congress Compared***

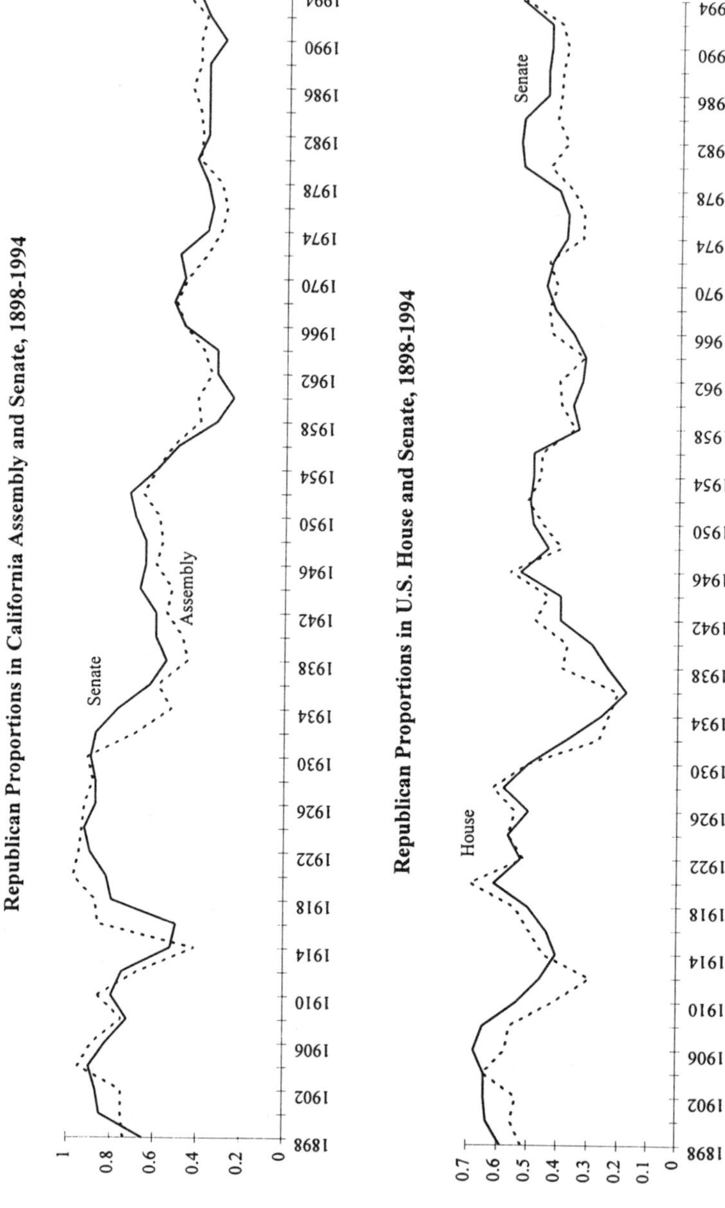

Table 3. ***Profiles of California Legislative Districts***

Variable	*Assembly Districts (n=80)* median	std deviation	*Senate Districts (n=40)* median	std deviation
% black	4.5 %	9.5 %	5. %	9.1 %
% Hispanic	19 %	18.1 %	21 %	16.2 %
% Asian	0.8 %	6.6 %	8. %	5.8 %
age 55 plus	18 %	3.6 %	18 %	2.9 %
average income	$43,155	$11,912	$43,595	$10,683
college educated	31 %	11.0 %	30.5 %	9.5 %
farm-employed	2. %	4.9 %	2. %	4.6 %
gov't-employed	4. %	2.4 %	4. %	2.6 %
service-employ'd	67 %	7.1 %	67 %	6.4 %
manuf-employed	24 %	7.4 %	23.5 %	6.6 %
soc'l sec. recip.s	21 %	4.2 %	22 %	3.3 %
reg'd Democrat	49.5 %	12.3 %	47.5 %	10.9 %
reg'd Republican	37 %	11.8 %	38.5 %	10.7 %

Sources: Lilley et al. 1994, 26-31, except partisan registration, from Green et al. (eds.) 1995.

chambers differ in regard to how much their districts vary from one another. The "standard deviation" statistic measures how much variance there is in a set of values: it would be 0 for the first case, indicating no variation from district to district, and about 40 in the second case, indicating a very large difference across some of the values.[11] A second statistic of interest is the median, the value of observations in the middle of the range when they are ordered from low to high for some measure. (For the senate, the median is the average of the 20th and 21st values; for

[11]Given values of some quality x for n observations, the standard deviation is $s = (\Sigma_i (x_i - \bar{x})^2 / (n - 1))^{1/2}$ where $\bar{x} = (\Sigma_i x_i) / n$. (In this instance, the existing districts may be thought of as one sample from the nearly infinite set of possible districts into which California could be separated.)

the assembly, the average of the 40th and 41st). In the first scenario above, the mean and median are both 20 percent. In the second, the median is 0 percent, and the mean 20 percent, this discrepancy indicating that there are a few very high values in the set.

Substantial differences between senate and assembly districts would not, of course, establish that their members differ in policy preferences or voting behavior, but they would at least alert us to probable differences, insofar as elected politicians are constrained by the traits of the populations they represent. In fact, Table 3 appears to offer little to pursue along those lines. In the respects for which we have data, the median senate and assembly district are all but indistinguishable. Furthermore, the standard deviations for the complete sets of district for each chamber vary little, with the larger body (the assembly) generally showing only a slightly larger internal variation. These gaps are small enough that one cannot say with confidence that they do not represent random variation. In short, the *Reynolds* decision has succeeded in making California's two chambers all but identical not only in terms of the size of the constituencies, but also in the patterns of social and economic profiles of the districts within the two chambers.

Finally, then, we turn to a direct comparison of legislators. Before we examine roll call voting, a unique source of data that is useful in this regard is the *California Journal* biennial surveys on the quality of state legislators. In 1990, 1992, and 1994, the *Journal* surveyed lobbyists, staff, the press, and legislators themselves, asking for rankings of all the legislators on a variety of desirable qualities such as integrity, intelligence, and effectiveness. They then compiled an overall score for each legislator (for full details, see Ziegler 1990, 1992, 1994). This rating is certainly open to charges of being deeply subjective, but it also allows a quick comparison to see whether those most knowledgeable about the workings of the legislature detect a difference in the nature of the two kinds of representatives at a fundamental and important level. The surveys were not designed to encourage respondents to make their ratings chamber-specific, and so if there is a general sense that one chamber or the other draws a better class of politician, it ought to be reflected in the average scores. Instead, Table 4 reveals yet another snapshot of sameness. Although senators have averaged slightly higher scores than assembly members each year, the gap

Table 4. ***California Journal Ratings of California's State Legislators***

	number rated	*mean*	*mean-median*	*low score*	*high score*	*standard deviation*
1990 Assembly	79	5.84	0.16	3.56	8.21	1.11
1990 Senate	40	6.08	0.00	3.59	7.80	1.02
1992 Assembly	80	5.53	0.09	2.97	7.84	0.99
1992 Senate	39	5.68	0.06	2.75	7.36	1.13
1994 Assembly	78	5.69	0.05	3.39	8.24	0.97
1994 Senate	37	5.78	0.12	3.97	7.75	1.01

Source: Ziegler (1990, 1992, 1994).

is very small. It is almost always true that the median scores are slightly lower than the means, but this is true for both chambers. In 1990, the spread of scores (standard deviation) was higher in the assembly; in 1992 and 1994 it was higher in the senate. The highest and lowest overall scores have not consistently been from the same house. None of the differences is large enough to represent a statistically significant gap. To the extent that these ratings do accurately reflect something about the quality of legislators, then, they do not reveal any important variation between the chambers.

Finally, therefore, we turn to ratings based on actual voting behavior of the members of California's two legislative houses. In Table 5, we report ratings compiled by various interest groups for the members of the assembly and the senate in recent years.[12] Various groups with specific

[12]Scores were retrieved from the *California Political Almanac* 2d ed. and 3d ed. (Green et al. 1991, 1993). One unfortunate feature of using that source is that the almanacs are compiled after an election and feature data from the prior session, so that scores are reported only for returned incumbents. Hence, our *n*'s in the table are never 80 and 40. We contacted interest groups to request reports, but while virtually every group promised to send information, we received material from only one group (the California Farm Bureau).

Table 5. ***Interest Group Ratings of Members of the Assembly and Senate***

Group	Session	Chamber	Number of Votes in Score	Party	Mean Rating	Standard Deviation	Number of Rated Members
CFB	1989-90	Assembly	12		43.3	19.9	66
		Senate	5		35.5	26.7	36
		Assembly		R	62.5	27.5	26
		Senate		R	58.2	14.7	11
		Assembly		D	30.8	10.8	40
		Senate		D	25.8	20.0	24
	1991-92	Assembly	20		45.5	24.3	55
		Senate	10		36.3	21.0	33
		Assembly		R	73.8	10.1	20
		Senate		R	49.8	27.1	11
		Assembly		D	29.4	28.1	35
		Senate		D	28.1	11.7	21
CLCV	1989-90	Assembly	20		66.4	37.9	66
		Senate	17		67.3	29.1	34
		Assembly		R	22.1	17.0	26
		Senate		R	35.8	20.2	10
		Assembly		D	95.1	6.7	40
		Senate		D	80.6	21.6	23

	1991	Assembly	39		64.7	38.8	53
		Senate	39		66.4	28.7	30
		Assembly		R	12.9	11.8	18
		Senate		R	26.2	15.5	9
		Assembly		D	91.3	9.2	35
		Senate		D	84.2	7.6	20
C of C	1989-90	Assembly	25		48.7	24.7	66
		Senate	24		41.0	20.2	36
		Assembly		R	77.7	8.9	26
		Senate		R	62.2	18.2	11
		Assembly		D	29.8	6.3	40
		Senate		D	31.2	12.7	24
	1991	Assembly	18		48.1	33.5	55
		Senate	19		39.7	25.0	33
		Assembly		R	90.5	9.7	20
		Senate		R	68.8	17.1	11
		Assembly		D	23.8	8.5	35
		Senate		D	23.8	10.7	21
NOW	1989-90	Assembly	10		70.1	30.8	66
		Senate	10		67.5	26.0	36
		Assembly		R	33.5	8.9	26
		Senate		R	37.3	16.2	11
		Assembly		D	94.0	7.1	40
		Senate		D	81.3	16.8	24
	1991-92	Assembly	10		76.0	91.6	55
		Senate	10		59.4	31.9	33
		Assembly		R	73.8	10.1	20

Table 5. ***Continued***

Group	Session	Chamber	Number of Votes in Score	Party	Mean Rating	Standard Deviation	Number of Rated Members
		Senate		R	49.8	27.1	11
		Assembly		D	29.4	28.1	35
		Senate		D	28.1	11.7	21
PIRG	1989-90	Assembly	22		42.9	43.7	66
		Senate	20		34.5	36.1	36
		Assembly		R	31.4	15.1	25
		Senate		R	52.9	17.4	11
		Assembly		D	93.3	7.3	39
		Senate		D	85.1	11.2	24
	1992	Assembly	22		69.1	32.3	64
		Senate	22		75.0	19.8	36
		Assembly		R	26.1	18.3	20
		Senate		R	34.5	18.3	11
		Assembly		D	93.5	6.1	35
		Senate		D	82.1	11.1	21

CTA	1989-90	Assembly	24		78.2	16.3	64
		Senate	24		90.6	11.4	36
		Assembly		R	59.7	8.1	25
		Senate		R	79.0	13.5	11
		Assembly		D	90.0	5.5	39
		Senate		D	96.1	4.7	24
FPAC	1991	Assembly	27		39.2	42.2	66
		Senate	25		33.3	31.5	36
		Assembly		R	90.3	7.9	26
		Senate		R	73.2	21.6	11
		Assembly		D	6.0	7.8	40
		Senate		D	14.8	13.8	24

CFB California Farm Bureau
CLCV California League of Conservation Voters
C of C Chamber of Commerce
NOW National Organization for Women
PIRG Public Interest Research Group
CTA California Teachers' Association
FPAC Free Market Political Action Committee

agendas watch roll call votes they deem important and score legislators as having voted the "right" or "wrong" way. The scores in Table 5 are averages across parties and chambers of the percentage of the time legislators voted in the manner the particular group recommended. We mark in bold the chamber that has the more extreme average. A first note of caution in making this comparison is that it is usually not true that the overall scores are based on exactly the same votes in the two chambers. In this sense, unlike the case of the *California Journal* scores just discussed, ratings are somewhat chamber-specific. A more subtle reason to worry about such scores is that there are undoubtedly cases of log rolling, wherein legislators will vote against their true preferences (whether these are based on personal ideology or a sense of the constituency's demands) in exchange for votes on other matters about which they care more. A thorough and careful scrutiny of ratings over legislators' careers and of all the bills that entered into the given scores could probably allay such fears. For now, we rely on the fact that we have several scores to examine and that our interest is not in the exact numbers assigned to any individual, but in whether there seems to be a general pattern of interchamber difference.

In every case, the standard deviations of the scores for each chamber taken as a whole (not divided into its partisan delegations) are very large in relation to the means—large enough that a statistical test could not reject the proposition that there is no systematic difference between assembly and senate members. Certainly, the breakdown of scores into party averages illustrates that party affiliation is a far more important predictor of a member's score than is chamber. Even for the partisan subsets, however, the size of the standard deviations, relative to the means, indicates that there is a good deal of variation from Republican to Republican and Democrat to Democrat within each chamber. The clearest difference between the chambers is that assembly Republicans are always more extreme than are the senate Republicans for these few years. Amongst Democrats, there is no such pattern.

Just how important a difference have we detected? It is hard to know exactly how to judge these data. There does not appear to be a major gap between the whole chambers. If assembly Republicans have consistently been somewhat more extreme than their senate colleagues, it might be asking too much to expect the small number of cases to yield a difference great enough to pass tests of statistical significance. Our sense is that this trend is somewhat time-bound, but we lack data to illustrate that point.

Nonetheless, historical comparison would seem the most obvious way to set these comparisons in a larger context.

After all, our implicit premise thus far has been that *Reynolds v. Sims* was an important event in terms of the operation of bicameralism in California politics. Certainly, historical descriptions of the legislature in the federal years indicate that it made a genuine difference to have most senators representing quite small populations. To cite just one example, the infamous lock-up in the summer of 1963, in which Speaker Unruh forced the Republicans to spend the night in the legislature after they refused to vote on a budget bill had its origin in the differences between the two chambers. Mills recounts:

> . . . most of the senators came from rural counties and represented vast herds of cattle, which are subject to property tax, and relatively few school children, who consume it. As long as state money was meted out to school districts on the basis of enrollment of students, the taxes on the cows remained low. However, if state school support came to be apportioned on the basis of the financial circumstances of the school districts, those districts that had lots of cows, orchards, and farmlands to tax would get less and would have to cover a larger percentage of the costs of their own schools out of their property taxes. The buckaroos in the Senate always wanted to make sure that a *pro rata* share, based on enrollment, of all new school moneys would go to rural areas. If they could do that, the property taxes, which were much lower in the rural areas of California than they were in urban areas, would always remain so (Mills 1987, 112).

He goes on to quote the Speaker insisting that the assembly not allow the senate to discover the details of their school bill, since, "the Senate members of the conference committee were Joe Rattigan from Santa Rosa and two other liberals who agreed with us that we should provide more money to improve the education of the children in the poor urban districts and they were in on the plot to keep the bill under wraps" (112). The very existence of such cabals indicates that those were years when the chambers were often at odds.

Unfortunately, data that would allow us to compare the assembly with the senate pre- and post-*Reynolds* are very hard to come by. Only one interest group, the AFL-CIO, has produced readily available legislator ratings that stretch back into the early 1960s. It is by no means obvious that labor issues are ideal to reveal the variation in preferences we expect between chambers that differ greatly in the degree to which they empower rural voters, especially because of the possibility of routine log rolling. However, we know of no better data to speak to the issue.

Figure 3 plots the average AFL-CIO score for each party for each chamber, from 1961 to 1993. (Data were not available for all years, so markers on the assembly-Democrats line indicate for which years we had ratings.) There is only a sliver of data from the federal period in the figure, and it offers a surprise. Contrary to our expectations, there is not a consistent senate-assembly gap in that period. In 1961, when Republican senators scored much higher than Republican assembly members, the Democrats were alike. In 1963, neither party demonstrated much of an interchamber gap. By 1965, it was the Democrats whose senate and assembly delegations looked different, the Republicans less so. In short, these data do not reflect a consistent ideological gap attributable to the very different constituencies. Oddly, though, the lines do illustrate again that assembly and senate Republicans have been fairly different at least since the 1980s, and perhaps as far back as the 1970s.

In Figures 4 and 5 we look beyond the means, examining a few years more fully. The figures are kernel density plots, which may be thought of as smoothed histograms. They show the distribution of legislators in each chamber on the AFL-CIO's scale of 0 ("bad" in their view) to 100 ("good") (see Silverman 1986 for technical details on density estimation). The figures are puzzling. Whereas the 1961 session seems to have featured quite different chambers (as we expected), the senate was a fairly liberal body, and it was the assembly that had a cluster on the right, near 0. Moreover, by 1963, the chambers look quite similar, the senate evidently having changed complexion dramatically. For comparison, Figure 5 plots the corresponding data from 30 years later. Our hunch was that the two bodies would look very similar in this post-*Reynolds* world, as indeed they

Figure 3. ***Mean AFL-CIO Ratings of California Legislators By Chamber, 1961-1993***

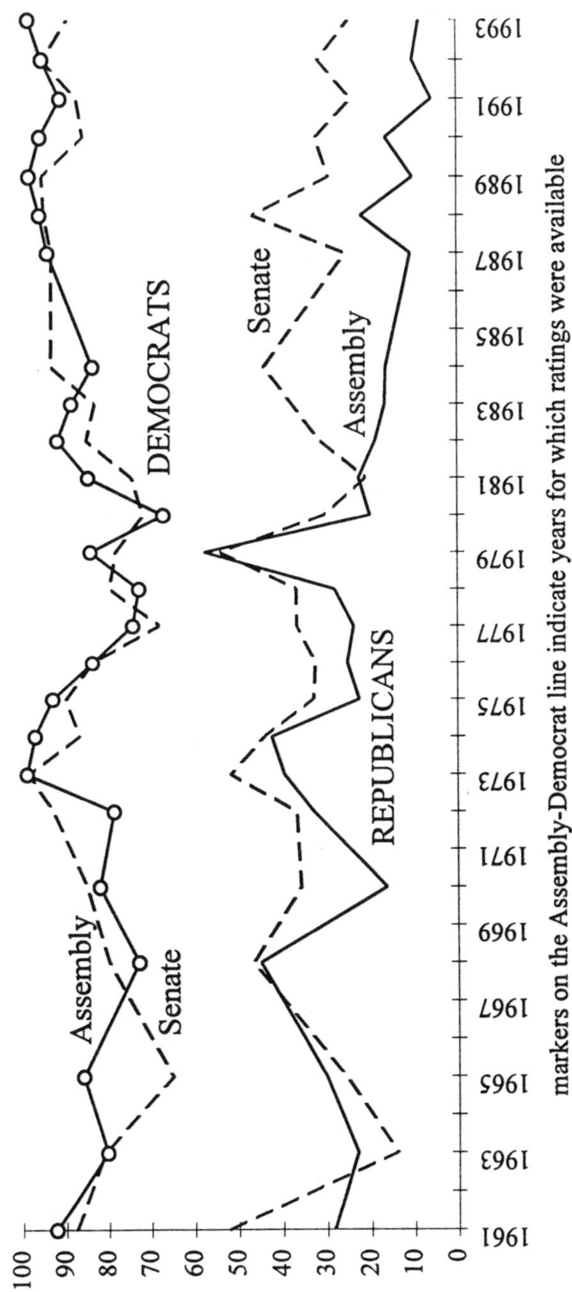

Figure 4

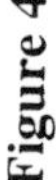

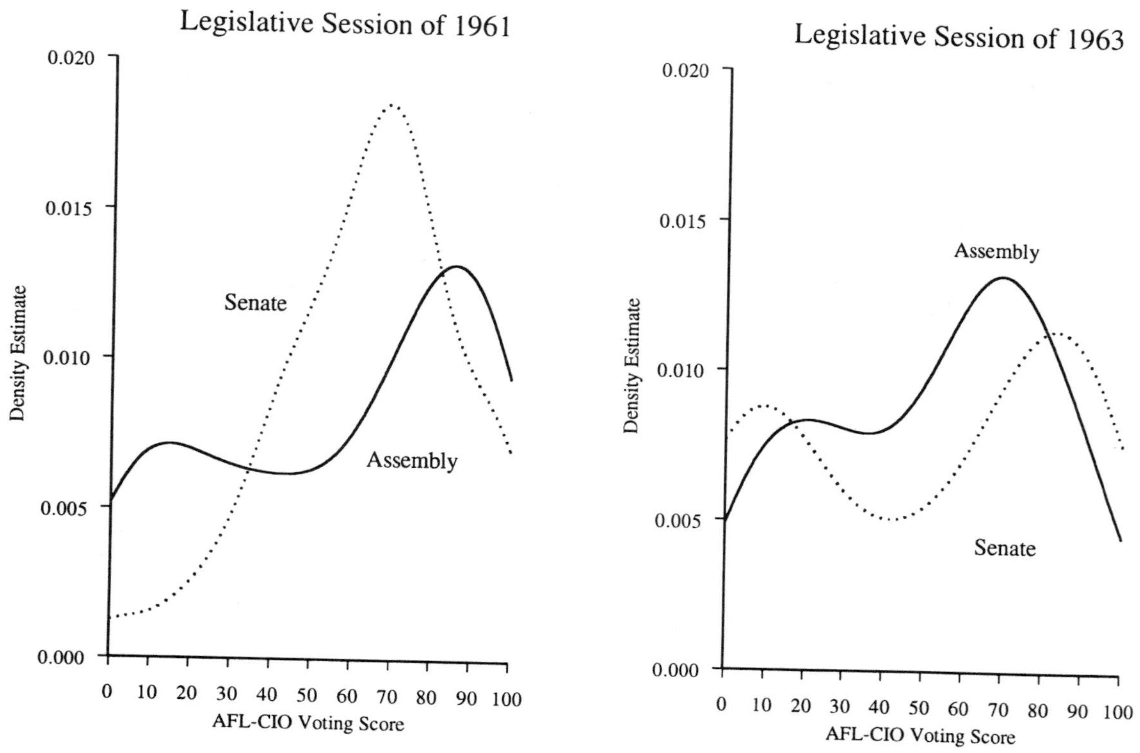

Legislative Session of 1961

Senate

Assembly

Density Estimate

0.000 0.005 0.010 0.015 0.020

0 10 20 30 40 50 60 70 80 90 100

AFL-CIO Voting Score

Legislative Session of 1963

Assembly

Senate

Density Estimate

0.000 0.005 0.010 0.015 0.020

0 10 20 30 40 50 60 70 80 90 100

AFL-CIO Voting Score

Figure 5

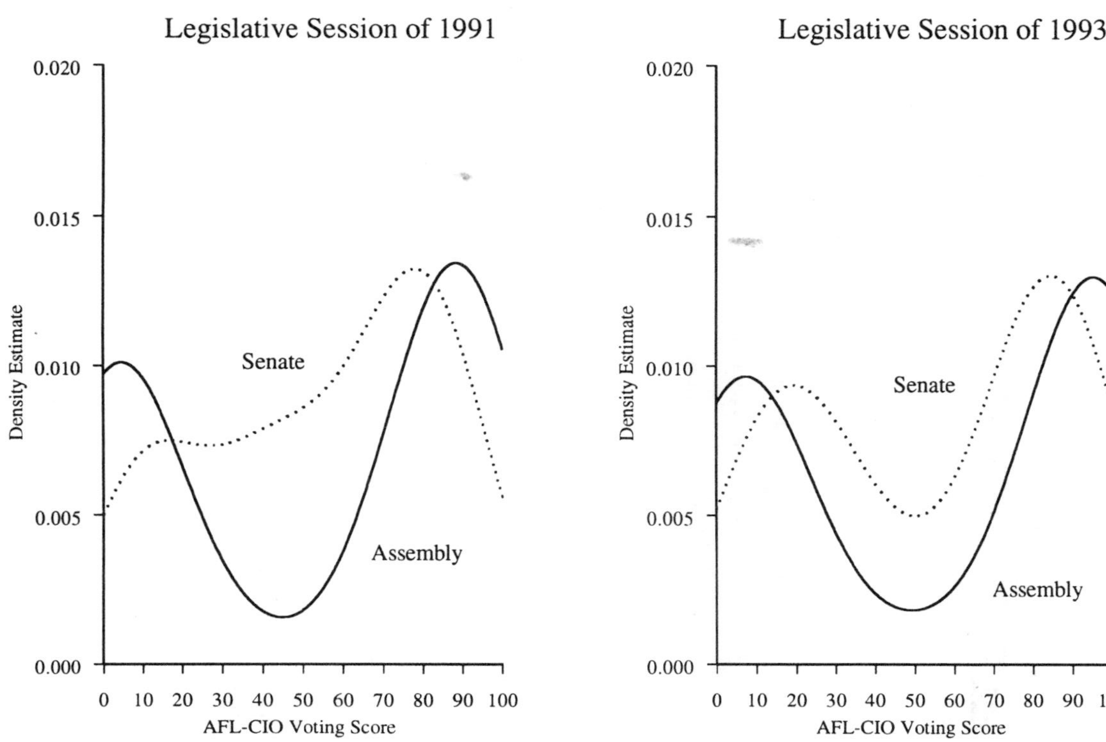
Legislative Session of 1991
Density Estimate
0.020
0.015
0.010
0.005
0.000
Senate
Assembly
0 10 20 30 40 50 60 70 80 90 100
AFL-CIO Voting Score
Legislative Session of 1993
Density Estimate
0.020
0.015
0.010
0.005
0.000
Senate
Assembly
0 10 20 30 40 50 60 70 80 90 100
AFL-CIO Voting Score

did in 1993. The plot for 1991, however, looks remarkably like its 1961 counterpart.[13]

Perhaps with broader data over longer periods we could illustrate that the 1961 and 1993 figures are the most accurate representations of how preferences have varied between chambers in the federal period and the postfederal period. For now, we must remain somewhat agnostic. Our sense is that it really is difficult to illustrate any long-standing, important variations between the typical member of the assembly and the typical member of the senate today. The one caveat is that it would seem worthwhile to examine further, in future research, the possible tendency for Republicans to differ by chamber. Whether the differences under the old apportionment regime were as striking as we expect, we cannot with confidence say. Nonetheless, the central point illustrated by this data is that there do not appear to be large, consistent differences in the two chambers of California's legislature at present. In that respect, this is a bicameral institution that does not really meet the conditions deemed essential by both the Founding Fathers and modern theorists for bicameralism to matter.

CONCLUSIONS AND PROPOSALS

We are left with two views regarding the effects of bicameralism on policy. The first, exemplified by Jesse Unruh's comments and by the present campaign for unicameralism in California, holds that bicameral

---

[13]We did not produce a separate figure, but we also obtained roughly comparable data for the 1911 and 1913 sessions, from tabulations of voting scores with respect to the "labor lobby" position (Hichborn 1911, 1913). Yet again, there is variation in contiguous sessions. In 1911, the chambers' scores were distributed in almost identical unimodal curves. In 1913, the assembly curve was lower and flatter, indicating more members at the extreme ends of the score distribution. The senate curve, meanwhile, shifted well to the left (literally, not politically, since the left of the diagram is the low-end of the labor rating) and became bimodal, with a remnant on the right. Districts in that period were neither as rigorously equal-sized as their present-day counterparts, nor as hugely diverse as were the federal-era senate districts. Our expectation was that the curves would therefore be roughly alike in both years. Those sessions were also, however, marked by intense Progressive-Machine battles, so that turnover of even a few members could result in enormous policy shifts.

inertia is excessive and crippling. Scholars writing on national and comparative politics have focused on the relationship between divided government and gridlock, and made divided government their preferred culprit. Analogous arguments posit that dividing a legislature internally also creates unnecessary blockades to policymaking and has the further defect of weakening the legislative branch with respect to the executive. In rebuttal to our argument that bicameralism has no such effects unless there are differences between chambers, critics might point to inherent transaction costs in legislating. Two like-minded individuals will probably take longer to act than one person alone. In the formal models we examined, making laws is costless and amounts to selecting a point in space. In real life, the existence of two chambers surely does delay legislation and force extra deliberation, regardless of how consonant the two sets of politicians are.

The second view, articulated by Riker and Buchanan and Tullock, is that bicameralism is laudable precisely because it makes policy change difficult, providing stability and insulating against quixotic shifts in public opinion and scheming minorities. In this view, major shifts in public policy ought not to be easily achieved, and safeguards against what proponents might deem "effective" or "responsive" government are deliberate and invaluable. In this stance, they follow Madison, who was greatly concerned on how "to protect the people against the transient impressions into which . . . they themselves might be led" and who suggested "an obvious precaution against [the danger of politicians betraying the people's trust] would be to divide the trust between different bodies of men, who might watch and check each other" (1987 [1840], 193).

We certainly are not the first to notice this contrast. Fred Riggs comments aptly that "proponents of unicameralism tend to stress the need for action whereas the advocates of bicameralism seem to be more concerned with the need for caution" (quoted in Longley and Olson 1991, 25). Ultimately, choosing between these antithetic portrayals of the nature of bicameralism requires a normative judgment about the value of legislative responsiveness. To the extent that one worries about government action, bicameralism ought not to be destroyed; if government seems frustratingly gridlocked, unicameralism might be an ideal lubricant.

Paradoxically, we view the conservative account as the more compelling, but we think that an experiment with unicameralism in California is now warranted. The resolution of this paradox is our central conclusion is that most of the inertia that originates in bicameralism follows from the two chambers being sufficiently different to be rivals, commonly at odds. With the *Reynolds* decision, the Supreme Court has made this condition greatly less likely to occur. We have not been able to prove in any thorough way that the pre-*Reynolds*, "federal" scheme of apportionment did fulfill the condition of interchamber variation, but it at least seems plausible that it might have done so. Now, however, the court has vitiated bicameralism as a protection against the evils Riker, Buchanan and Tullock, and Madison feared.[14] In our view, the supermajority requirement in place for California's budget is now a more important inducer of stability.[15] Hence, an important qualifier to our endorsement of unicameralism is that the requirement of supermajorities ought to be maintained at least to the same degree as in the present system. Super majoritarianism is in many ways comparable to bicameralism as a stabilizer, and with representational differences having been largely wiped away, it is likely to be a more important institution in this regard.

If there are few reasons not to try unicameralism, are there also gains to be had in making the change? In our view, the need for greatly increased responsiveness is not the selling point for legislating in a single-chamber. Rather, the main bonuses in dropping one chamber are gains in visibility and accountability. In a unicameral system, constituents are directly tied to a single representative. It is harder, therefore, for representatives in a single house to duck responsibility for their actions, and it is easier for the voters to assign responsibility for policies to particular politicians or parties. The possibility for divided partisan control of the legislature is removed (at least insofar as the system continues to be dominated by two major parties), and so are the secret gardens of conference committees and cabals like the one Mills described above.

Our proposal, accordingly, is that California adopt a one-house legislature with a supermajority requirement of two-thirds for passage of

---

[14]The reader will probably have guessed that we judge *Reynolds* to have been a bad decision. It would take us far astray to defend this claim, but in our view Justice Harlan's dissent demolishes the constitutional basis for the majority decision. As a matter of public policy, it could simply be described as myopic.

[15]It is probably also true at the national level that the Senate's cloture rule is a source of important House-Senate differences beyond any already induced by the different terms or bases of apportionment.

the budget (and possibly for other important matters). We are reasonably indifferent to its size, provided it falls somewhere between 80 and 120 members. Although we could not detect much effect from the staggering of terms in the present senate, we would maintain a staggered system wherein half of the legislature stands for election each year. There are theoretical reasons to expect this arrangement to dampen wild and possibly fleeting public enthusiasms.[16]

Political scientists almost cannot help but hope for periodic reforms of the sort proposed here. We rely on variation in institutions to test theories about the effects of different political arrangements, and so variance is always a delight. Of course, politicians who hope to be reelected will instinctively be much less enamored with experiments in governmental design. Accordingly, one objection we should answer, in closing, is: Just how weird a proposal is this? Among the American states, only Nebraska is unicameral. Is that fact perhaps not evidence in itself that the elimination of one legislative house is a strange and risky move? One quick answer is that the American states actually do vary quite a lot in several other, rather fundamental respects. The precise electoral laws in states, for example, still differ widely, despite much Court-enforced homogenization.

---

[16]There is one odd and troubling consequence of having both staggered terms and adjustable boundaries that occasionally crops up in California politics. Since new boundaries take effect two years apart in even and odd districts, it can happen that, for the two years that the "old" and "new" districts coincide, one set of voters enjoys two representatives while another is not represented at all. This anomaly is made worse still by the incentive for politicians to jump from districts which, having been redrawn, are about to become much harder to win, into safer, open seats, even if it means running for reelection early. Voters can even be subject to a strange variety of double jeopardy in which a member who attempts to parachute into a safer seat early loses that election, but then continues to sit for the old seat, and eventually gets a second chance to find a more hospitable district two years later. (Thus, for example, in 1990 Herschel Rosenthal (D) won re-election to a third term in the 22nd Senate district. He then decided to run early and jump into the new 23rd district in 1992, since that district would include his home turf of West L.A. However, he lost that primary contest to Tom Hayden, stayed on in the 22nd until 1994, and then at that point moved into the vacated (new) 20th district, and won.) We draw attention to these peculiar outcomes, though we have no specific remedy to propose at present.

Moreover, a quick glance around the democratic world reveals that institutional variation is rampant, and that variation even among sub-national governments in federal states is not rare. Several legislatures worldwide have made the transition from bi- to unicameralism in the past century, including those of New Zealand, Denmark, Sweden, and many Canadian provinces. Table 6 reveals a smorgasbord of government arrangements that might offer some comfort to those wary of the "untried" nature of unicameralism in the American states.

Table 6. ***Institutions of Democratic Government Worldwide, 1995***

	Unicameral Legislature	Asymmetrically Bicameral Legislature	Symmetrically Bicameral Legislature
Independent Executive/ Separation of Powers	Finland[P] Nebraska[F†*] 21 Swiss cantons[P†] 5 Swiss cantons[F†]	France[F/M]	49 American states[F†] *Switzerland*[P] *United States*[F]
Executive Dependent upon Legislature's Confidence	Canadian provinces[F†] Denmark[P] 15 German states[M†] Iceland[P] Israel[P] Luxembourg[P] New Zealand[F/M] Norway[P] Queensland[A†] Sweden[P]	4 Australian states[AP†] *Austria*[P] Austrian provinces[P†] Bavaria[M†] *Canada*[F] Great Britain[F] Ireland[T] Tasmania[T†]	*Australia*[A,P] Belgium[P] *Germany*[M] Italy[M] Japan[N] Netherlands[P]

Superscripts indicate basic electoral system of the legislature, federal systems are indicated by italics.
[F] “first-past-the-post,” seats awarded to candidates receiving the most votes by district
[P] seats allocated to parties in proportion to their total vote share (sometimes by district)
[M] mixture of [F] and [P]
[A] seats won using alternative-vote system
[T] seats won using single-transferable-vote system
[N] seats won using single-nontransferable-vote system
* nonpartisan elections
† subnational political system

Notes: This table is not exhaustive, including only those countries that have been continuously democratic since about World War II, and relevant subnational units. Australia uses the alternative-vote system (which works much like a straight plurality system) for its lower house and proportional representation for its upper house. New Zealand held elections using a first-past-the-post system until 1993. In that election, however, voters approved a plan to switch to a mixed scheme incorporating some proportional representation for future elections. Norway and Iceland are formally bicameral, but functionally unicameral. The most recent changes to Belgium's constitution are ignored here. On all of the distinctions drawn in this table, see Lijphart (1984).

REFERENCES

Allen, Don A., Sr. 1965. *Legislative Sourcebook: The California Legislature and Reapportionment 1849-1965*. Sacramento, Calif.: Assembly of the State of California.

Arrow, Kenneth. 1963 [1951]. *Social Choice and Individual Values*, 2d ed. New Haven, Conn.: Yale University Press.

"'Big Daddy' of California: He Has the Assembly in His Pocket." *Life* 55, 13 (September 27): 47-52.

Black, Duncan. 1958. *The Theory of Committees and Elections*. Cambridge: Cambridge University Press.

Brennan, Geoffrey, and Alan Hamlin. 1992. "Bicameralism and Majoritarian Equilibrium." *Public Choice* 74, no. 2 (September): 169-79.

Browne, J. Ross. 1850. *Report of the Debates in the Convention of California on the Formation of the State Constitution In September and October, 1849*. Washington, D.C.: John T. Towers.

Buchanan, James M., and Gordon Tullock. 1969 [1962]. *The Calculus of Consent: Logical Foundations of Constitutional Democracy*. Ann Arbor, Mich.: The University of Michigan Press.

California Labor Federation. 1961-1972. *AFL-CIO Legislative Report*. San Francisco, Calif.: AFL-CIO.

_________. 1973-1994. *Force for Progress*. San Francisco, Calif.: AFL-CIO.

Cannon, Lou. 1969. *Ronnie and Jesse: A Political Odyssey*. Garden City, New York: Doubleday.

Commonwealth Club of California. 1943. *The Legislature of California: Its Membership, Procedure, and Work*. San Francisco, Calif.: Parker Press.

Frickey, Philip P. 1992. "Constitutional Structure, Public Choice, and Public Law." *International Review of Law and Economics* 12, no. 1 (March): 163-65.

Gerston, Larry N., and Terry Christensen. 1995. *California Politics and Government: A Practical Approach*, 3d ed. Belmont, Calif.: Wads-worth.

Grant, James Allan Clifford. 1927. "The Bicameral Principle in the California Legislature." Doctoral dissertation, Stanford University.

Green, Stephen, et al. 1991. *California Political Almanac 1991-1992*, 2d ed. Sacramento, Calif.: California Journal Press.

_________. 1993. *California Political Almanac 1993-1994*, 3d ed. Sacramento, Calif.: California Journal Press.

_________. 1995. *California Political Almanac 1995-1996*, 4th ed. Sacramento, Calif.: California Journal Press.

Hammond, Thomas H., and Gary J. Miller. 1987. "The Core of the Constitution." *American Political Science Review* 81, no. 4 (December): 1155-74.

Hichborn, Franklin. 1911. *Story of the Session of the California Legislature of 1911*. San Francisco, Calif.: Press of the James H. Barry Company.

________. 1913. *Story of the Session of the California Legislature of 1913*. San Francisco, Calif.: Press of the James H. Barry Company.

________. 1916. *Story of the Session of the California Legislature of 1915*. San Francisco, Calif.: Press of the James H. Barry Company.

________. 1922. *Story of the Session of the California Legislature of 1921*. San Francisco, Calif.: Press of the James H. Barry Company.

Lee, Eugene C and Larry L. Berg. 1976. *The Challenge of California,* 2d. ed. Boston: Little, Brown.

Levmore, Saul. 1992. "Bicameralism: When Are Two Decisions Better than One?" *International Review of Law and Economics* 12, no. 1 (March): 145-62.

Lijphart, Arend. 1984. *Democracies: Patterns of Majoritarian and Consensus Government in Twenty-One Countries*. New Haven, Conn.: Yale University Press.

Lilley, William, III, Laurence J. DeFranco, and William M. Diefenderfer III. 1994. *The Almanac of State Legislatures*. Washington, D.C.: Congressional Quarterly, Inc.

Longley, Lawrence D., and David M. Olson. 1991. *Two Into One: The Politics and Processes of National Legislative Cameral Change*. Boulder, Colorado: Westview Press.

Madison, James. 1987 [1840]. *Notes of Debates in the Federal Convention of 1787*. New York, New York: W. W. Norton & Company.

________, Alexander Hamilton, and John Jay. 1987 [1788]. *The Federalist Papers*. New York, New York: Penguin.

McKelvey, Richard D. 1976. "Intransitivities in Multidimensional Voting Models and Some Implications for Agenda Control." *Journal of Economic Theory* 12: 472-82.

________. 1979. "General Conditions for Global Intransitivities in Formal Voting Models." *Econometrica* 47: 1085-1111.

Miller, Gary J., and Thomas H. Hammond. 1989. "Stability and Efficiency in a Separation-of-Powers Constitutional System." In *The Federalist Papers and the New Institutionalism*, ed. Bernard Grofman and Donald Wittman. New York, New York: Agathon Press.

________. 1990. "Committees and the Core of the Constitution." *Public Choice* 66, no. 3 (September): 201-27.

Mills, James R. 1987. *A Disorderly House: The Brown-Unruh Years in Sacramento*. Berkeley, Calif.: Heyday Books.

Money, Jeannette, and George Tsebelis. 1992. "Cicero's Puzzle: Upper House Power in Comparative Perspective." *International Political Science Review* 13, no. 1 (January): 25-43.

Muir, William K., Jr. 1982. *Legislature: California's School for Politics*. Chicago, Ill.: The University of Chicago Press.

Opatrny, Dennis J. 1974. "Nebraska's Unicameral—Would it Work Here?" *California Journal* 5, no. 5 (May): 167-68.

Richardson, Jim. 1991. "The Unicameral Legislature." *California Journal* 22, no. 5 (May): 211-13.

Riker, William H. 1955. "The Senate and American Federalism." *American Political Science Review* 49, no. 2 (June): 452-69.

_________. 1992a. "The Justification of Bicameralism." *International Political Science Review* 13, no. 1 (January): 101-16.

_________. 1992b. "The Merits of Bicameralism." *International Review of Law and Economics* 12, no. 1 (March): 166-68.

Schrag, Peter. 1995. "When Government Goes on Autopilot." *The New York Times* (February 16): A15.

Silverman, B. W. 1986. *Density Estimation for Statistics and Data Analysis*. London: Chapman & Hall.

Swift, Elaine K. 1993. "The Making of an American House of Lords: The U.S. Senate in the Constitutional Convention of 1787." *Studies in American Political Development* 7 (Fall): 177-224.

Tsebelis, George. 1993. "Decisionmaking in Political Systems: Comparison of Presidentialism, Parliamentarism, Multicameralism, and Multipartism." Unpublished manuscript.

Unruh, Jess. 1971. "Unicameralism—The Wave of the Future." In *Strengthening the States: Essays on Legislative Reform*, ed. Donald G. Herzberg and Alan Rosenthal. New York, New York: Doubleday & Company, Inc.

Wilson, E. Dotson. 1994. *California's Legislature*. Sacramento, Calif.: Office of the Chief Clerk of the Assembly.

Ziegler, Richard. 1990. "Rating the Legislators." *California Journal* 21, no. 3 (March): 133-41.

_________. 1992. "The Capitol's Best: Rating the Legislators." *California Journal* 23, no. 4 (April): 173-80.

_________. 1994. "California Journal's Third Biennial Survey Spotlights the Legislature's Best." *California Journal* 25, no. 3 (March): 9-16.

Terms of Office, Legislative Structure, and Collective Incentives

Linda R. Cohen

In 1990, Proposition 140 amended the California Constitution to limit the number of terms that legislators can serve in the state assembly and senate. Article IV, Section 1.5 now reads:

> The ability of legislators to serve unlimited number of terms, to establish their own retirement system, and to pay for staff and support services at state expense contribute heavily to the extremely high number of incumbents who are reelected. These unfair incumbent advantages discourage qualified candidates from seeking public office and create a class of career politicians, instead of the citizen representatives envisioned by the Founding Fathers. These career politicians become representatives of the bureaucracy, rather than of the people whom they are elected to represent.
>
> To restore a free and democratic system of fair elections, and to encourage qualified candidates to seek public office, the people find and declare that the powers of incumbency must be limited. Retirement benefits must be restricted, state-financed staff and support services limited, and limitations placed upon the number of terms which may be served.

Legislative term limits are a nationwide phenomena, and are supported by an overwhelming majority of voters. Since 1990, voters in 22 states have passed amendments to their state constitutions to limit terms of state and congressional representatives.[1] The movement has spawned a large literature that argues the merits and perils of the policy.[2] In contrast, I address an implementation issue: within the constraint of a short overall career limit for legislators, how do different electoral arrangements effect the composition of the legislature? The primary objective of my analysis is to identify the likely share of the legislature occupied by novices (people with no previous legislative experience) or by legislators who are in the final years of their last (term-limited) term.

Lack of legislative experience is one of the problems identified by term limit opponents. Their focus, however, is on long-run experience: for example, the benefits of legislators who have served for many years and who, in the past, occupied key leadership positions in state legislatures and in the U.S. Congress. Without such individuals, it is claimed, the ability of legislatures to formulate complicated legislation, to play a powerful role relative to the executive departments, and to organize and maintain coalitions to address and institute necessary long-term problems is compromised. Term limit proponents counter such arguments both directly and indirectly. The direct argument rests on the proposition that the learning curve in legislatures is steep, so that many years of experience is not a prerequisite for legislative effectiveness. The indirect argument is more subtle, resting in part on views of the proper role of the legislature (for example, that the executive branch is more important for the formulation and institution of wise public policies), and in part on the desired nature of policies and legislative process—e.g., that they should not be so complex in the first instance that such expertise is required.[3] And, even if

---

[1]In 1995 the Supreme Court ruled that state-imposed limits on congressional members are invalid; such limits require an amendment to the federal Constitution. Its ruling does not effect limits on state legislators. *U.S. Term Limits Inc., et al. v. Thornton et al.*, No. 93-1456, decided May 22, 1995.

[2]Academic papers presented at two national conferences on term limits are contained in Benjamin and Malbin (1992) and Grofman (forthcoming). Influential books that argue the case for term limits in the U.S. Congress are Will (1992), Coyne and Fund (1992), and Ehrenhalt (1991). An excellent discussion of Will's book is contained in Polsby's review (1993). Further discussion of the case against term limits is contained in Fiorina (1992) and Cohen and Spitzer (1992). A notable effort to present both sides is the debate between Frenzel and Mann (1992).

[3]See Cain (1995) for a discussion of these issues.

expertise based on long service might in principle be desirable, the disadvantages of allowing lengthy careers more than offset such benefits.

The proposal offered here maintains the career limit and so does not represent a solution to the expertise problem as identified by term limits opponents, nor does it compromise the immediate goal of their supporters. But unless learning about legislative opportunities and procedures is extraordinarily simple, a very large number of newly elected novices poses a problem. Indeed, no one recommends a two-year career limit for U.S. legislatures. California's three-term, six-year limit in the state assembly is among the shortest of the limits adopted by the states.[4]

Thirty of the 79 members of California's assembly were first elected in 1994. In the subsequent section, it is shown that (in the long run) the share of assembly members serving in their first two years will always exceed one third and is likely to approach one-half.[5] To put these numbers in perspective, the assembly has 25 standing committees and five standing budget subcommittees. Under close partisan division, as currently exists in the legislature, and, for reasons discussed below, as is likely to continue, if the majority party wishes to retain control over committees, some freshmen will chair important committees from the first day they arrive in the legislature.

However, the analysis below shows that only small changes in the term limit rules—from three terms to four, as is consistent with limits in most of the states—result in a substantial reduction in the share of novices in the

---

[4]Only Nevada has a shorter limit of two terms, or four years, in the state assembly. Six year (three terms) state assembly careers have been adopted by Arkansas, Michigan, and Oregon; Washington and Montana both also specify six years but allow rotation so that people can reenter the assembly after sitting out a full term. Missouri allows for eight years (four terms), as do Arizona, Colorado, Massachusetts, Florida, Ohio, and South Dakota with rotation. Two states set 12-year (six terms) limits; Utah with rotation and Oklahoma without rotation. In all of these states, state senate limits are comparable or longer.

[5]Composition issues are also addressed by Opheim (1994) and Reed and Schansberg (forthcoming). These authors use a different methodology to predict cohort size. They start from the current legislature and examine adjustments, rather than long-term conditions focused on here. Second, they use current reelectoral rates for elections in which incumbents are not precluded from seeking reelection by term limits. For reasons discussed in the text, this assumption is problematic.

legislature. I recommend that this change be adopted. The concluding section, which contains discussions of the recommendations, considers in more detail the impact of a two-year extension on the aspects of careerism that constitute the major arguments in favor of term limits.

Under current rules and structure, the California senate does not rely as critically on the wisdom of novices. Three features account for the difference. The career limit in the senate is currently eight years (2 terms), rather than the six years in the assembly. It is the other two features, however, that suggest valuable reforms for the current assembly and, more critically, for California if it adopts a unicameral structure. First, senate elections are staggered: only half of the seats are chosen in each election year. Election staggering introduces an important component of short-run stability into a legislature, even if individual careers are subject to shortened terms. As is shown below, staggering has an even more significant impact on the likely size of the novice cohort than a simple one-term extension of the term limit. Second, nearly all of the state senators have previous experience in elected positions, usually in the state assembly. Currently, 31 of the 40 state senators served in the assembly, a few for one or two terms, but 25 of them had prior assembly service of at least six years. Of the eight senators newly elected in 1994, all but one has served in the assembly.

Consequently, there exists a potential problem with the suggestion that California move to a unicameral legislature, for prior state legislative experience would not be available. However, the ubiquitous presence of assembly experience in the senate also suggests a possible solution, based on the preferences apparent in California's term limit law. The effective limit for many legislators in the state government is not six or eight years but rather their sum: 14 years, or six in the assembly and eight in the senate. Furthermore, prior assembly experience is a long-standing tradition for state senators, so that the current outcome was well-known at the time that Proposition 140 was approved by the voters. Combining these observations with the arguments in favor of staggering leads to the recommendation that a unicameral proposal be combined with reforming the term limit laws to provide for first, senate electoral rules (four-year terms with staggering), and second, an extension of the term limit to three terms, or 12 years.[6]

A consideration of the role of elections lends further support to these recommendations. The term limit debate reveals a divergence in views about the role of elections in representation. Term limit opponents emphasize the incentives that reelections yield *ex ante* for sitting legislators. Threat of future electoral defeat is claimed to induce legislators to represent the interests of constituents. Alternatively, proponents focus on the role of elections in choosing legislators who will represent districts even if they do not plan, or cannot, run for reelection. The second argument is of interest to the reforms proposed here. If elections are choice mechanisms, their success depends on information available about the candidates. Information about the legislative effectiveness of many senate candidates is now available, based on their assembly records. A term-limited unicameral legislature poses greater problems in this regard. Another argument in favor of multiple, though few, allowed terms is that a certain amount of sorting—getting rid of legislators who perform worse than expected; keeping those that are effective—is desirable.

Because sorting possibilities are desirable for all first-term legislators, not just those in their first two years, the relevant cohort is not the novices identified above, but all freshmen. Four-year terms, recommended here over the two-year terms of the current assembly, are thus less desirable on these grounds, although their establishment appears necessary in order for staggered elections to be viable. In the conclusions, the makeup of a legislature limited to six two-year terms is compared to three four-year terms (thus keeping a constant career limit of 12 years). The latter has many fewer novices, but substantially more freshmen—an unavoidable trade-off. Mitigating the trade-off would be ways to increase information about candidates in elections, so that the size of the freshmen cohort would be of less concern. One possibility, discussed by Bawn in this volume, is to decrease the size of districts and increase the size of the legislature.

Another cohort that may be problematic for smooth functioning of the legislature is those members who are in their last years of office, i.e., their

---

[6]It is important to distinguish between length of time spent in elected office—the political career—and length of time spent in a single institution. The conclusion section considers some options that can mitigate problems from increased institutional tenure.

third term in the assembly or the final two years of their second term in the senate. Some of them will seek other elected offices, but not enough seats are available for all. When the music stops at successively higher levels in the electoral hierarchy, the number of chairs decreases. A fraction of legislators will recognize that *this* term is their last foray into the electoral arena. Indeed, if the proponents of term limits are correct that the legislature will not be composed of career politicians, many members will be uninterested in continued elected office.

My concern with these "terminal cases" does not rest on the arguments that term limit opponents usually make about the behavior of lame ducks.[7] Rather, it is with the fact that such representatives will need a job after finishing their term.[8] If an opportunity arises, at least some of the legislators might choose to pursue it rather than complete their elected term. As a result, the phenomenon of empty seats and special elections to fill them, witnessed in the current assembly, may become yet more common.[9]

The 1995 California assembly has been a zoo. While press reports focus on the parliamentary prowess of former Speaker Willie Brown—whose power, or at least experience, will not be duplicated in a term-limited legislature—his manipulations required two conditions that probably will be: empty seats, discussed above, and close partisan

---

[7]The standard argument rests on the view that elections are necessary to induce "good" behavior by representatives. Without the threat of future electoral defeat, the opponents claim that legislators will shirk their duties to the detriment of the public good. Proponents of term limits present a panoply of counter-arguments, the most fundamental of which relates again to the role of elections in incentive formation. They argue that the legislators elected in a term-limited regime, not motivated by legislative career, will be a different sort of person than our current elected representatives: people who act for the public without the reelectoral incentive. The discussion in the text is consistent with both philosophies.

[8]See Polsby (1993) for a colorful development of this point.

[9]To the extent that the opponents are correct about lame duck incentives, at least regarding some of the legislators, another reason for empty seats and special elections might be recalls mounted to remove an errant legislator—again as observed in the current assembly. But the point remains even if the "new politician" refrains from such behavior.

division.[10] If term limits, as expected, cause elections to be much more competitive, then in many districts, candidates of either party will have roughly equal chances of winning. An immediate consequence is that close party division within the assembly will be a permanent feature of the legislature. Hence, a single special election can change the majority party in the assembly, and, with it, the Speaker. The Speaker's job may be reduced not just from the apparently permanent tenure enjoyed by Willie Brown to a period of time that strikes many as more reasonable—a single term, for example—but to only a fraction of a term. Indeed, the majority party in the assembly is likely to change regularly within a single budgetary cycle.

The probability that voters elect a legislature where changing the party of a single seat switches the majority party declines rapidly with increases in the size of the legislature. Some calculations illustrate this point. Suppose that both parties have equal probabilities of winning each seat. Then the probability of a legislature where one party has a one-seat majority, or where the parties are equally represented, is about 36 percent for a legislature of 40, 27 percent for a legislature of 80, 22 percent for a legislature of 120, and only about 17 percent for a legislature of size 200 (see Figure 1). Thus, increasing the size of the legislature, as recommended above, carries additional short-run stability benefits in a term-limited world.

As is developed below, the expected size of the terminal cohort is substantially larger in a legislature limited to three two-year terms than in one that allows four two-year terms. Also, the cohort is larger in a three two-year term legislature than one that allows two four-year terms with staggered elections. A comparison of the 12-year career options (six two-year terms versus three four-year terms with staggering) reveals that the share of terminal legislators is virtually identical. Thus there is no penalty from an increase in terminal legislators associated with the staggering recommendation, and a significant advantage from a small extension in the career length.[11]

---

[10]Term limit opponents would add a third condition that will also be present in the future: legislators with only a short time to serve in the assembly.

[11]There are many more lame ducks in a four-year term staggered legislature than in a two-year term legislature with equal allowed career lengths, which may cause concern to term limit opponents. However, the lame duck incentives apply

Figure 1. ***Probability of Closely Divided Legislature***

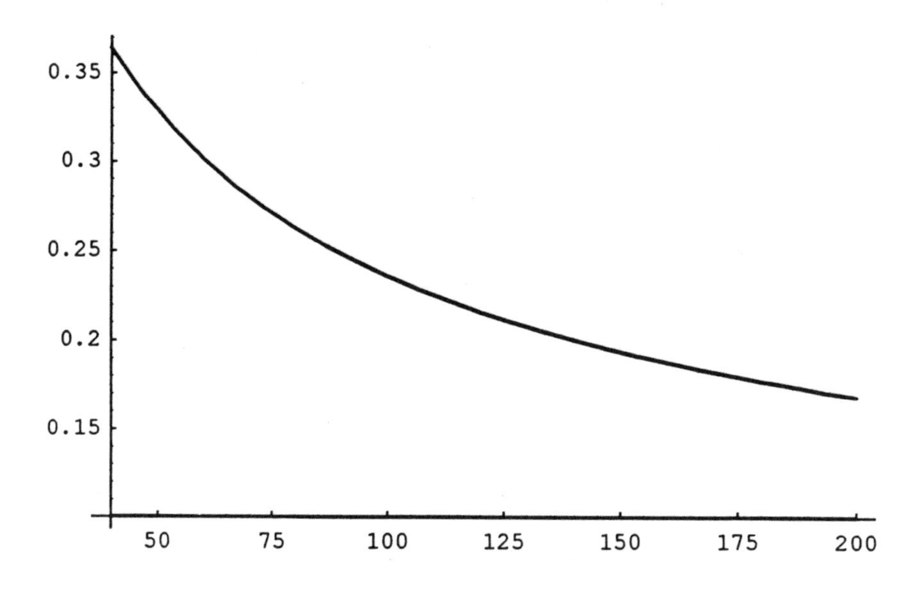

COHORT SIZES IN TERM-LIMITED ASSEMBLIES

This section contains predictions about the size of different cohorts in legislatures subject to varying term limit rules. The basic strategy is to start with some distribution of legislators, consider how many are replaced through electoral defeat, resignation, or term limit restrictions, and then recalculate the distribution in the subsequent electoral period. Thus, assumptions are needed about (1) initial shares, and (2) replacement rates.

Two strategies are possible for setting initial shares. Previous work has predicted a 10- or 15-year evolution of cohorts starting from current shares.[12] This strategy characterizes the transition from nonterm-limited legislatures to term-limited regimes. Because the purpose of this chapter is to inform constitutional reform, and because constitutions are ideally semipermanent documents, I am less interested in the transition than in

---

not just to lame ducks, but also to some degree to members in their penultimate term, and are exacerbated by the shortness of terms. Recall possibilities further muddy the comparison. Thus, there is ambiguity in comparing the two regimes.

[12]See footnote 5.

long-run predictions. As a result, I employ a second strategy and assume a steady state, where the number of entering legislators is constant from one electoral period to the next.

For example, consider a legislature with a three-term limit and two-year terms. After an election, some members will advance from their second to third year, some from fourth to fifth, and some new members will enter the legislature to serve their first year, either defeating first- or second-term legislators or winning an open seat. In steady state, the expected number of new legislators is constant over time, as is the expected number of second-term and third-term (and etc. as appropriate) legislators.

Choosing an appropriate reelectoral probability is, at this point, speculative at best. Historically, replacement rates in two-year state assemblies declined steadily in the postwar period.[13] Average turnover in the 1950s was 47.1 percent, 37.3 percent in the 1960s, 28.7 percent in the 1970s, and 24.2 percent in the first half of the 1980s.[14] In California, the turnover rate in the state assembly was 27 percent in the 1970s and had fallen to 17.5 percent in the early 1980s. However, it is hoped that term limits will reverse the trend towards increased incumbency and return turnover rates to their earlier levels. Indeed, in 1994, the turnover in the California assembly was nearly 39 percent. Results are presented here for a wide range of reelectoral probabilities; the text focuses on the range between 60 and 80 percent.

Theory predicts that the reelectoral probabilities for second, third, and subsequent elections might increase or decline. On the one hand, it might increase due to residual incumbency advantage, even in a term-limited world. In addition, defeat rates for freshmen might be higher if voters employ sorting strategies and weed out weak representatives at the first

---

[13]This covers a period when no legislatures were term limited, so that replacement is a combination of electoral defeats and retirements. Some retirements are motivated by anticipated defeat, so that the probability of reelection falls in between the rate of defeat and the rate of replacement. See Cohen and Noll (1992). Information is readily available at the state level only for replacements. If legislators choose to retire only at the end of their term-limited term, historical replacement rates are an underestimate of reelectoral rates. Alternatively, if elections are much more competitive, historical rates may be a serious overestimate.

[14]Niemi and Winsky (1987).

opportunity. Alternatively, there are good reasons why the probability of defeat for a legislator seeking reelection to his or her last term might be higher. If constituents are worried about actions of lame duck representatives, they might be less likely to elect a representative who will be term-limited. Some political scientists have suggested that legislators in their penultimate term will face greater electoral competition. The rationale is that a candidate without experience has his or her best chance at success when running for an open seat. Running against the incumbent in the previous election is one way to establish an organization, gain name recognition, and test the waters. But when serious candidates run for election, they might win—thus, an incumbent running for his or her third term in a three-term legislature could face a diminished likelihood of success.

I assume that the reelectoral probabilities are constant across elections. The steady state and constant reelectoral rate assumptions completely identify the number of legislators in different cohorts for each reelectoral probability.[15] Figure 2 plots the share of novice legislators for different reelectoral probabilities in legislatures with three, four, and six two-year term limits. The graph shows several notable features. First, for low reelectoral probabilities, the share of novices in the legislature is very high. Under California's three-term arrangement in the assembly, the legislators who will be in office for two years or less are a majority if the likelihood

---

[15]Suppose the legislators are limited to n terms in total, and that the reelectoral probability is p. Then the expected share of the legislature composed of members in their *i-th* term is given by:

$$Share(i|\ n,p) = \frac{p^{i-1}}{1+p+p^{2}+...+p^{n-1}}$$

The formula is generalized to nonconstant probabilities of reelection as follows. Let $p_1, p_2, ..., p_{n-1}$ be the probabilities of reelection at the end of the first, second, ..., n-1-th terms. The expected share of the legislature composed of members in their *i-th* term is:

$$\frac{p_1 p_2 \cdots p_{i-1}}{1+\sum_{j=1}^{n-1} p_1 p_2 \cdots p_j}$$

Figure 2.

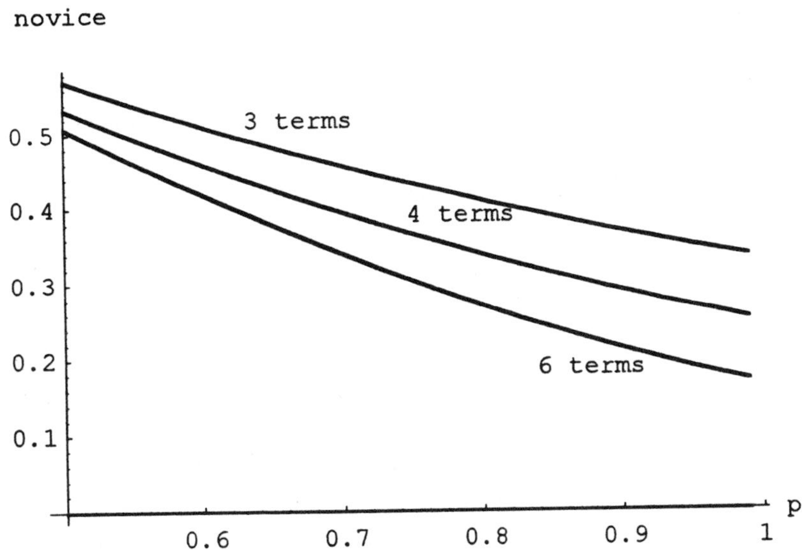

of reelection is less than 63 percent. The median legislator is in his or her first term. For a reelectoral probability of .8, novices still constitute 42 percent of the assembly.

The number of novices declines steadily as reelectoral probabilities increase, since a greater share of legislators (who are not, of course, in their term-limited term) succeed in retaining office. Given the best possible conditions for experienced legislators to hold onto their jobs—a reelectoral probability of one—the number of novices in a n-term limited legislature is 1/n. Thus, in California, *at least* one-third of the assembly will necessarily be composed of legislators who have held office for two years or less.

For higher reelectoral probabilities the difference in the number of novices in the different term-limit regimes is significant. For example, an increase in maximum allowed terms from three to four decreases the share of novices at a reelectoral probability of .8 to 35 percent—a reduction of seven points, or 17 percent. Thus, fairly modest changes in term limit laws have a substantial impact on the extent to which the assembly is dominated by inexperienced legislators.

Figure 3 plots the share of terminal legislators in legislatures with term limits of three, four, and six two-year terms. (For this case, the terminal classification is equivalent to the lame duck cohort.) The number of terminal legislators increases with the reelectoral probability. Of course, the number of novices declines with higher reelectoral probabilities, so that we trade the problem of inexperience for one of end-period incentives.

The relationship between reelectoral probabilities and the problems associated with terminal legislators is more complex than the graph suggests. If reelectoral chances are low, a legislator in the penultimate term may rank his chances at retaining office as small, and actively seek, and perhaps accept, outside employment. As reelectoral rates decline, the extent to which we should be concerned not only with terminal cases, but also with legislators who are not term-limited increases, so that the smaller number of actual terminals is not the sole consideration. Therefore, the comparison of terminal shares across reelectoral probabilities but within single regimes is of limited value.

Comparing across regimes for identical reelectoral probabilities is a useful exercise. For a reelectoral probability of .8, 26 percent of the legislators in a three-term limit legislature can be expected to be in their third term, whereas 17 percent of the legislators in a four-term limit legislature are in their terminal period: a reduction of over a third. For smaller reelectoral probabilities the absolute shares are smaller in both cases, but the proportionate reduction from increasing the limit by one term is significantly larger.

Figure 4 presents cumulative shares of legislators by terms of office for three-, four-, and six-term limit legislatures and a reelectoral probability of 0.8. The number of legislators in intermediate terms—neither freshmen nor lame ducks—increases with the number of allowed terms. For this case, the median number of terms in office for both the three- and four-term limit cases is two terms; for the six-term limit legislature, the median is at three terms in office.

Figure 3.

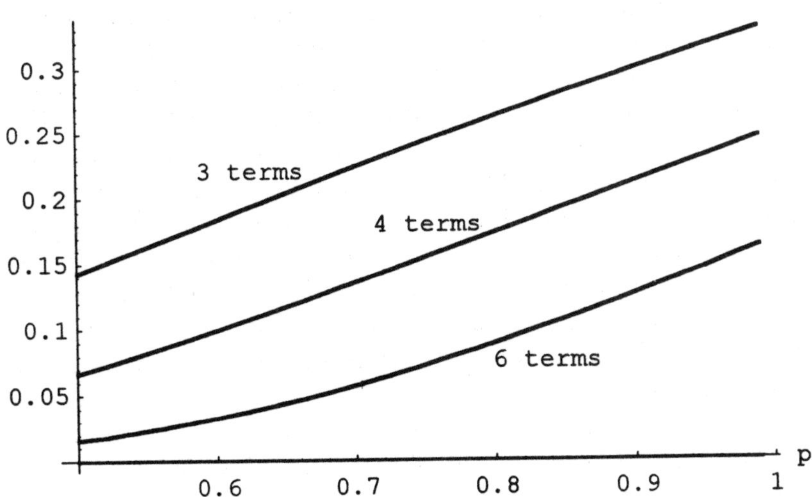

Figure 4.

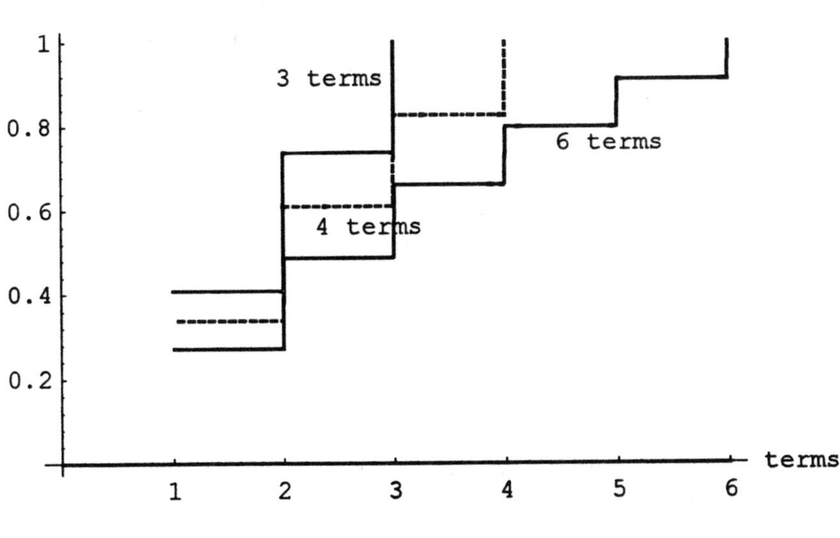

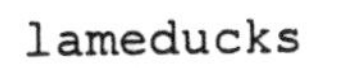

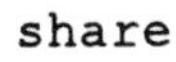

COMPARING COHORT SIZES IN THE SENATE AND ASSEMBLY

The California state senate (and other state senates) operates under a different term-limit regime. The important formal distinctions between it and the assembly are: (1) senators are limited to a single reelectoral opportunity, or two terms in total; (2) terms are four years, rather than two; (3) elections are staggered across districts. Elections are held for half of the senate seats every two years. Vacancies are filled by special election, but only for the remainder of the term, so that the staggering schedule is maintained. Thus, at most half of the senate could be occupied by novices at any time, although for low reelectoral rates substantially more than half of the senate may be composed of freshmen. Similarly, of the lame ducks, only half of them qualify for terminal status. (Exactly half of the lame ducks are terminal, and half of the freshmen are novices, under the steady state assumption.)[16]

Because election to the senate guarantees four years of employment, rather than the two years guaranteed by an assembly election, it is not reasonable to assume that reelectoral probabilities would be identical in the two cases. The senate seat is a better job—hence, elections are expected to be more highly contested, and reelectoral rates lower. Aggregate reelectoral rates in the U.S. Senate, where success brings a term three times as long as in the House of Representatives, is approximately the cube of the reelectoral rate to the House. In other words, the probability of serving six years is nearly identical in the two houses of Congress, as the likelihood of winning reelection to the Senate is equivalent to winning reelection three times to the House.[17]

---

[16]The share of senators is given by:

$$\frac{1}{2+2p}$$

for senators in their first two years and second two years, and

$$\frac{p}{2+2p}$$

for senators in their third two years and fourth two years.

[17]See Glazer and Grofman (1987).

Table 1. ***Return Rates in State Senates and Assemblies***

Year	Senate Rate*	Senate Rate	Assembly Rate	Assembly Rate
1951-1960	.434	.362	.529	.28
1961-1970	.474	.512	.627	.393
1971-1980	.542	.554	.713	.508
1980	.618	.649	.768	.590
1982	.593	.594	.763	.582

*Calculated from data in Niemi and Winsky (1987). Rates in Niemi and Winsky are defined to be one minus the ratio of new members to the total number of members in the legislative body. Only half the seats are contested in staggered Senates. The number of new members is doubled here to make the rate comparable to the other columns.

Applying this logic to states implies that the reelectoral probabilities in senates would be about the square of the probability in assemblies. The following table suggests that this relationship is a reasonable approximation: average return rates in (nonterm-limited) two-year term assemblies are systematically higher than in four-year term senates; recently, the square relationship holds well.

Figure 5 shows the share of novices in a two-term limit, four-year term, staggered legislature (labelled, "staggered terms"), compared to the two-year term legislatures with three-term, four-term, and six-term limits. The x-axis gives the probability of reelection to the two year terms; for staggered terms the probability of reelection is assumed to be p^2.

Consider first the staggered terms and four-terms cases. For them, the maximum number of years in office is eight years, so this comparison holds "careerism" constant. The share of novices is substantially lower when electoral rules specify longer terms and staggering. The difference is more pronounced at low reelectoral rates, where the share of novices in the staggered case is lower than even the share in the six-term limit, 12-year career limit legislature. Note that this difference exists even though it is assumed that the probability of reelection to the senate is lower than that in the assembly. Without the reelectoral probability adjustment employed

Figure 5.

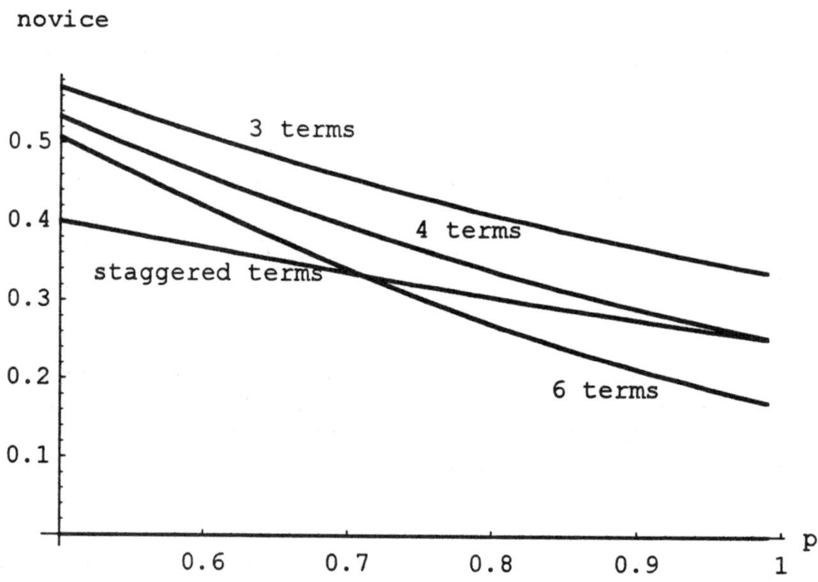

here, the discrepancies would be larger. Thus, longer terms with staggering buys the legislature considerable experience—more, even, than relaxing the term limit constraint.

What staggering costs is an increase in the number of freshmen. Thus, if election-sorting is an important consideration—if there is significant uncertainty about the characteristics of first-term legislators—staggering creates a problem. The electorate must wait four years, rather than two, to weed out electoral mistakes. The importance of this problem rests on the availability of information about candidates. In the present electoral structure in California it is probably not a major concern: most state senators have held previous office in the assembly. However, it is an issue for a unicameral legislature.

Terminal cases in the staggered arrangement are slightly higher than for a four-term limit legislature, although still lower than for a three-term arrangement, as shown in Figure 6. The difference increases at low reelectoral rates, although, as discussed above, this is difficult to interpret.

Figure 6.

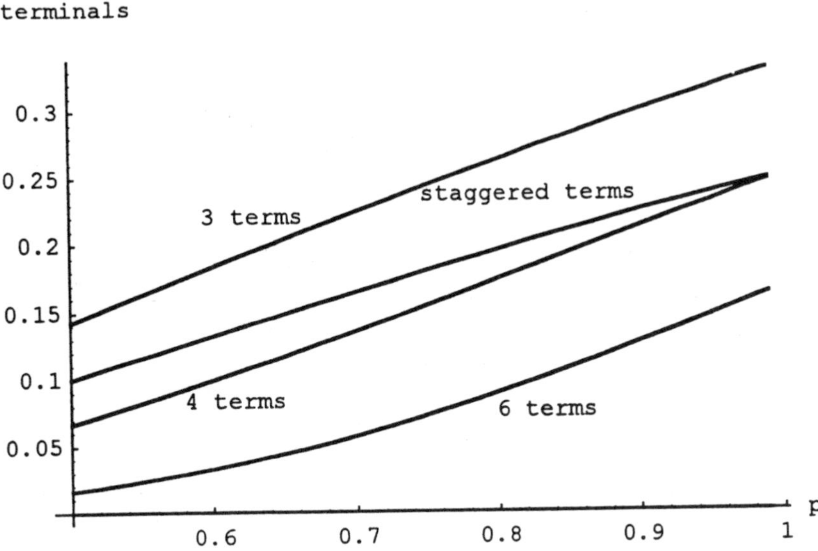

If legislators in their third term of office face uncertainty over reelection to a fourth term, they may initiate terminal behavior early. Alternatively, legislators in their fifth and sixth years in the staggered term case have the final two years in office more or less assured. Thus the number of terminal "types" in the two-year term cases is underestimated relative to the four-year term case in Figure 6, particularly for low reelectoral probabilities.

Four-year term legislatures have a greater number of lame ducks (Figure 7). The importance of the discrepancy depends on how detrimental lame duck incentives are in the first two years of the lame duck term. Term limit proponents tend to discount the importance of shirking by lame ducks who were first selected under term limit conditions; opponents perhaps can take some comfort from the possibility that recall threats deter gross misbehavior. Again, the discrepancy between the two regimes is tempered by the extent to which legislators in their third term have lame duck incentives even though they can run for office one more time. The classic

Figure 7.

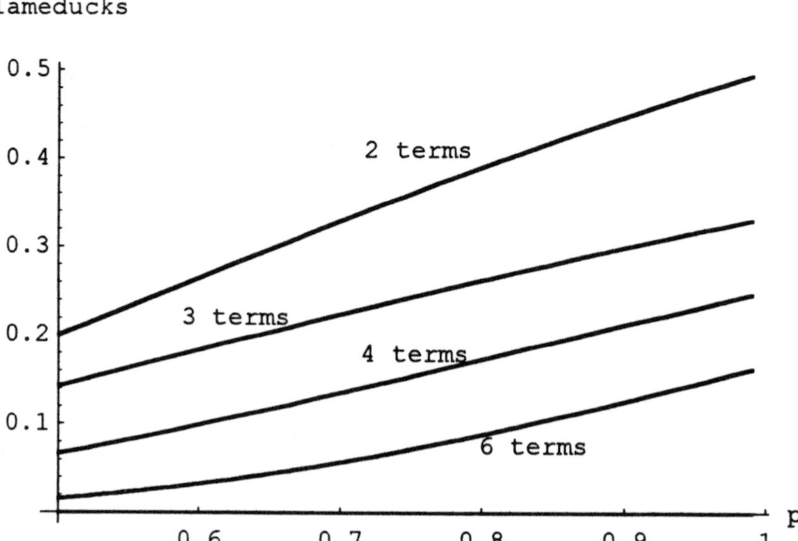

repeated game theory model, on which bad lame duck behavior is predicated, finds no difference in behavior between legislators in their last and next-to-last terms.

In sum, staggering elections, together with longer terms, appears to have some significant advantages along the two key dimensions emphasized here—the share of novices and terminals. These are more pronounced in the actual arrangements in California (six-year maximum in the assembly versus eight years in the senate). The state senate is likely, in the long run, to be a more effective institution than the assembly.

CONCLUSIONS

The preceding discussion suggests that the term limit arrangements in the California assembly are so restrictive that over the long run it will be unable to perform in any reasonably effective fashion. The share of legislators at the beginning and end of their tenure in office will be exceptionally high: perhaps higher than envisioned by the reform movement that brought the limits into existence. But only minor modifications yield substantial improvements: an increase of one term to a four-term limit, or longer electoral periods with staggering.

Does an extension from six years to eight significantly breach the term limit rationale? Voters in California did not choose six years over eight; the initiative process only gives an up-or-down choice on each proposed amendment. Eight years have been chosen by a plurality of states for the legislative career limit.

The term limit literature does not address whether six years is optimal, or eight is too many (with one exception, discussed below). The argument in favor of term limits is that legislators who have the possibility for long-term careers distort government so as to build incumbency advantages and allow them to realize the potential career. Fundraising, catering to special interests, abetting and encouraging lobbyists, and pork-barrel politics follow. Furthermore, certain interests become entrenched, as leadership positions rest for long periods of time with the same individuals.

The two-year extension has, I believe, little relevance for the last point—examples given are to legislators who have served 20 years or more. One more election, however, does represent a move towards greater potential incumbency, and thus increases the value of attempting to assure it. However, it would not appear to compromise the most fundamental point: in neither the six- nor eight-year case could an individual equate his or her legislative service in the assembly with a life-time career. The new "type" of representative would run for office in both regimes; to the extent that this is the critical component in limiting the search for incumbency advantages, the goal of term limits is maintained.

Doug Bandow, of the Cato Institute, specifically makes a case for six-year terms.[18] The context for his piece was the amendments considered by the U.S. Congress, most of which incorporated a 12-year limit. Bandow argues that the short career limit is more than adequate to develop expertise. That, of course, is not contested here; he does not address whether novices have such expertise, nor does he consider the potential

---

[18]Bandow (1995) claims, in addition to the arguments in the text, that voters have indicated a preference for six-year career limits by choosing them in 15 of the 22 states with limits. This is contrary to other published sources (e.g., Benjamin and Malbin) and my survey of state laws on Lexis. Also, most states with term limits allow rotation.

problems that a large novice cohort would present. Second, he argues that three terms would reinforce competitive elections, whereas six is too many:

> In [a three-term] system, initial reelection would probably remain relatively tough, as it is today, and the final election might be more difficult than expected as challengers ran in an attempt to position themselves for the next election, when the seat would be empty. A six-term limit, in contrast, would give incumbents relatively easy rides in elections three, four, and five.

A four-term limit might present an "easy ride" in one election: number three, by his reckoning. However, elections one, two, and four are not problematic. Note that for the recommendation given here for a unicameral legislature (four-year terms; three-term limit), the number of elections is consistent with Bandow's recommendation and conclusion about maintaining adequate competition.

Finally, Bandow states that, "The third, and most important, reason for three-term limits is that they would reestablish a citizen legislature rather than a professional one." The point relates to whether members perceived the legislature as their sole career. As discussed above, eight years does not fall in that category.

A unicameral legislature is recommended by other chapters in this volume. The analysis here suggests that appropriate guidelines for term limits in that case would be to abide by senate rules (four-year terms; election staggering), and to increase the career limit to 12. To reiterate, this switch is consistent with effective career limits in California, which currently stand at 14 years for many senators. But it does allow for greater entrenchment within a single legislative body. That is, in moving from the assembly to the senate, members lose institutional seniority. More could exist in a single 12-year legislative body.

A formal mechanism to reduce such possibilities is requiring rotation of leadership positions and committee chairs within the legislature. For example, the U.S. House of Representatives adopted term limits for all committee chairs in 1995; it has limited membership on the Budget Committee to six years since that committee was established.

Both the advantages and disadvantages of staggering apply to a 12-year potential career. As Figure 8 shows, the share of terminal cases for six two-

Figure 8.

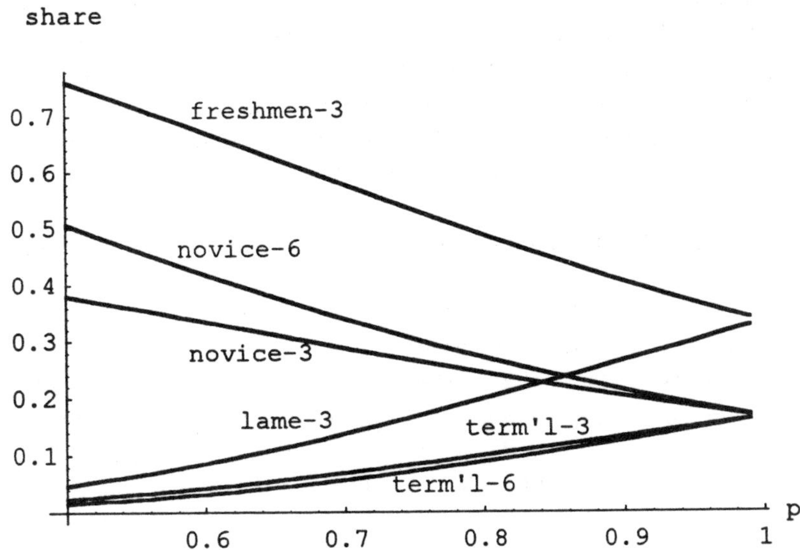

year terms ("term'l-6") and three four-year terms ("term'l-3") are virtually identical; the number of novices is greater in the six-term case; and the share of lame ducks and freshmen is greatly reduced. Because the lame duck incentives of legislators in their penultimate fifth term are unclear, the end-period differences in the two cases are not very different. Therefore, the case turns on the first-period differences.

For low reelectoral probabilities, the difference in the share of novices is substantial. Even in the six-term case, close to a majority of legislators may be very inexperienced. While this needs to be balanced against the importance of sorting freshmen, the advantage of the three-term case is significant.

REFERENCES

Bandow, Doug. 1995. "Real Term Limits: Now More Than Ever." *Studies in the Policy Analysis Series*, no. 221. The Cato Institute, March 28.

Benjamin, Gerald, and Michael J. Malbin, eds. 1992. *Limiting Legislative Terms*. Washington, D.C.: Congressional Quarterly Press.

Cain, Bruce E. (forthcoming). "The Varying Impact of Legislative Term Limits." In *Legislative Term Limits: Public Choice Perspectives,* ed. Bernard Grofman.

Cohen, Linda R., and Roger G. Noll. 1992. "The Political Discount Rate." MS.

Cohen, Linda R., and Matthew Spitzer. 1992. "Term Limits." *Georgetown Law Journal* 80, no. 3 (February).

Coyne, James K., and John H. Fund. 1992. *Cleaning House: America's Campaign for Term Limits*. Washington, D.C.: Regnery Gateway.

Ehrenhalt, Alan. 1991. *The United States of Ambition: Politicians, Power, and the Pursuit of Office*. New York: Times Books.

Fiorina, Morris. 1992. *Divided Government*. New York: MacMillan Publishing Co.

Frenzel, Bill. 1992. "Term Limits and the Immortal Congress." *The Brookings Review* 10 (Spring): 18-22.

Glazer, Amihai, and Bernard Grofman. 1987. "Two Plus Two Plus Two Equals Six: Tenure in Office of Senators and Representatives, 1953-1983." *Legislative Studies Quarterly* 12, no. 4 (Nov.) 555-63.

Grofman, Bernard, ed. (forthcoming) *Legislative Term Limits: Public Choice Perspectives*. Kluwer Press

Mann, Thomas E. 1992. "The Wrong Medicine." *The Brookings Review* 10 (Spring): 23-25.

Niemi, Richard G., and Laura Winsky. 1987. "Membership Turnover in U.S. State Legislatures: Trends and Effects of Districting." *Legislative Studies Quarterly* 12, no. 1 (February).

Opheim, Cynthia. 1994."The Effect of U.S. State Legislative Term Limits Revisited." *Legislative Studies Quarterly* 12, no. 1 (February): 49-59.

Polsby, Nelson W. 1993. "Restoration Comedy." *Yale Law Journal* 102: 1515-26.

Reed, W. Robert, and D. Eric Schansberg. (forthcoming). "An Analysis of the Impact of Congressional Term Limits." *Economic Inquiry.*

Will, George F. 1992. *Restoration: Congress, Term Limits and the Recovery of Deliberative Democracy*. New York, N.Y.: The Free Press.

IV. INITIATIVE REFORM

Constitutional Change: Is It Too Easy to Amend our State Constitution?

Bruce E. Cain
Sara Ferejohn
Margarita Najar
Mary Walther

California's initiative has two functions: to make statutory law and to amend the constitution. Of the 23 states that have the popular initiative, only 17 permit initiative constitutional amendment (ICAs).[1] By any standard, California puts the fewest restrictions of all states on what can be decided by the initiative, and as a consequence, Californians use the ICA process often and in many varied ways. Another unusual feature of California government is its high rate of constitutional amendment activity. As Table 1 indicates, California changes its constitution as a whole less frequently than other states, but amends it in part more often. California has had only 2 constitutions in its history as compared to an average of 2.9 for all the states, but the current constitution, adopted in 1879, has been amended 489 times (the second highest rate in the country). In all, there have been 817 proposed changes (first in the country) and an average of 4.29 amendments adopted on a yearly average (third in the nation). An average of over four amendments per year to a state constitution seems like quite a lot by any standard, and it prompts us to ask some obvious questions: is it too easy to amend the California Constitution (i.e., does it suffer from hyper-amendability), and what role does the initiative process play in this?

In addition to the amendment rate issue, many people have some qualitative concerns about the types of constitutional amendments that the

---

[1]Philip L. Dubois, and Floyd F. Feeney, "Improving the California Initiative Process: Options for Change" Report 14 (Berkeley, Calif.: California Policy Seminar, University of California, 1991).

Table 1. ***General Statistics for Comparative States***

State	Effective Date	Number of Constitutions	Estimated Length (Number of Words)	Number of Amendments			Percentage of Proposed Amendments Adopted	Initiative Method of Constitutional Amendment?
				Proposed	Adopted	Adopted/ Year		
California	July 4, 1879	2	33,350 (12th)	817 (1st)	489 (2nd)	4.26) (3rd)	59.9% (27th)	yes
Illinois	July 1, 1971	4	13,200	14	8	.35	57.1%	yes
Michigan	Jan. 1, 1964	4	20,000	51	17	.57	33.3%	yes
New York	Jan. 1, 1895	4	80,000	280	213	2.15	76.1%	no
Ohio	Sept. 1, 1851	2	36,900	253	151	1.06	59.7%	yes
Texas	Feb. 15, 1876	5	76,000	518	353	2.99	68.1%	no
National Average	1896	2.9	28,590	189	118	1.34	62.5%	----

The Book of the States, 1994-1995. The Council of State Governments, Lexington, Kent., v. 30, 1994.

initiative produces. Critics of the current initiative process argue that initiative constitutional amendments (ICAs) tend to be flawed in a number of ways: they are often poorly drafted, they constrain flexible policymaking with constitutionally protected mandates and limits, they allow small groups of citizens to revise the structure of government for political advantage, and they lead to an incoherent and logically unsound constitutional document.[2] Are these criticisms valid, and if so, should the power of the initiative to amend the constitution be curbed in some way? In the sections that follow, we will first consider the hyper-amendability problem, and then the qualitative issues about ICAs as they affect governmental structure and public policy.

HYPER-AMENDABILITY: CAUSES AND CONSEQUENCES

The fact that Californians have amended their constitution 489 times in the 116 years of its existence startles people when they hear this for the first time. Given the relative infrequency of amendments to the federal constitution, the contrast with the California Constitution is quite stark and makes one a bit uneasy. The federal constitution is an enduring document that covers rights and structure but not policy, and that is procedurally difficult to amend (requiring a supermajority vote in both houses of Congress and three quarters of the state legislatures). The reality of current state constitutions generally is that most are not the original document, they are full of detailed policy prescriptions, and they are frequently and easily amended. The logic behind state constitutions is discussed elsewhere. The question we consider is whether the California Constitution's *susceptibility to amendment* is caused by the initiative process per se.

Counterintuitively, we argue that the initiative process contributes little if anything to the rate at which state constitutions are changed. The first indication that this is so comes from Table 2, a histogram that plots the number of adopted constitutional amendments in California by decade and

---

[2]Eugene Lee, "Representative Government and the Initiative Process," in *California Policy Choices*, ed. J. J. Kirlin and D. R. Winkler, vol. 6, (L.A.: Sacramento Center, School of Public Administration, USC, 1990). See also report by California Commission on Campaign Financing, *Democracy by Initiative* (Los Angeles: Center for Responsive Government, 1992).

Table 2. ***Adopted Constitutional Amendments by Decade and Process***

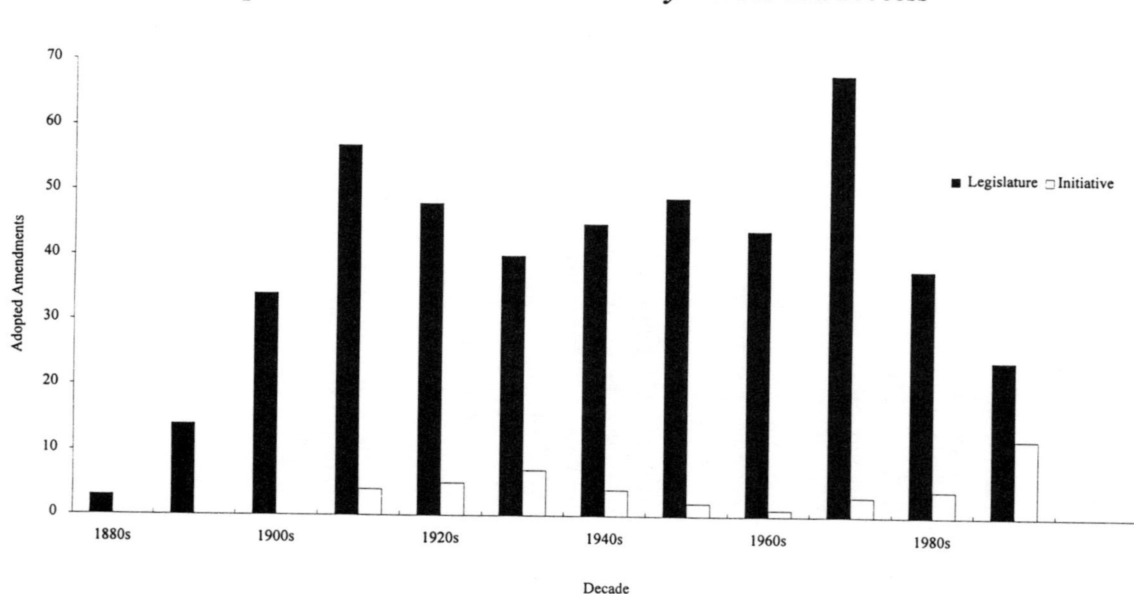

"A Study of California Ballot Measures, 1884-1992," Compiled by March Fong Eu, California Secretary of State. Sacramento, CA.: January, 1993

"Statement of Vote for November 2, 1993 General Election," Compiled by March Fong Eu, California Secretary of State. Sacramento, CA.: 1994.

"Statement of Vote, November 8, 1994, General Election," Compiled by Tony Miller, Acting Secretary of State. Sacramento, CA.: 1994.

divides them into legislative constitutional amendments (LCAs) and initiative constitutional amendments (ICAs). The first observation is that in every decade since the adoption of the initiative in the early twentieth century, the number of amendments generated by the legislature (LCAs) exceeds the number generated by the initiative process (ICAs) by wide margins. There is some variation over time. In particular, there has been an upsurge in the adoption of ICAs since the sixties, and if the pattern of the first elections in the nineties were to continue, it would lead to a projected record number of ICAs. Also, there seems to be a small inverse relationship between the frequency of adopted LCAs and ICAs: i.e., when the number of adopted LCAs goes up, the number of adopted ICAs goes down, possibly tracking the flow of trust to and from the legislature.

LCAs have a higher probability of succeeding than ICAs (see Table 3). On average, 65 percent of proposed LCAs have been approved by the voters since 1880. Only two decades—1930-39 and the first years of the 1990s—demonstrate unusually low LCA adoption rates. By contrast, the average passage rate for ICAs since 1910 is 31 percent (meaning that on average an ICA is half as likely as an LCA to pass) and appears to vary more from decade to decade. Indeed, in the first three elections of the 1990s, LCAs and ICAs had relatively similar passage rates as compared to the 50-point difference in the 1960s.

Returning then to the question of whether the initiative process is the source of California's high rate of amendability (which we have termed hyper-amendability), we can summarize the evidence as follows: there have been more proposed LCAs than ICAs over time in California, the LCAs have on average been more likely to pass than the ICAs, and, as a consequence, only 118 of the total 817 proposed amendments (i.e., 14 percent) and only 36 of the 489 total adopted amendments since 1880 (i.e., 7 percent) can be attributed to the initiative process. Even if we were to eliminate ICAs from the total, California would still have one of the highest amendability rates in the country.

But perhaps this evidence underestimates the effects that the initiative process has on amendability. For instance, as Professor Gerber has sug-

Table 3. ***California Constitutional Amendments, Proposed and Adopted***

Decade	Amendments Proposed	Amendments Adopted	percentage	LCA Proposed	LCA Adopted	percentage	ICA Proposed	ICA Adopted	percentage
1880-89	7	4	57%	7	4	57%	*	*	*
1890-99	28	14	50	28	14	50	*	*	*
1900-09	51	34	67	51	34	67	*	*	*
1910-19	98	61	62	83	57	69	15	4	27
1920-29	89	53	60	68	48	71	21	5	24
1930-39	107	47	44	86	40	47	21	7	33
1940-49	83	49	59	72	45	63	11	4	36
1950-59	80	51	64	72	49	68	8	2	25
1960-69	75	45	60	68	44	65	7	1	14
1970-79	102	71	70	94	68	72	8	3	38
1980-89	60	42	70	48	38	79	12	4	33
1990-94	37	18	49	22	12	55	15	6	40
Overall	817	489	60	699	453	65	118	36	31

*ICA procedure not introduced yet.

"A Study of California Ballot Measures, 1884-1992," compiled by March Fong Eu, California Secretary of State. Sacramento, Calif.: January 1993. "Statement of Vote for November 2, 1993 General Election," compiled by March Fong Eu, California Secretary of State. Sacramento, Calif.: 1994. "Statement of Vote, November 8, 1994, General Election," compiled by Tony Miller, Acting Secretary of State. Sacramento, Calif.: 1994.

gested in her scholarship, the existence of the initiative could have indirect as well as direct effects.[3] The direct effect of the initiative process on the rate of constitutional amendment is measured by the number of ICAs proposed and adopted. The indirect effects might include such things as the influence that the existence of the ICA option has on the legislature's propensity to offer an amendment of its own. In other words, the threat of being preempted by an ICA might force state legislatures to offer more LCAs.

The best way to examine this possibility is to compare states with the ICA option and those without it. If there were a relationship between the ICA option and the prevalence of LCAs, the LCA rate should be higher in states with ICA options than in states without it. Contrary to this hypothesis, Table 4 shows that in fact states with the initiative process have a slightly lower LCA rate per year (1.17) than states without the initiative process (1.37). Moreover, the data shows that, just as we found in California, the ICA yearly adoption rate in other states never exceeds the LCA rate and on average is about 7 times lower.

Given that LCAs are such a major portion of the total number of amendments both in California and in other states, the question then becomes the following: do the number of LCAs produced in the different states have anything to do with the ease of putting LCAs on the ballot? In other words, is the amendment rate of state constitutions in any way a function of the rules governing the introduction of LCAs to the ballot. Conventional political science logic suggests that *ceterus paribus*, the higher the threshold of consensus needed in order to pass a measure, the lower the probability of success: to take extreme examples, everything else being equal, a simple plurality requirement (i.e., a measure only needs more yes than no votes) should be easier to meet than a unanimity requirement, and hence, one might expect more measures adopted in legislatures that have the former rather than the latter procedure.

There are four common procedures for LCAs in 44 states (and one residual category of six other states in which contingencies exist for the LCA procedures). The most common method (used by 17 states) is the one

---

[3]Elisabeth R. Gerber, "Legislative Response to the Threat of Initiatives," *American Journal of Political Science,* forthcoming.

Table 4. ***States with Initiative Constitutional Amendment Process***

State	Number of Amendments					Percent of Proposed Amend-ments Adopted
	Proposed	Adopted	Adopted /Year	ICAs /Year	LCAs /Year	
Arizona	204	111	1.39	.21	1.15	54.4
Arkansas	167	77	.69	.27	.38	48.5
California	817	489	4.26	.32	3.94	59.9
Colorado	243	118	1.02	.27	.75	48.6
Florida	83	57	2.48	.21	2.17	68.7
Illinois	12	7	.33	.05	.27	58.3
Massachusetts	144	117	.55	.01	.40**	81.3
Michigan	47	16	.57	.20	.44	34.0
Missouri	119	76	1.62	*	*	63.9
Montana	27	16	.84	.15	.65	59.3
Nebraska	289	193	1.65	.09	1.21***	66.8
Nevada	178	111	.87	.03	.84	62.4
North Dakota	231	127	1.23	.19	1.03	55.0
Ohio	248	147	1.04	*	*	59.3
Oklahoma	287	141	1.66	*	*	49.1
Oregon	375	192	1.44	*	*	51.2
South Dakota	190	98	.95	*	*	51.6
Average	215	123	1.33	.17	1.17	57.2
Average for States without Initiative	169	112	1.37	*	1.37	67.7
Overall Average	185	116	1.36	*	1.30	64.0

*Information not available. Unable to distinguish between ICAs and LCAs.
**Constitutional convention amendments per year is .15.
***Constitutional convention amendments per year is .35.

that California employs; namely, an LCA needs the approval of two-thirds of each house in the state legislature. Nine states require three-fifths of each house, seven states require a majority in consecutive sessions, and nine others require a majority in each house. Two states require a two-thirds vote in consecutive sessions. If we were to arrange legislative procedures in terms of expected difficulty from most to least, a plausible order would be as follows: two-thirds in consecutive session, two-thirds of each house, three-fifths of each house, a majority in each house in consecutive sessions and a majority in each house (the only possible question being how to trade-off the consecutive session feature with the vote threshold level). Do we find that the rate of adoption of LCAs varies with our expectations about the relative difficulty of the adoption procedures?

The answer would appear to be no. States with more onerous procedures have yearly adopted LCA rates that are as great as or greater than those with less onerous procedures. Specifically, the 11 states that require two-thirds of each house have an LCA adoption rate of 1.25 while six states that demand a simple majority vote in each house had a rate of .88. There is no linear relationship one way or the other (see Table 5).

There is, however, another interesting aspect to these rules. It would appear from the data that there is a relationship between the difficulty of the voting rule and the subsequent electoral success of LCAs. States that make it more difficult to pass LCAs out of the legislature tend to have the highest LCA success rates. The consecutive sessions requirement appears to be particularly important in this regard (see Table 6). This makes sense. It will take a greater and more stable consensus to pass a measure by two-thirds or even a majority of each house in consecutive sessions than a majority of each house in a single session, and that will be reflected in higher success rates at the ballot box.

If the constitutional amendment rate cannot be traced to the availability of the initiative option or to the rules that govern how the legislature places constitutional amendments onto the ballot, then what are we to make of this phenomenon? The answer most likely lies in the complexity and scope of state constitutions: the more topics covered by a constitution, the greater the likely perceived need for amendment over time. Since certain state constitutions as originally written contain many policy items, there is a greater need to amend those than there is in constitutions that originally contain few or no policy prescriptions.

Table 5. ***Legislative Constitutional Amendment Procedure and Number of Legislative Amendments Adopted per Year***

Method	Average number of LCAs adopted per year	Cases
1. 2/3 of each house	1.25	11
2. 2/3 of each house in consecutive sessions	--	1
3. 3/5 of each house	1.93	6
4. majority of each house	.88	6
5. majority of each house in consecutive sessions	.87	6
6. Other	.71	3
average	1.19	33

State-by-state average number of LCAs adopted per year.

1.		2.		3.	
AK	.70	DE	--	AL	5.91
CA	3.94			FL	2.17
CO	.75			KE	.30
ID	1.06			NE	1.21
KA	.67			NH	.69
ME	.92			NC	1.29
MI	.44				
MS	1.06				
MT	.65				
TX	2.92				
WY	.60				

4.		5.		6.	
AZ	1.15	IN	.27	CN	.96
AR	.38	MA	.40	NJ	.91
MN	.84	NV	.84	VT	.25
NM	1.51	NY	2.03		
ND	1.03	PA	.79		
RI	.36	WI	.87		

--Data not available because unable to distinguish between legislative, initiative, and convention constitutional amendments to the Delaware Constitution.

Table 6.

Method	Average Passage Rate of Legislative Constitutional Amendments	Cases
1. 2/3 of each house	64.8%	11
2. 2/3 of each house in consecutive sessions	--	--
3. 3/5 of each house	65.4%	6
4. majority of each house	55.3%	5
5. majority of each house in consecutive sessions	71.6%	5
6. other	65.2%	3
average	64.5%	30

-- Data not available because unable to distinguish between legislative, initiative, and convention constitutional amendments.

Even among state constitutions, however, there is variation, and here we would point to two factors: age and constitutional complexity. We think it likely that states that have (1) constitutions adopted in the late 19th century that reflect the populist sentiments of the time, and (2) greater scope and specificity of coverage in them, may be more prone to high rates of amendability. Returning to Table 1, the two states with the lowest yearly averages for adopted amendments are Illinois and Michigan, both of which adopted their latest constitutions after World War II. Plausibly, there may be some trade-off between scrapping a constitution entirely (and thereby eliminating the need for constant revision) and sticking with the original document by adapting it to changing circumstances through constant amendment.

The second factor is the scope and specificity of a state's constitution. State constitutions vary significantly in the topics that they cover and the degree of specificity devoted to each area. For comparative purposes, we coded the constitutions of the six states in Table 1, arranging items by 35 major topics and 187 more specific subtopics. It should come as no surprise to discover that California's constitution covers the widest range of topics with the greatest degree of specificity. The California Constitution includes 31 of the total 35 major topics identified in our coding scheme: omissions are in the areas of indebtedness, the organization of law enforcement/prison labor, the militia and veterans benefits. By comparison, California's constitution is uniquely specific in the areas of civil rights, liquor, recall powers, issues of statehood (boundaries, languages, symbols, etc.), statutes, taxation, and usury.

At the other end of the spectrum is the Illinois constitution, which was enacted almost a century later and in size is about a third of the California document. It covers only 24 of the 35 major constitutional topics, omitting such subjects as criminal behavior, federal issues, indebtedness, labor, liquor, recall, nontax revenues, usury, and veterans. Note that two of these topics are areas in which the California Constitution is uniquely detailed. The Illinois constitution is also less specific than the California one: it covers only 102 of the 187 coded subtopics. Ohio and Texas are a little bit closer to the California model while Michigan and New York fall a bit closer to the Illinois model. Ohio's constitution, for instance, also covers 30 of the 35 major topics (missing environmental protection, federal issues, liquor, criminal behavior, and gambling) with a fairly high level of specificity (120 out of 187 subtopics). Texas covers 27 major topics (missing environmental protection, federal issues, initiative provisions, labor, militia, recall, referendum, and veterans) and 126 subtopics. Michigan's constitution, adopted in 1964, covers 28 of 35 topics (excluding environmental protection, labor, law enforcement, nontax revenues, social health and welfare, usury, and veterans) and 100 subtopics while New York's document covers 29 major subjects (excluding criminal behavior, federal issues, the initiative, liquor, recall referendum, and non-tax revenues) and 98 subtopics. In short, the three oldest (California, Ohio, and Texas), which were products of the populist era, have the highest levels of specificity and highest yearly amendability rates. The newer constitutions of Michigan and Illinois have less specificity and lower yearly rates of amendability.

What we think this means is that the main causes of California's constitutional hyper-amendability are the era in which it was adopted and the influence that the populist and Progressive movements had on its contents. To put it another way, we think it is likely that California's constitution changes as frequently as it does because it has so much in it that invites changing, and because Californians have come to expect everything but the kitchen sink to be in it. Stemming from a long-standing mistrust of representative government in California, the constitution has been used to express the majority will on various policy subjects and to constrain representative government in its powers and freedom to make policy. The initiative has contributed to this tradition in significant qualitative ways that we will discuss shortly, but it would be wrong to blame the policy orientation of the California Constitution per se or its high rate of amendability on the initiative. If the ICA process needs to be curbed or reformed, the reasons have more to do with qualitative than quantitative problems.

ICAS AND STRUCTURAL REFORM

If we take as a given that the California Constitution will have things in it that we would not expect in a federal constitution, and that amendments will therefore occur frequently in order to meet the changing needs of a fast-growing and complex state, we can still ask whether the ICA process is functioning properly as an instrument of structural and policy change. A significant number of LCAs and ICAs deal with institutional structure issues such as: the compensation, terms and eligibility of elected officials; the organization of the judiciary, the legislature, and the executive; the procedures governing elections; the operation of direct democracy options; and even the process of constitutional revision itself. Clearly, all state constitutions need to cover questions of institutional organization, and just as clearly, there have to be mechanisms for making institutional changes when they are needed. The critical questions are how these changes should be generated and what the proper threshold of agreement should be before they are adopted into the constitution.

The first issue concerns how institutional changes are proposed. Both the federal and the California Constitution were devised by a constitutional convention. The model of a convention or commission based revision contains certain key elements. A convention or a commission typically has expertise: some or many of its members will be individuals who have practical or theoretical knowledge about the principles and practices of government. Drawing upon what they know to be the failures of the current system, the advantages and disadvantages of other constitutional forms, and their expectations of what would happen if changes were made, commission or convention members try to make informed choices. When they do not already possess the necessary expertise about a given matter, they have the time, opportunity, and incentive to inform themselves. Often, they have staff and other resources to which average citizens would not have access.

Another element of the commission or convention model is deliberation. Members with differing viewpoints are brought together to exchange ideas and to try to persuade one another about the merits of their ideas. This interaction allows those who are making proposals to hear objections to their ideas and opens up the possibility of compromise. Those with opposing perspectives can have input into the proposal itself. One of the central premises of modern social science is that cooperation is difficult to forge in the absence of communication (particularly when actions lack the properties of markets).[4] A chief advantage of the commission or revision model is that it provides a forum for informed communication and thereby facilitates cooperation.

By contrast, the initiative constitutional amendment process has less guarantee of expertise or deliberation. Initiatives might be proposed by people who have considerable expertise and knowledge of government, or they might not. ICAs also do not undergo any systematic deliberation before they are placed on the ballot. When the petition begins to circulate, there might be a public exchange of views in the press or through campaign literature, but once the measure is qualified, there is no room for compromise or reconciliation. The chief advantage that the ICA process has over the commission or revision model is that it is a far more convenient and less costly method of making changes.

Why might one prefer a less convenient, more costly procedure to one with the opposite traits? The answer lies with the benefits that derive from expertise and deliberation in designing government structure as opposed to normal policy. If the normal decisions of government had to be subjected to a constitutional convention before they were enacted, California government would be extremely limited in its ability to deal in a timely manner with changing conditions and crises. Flexibility and adaptability would be sacrificed, and the gain in either better policies or enhanced legitimacy would be minimal. On the other hand, we have different criteria

---

[4]Mancur Olson, *The Logic of Collective Action* (New York: Schocken, 1965).

for institutional design than for policymaking. There are real dangers if institutions are not designed properly and real advantages to making institutional changes more difficult. Poorly designed institutions can result in the multiplication of bad policy in a number of areas simultaneously. They can also be perceived as unfair (e.g., favoring one group over another) and consequently as illegitimate, and, depending upon the seriousness of the perceived injustice, ultimately destabilizing. For these reasons, political scientists have traditionally treated the requirements of institutional design and policymaking differently.

In this spirit, the California Constitution distinguishes between revisions and amendments: amendments can be made by initiative, but revisions can be made in one of only two ways: by convening a constitutional convention and obtaining popular ratification or by legislative submission to the voters. Given the vagueness of the constitutional language, the courts have played a major role in defining what constitutes a revision and what constitutes an amendment. In its pronouncements on this subject, including its most recent decision in the *Legislature of the State of California v. March Fong Eu* 54 Cal. 3d 492 (1991) the California Supreme Court discussed both a quantitative and qualitative standard for determining when a change constituted a revision as opposed to an amendment. An impermissible quantitative change for an ICA would be one that changed a substantial number of words or articles of the constitution—e.g., the measure in *McFadden v. Jordan* 32 Cal. 2nd 330 (1948) involving 21,000 words and 15 out of 25 articles. An impermissible qualitative change for an ICA would be one that involved a substantial shift of formal power from one branch or level of government to another. In *Raven v. Deukmejian* 52 Cal. 3d 336 (1990), the court held that the Victims Bill of Rights (Proposition 24) went beyond the permissible qualitative standard, because it would have limited the exercise of judicial power so that the California courts could no longer interpret rights in the California Constitution "in a manner more protective of defendant's rights than extended by the federal constitution." In the *Legislature v. Eu*, however, the court held that Proposition 140 had no impact upon the exercise of legislative power despite the fact that it limited legislative terms of office to six to eight years and slashed the legislature's budget by almost 40 percent. One cannot help but wonder whether the court would have ruled the same way had either proposition limited judicial terms of office or cut the judiciary's budget by a third or more.

Whether the decision was a good one or not, and whether term limits is a good reform or not, there is an overriding issue of design—should reforms that alter governmental structure be treated as revisions or amendments? The danger with setting the standard for revision as high as the courts have is that it means that a great deal of governmental restructuring can occur as mere amendments—i.e., outside the deliberative process of a constitutional convention or a revision commission. Unless a measure affects a large (but as yet unspecified) number of articles, or unless it takes powers formally away from one of the branches, the court will allow the proposed change to be introduced as an ICA. Diminished capacity apparently does not equate in the California Supreme Court's view with formal changes in the exercise of power. From a political science perspective, the court's position is naive at best. There is a long tradition of literature about power that points to informal power and capacity as being as important as formal power in determining the operation of government.

However, to be fair to the court, changes in formal powers are more certain and easily predictable whereas changes in capacity or operation have more speculative effects. In essence, the court's position gives the benefit of doubt to all structural changes short of formal shifts in powers and responsibilities. Given that the electoral majority that approves ICAs is the same one that controls whether justices are confirmed or not, the court is understandably cautious when it comes to overturning the expressed will of the majority.

What are the advantages and problems with allowing such a wide latitude for structural reform through the ICA process? The advantages have to do with making it easier to implement reforms that the electoral majority prefer. If the term limits proposal had to go through the constitutional convention or commission process, it would not have been implemented as rapidly as it was, and perhaps, would not have been implemented at all. And needless to say, it is even less likely that term limits would have been put on the ballot through the LCA process—no state without the initiative has adopted term limits for its legislature. A key issue, then, is how easy one wants it to be to make changes in the structure of government. Those who favor frequent reform and immediate responsiveness to the majority's preferences will see the removal of the ICA option as an enormous setback. Those who prefer that changes be less frequent and that governmental institutions should change very slowly (if at all) will see the ICA option as problematic.

However, it is not simply a question of California's relative vulnerability to structural change due to the ICA option—it is also a question of how such changes become considered. Structural reform through the ICA is necessarily piecemeal and ad hoc. Since reforms are proposed by different groups or individuals at differing points in time, there is little chance for consistency or consideration of the whole. However problematic this is for policymaking, it is even more so for institutional structures. Structural change through the ICA is also less deliberative in the sense defined earlier. The contrast between the deliberative process of a constitutional commission or convention versus the normal ICA process is particularly sharp when we consider some of the recent developments in California initiatives:

1. Initiatives are normally qualified by professional signature gatherers, and people often sign these petitions despite knowing little about the contents.[5]
2. Election outcomes are often determined by slick media campaigns that appeal to emotions and fears.[6]
3. The side that has the advantage in money does not always win, but is better able to get its message across.[7]
4. Voter knowledge about measures is often shallow even when great sums of money are spent by both sides.[8]

Given all these considerations—the level of voter knowledge, the role of money and consultants, the superficial nature of TV and radio campaigning—it is reasonable to ask whether the permissible line between revision and amendment should be set as high as the court has placed it. As Gerber argues elsewhere in this volume, the problems that the initiative poses for policymaking are substantial. Given the importance of decisions

---

[5]Daniel H. Lowenstein and Robert M. Stern "The First Amendment and Paid Initiative Circulators: A Dissenting View and a Proposal," *Hastings Constitutional Law Quarterly* 17 (Fall 1989).

[6]Lee, *op. cit.*

[7]David B. Magleby, *Direct Legislation: Voting on Ballot Propositions in the United States* (Baltimore: Johns Hopkins Press, 1984).

[8]Arthur Lupia, "Busy Voters Agenda Control and the Power of Information," *American Political Science Review*, vol. 86 (June 1992): 390-413.

about governmental structure, the problems ICAs pose in this area are even greater. Significant changes in basic government structure can be adopted by an electorate that is not well-informed about their meaning or effects, or that responds emotionally to slick campaigns and the influence of money, or that is excessively influenced by transient concerns as publicized in the media and exploited by opportunistic politicians. Such amendments could undermine the effectiveness of the institutions they alter, or promote a series of strategically motivated amendments intended to advantage one political faction over another.

What then are the options? There are two. First, one could put more explicit language in the constitution (in Article XVIII) to distinguish amendments from revisions. Currently, the constitution is vague on the subject, and the California courts have been left with the task of devising an operational distinction between the two. As discussed already, there are several problems with this. To begin with, the courts, as is often their habit, have not provided any clear numerical definition of what constitutes sufficient quantitative change. This is less of a problem at the extremes (several thousand words and twenty thousand words) than in the middle ranges. More importantly, the California Supreme Court's distinction between changes in the formal exercise of power versus changes in the capacity to exercise this power is a ludicrous and ultimately untenable distinction. Without more explicit constitutional guidance, the courts are in a politically vulnerable position, deciding "political" questions in ways that could advantage some groups over others. This can only lead to further politicization of the court, especially in a state that puts its judges up for electoral confirmation.

The logical solution is to sharpen the language in the constitution to include, for instance, all changes in government structure as revisions (in essence, banning ICAs that alter the organization of the government), but we believe this approach would have at least two drawbacks. First, it still leaves the court to decide the grey areas between revision and amendment—for instance, would campaign finance reform be considered an amendment? But second and more important, classifying structural reforms as revisions would effectively shut off an important avenue for government reform (i.e., through popular initiative). Since commission proposals have to pass through both houses of the legislature, the legislature would be in a position to kill any reform that it did not like. The experience with term limits, campaign finance, and redistricting reforms are illustrative of the legislature's inherent lack of enthusiasm for certain kinds of reforms.

We believe that a more sensible proposal would be to allow amendment or revision of governmental structure through the ICA process, but require the kind of high level of consensus that we currently require of the legislature. There are two devices California should consider: the supermajority rule and a successive elections provision. Both of these—separately or in combination—are commonly used for legislative votes on constitutional amendments. Thus, changes to the constitution that alter the organization, powers or structure of branches of the state government might have to pass a three-fifths or two-thirds vote requirement. Or, California could keep the majority vote requirement and require that ICAs dealing with government structure pass in successive November elections. Or, we might consider a supermajority vote in successive general elections. The purpose of the supermajority requirement is to confer the highest level of legitimacy possible on institutional changes and to prevent transient majorities from changing the rules to gain advantages over other groups. The purpose of the successive elections requirement is to give the electorate a chance to reconsider proposals in the light of further reflection and debate and to guard against changes that are driven by temporary emotions and events.

Finally, and this is a point that will be taken up in greater detail in a moment, there are real dangers with allowing asymmetries in the rules that govern LCAs and commission generated proposals versus those that govern ICAs. As we will argue in a moment, if it is easier to make significant policy or institutional change through the ICA process than the LCA or commission/convention route, then we are in effect setting up a situation that encourages reform through the ICA process. Political action tends to follow the path of least resistance, and the path of least resistance to significant reform is through the ICA (we are talking of significance in qualitative not quantitative terms). As stated earlier, the ICA, whatever its merits, is a nondeliberative process prone to abuse and manipulation. The successive election and supermajority vote requirements would at least ensure that *large stable majorities* approve of changes before they are implemented.

MAKING POLICY IN THE CONSTITUTION

Perhaps the greatest difference between the federal and state constitutional models is the prevalence of policy items in the state constitutions. Consider the range of policy subjects covered by the California Constitution: the regulation of business, criminal behavior, education, environmental protection, gambling, housing, labor, liquor, natural resource management, social health and welfare, taxation and fiscal matters, usury, and veterans affairs. Elsewhere, Cain and Noll consider the justifications for embedding policy in the constitution as opposed to making it in statutory form. Here, we consider issues about amending or placing policy in the constitution through the initiative process.

As part of this project, we have coded the subject matter of all amendments to current constitutions in the states where this information was available. Among other things, this allows us to examine the frequency of all amendments (including ICA and LCA) to the California Constitution by subject matter and to compare this with other states. Table 7 is a comparison of the frequency of amendments by subject categories for California and the other 49 states. The columns show the percentage of all passed constitutional amendments that pertain to a particular subject category. So, for instance, the data show that amendments relating to energy, public utilities, water, and highways represent 5.6 percent of the total amendments to the California Constitution and only 2.8 percent of amendments for the other 49 state constitutions.

The areas that generate the most amendments in California are education, fiscal matters, and above all taxation. Eighteen percent of the total amendments to the California Constitution deal with taxation alone compared to slightly over 13 percent for the other 49 states. What might explain this? One possibility is the prevalence of well-organized interest groups in the state who have the finances and incentives to put these measures on the ballot. In other words, it could be the efficacy of groups like Caltax and the CTA that is in evidence here. On the other hand, the doctors, law enforcement, and gambling lobbies are also very powerful in California, and the relative frequency of amendments in these areas is not exceptionally high. Still, we should not discount the role that special interests play in generating amendments. Of the 87 amendments we identified as dealing with taxation, all but four were put onto the ballot in

Table 7. ***Percentage of Amendments by Subject Area***

Subject Area of Amendment	Percentage of Total Amendments and Actual Number of Amendments	
	California	Other 49 States
Bonds	3.3% (16)	4.2% (187)
Business/Commerce	2.1% (10)	3.5% (154)
Civil Service	0.6% (3)	0.3% (12)
Consitutional Conventions	0.2% (1)	0.1% (4)
Constitutional Revisions	0.6% (3)	1.4% (63)
Criminal Behavior	0.6% (3)	0.3% (13)
Education	5.6% (27)	2.9% (127)
Elected and State Officials		
Compensation	3.3% (16)	3.1% (136)
Eligibility	2.7% (13)	3.1% (138)
Terms	0.6% (3)	1.9% (82)
Elections	2.5% (12)	1.8% (80)
Energy/Public Utilities/ Water/ Highways	5.6% (27)	2.8%(124)
Environmental Issues	0.6% (3)	0.3% (12)
Fiscal Matters Local	1.0% (5)	1.0% (42)
Fiscal Matters State	4.8% (23)	3.8% (166)
Gambling/Sports	1.2% (6)	1.7% (73)
Grammatical/Technical Changes	0.2% (1)	1.2% (51)
Health/Medicine/Science	0.4% (2)	0.4% (19)
Indebtedness	2.1% (10)	3.0% (132)
Judiciary		
Compensation	1.0% (5)	1.6% (70)
Jurisdiction/New Courts	2.3% (11)	3.0% (134)
Eligibility	2.1% (10)	1.6% (70)
Administration/Process	2.7% (13)	3.6% (159)
Terms	0.2% (1)	0.9% (41)

Table 7. ***Continued***

Subject Area of Amendment	Percentage of Total Amendments followed by Number of Amendments	
	California	Other 49 States
Labor Issues	0.8% (4)	0.7% (32)
Law Enforcement	0.8% (4)	0.9% (38)
Miscellaneous	2.5% (12)	1.2% (55)
Moral Issues	1.2% (6)	2.5% (110)
Municipal/County Government	8.1% (39)	5.8% (256)
Organizational Changes	0.4% (2)	0.3% (13)
Prohibition/Alcohol/Drugs	1.0% (5)	1.1% (49)
Property Ownership/Housing	2.7% (13)	1.8% (78)
Social Health and Welfare Aids/Pensions	3.1% (15)	1.9% (84)
State Bureaucracy	1.2% (6)	1.7% (73)
State Executive Organization	0.4% (2)	2.1% (95)
State Executive Powers	1.0% (5)	1.4% (64)
State Legislature Organization	2.5% (12)	5.6% (248)
State Legislature Powers	0.4% (2)	2.9% (130)
Taxation	18.0% (87)	13.1% (579)
Veterans	3.9% (19)	1.0% (44)
Voting	3.1% (15)	5.2% (231)
Wildlife/Parks/Beaches/ Forests/Fishing	1.2% (6)	1.1% (47)
Statutes/Initiative/Referenda	1.0% (5)	1.8% (78)
Militia	0.0% (0)	0.4% (19)
Statehood	0.0% (0)	0.2% (8)

the form of LCAs, and 36 of these dealt with creating new tax exemptions while only one eliminated an exemption.

Once again, however, the more important question is qualitative, not quantitative: what are the problems associated with making fiscal and taxation policy by ICA? In the area of taxation, ICAs only account for four of the successful changes, but all of them were adopted on or after 1978. Prior to that time, all ICAs dealing with taxation matters had failed at the polls. Only one of these measures, Proposition 99, created new taxes, and even then, the money was earmarked for tobacco-related education, treatment, and research. The others limited deductions on prison labor (Proposition 139), capped taxes on property (Proposition 13) and eliminated taxes on certain food products (Proposition 163).

Another area of concern for many informed observers of California politics are mandated expenditures such as Proposition 98, which allocated a fixed share of the state budget to K-12 education. Of the nine successful ICAs that mandated expenditures, historically six have dealt with education and three with health/welfare. Unlike the trend in taxation, the history of mandated expenditures through the ICA process dates back to 1920 when Proposition 16 mandated a minimum per-pupil expenditure level. Other measures in 1944, 1946, 1952, and 1984 also dealt with mandated money for education.

Critics of direct democracy argue that while the number of successful ICAs dealing with fiscal and taxation matters is relatively low, the impact that they have had has been quite large. No measure, for instance, has more fundamentally altered the fiscal situation for both state and local governments in California than Proposition 13. Propositions 98 and 99 have also severely constrained the flexibility of California's elected officials to deal with fiscal crises. Given the uncertainties of economic conditions and the difficulties that are inherent in balancing the state budget every year, is it a good idea to bind the hands of elected officials in this way? According to Leroy Graymer's report on governance in California, a large number of knowledgeable people both inside and outside government think not.[9] But our focus here is procedural—rather than

---

[9]LeRoy Graymer, "Options for Reforming California Governance," Working Paper (Berkeley, Calif.: California Policy Seminar, University of California, 1995).

debate the merits of these measures, we will concentrate on the process that generated them.

There are two disturbing aspects of making fiscal and taxation policy through the ICA. The first, which we discussed at length in the previous section on structural reform, is that the ICA process is nondeliberative, and thus ICA proposals do not emerge out of a situation in which a particular tax and fiscal policy is put in the context of the entire budget. This maximizes the probability of people going after their share of the budget or protecting their resources at the expense of other programs or individuals. The sponsors of Proposition 98, for instance, did not have to consider or take responsibility for the implications that their measure would have for higher education, prisons, or health care. In this sense, the ICA option precludes the possibility of compromise and adjustment and fosters a zero sum competition for funding.

A second issue is the problem of rule asymmetry in fiscal matters and the incentives that it creates for undermining representative government. It currently takes a two-thirds vote of the legislature to pass a budget, and since it is rare that either party has the votes to pass a budget without the cooperation of some members of the minority party, a successful budget requires some bipartisan compromise. A successful ICA only requires a majority of those voting, and in some elections that represents far less than half the eligible voters. Groups that get impatient with fiscal deliberations in the legislature can take their preferred position to the people and need only obtain a majority of those voting. Coupled with the professionalization of initiative campaigns and the information problems associated with initiative voting, it is not surprising that some groups will take their case directly to the people. The question is whether it is appropriate to have a higher threshold of required agreement for legislative action than we do for initiative action. The asymmetry of legislative and ICA rules sets up a situation in which the stronger incentives are to do fiscal business by ICA—groups that can will follow the path of least political resistance. Unless one purposely wants to undercut legislative responsibility for fiscal matters, this asymmetry should be resolved.

The resolution can be in either direction. It makes sense either to lower the threshold needed to pass a budget in the legislature, as some have suggested, or to raise the threshold for passing fiscal measures through the ICA process to the two-thirds level. The original concept of the initiative was to provide a check on elected officials, not to replace representative government. In the area of taxation and fiscal matters, several of the most important and constraining fiscal decisions have been made at the ballot box. Placing legislative and ICA policymaking on this subject on the same footing would be more in keeping with the original purposes of the initiative and, we hope, will allow for a more deliberative and integrated approach to fiscal planning.

What about nonfiscal and taxation matters? The problem of rule asymmetry does not apply here. The problems that arise here have more to do with many of the themes raised in Gerber's paper—namely, the need to give the legislature a chance to respond before the fact and to amend when necessary after the fact. Clearly, giving a policy constitutional standing builds in a higher commitment to that policy than handling the matter as a statute. For that reason, it might make sense to consider some of the reforms that Gerber has proposed for statutory initiatives as possible reforms for ICAs as well; i.e., referral after qualification to the legislature for consideration, and allowing the legislature to amend the amendment and to place it on the ballot as an LCA if the original authors do not approve of the changes.

CONCLUSION

Is it too easy to amend the California Constitution? The answer is a qualified yes. On the one hand, we have to expect that the California Constitution will be changed frequently because it covers so many subjects in a high degree of specificity. On the other, the ICA option has made a qualitative difference in terms of structure and policy. With regard to the former, the ICA option has opened up the possibility of passing government reforms that elected officials might oppose for reasons of self-interest, but it also brings changes that are formulated in an ad hoc, nondeliberative fashion. We have recommended that the ICA option be kept but that either or both a supermajority and successive election requirements be added to ICAs that change government powers or organization. In terms of policy, amendments to the California Constitution have heavily focused on fiscal and taxation measures. Some of the most critical fiscal decisions have been put into the constitution by the ICA process, and this has limited the ability of elected officials to deal with fiscal crises. Again, the asymmetry of what is required of the legislature and what is required of the electorate is partly to blame. We need to have

a consistent standard for making fiscal decisions to avoid the inevitable flow in the direction of the political path of least resistance.

Reforming the California Initiative Process: A Proposal to Increase Flexibility and Legislative Accountability

Elisabeth R. Gerber

As Californians confront the daunting prospect of revising their state constitution, one feature of the state's political landscape that is bound to receive a great deal of attention is the initiative process. Initiatives are a form of direct legislation in which regular citizens make policy by voting on ballot propositions. Initiatives are propositions that are placed on the ballot by nonlegislative actors—typically regular citizens or established interest groups.[1] Initiatives may be either statutory or constitutional. California is one of 23 states that use initiatives at the statewide level.[2]

The initiative process plays a key role in contemporary California politics. Between 1974 and 1990, California voters considered 73 statewide initiatives, of which 32 passed.[3] These initiatives covered policy areas as diverse as taxation, insurance regulation, government reform, gambling, environmental policy, criminal law, and school funding. Further, many laws passed by initiative have had important consequences on government operations. For example, the combined effect of Proposition 13 (1978) and

---

The author gratefully acknowledges the research assistance of Tim Groeling, Thomas Kim, Jennifer Kuhn, and Mark Sniderman.

[1]In recent years, legislative actors and other officeholders have proposed or sponsored initiatives, typically linking their campaign to the initiative. Such involvement in the initiative process, however, is informal, with the officeholders acting unofficially as regular citizens.

[2]Other forms of direct legislation include referendums, which are laws passed by the legislature and then ratified or rejected by the electorate, and the recall, where citizens petition to subject an elected official to removal. See Magleby, 1984, for a description of types of direct legislation.

[3]California Secretary of State, *Statement of the Vote*, selected years.

Proposition 4 (1979) has been to severely constrain the ability of state and local governments to raise taxes and provide public services. Other initiatives, such as 1988's Proposition 98 (K-14 school funding) and Proposition 99 (cigarette tax) further constrain the legislature's flexibility by earmarking general fund revenues for narrowly specified purposes. In sum, the effects of direct legislation permeate the entire political system. No meaningful constitutional reform or revision can proceed without considering the role and effects of direct legislation.

Many people believe that direct legislation, especially the initiative, is at odds with a well-functioning representative democracy. They argue that initiatives undermine the legislative process by tying legislators' hands and diminishing their ability to respond to the needs of their constituents. Others argue that the possibility that issues will make their way to the ballot allows legislators to avoid taking positions on politically tough issues like gun control, abortion, and immigration reform. In other words, legislators may duck their responsibilities behind the facade of "letting the voters decide."

Indeed, much truth lies in these arguments. The initiative process, as it currently operates in California, affords little opportunity for input by the legislature. Formally, the legislature is required to hold hearings on qualified propositions, but it cannot amend a qualified initiative as a result of a hearing. The sole consequence of a hearing is therefore to inform members of the assembly and senate that an initiative has qualified. The legislature may pass laws on issues that will be appearing on upcoming ballots, but there is no procedure for removing initiatives from the ballot if the legislature passes an identical measure. The legislature may also place a competing measure on the ballot, but it may not amend, revise, update, or improve an initiative once it has been enrolled, except by submitting the amended version again to the people. Consequently, the legislature has little opportunity or incentive to seek compromises, take positions, or draft legislation on issues that may qualify as initiatives.

This need not be the case. In other states, the initiative has been used to enhance, rather than undermine the legislative process. For instance, many states allow or require the state legislature to hold meaningful, formal hearings on issues that have qualified for the ballot. The legislature may then pass amendments to the initiative, or recommend amendments to the initiatives' sponsors, or pass the measure itself. Such review and amendment procedures provide an opportunity for the legislature to do its job—to assess public support, research the issue, gain input and expertise from interested parties, and perhaps pass a law. Other states have provisions for the indirect initiative, in which qualified measures must first be considered by the legislature. The measure goes to the ballot only if it fails to garner legislative support. Still other states allow the legislature to amend initiatives after they have passed. All of these provisions allow state legislatures, staffed with people who have the resources and expertise to decide complex issues of public policy, the opportunity to make laws that reflect both broad public sentiment and the concerns of intensely interested parties.

Table 1 reports provisions for pre- and postelection review and amendments for the 23 states that allow initiatives. California is one of 10 states that provide for pre-election legislative review, although it is unique in not also allowing pre-election legislative amendments. It is one of only two states that provides no provision for postelection legislative amendment.[4]

Several proposals for reforming the initiative have already been made and are likely to receive careful attention by the current California Constitution Revision Commission. Some of these proposals attempt to enhance the role of the legislature in the initiative process by allowing for some type of pre- or postelection review and amendment power. In general, I believe such reforms would greatly improve the California initiative process by allowing it to function more as a tool for making the legislature responsive to the public. In particular, I recommend that an en-

---

[4]Arizona's postelection legislative amendment restriction applies only to those measures that receive a majority of *all* registered voters. See California Commission on Campaign Financing, 1992. Since the inception of the initiative in Arizona, this has never happened. Therefore, in practice, California is the only state in which the legislature cannot itself amend initiatives.

The exception to this rule in California is that the legislature may amend initiatives *if explicitly permitted* in the measure's text. According to the California Commission on Campaign Financing, 1992, of the 55 initiatives that qualified for the California statewide ballot between 1976 and 1990, 38 contained such provisions. Most required supermajority votes. This possibility for amendment, however, is at the discretion of the initiative's sponsors and is absent from many substantively important initiatives.

Table 1. ***Provisions for Review and Amendments***

	Pre-election		Postelection		
State	Review	Amendment	No Restrictions	Waiting Period	Supermajority
AK	YES	YES	R	2YR*	NO
AZ	YES	NO	R	NO	NO
AR	NO	-	R	NO	2/3
CA	YES	NO	R	NO	NO
CO	NO	-	NR	NO	NO
FL	NO	-	R	NO	NO
ID	NO	-	NR	NO	NO
IL	NO	-	R	NO	NO
ME	YES	YES	NR	NO	NO
MA	YES	YES	NR	NO	NO
MI	YES	YES	R	NO	3/4
MO	NO	-	NR	NO	NO
MT	NO	-	NR	NO	NO
NE	NO	-	NR	NO	NO
NV	YES	YES	R	3YR	NO
ND	NO	-	R	7YR	2/3
OH	NO	-	NR	NO	NO
OK	NO	-	NR	NO	NO
OR	NO	-	NR	NO	NO
SD	NO	-	NR	NO	NO
UT	YES	YES	NR	NO	NO
WA	YES	YES	R	2YR	2/3
WY	YES	YES	R	2YR*	NO

Source: Philip Dubois and Floyd Feeney, *Improving the California Initiative Process* (Berkeley: California Policy Seminar, 1992).

*Waiting period applies to repeals only.

hanced pre-election legislative review and amendment procedure, coupled with a postelection legislative amendment, be adopted in California. Contrary to opponents of such a reform, I believe these proposed revisions will provide the legislature with the necessary incentives to participate in the policy process while still preserving an important agenda-setting role for the initiative.

BACKGROUND

The initiative was adopted in California in 1911 as one of several Progressive reforms. The Progressive movement in California was part of a nationwide reform movement at the beginning of the twentieth century. This reform movement was largely a reaction to the power of wealthy, big business and the uneven distribution of wealth caused by rapid industrialization.[5] The Progressives were mostly middle-class reformers whose political agenda focused on ways of reducing corruption and the influence of special interests in state and local government. In California, the Progressive reforms were directed at weakening the Southern Pacific Railroad's virtual usurpation of the state government. Accounts reveal that the railroad was literally able to buy their own representatives in the state assembly and effectively prevent the passage of popular government reform and regulatory legislation. The initiative in particular was intended to give a voice to the voting majority to pass these popular laws. Early advocates also argued that the initiative would provide a means for the passage of subsequent reforms. It was envisioned that the initiative would also empower regular people, making them better citizens. Hence, it was hoped that the initiative would lead to more representative laws.

Support for the initiative, however, was not universal. Early opponents feared that regular citizens were unfit for the challenges of lawmaking. Others argued that the initiative would lead to poorly written laws with many negative unintended consequences. They also argued that initiatives

---

[5]Literally hundreds of scholars have written about the sources of the Progressive movement. Most but not all would concur with this characterization. See Deverell and Sitton, 1994, for a recent treatment of the Progressive movement in California.

would deprive minorities of their rights and would undermine representative government.[6]

More than eight decades of experience has provided Californians with ample opportunity to observe and evaluate the effects of the initiative. Some consequences are clear. Political reforms such as state legislative term limits almost surely would not have been passed except by initiative. In fact, state legislative term limits laws have passed by popularly initiated measures in 16 states, while none have been passed by the state legislatures themselves. Other effects are less clear. Hence, reformers, commentators, and the public disagree about the net value of the initiative in modern California politics. Many of the same issues that led to the Progressive reforms, such as the power of special interests, are still important in the debate over the initiative today. Other concerns are new or are of much greater importance today than they were during the Progressive Era. Two of the most important issues in the current debate over the initiative are the problems of legislative accountability and legislative flexibility.

Legislative Accountability

Many opponents of the initiative argue that the initiative process reduces legislative accountability. Accountability refers to the ability of legislators to justify their actions and the concurrent ability of the electorate to hold legislators responsible for the content of policy. Thus, for legislators to be held accountable, they must be closely involved in the legislative process. In addition, citizens must be able to recognize this involvement in order to provide electoral rewards or punishments.

The initiative can reduce both components of legislative accountability. First, legislators in states that have initiatives can avoid participating in the policy process. Legislators know in advance when initiatives are likely to be proposed, especially on contentious issues or issues of great public interest. Legislators may find it easier to not take a firm position on such an issue and risk alienating important constituencies. They may opt simply to do nothing and "let the public decide." This is certainly not to say that every case of direct democracy represents an irresponsible abdication of

---

[6]See Cronin, 1989, for a history of the adoption of direct legislation, and Magleby, 1984, for a summary of arguments for and against the initiative.

legislative responsibility. Sometimes legislators sincerely believe that the public is better suited to decide some issues, such as raising taxes, issuing debt, or otherwise extracting resources from the public. Other times, however, legislators "embrace" direct democracy when legislative politics promises to be rancorous or personally damaging. The effects of such behavior for the long-term health of democracy are difficult to assess. One likely consequence is that, to the extent that such issues are framed in starker terms as initiatives, they may be more contentious and divisive in the electorate than in the legislature. Thus, the legislature fails to provide its moderating influence in finding points of agreement and compromise.

Recent experiences in California and several other states provide examples of legislative shirking leading to divisive electoral politics. Perhaps the most famous example is the controversy over tax relief in the 1970s that led to the passage of Proposition 13 of 1978. For years, the legislature failed to pass meaningful tax reform in the face of skyrocketing property taxes and public pressure. Voters responded with the draconian Prop. 13, and while the legislature finally passed some meaningful tax reform early in 1978, most observers (and voters) felt this was too little, too late.[7] A second illustration of legislative inaction leading to divisive initiative politics is in the area of automobile insurance reform. The legislature repeatedly failed to pass auto insurance reform legislation in the 1980s until finally consumers, the insurance industry, and trial lawyers took matters into their own hands with the introduction of Propositions 100, 101, 103, 104, and 106. Groups in recent years have also successfully used the initiative process to pass initiative legislation that restricts the civil rights and/or human rights of minority groups, rights that the state legislatures have been slow to protect. Perhaps the most salient example is California's Proposition 187 of 1994, which denies basic social services to a minority population of illegal immigrants. The anticipated California Civil Rights Initiative and antigay rights initiatives considered in Colorado, Idaho, and other states are further examples. Electoral politics on all of the issues have been divisive and stark, leading to conflict and bitterness among social groups. In each case, failure of the legislature to respond to increasing public pressure has resulted in costly, extreme, and divisive initiatives.

---

[7]See Sears and Citrin, 1982.

A second consequence of the initiative is that responsibility for policy outcomes is often ambiguous and dispersed. Especially in modern government with overlapping jurisdictions and multiple points of access into the political system, it can be very difficult for individuals to know who is responsible for policies. This becomes even more problematic when the voters themselves are passing laws. Citizens cannot electorally reward or punish lawmakers when they either cannot identify the lawmakers or are the lawmakers themselves.

The problem of legislative accountability is especially severe in the current California system. Legislators have neither the opportunity nor the incentive to participate in the initiative process or to pass laws themselves when they believe an initiative will be proposed. Citizens are deeply confused about the mechanics of the legislative process and about who is responsible for particular policies.

Legislative Flexibility

Other opponents of the initiative argue that the use of initiatives reduces policy flexibility. By flexibility, I mean the ability of policy actors to alter legislation that has unintended consequences, that is poorly written, or that ceases to attract popular support. When laws are made by initiative, the need for flexibility is greater, but the opportunities are few.

Initiative laws may be uniquely prone to containing unintended consequences. To insulate initiative laws from infringement or reversal by the legislature, the Progressive reformers designed the California initiative process to completely circumvent the legislative process, providing no provisions for the legislature to amend initiative legislation, except as permitted in the language of the initiatives. As a result, initiatives are uniquely permanent: the only way to amend an initiative in California is with another popular vote on an initiative or referendum or with a court decision. California is one of only two states with no provision for some type of legislative amendment.[8]

Experience with several recent initiatives clearly illustrates the problem of unintended consequences with laws that are difficult to amend. Initiatives such as Proposition 13 of 1978 have dramatically affected the

---

[8]See note above regarding Arizona.

entire system of state public finance and the distribution of wealth, beyond possible anticipation. Worse, many people believe the resulting effects on property values in particular have been unfair and inequitable, yet little opportunity exists for addressing those effects short of repealing the initiative with another initiative or referendum.

Closely related to this problem is the issue of poorly written laws. Many initiatives are written by citizens groups with little or no legislative experience. Unlike several other states that provide pre-election administrative or judicial review, qualified California initiatives go directly to the ballot. As a result, many of the laws passed by California voters have either been hung up in costly court battles for many years, struck down in court for technical reasons, or stripped of some important but poorly written provisions. With the professionalization of the California initiative process in recent years and the involvement of professional campaign consultants, "errors" in writing initiatives may be more rare. However, even with experienced initiative drafters, the nature of the initiative process is such that initiative propositions are typically not subjected to the extensive writing and rewriting that occurs in the legislative markup process.

These concerns—legislative accountability and legislative flexibility—are widely held; they come both from people who argue that the initiative produces favorable policy outcomes and should be strengthened, and from those who argue that the initiative has mainly detrimental consequences and should be weakened. A common solution to all of these concerns is a greater role for the legislature. Several studies and individuals have proposed specific reforms that provide for a more active role for the legislature in the initiative process.[9] These reforms range from a relatively minor increase in the legislature's involvement to a rather large increase. I propose a revision to the California initiative process below that directly addresses the problems of legislative accountability and legislative flexibility. I then compare my recommendation with the four major reform proposals currently under consideration.

---

[9]The four major reform proposals that have received a great deal of attention are Dubois and Feeney, "Improving the California Initiative Process"; California Commission on Campaign Financing, "Democracy By Initiative"; Citizen's Commission on Ballot Initiatives, "Report and Recommendations"; and Costa, SCA 22, 1995.

RECOMMENDATION

I believe there is a pressing need to more closely involve the legislature in the California initiative process. I recommend that California adopt reforms to its initiative process with the following features. The sequence of events under the proposed reform is represented in Figure 1. In the figure, the first stage of the initiative process (qualification of the initiative) is denoted at the far left of the tree, and the process proceeds to the right. Each branch in the tree represents a choice or "path" down which the process may proceed.

- Mandatory pre-election legislative review and recorded vote (with possibility for legislative amendments).
- Pre-election legislative amendments, either technical or substantive.
- Postelection legislative amendments subject to:
  - 3 year waiting period for measures passed by the legislature;
  - 5 year waiting period for measures passed by voters.

Under this reform, the legislature is required to review and vote on all qualified initiatives. After an initiative receives a required number of signatures, equal to 5 percent of the turnout for the last gubernatorial vote, the legislature is obliged to hold hearings to evaluate the initiative. The legislature must then take a recorded vote on either the original legislation (subject to minor "technical" changes) or an amended but related version of the legislation. A nonlegislative body such as the state attorney general's office will determine whether the legislature's measure is consistent with the "intents and purposes" of the original initiative or whether it represents an amendment to the legislation.

If the legislature passes the original initiative (and it is signed by the governor), the measure is automatically removed from the ballot. The initiative then becomes more like regular legislation; that is, the legislature can amend the law in the future. Thus, if there are unfavorable unintended consequences, or if support for the policy subsides, the legislature can modify or eliminate the measure. I recommend a three-year waiting period during which time legislation that the legislature passes as a result of the initiative process cannot be amended. This will prevent the legislature from immediately stripping the measure of its original intent and will allow sufficient time for the consequences of the legislation to become known.

Figure 1. *Sequence of Events Under Proposed Reforms*

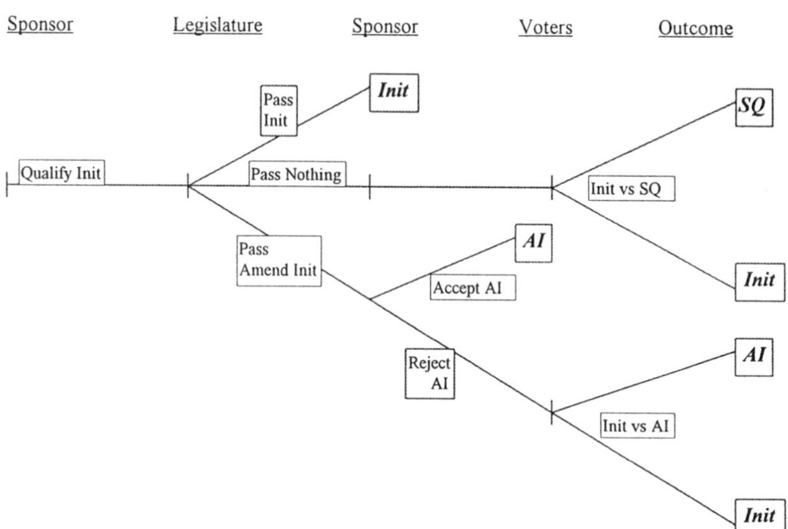

After the waiting period, the legislature can then amend or repeal the legislation with a simple majority vote, according to its established procedures.

If the legislature fails to pass either the original initiative or an amended version, or if the governor vetoes the legislation, the initiative remains on the ballot as under the current system. The primary difference is that the result of the roll call vote is reported in the official ballot pamphlet. A similar practice is currently used for statutes or constitutional amendments placed on the ballot by the legislature. In the current ballot pamphlet, however, only the aggregate vote totals are reported, whereas under the proposed reform, the ballot pamphlet will report each individual legislator's vote.

If the legislature passes an amended version of the initiative, the initiative's sponsor has the option of withdrawing the original initiative or leaving it on the ballot. From the sponsor's perspective, settling for the amended version of the initiative passed by the legislature may be preferable to waging an expensive campaign for a marginally preferred initiative. However, an important component of this recommended reform is to retain this as the sponsor's choice. Then, if the legislature makes changes that are contrary to the sponsor's intent, there is still a non-legislative means for pursuing the policy.

Three possible outcomes may result from this last option. First, the initiative's sponsor accepts the amended initiative and withdraws the original initiative, in which case the legislature's amended version remains the law. This law is subject to the same three year waiting period and simple majority amendability as when the legislature passes the original initiative. Second, the sponsor leaves the original initiative on the ballot but the initiative fails to win a majority vote in the election. In this case, the vote is now effectively between the original initiative and the amended version passed by the legislature. Again, the legislature's amended version remains the law, subject to the waiting period and amendability described above. Third, the sponsor leaves the original initiative on the ballot and the initiative wins. In this case, since the electorate decisively chose the initiative over the legislature's alternative, I recommend a longer waiting period of five years, after which the initiative is subject to legislative amendment by a majority vote. In this third case, the longer waiting period is included for two reasons: it provides an incentive for the legislature to pass the law, since it is amendable sooner; and it protects measures that have broad public support from immediate amendment or repeal by the legislature.

In all cases, initiative sponsors or other actors are permitted to requalify an initiative after the three- or five-year waiting period to prolong its immunity from legislative amendment. The sponsor must again gather the required number of signatures for qualification. In many cases, however, this will be easier the second or subsequent times, since the original organizational and fundraising apparatus may still be in place.

Note that the proposed reform applies strictly to statutory initiatives. In California, like many other initiative states, policy advocates may also pursue their policy agendas through initiative constitutional amendments. By making statutory initiatives less permanent (and therefore less valuable) through the current reform, there is the possibility that interest groups will simply shift their efforts to initiative constitutional amendments. This situation is undesirable for several reasons. First, the substitution of initiative constitutional amendments for initiative statutes undermines the intentions of the current reform by making policy less flexible and removing the legislature from the process. Second, the excessive use of constitutional amendments for statutory purposes is contrary to legal principles of state constitutions. Therefore, I recommend simultaneously reforming the initiative constitutional amendment process by requiring 60 percent of the votes cast on that measure for passage. The electoral supermajority requirement clearly makes it harder to pass initiative constitutional amendments and reduces their relative attractiveness as ways of circumventing the initiative process. It also addresses the problem of constitutional hyper-amendability, independent of the effects on statutory initiatives.[10]

CONSEQUENCES

This proposed reform provides several incentives for the legislature to play an active role in the initiative process. First, by requiring the legislature to vote on all qualified initiatives, the legislature can directly affect the content of popularly initiated laws. In fact, since each legislator's roll call vote is published in the voter information pamphlet, the ability to take credit for legislation is improved, making the review process potentially more valuable for the legislators. Second, by allowing legislative amendments to popularly initiated measures passed by either the legislature or the electorate, the legislature is no longer written out of the policy process on legislation that results from the initiative process. Third, by making it easier to amend those measures originally passed by the legislature, the legislature can buy increased future flexibility by entering into the process early. In all of these respects, the proposed reform provides incentives for the legislature to take primary lawmaking responsibility while still allowing citizens and interest groups to use the initiative process to force issues onto the legislative agenda.

---

[10]An alternative proposal is to subject constitutional initiatives to the same legislative review and amendment as statutory initiatives, perhaps with a legislative supermajority vote requirement. Such a reform would mitigate the relative advantage of constitutional initiatives. However, many argue that there are some issues that should be exempt from legislative revisions such as issues relating to the structure of government and broad "constitutional" principles. Under the alternative proposal, there is no means for protecting these constitutional issues from legislative amendment. Under the original reform proposed here, the constitutional initiative would effectively be reserved for such issues.

From an accountability perspective, requiring the legislature to vote on all qualified initiatives forces legislators to take the review process seriously. Under the proposed reform, legislators must take positions on all initiative measures and be prepared to defend their actions. These positions are reported in the official ballot pamphlet, which is readily accessible to both voters and the media. To the extent that citizens hold legislators electorally accountable for their positions, forcing them to take positions and reporting those positions to voters may increase legislative accountability.

From a technical perspective, providing the legislature with the power to review, amend, and adopt initiatives before the election means that it may be more likely to detect and fix technical problems with initiative legislation. Legislators often have knowledge and experience with legislation similar to the laws contained in ballot propositions. They may therefore be able to anticipate problems with laws even before they are enacted. Further, when the legislature is an important player in the initiative process, it may gain information from experts and interested parties regarding the likely consequences of aspects of an initiative. Simply having the opportunity to scrutinize initiative proposals may bring to light technical flaws in initiative legislation. It is also important, however, that the legislature can act on their information—purely advisory reviews provide few incentives for the legislature to take the review process seriously or for other actors to abide by the legislature's recommendations.

Providing the legislature with the opportunity to amend and pass propositions before the election may also have the effect of encouraging initiative sponsors to write better laws in the first place. Although it is difficult to infer precisely an initiative sponsors' motives, many observers argue that sponsors intentionally include technically unsound but popular provisions in their initiatives. An example is Proposition 103, which included a popular but infeasible (and perhaps unconstitutional) provision to mandate lower auto insurance rates for many drivers. Whether or not the authors of Proposition 103 knew that such a provision would be impossible to enforce, it is nevertheless likely that pre-election legislative review would have led to that clause being identified and perhaps modified or removed. It is also possible that the authors may have anticipated a legislative review and reworked that problematic provision before ever qualifying the initiative.

The proposed reform may have other consequences as well. From a representational perspective, involving the legislature in the initiative process increases the potential for a broader set of interests to be represented in initiative policies. By design, the legislature embodies the aggregation of preferences and interests across a wide range of groups. Each individual legislator must cultivate support from many types of constituents (both voters and financial contributors) to win and keep his or her seat; and each legislative coalition must respond to the interests of its many members to keep the coalition together. By contrast, interest groups and other initiative sponsors tend to represent a much narrower set of interests.

Forcing the legislature to review, possibly amend, and vote on each qualified initiative ensures that a broader set of interests will be reflected in the ultimate policy. This may be important for protecting the rights of minorities. That is, an initiative sponsor and the majority of voters may prefer an initiative that severely harms some minority group. Given the nature of the initiative process, with a binary policy agenda and majority rule voting, there is little opportunity for the minority to protect its own interests through the initiative. By involving the legislature, those minority groups gain access to the policy agenda and at least have the opportunity to make their case.[11]

This form of legislative review may also be important for reducing the power of special interests. In the initiative process as it currently exists, interest groups have exclusive power to set the policy agenda once the legislature has established its own position. This means that initiative sponsors may place on the ballot measures that diverge significantly from the policy ideally preferred by a majority of voters, but that are still preferred to the status quo. The legislature may be able to amend the initiative in a way that makes the majority of voters better off than under the original initiative.

---

[11]The other side of this coin, however, is that including a broader set of interests through the legislative process may result in "fatter" bills that contain benefits for more groups.

COMPARISON WITH EXISTING PROPOSALS

Certainly, this is not the first proposal to recommend an increased role for the legislature in the initiative process through more meaningful legislative review and amendment powers. At least four other reform proposals are known to the author: two published reports, one citizen's commission report, and one pending legislative constitutional amendment. Each of these proposals share important features with my proposal.[12] I believe my proposal, however, provides the most coherent set of reforms that most directly address the constitutional principles of increasing legislative accountability and flexibility. I briefly describe the legislative review and amendment provisions of the four proposals below, emphasizing the features that differ from my proposal.

Dubois and Feeney Proposal

The Dubois and Feeney proposal is contained in their 1992 California Policy Seminar Report, *Improving the California Initiative Process: Options for Change*. The pre-election review and amendment provisions of this proposal are quite limited relative to my proposal, restricted to amendments by the legislature and limited to the intents and purposes of the original initiative. Incentives for the legislature to take an early active role in the policy process are therefore weaker: the roll call vote is not mandatory; results of the roll call, if taken, are not necessarily made public; and the legislature can amend any legislation resulting from the initiative process, whether it is passed by the legislature or the electorate. The postelection review and amendment powers, conversely, are substantial. The Dubois and Feeney proposal recommends unlimited postelection legislative amendments, both to amend the legislation (not restricted to the original intents and purposes) and to repeal the legislation entirely. Further, there are no requirements for a waiting period or supermajority vote or other restrictions on the legislative amendment. Such unrestricted

[12]Most of these proposals also make other recommendations besides enhancing the power of legislative review and amendment.

Table 2. *Comparison of Reform Proposals*

Provision	SQ	**Gerber**	SCA22	Citizen's	CCCF	D&F
	Reform Proposal					
Mandatory Pre-election Legislative Review	YES	**YES**	YES	YES	YES	NO
Mandatory Roll Call Vote	NO	**YES**	NO	YES	YES	NO
Roll Call Results in Voter Pamphlet	NO	**YES**	NO	NO	YES	NO
Pre-election Sponsor Amendment (I & P)	NO	**NO**	YES	YES	YES	NO
Pre-election Legislative Amendment (I & P)	NO	**YES**	YES	YES	YES	YES
Pre-election Legislative Amendment (Not I &P)	NO	**YES**	YES	YES	YES	YES
Pre-election Legislative Amendment (Not I &P) Subject to Sponsor's OK	NO	**NO**	YES	YES	YES	NO
Postelection Legislative Amendment (I &P)	NO	**YES**	YES	YES	YES	YES
Postelection Legislative Amendment (Not I & P)	NO	**YES**	NO	NO	NO	YES
Postelection Legislative Repeal	NO	**YES**	NO	NO	NO	YES
Supermajority for Post-election Legis. Amend.	NO	**NO**	NO	YES	YES	NO
Waiting Period for Post-election Legis. Amend.	NO	**YES**	NO	YES	NO	NO
Graduated Waiting Period	NO	**YES**	NO	NO	NO	NO

amendment power will no doubt increase flexibility. It will likely do so, however, at the expense of undermining any real power to use the initiative to force the legislature to respond to citizens and interest groups.

California Commission on Campaign Financing Proposal

The California Commission on Campaign Financing proposal (hereafter referred to as "CCCF") is contained in its 1992 report *Democracy By Initiative: Shaping California's Fourth Branch of Government*. By comparison to the Dubois and Feeney proposal, the CCCF proposal recommends greatly expanded pre-election review and amendment powers, including a mandatory pre-election legislative review; mandatory roll call vote; pre-election amendments by either the sponsor or the legislature (limited to the initiative's intents and purposes); and pre-election legislative amendments not restricted to the initiative's intents and purposes, subject to the sponsor's approval. The CCCF's pre-election review and amendment provisions are nearly identical to those in my proposal, except that I do not restrict legislative amendments that conflict with the initiative's intents and purposes to those approved by the sponsor. Such a restriction, I argue, unduly empowers the initiative's sponsor, who is neither elected nor otherwise accountable to the people, to bargain and make deals with the legislature. Rather, in my proposal, the majority of voters effectively mediates disagreements between the legislature and the initiative's sponsor by choosing between their respective proposals.

The CCCF's postelection amendment provisions, by contrast, are quite limited. The CCCF recommends only postelection legislative amendments restricted to the initiative's original intents and purposes, with a 60 percent supermajority required for such amendments. It prohibits legislative amendments that conflict with the initiative's intents and purposes, or that entirely repeal the initiative. These provisions, while allowing the legislature to make technical improvements to the measures passed through the initiative process, do not provide the means for legislative flexibility as in my proposal.

Citizen's Commission Proposal

The Citizen's Commission proposal is nearly identical to the CCCF's proposal. It recommends strong pre-election review and amendment powers, with amendments restricted to the initiative's intents and purposes and/or the sponsor's approval. It also recommends limited postelection legislative amendment power, restricted to the initiative's intents and purposes. In addition to a two-thirds supermajority, legislative amendments are prohibited within the first three years after enactment. Thus, legislative flexibility through postelection amendments is even further reduced.

SCA 22

SCA 22 is a legislative constitutional amendment co-authored by state Senators Costa and Kopp. The bill was introduced in March 1995, and at the time of this writing, is still under committee consideration. The measure's pre-election review and amendment provisions are similar to those in my proposal, as well as those advocated by the CCCF and the Citizen's Commission, except that the roll call vote is not mandatory. While this provision at first appears rather innocuous, it raises the strong possibility of fundamentally undermining the benefits of increased accountability by allowing legislators to opt out of the pre-election review process. Like the other proposals (but in contrast to mine), SCA 22 limits legislative amendments that conflict with the initiative's intents and purposes to those approved by the initiative's sponsor. Again, this limitation means that legislators have little opportunity to join in the pre-election agenda setting phase in a meaningful way. Finally, SCA 22's provisions for postelection legislative amendments are limited to the initiative's intents and purposes. There is, however, no check such as a supermajority requirement or waiting period for such amendments. Thus, technical amendments will be relatively easy, but legislative flexibility will be enhanced only in a very limited way.

CONCLUSION

The reform proposed in this chapter addresses several pressing problems with the contemporary California initiative process. By providing the legislature with a meaningful opportunity to scrutinize and amend initiative propositions, the reformed initiative process is expected to increase legislative involvement in the initiative process and therefore to increase accountability. The proposed reform will also improve policy flexibility by reducing the probability of poorly written laws or laws with unforeseen and unintended consequences, and by providing the legislature with a means for improving and updating legislation. The expected increase in the legislature's power, however, is limited. Under most plausible circumstances, the legislature is severely constrained in its ability to take the bite out of initiative legislation. While the legislature may be able to pass policies that it prefers to proposed initiatives, this will usually only be the case when the legislature's interests are similar to those of the majority of the electorate. In this sense, the proposed reform improves the representation of the voting majority.

The proposed reform contains several familiar elements that have been proposed in other reports and recommendations. Why, then, have these sorts of reforms not already been adopted? One reason is that special interests who have successfully used the initiative process to their advantage oppose such reforms. These groups often have vast resources at their disposal to block such reform efforts, either explicitly or implicitly. In general, greater involvement by the legislature reduces the relative power of special interests to make policy by initiative. At a minimum, special interests must compete with the legislature for majority voter support. This implies a much more complex game between special interests, the legislature, and citizens. In such a game, special interests may lose out, but the ultimate winners are the majority of citizens (or at least voters). It should also be noted that the specific reforms proposed here retain an important role for special interests. This role, however, is more one of agenda-setting, rather than lawmaking per se.

A second reason such reforms are yet to be adopted is that citizens may be suspicious of reforms that increase the power of the legislature. Throughout American history, there has been a widespread distrust of governmental power, especially legislative power. This distrust lay at the base of many of the Progressive Era reforms such as the initiative. Supporters of a strong initiative process fear that involving the legislature in the initiative process will reduce their ability to protect their own interests via initiatives. There are several reasons to discount this objection. Multiple safeguards are built into the proposed reform to guard against legislative dominance. By retaining the sponsor's option of leaving the original initiative on the ballot, the legislature is prevented from substituting the original initiative with unrelated legislation or legislation opposed by the initiative's sponsor. Furthermore, by imposing the three- or five-year waiting period for legislative amendments, the legislature is prevented from immediately reversing legislation introduced through the initiative process. Each of these provisions is intended to protect the right of the people to make laws by initiative and to prevent the legislature from stripping that legislation of important components. The increased power of the legislature under this reform is, indeed, quite limited.

While each provision of the reform package is important in and of itself, it is critical that readers and reformers consider the current reform as a coherent package that together will achieve the purposes of increasing legislative accountability and policy flexibility. The danger of political reform in general, and of considering elements of this proposal in particular, is that individual components of a reform package, taken alone or out of context, often fail to accomplish their intended objective. Indeed, picking and choosing elements of a reform package and discarding other components is likely to produce a reform with perverse effects that fails to address the very problems it is designed to solve.

California can learn from the different ways the initiative process is used in other states. States that have legislative review and amendment powers similar to those proposed here seem to have fewer problems with legislative accountability and policy flexibility. This is not to say, however, that California should adopt wholesale the initiative process as it is used in other states. California is unique in terms of its sheer size and the diversity of its people, its history, culture, and economic composition. This texture is reflected in the state's political institutions and customs. The way the initiative process is used in California however, is atypical and uniquely antagonistic towards the legislature. California has much to learn from other states about how to make both the initiative process and the legislative process work better.

REFERENCES

Butler, David, and Austin Ranney. 1994. *Referendums Around the World.* Washington, D.C.: American Enterprise Institute.

California Commission on Campaign Financing. 1992. *Democracy By Initiative: Shaping California's Fourth Branch of Government.* Los Angeles: Center for Responsive Government.

California Secretary of State. Selected years. *Statement of the Vote.*

Citizen's Commission on Ballot Initiatives. 1994. *Report and Recommendations.*

Cronin, Thomas E. 1989. *Direct Democracy: The Politics of Initiative, Referendum, and Recall.* Cambridge: Harvard University Press.

Deverell, William, and Tom Sitton. 1994. *California Progressivism Revisited.* Berkeley: University of California Press.

Dubois, Philip L., and Floyd F. Feeney. 1992. *Improving the California Initiative Process: Options for Change.* Berkeley: California Policy Seminar, University of California.

Magleby, David. 1984. *Direct Legislation: Voting on Ballot Propositions in the United States.* Baltimore: Johns Hopkins University Press.

Sears, David O., and Jack Citrin. 1982. *Tax Revolt: Something for Nothing in California.* Cambridge: Harvard University Press.

Senate Constitutional Amendment 22. 1995. California State Senate.

Reforming the Initiative Process

John Ferejohn

INTRODUCTION

It is dangerous to tamper with the initiative process. Public interest groups and the press are always ready to discredit attempts to weaken or limit the initiative process through the usual means (increasing signature requirements, limiting the topics that can be included in initiatives, and the like). Such efforts bear the marks of self interest so clearly as to arouse immediate suspicions no matter what their merits. "Of course elected politicians want to limit the effects of the initiative," so the complaint goes, "it is in their interest to do so." The gingerly handling of Proposition 13 by elected officials is testimony to the general fear in Sacramento of fooling around with the initiative process. Following the passage of a particularly troubling initiative, elected officials must simply resign themselves to prayer that (elected) state or federal judges will undertake to limit or overturn the measure. Lacking judicial relief, they can only resort to hand wringing and abstract complaints about the process; direct attempts to modify the people's judgment are generally doomed to failure.

Reforming the initiative process can be politically dangerous because such attempts often appear to be undemocratic and high handed. The initiative seems so obviously democratic and self-justifying, that those who would limit it appear to be self seeking, corrupt, arrogant or simply out of touch with the people. Such attempts appear, at best, to be "counter-majoritarian," in urging that limits be placed on majority judgments. And, there is little question that many of those who would reform or limit the initiative would do so on explicitly antidemocratic grounds. When Judge Linde urged that the federal constitution's "Guarantee Clause" be used to strike down the anti Gay Rights initiative in Oregon, he based his argument on the claim that the initiative in such cases was not consistent with

---

I wish to thank Tino Cuellar for helpful comments and assistance.

"republican" deliberative norms.[1] The federal Constitution's guarantee clause, according to Linde, was designed to protect citizens of the states against direct democracy as well as against a re-imposition of monarchy. No matter how meritorious, such arguments are bound to appear high handed and arrogant to those who distrust public officials and are unlikely to be politically attractive grounds for reform.

Indeed, the initiative, while certainly the most prominent intrusion of direct democracy into state government, is not alone. Recall and referendum and the election of state and local judges are all majoritarian processes, animated by the same populist spirit. Each rests on a background of suspicion of professional politicians who the public thinks are prone to be isolated from their constituents and captured by special interests. Because each of these institutions are justified by the popular fear that their representatives will be captured, people distrust reform proposals originating in Sacramento. In view of these perceptions it is easy to think that there is simply no place to stand, within a democratic conception of public life, that permits reform of any of the institutions of direct democracy.[2]

This diagnosis is badly misconceived. It rests on the idea—the misconception—that because initiative, recall, and referendum provisions have the purpose of increasing influence of popular opinion on public policy they actually have these effects. This turns out to require argument and such argument is hard to provide. Like representative institutions, institutions of direct democracy are corruptible by interest groups. The forms this corruption takes vary with the specific institution, but there should be no doubt that groups with resources can use the rules of direct democracy to their advantage just as they can use legislative rules. There is simply no guarantee that the use of such institutions, by themselves, will produce policy that is more popular or majoritarian than that which emerges from the ordinary legislative process. This does not mean we

---

[1]Hans A. Linde, "When Initiative Lawmaking is Not 'Republican Government': The Campaign Against Homosexuality," *Oregon Law Review*, vol. 72 (1993): 10-36.

[2]Proposals to invalidate initiatives on account of their subject matter are among the franker judicial techniques for limiting their effects. Various states have created interpretive doctrines that construe initiatives narrowly, or have been ready to find them unconstitutional on various grounds.

should abandon populist practices. Rather, it suggests we try to reform or perfect them to improve their *democratic* performance. Such reforms, like reforms of the legislative process, must rest on a theory of democratic government that permits us to see how institutional reforms will actually work. It is possible to construct a plausible democratic theory within which the initiative process—at least as practiced in California and other states—is defective on purely *democratic* grounds. The theory may not completely specify exactly how to reform the initiative process to improve its democratic character but it will open up a space for legitimate debate and discussion. And it will permit us to suggest some general directions for reform.

The simple democratic theory presented here allows us to consider three characteristic kinds of reform of the initiative process, each of which has the potential for improving its performance as a democratic institution: first, the use of supermajority rules for approving initiatives; second, increasing the signature requirements for ballot access; and, third, permitting amendments to initiative proposals. All three of these ideas would, in theory, have the effect of making the initiative a more effective and responsive democratic instrument. All three fit the majoritarian spirit in our state constitutional traditions. All three are conceivable, and therefore, salable to "We the People" as genuinely democratic reforms that would improve the responsiveness of state governments in ways that Californians seem to want.

The problem is that, for various reasons, none of the three theoretically attractive reforms seems practical. The first two—the imposition of supermajority requirements and increasing the signature requirement—would appear as blatant efforts to diminish the majoritarian force of the initiative even though their effects would be to increase it. The third would seem to dilute the wishes of the initiative sponsors. There is, however, a simple modification of current initiative law that contains aspects of each of the three reform ideas. It is the following: once an initiative has been qualified for inclusion on the ballot according to the current signature requirements, new initiative proposals on the same subject should be subjected to a substantially *lower* signature requirement to go on the ballot. This proposal would stimulate a deliberative process within the electorate by encouraging open competition among interest groups. It should improve the democratic performance of the initiative

process by reducing the prospects for interest group capture of the initiative and increasing the chance that majority preferences prevail.

TWO CONSTITUTIONAL TRADITIONS: FEDERAL AND STATE CONSTITUTIONAL POLITICS

There are two very different constitutional traditions in the United States. One, by far the more familiar to most Americans, is found at the federal level and is centered around the relatively brief, seldom amended federal Constitution. The federal Constitution stands almost alone among world constitutions in its simplicity and flexibility in changing political circumstances. Whether because of the difficulty of constitutional amendment under the Article V procedures or because, as Madison hoped, Americans have come to venerate their Constitution and are loathe to undermine its elegant formulations, the federal Constitution has evolved exceedingly slowly and the character of constitutional law has taken on the character of a "higher" law that commands a different kind of respect than mere statutory rules.[3]

At the state level, things are completely different. Unlike the stringent Article V procedures in the federal Constitution, state constitutions are easily amended, often by majoritarian processes within the legislature or the electorate. As a result state constitutions are not only frequently amended, they are sometimes replaced altogether. Indeed, over the course of their histories, most states have had three separate constitutions.[4] The relative ease of amendment also means that the sharp line between constitutional and statutory law and politics at the federal level is much more blurred in the states.

Theoretically, the federal Constitution can be understood as an attempt to address certain characteristic weaknesses in a liberal state, principally, the problems of faction, majority tyranny, and the corruption of public officials. Madison's defense of an extended and compound republic (in Federalist #10) and the structure of checks and balances (defended in #51) do not merely stand as justifications of the structure of the national

---

[3]Bruce Ackerman, *We The People* (Cambridge: Harvard Press, 1991).

[4]Donald Lutz, "Toward a Theory of Constitutional Amendment," in *Responding to Imperfection: The Theory and Practice of Constitutional Amendment*, ed. Sanford Levinson (Princeton: Princeton University Press, 1995), 237-74.

government, they serve as a diagnosis of the ills that would likely plague a large liberal state and as formulas for future attempts at reform. Madison and the other founders expected future constitutional politics to be guided by the kinds of solutions they built into the structure of the federal Constitution—principally, the use of checks and balances to oppose tyranny.

While many citizens, when (if ever) they first learn about state constitutions, are dismayed by the confusion and disorder of state constitutional politics, it is important to understand that state constitutional practices are rooted as deeply in American political life as federal ones are. If federal constitutional politics may be termed Madisonian in its emphasis on checks and balances and on the creation of an extended and compound republic, state traditions fit the Jeffersonian tradition of small governments kept close to the people and open to new ideas and participants. While Madison fought for a powerful national government that would attract talented and virtuous leaders, governed by balanced constitutional structure in order to prevent the development of tyranny, Jefferson's preferred solution was to emphasize majority control of small governments—short terms of office, frequent elections, elected judges, and the like—in the belief that constitutional defects would be eliminated by an attentive and vigilant electorate. It is important to see that both traditions are based on a suspicion of officials, but that each has generated its own characteristic techniques of control and its own preferred pathway to reform.

Although Jeffersonian tradition may be traced back to the establishment of most state governments, Progressive Era reforms introduced new institutional mechanisms that fit well within this tradition. From the standpoint of state government, the most important of these mechanisms are the referendum, the recall and, above all, the popular initiative. The initiative is particularly interesting in that it opens a route to lawmaking that avoids the legislature altogether and whatever deliberative practices and institutions the legislature has evolved, while it permits the people directly to enact constitutional provisions as well as ordinary legislation. It is difficult to conceive of any institution more Jeffersonian in its aspirations. Initiatives are, in the most direct sense, the unmediated commands of the people and would seem to have a stronger claim to respect than ordinary legislation. Initiatives are, in Ackerman's expression, "We the People" directly expressing their desires and aspirations.

A DEMOCRATIC THEORY FOR REFORMING THE INITIATIVE

Both the federal and state constitutional traditions envision the possibility of tyranny or corruption, and reform attempts in both traditions are best understood as efforts to alleviate this possibility. The initiative, in this view, is an attempt to address the possibility (or likelihood) that elected officials might lose touch with the people or be captured by special interests.[5] In cases where popular sentiment is very different from that of elected politicians, the initiative permits the people to intervene directly in the political process and directly draft laws they want. Because it is difficult to mobilize the electorate even in a popular cause and because elected politicians meet all the time, popular pronouncements should be made hard to amend by giving them constitutional status. Thus the initiative supplements ordinary lawmaking, permitting a regular form of "higher lawmaking" by resorting to the people. That is the theory anyhow.

Like any institution, however, the initiative process has its own peculiar operating characteristics. While its intended purpose might be to cure a problem of corruption or capture, it is not obvious that it succeeds in this purpose. Traditional criticisms of the initiative point to its characteristic institutional defect: unlike the legislative process, the initiative is not deliberative.[6] Ordinary citizens simply do not have the time or attention span to focus on complex political issues and their judgment is likely to be erratic and capricious, swayed by momentary passions and prejudices.[7] For the same reason, it is relatively easy for well-funded

---

[5]This motivation is especially clear in California where a chief motivation for the adoption of the initiative process was to break the control of lobbyists of the Southern Pacific Railroad over the state legislature.

[6]"One problem is that voters are not permitted to vote on alternate bills; another is that voters cannot attempt to amend the proposed legislation to make it more acceptable. An additional problem is that voters are limited to an affirmative vote, a negative vote, or an abstention. Because of the way in which propositions are worded, voters often must choose the least inaccurate expression of their opinion." David Magleby, *Direct Legislation* (Baltimore: Johns Hopkins University Press, 1984), 183.

[7]"By their nature, referendum campaigns appeal to passions and prejudices, spotlight tensions, and may foster even greater conflict and disagreement. This has

interests to manipulate information to their advantage and thereby to corrupt the process. Moreover, even in the absence of corruption, the initiative process is poorly suited to make complex policy trade-offs of the kind often required by modern government.[8] Initiatives are characteristically likely to produce bad policy because they are overwhelmed by passions, corrupt, or merely inapt.

While each of these criticisms is valid, they do not furnish useful advice for reform. If problems with the initiative all stem from its institutional features, then the way to fix it would be either to correct these basic features, or to limit its bad effects (à la Madison). Proposals of the first kind, which aim to make direct democracy more deliberative by making citizens more informed and responsible, are vulnerable to charges of utopianism. Proposals of the second kind, which usually aim to limit the use of the initiative to safe issues or to make it harder to use, appear to be elitist and antidemocratic.

By making use of recent advances in the positive theory of politics, we can understand the defects of the initiative in another way. Initiatives are essentially take-it-or-leave-it offers to the electorate.[9] Either a majority of voters approves the specific wording of the initiative or the *status quo ante* prevails. This feature of an initiative resembles the "closed rule" procedure occasionally used in legislatures, in which a person or committee gets to propose a bill that cannot be amended.[10] Such rules are rarely used

---

been the case in referendums involving race relations and the rights of homosexuals. . . . The tendency for majority passions to be excited against unpopular minorities is a real danger of expanded use of the initiative, as evidenced by Colorado's 1992 Amendment Two, which called for "no protected status" to be given to homosexuals." David Magleby, "Governing by Initiative: Let the Voters Decide?" *Colorado Law Review,* vol. 66 (1995): 44.

[8]In a recent article, Magleby writes, "The very nature of the initiative is to ask voters to make "temporary" and "partial" considerations. A voter is asked, for instance, to raise or lower taxes without regard for what programs will be cut as a result. Legislators, on the other hand, are more likely to confront the trade-offs and implications of any given policy question." *ibid.* 20.

[9]The California Constitution provides for "the power of the electors to propose statutes and amendments to the constitution and to adopt or reject them." Art. II, @ 8(a).

[10]Article. II, @ 10(c) of the California Constitution says that the legislators can only amend a statutory initiative if they have the voters' permission (in the

because members of legislatures appreciate the potential for abuse, but they are employed in the House of Representatives to consider tax and tariff bills. But, as Keith Krehbiel has emphasized, those legislative committees that are able to obtain closed rules (the House Ways and Means committee, to take the most prominent example) are quite representative of their parent chamber.[11] Because the committee is representative of the parent chamber it is unlikely to make an opportunistic proposal to the chamber under a closed rule, *which is why the legislature is willing to consider the legislation under a closed rule.*[12] In the case of the initiative there is no such assurance: there is no reason to believe that the proposers of an amendment are representative of the electorate as a whole. Indeed, there are good reasons to doubt this will be the case.

To appreciate the nature of the problem, it is helpful to introduce a simple model of an electorate that is to choose a policy of some kind through an initiative. Suppose the set of possible policies may be arrayed along a line, where M represents the most preferred policy of the "median" voter—the voter who has exactly half the electorate on each side. Suppose, further, that each voter (including the median) prefers policies closer to her most preferred policy to those further away. In this case, it is easy to see that policy M, the preferred policy of the median voter, would defeat each other policy in a majority vote. Policy M is, thus, the preferred outcome of this electorate under majority rule. Now suppose there is already a policy Q in place that will continue to be governmental policy unless the electorate votes to introduce a new policy. Figure 1 represents this simple situation.

Under the rules for the initiative, we may suppose that someone is able to qualify policy proposal y for the ballot and that there will be competition for the right to place such a proposal on the ballot. Consider what would happen for each possible policy proposal. If y is to the left of Q, it would

---

initiative itself) or subject to referendum approval.

[11]Keith Krehbiel, *Information and Legislative Organization* (Ann Arbor: University of Michigan Press, 1991).

[12]Krehbiel also points out that the House does not provide a rule before seeing the actual legislative proposal. It does not give a procedural "blank check" to the proposers to fill in as they see fit.

Figure 1

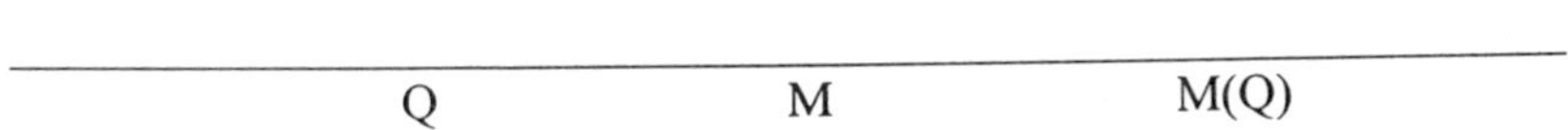

certainly lose in the balloting. This is because half of the voters are to the right of M and all of them prefer Q to y, as does the median voter and this is enough to defeat y. If y is between Q and M, y will defeat Q by the same logic. If y is to the right of M but is closer to M than Q is, it will also defeat Q in a majority vote. But if y is further right than this position, M(Q), it will not pass. Thus, the only proposals that could defeat the status quo lie between Q and M(Q).

The important result of the analysis is this: if the status quo is different from the preference of the median voter, *there is no reason to think that the outcome of the initiative process will be the majority preferred outcome.* The result of the process depends on who makes proposals and, at present, we do not have a theory telling us who is likely to take advantage of the opportunity presented by the initiative process. Though one could easily spin out such theories—and various forms of "capture theory" have been proposed as hypotheses as to who ends up proposing initiatives—we do not need to commit ourselves to any particular theory to make our argument.

What opportunities exist to improve the performance of the initiative process? The first possibility would be a direct attack on the take-it-or-leave-it aspect of initiatives. If initiatives could be freely amended or if the process could be used often enough, there might be reason to think that initiative process outcomes would "converge" to the preferred policy of the median voter. The easiest way to see this is to reconsider Figure 1. Note that any proposal that would defeat Q must be between Q and M(Q), and thus be closer to M than Q is. This proposal, once passed, then becomes the new status quo and a new successful initiative put against it would have to be yet closer to M. Thus, if the initiative is sufficiently easy and quick to employ, outcomes should tend toward the position of the median voter.

A similar analysis would show that permitting amendments to initiatives would support the same result. For example, assume that x is an initiative proposal and y is a proposed amendment, with $M < y < x < M(Q)$. Either x or y would pass if it were the final proposal. But it is easy to see that if a vote were held between x and y to determine which should stand as the initiative, y would defeat x. This is because everyone to the left of y prefers y to x, and by the definition of M this constitutes a majority. Thus, an ordinary legislative amendment process would produce convergence to the preferred policy of the median voter. The problem is that it is difficult to see how amendments or revisions could be made practical within the initiative process. To my knowledge, the only institutionally plausible process involves legislative amendment of initiatives and this proposal is politically vulnerable to the charge of antimajoritarian opportunism and, for that reason, a nonstarter.

But our technique can be used to show how the process might be improved from a majoritarian point of view. In Figure 2 we examine the consequence of requiring a supermajority to overturn the status quo.If a fraction (s > ½) of the electorate is required to approve an initiative, let S stand for the voter who has the fraction s voters to the right and the fraction 1-s to the left. Clearly S < M as in the figure. Now let S(Q) be the policy position that is the same distance from S as Q is. The set of proposals that could defeat Q under the supermajority rule is the interval between S and S(Q). Note that this is a smaller set than the one that arises under majority rule, and if this interval is not empty, it must contain M. Thus, there is less of an opportunity under a supermajoritarian rule for an interest group to use the initiative process to exploit the take-it-or-leave-it aspects of the initiative process to the disadvantage of the median voter.

The conclusion I want to draw is this: *If the status quo is different from the preferred policy of the median voter, there is always a supermajority requirement that is "better" for the median voter than is the majority requirement.* Moreover, the best supermajority rule, from the standpoint of the median voter, would be one that produced the preferred policy of the median voter as the unique equilibrium of the initiative process. It is easy to compute which rule this is: let S* be the midpoint between Q and M, and s* the fraction of voters to right of S*. Then under s*-majority rule, M is the unique policy that would defeat Q.

This analysis cannot specify a special majority rule that would be best in every case—the appropriate rule depends on how far the status quo is from M. When M and Q are not too far apart, small increases in the majority requirement would be appropriate. When these policies diverge greatly, larger majorities should be employed. What is needed, therefore, is an *endogenous* majority requirement: the best rule depends on the parameters of the situation.

Figure 2

Q S M S(Q) M(Q)

While the formulation of such a rule may seem difficult, current California initiative law actually contains a procedure that, with some modification, would essentially implement the endogenous majority requirement. The California rule states that if two conflicting initiatives, dealing with the same subject, receive majorities, the one with the largest vote total takes effect.[13] Referring back to Figure 1, consider what happens if x and y are both proposed and $M < x < y < M(Q)$. In this case both x and y would defeat the status quo by a majority vote but x would receive a higher vote total. More generally, if k proposals appear on the ballot, the one that is closest to the median will receive the largest number of votes. Note that if we could guarantee that the median voter's preferred position would be offered as a proposal, this procedure is essentially the optimal endogenous supermajority rule. This is because the median policy position would obtain the largest number of votes against the status quo and would be the unique outcome under the California procedure.

Of course, it is costly to make proposals and these costs inhibit the kind of competition needed to make the initiative process truly majoritarian. On the present analysis there are two plausible routes to reform. One possibility is to reduce the costs of offering competing proposals, possibly by lowering the signature requirement for competing proposals. In other words, the current signature requirement for the first initiative proposal on a given subject might be kept at five percent and eight percent for statutory and constitutional initiatives respectively. But once an initiative is proposed on a topic, additional proposals would be required to meet a much lower signature requirement—just enough to deter nuisance initiatives. Such an alteration in initiative procedures would effectively install a popular deliberative process that would substitute for the more cumbersome amendment rules found in legislatures.

---

[13]Article II, section 10, part (b): "If provisions of 2 or more measures approved at the same election conflict, those of the measure receiving the highest affirmative vote shall prevail."

By encouraging a free and open competition on a topic of a proposed initiative among all the effected interests, the chances are increased that the majoritarian outcome or something close to it will be the result. This would work in two ways: if there are several proposals on the ballot, the one nearest to the median would prevail. In anticipation of this competition, only moderate proposals will be made in the first place. Those preferring extreme outcomes would be reluctant to pay the costs of meeting the high signature requirement of introducing an initial proposal, only to see their investment wiped out when more moderate alternatives are proposed.

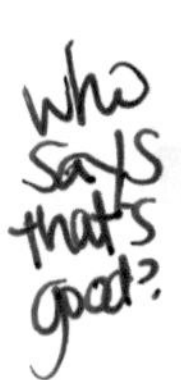

There are costs to adopting this alternative. Foremost among them is the difficulty that voters would face in sorting through and informing themselves on numerous similar technical proposals to find the one they actually prefer. If these costs seem too high, we could follow a second best procedure of specifying a supermajority rule that seems likely to work in most cases. The question of how to set this rule would require some empirical investigation. But a reasonable rule of thumb could be found that would moderate the influence of extreme groups while not overinsulating the status quo. This is an inferior course of action for two reasons. First, it is not clear how to go about finding a supermajority requirement that would work "well enough." And, second, this proposal seems politically vulnerable for reasons already presented.

CONCLUSION

Lowering the signature requirement for a second initiative proposal on a subject should improve the performance of the initiative process from a majoritarian perspective. It should do so for two reasons. First, proposals nearer the median voter's policy position will tend to defeat those further away. Second, because this is true, interest groups preferring relatively extreme positions will not want to offer proposals that will be undercut easily. If they fail to anticipate how the initiative system works, first movers will incur a high price for their folly.

There are additional issues that need to considered. It is possible that the presence of many proposals on the ballot will confuse voters leading them to reject all of the alternatives. If this occurred it would tend to insulate the status quo even if it were quite distant from M, and this would surely be a defect of the system. But, to the extent that interest groups rationally anticipate the performance of the system, one would not expect to see many initiative proposals and certainly not many that are far from M.

Whether or not the specific suggestions made here are deemed useful, the general idea of approaching the idea of reforming democratic processes from the standpoint of a democratic theory seems useful and attractive. It leads us to consider the ways that democratic institutions can be and have been corrupted and seeks to correct their deficiencies. The way to do this is to tailor institutions to permit the development of appropriate forms of deliberation within whole electorates. The reformed institutions will not look exactly like the kinds of institutions and procedures we use in small and medium voting bodies. Deliberative practices found in legislatures—amendment processes, legislative committees, etc.—are not likely to be of much use in electoral deliberation. Rather reformed deliberative electoral mechanisms will make more use of a competitive process among groups and attempt to structure this competition in ways that it is self correcting.

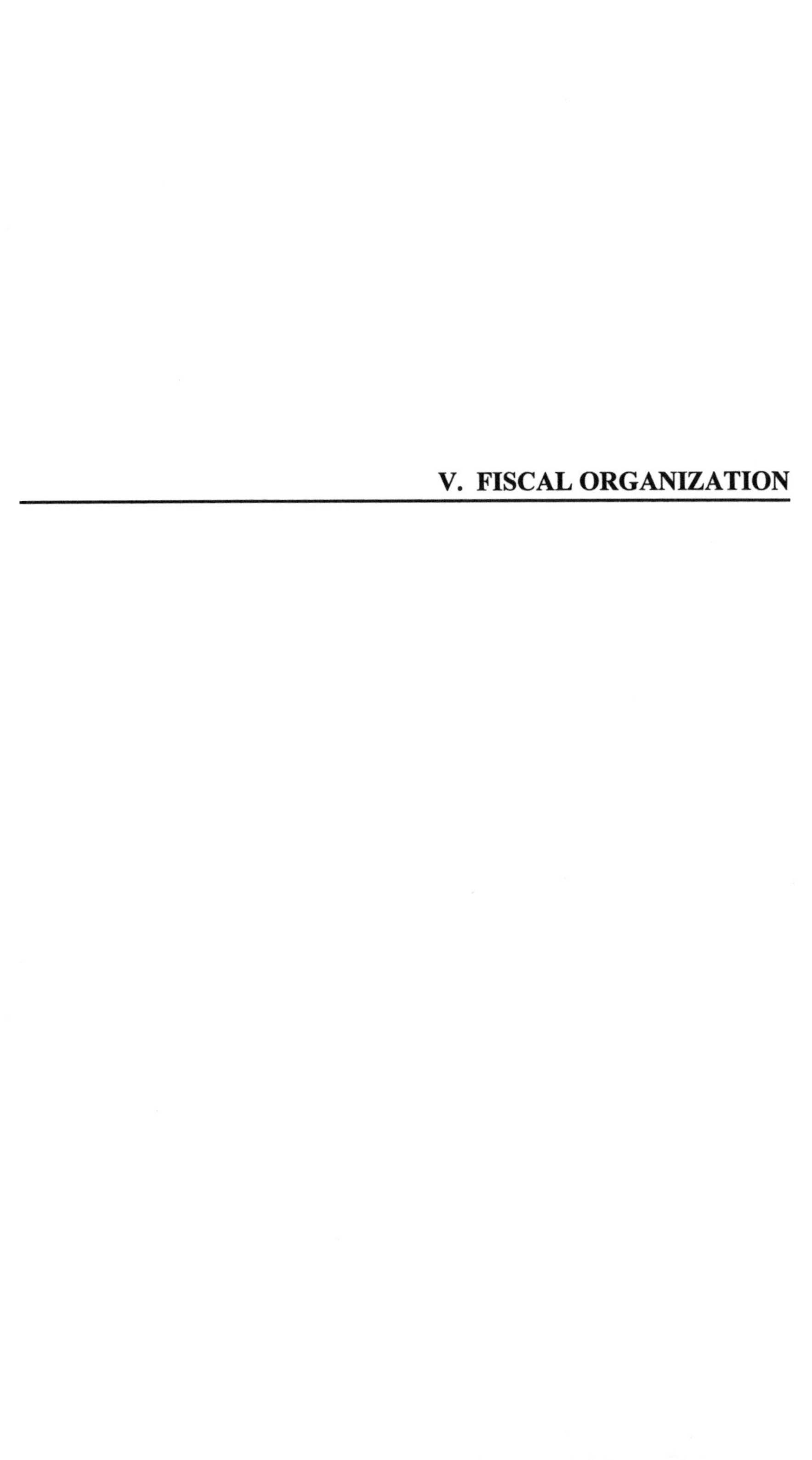

V. FISCAL ORGANIZATION

Options for Reforming the California State Budget Process

John W. Ellwood
Mary Sprague

INTRODUCTION: PERCEIVED PROBLEMS

Since 1990 California has experienced its worst sustained economic performance since the Great Depression. The poor performance of the economy has caused a series of persistent budget deficits in the state's General Fund. Poor economic performance coupled with an inability to gain the necessary votes to raise taxes and/or make permanent spending reductions led to a series of very large projected General Fund deficits—$14.3 billion in 1991-1992 (or some 34 percent of General Fund expenditures), $11.2 billion in 1992-1993 (or some 27 percent of General Fund expenditures), $8.0 billion in 1993-1994 (or some 21 percent of General Fund expenditures), and $4.9 billion (or 11.8 percent of General Fund expenditures) in 1994-1995. Most of the state's budget analysts believe that even though the economy is in recovery the state continues to roll over year-end deficit balances of up to $3 billion.

In the first year of the budget crisis the Republican governor and the Democratic-controlled legislature responded with a combination of tax increases, the rolling forward of some expenditures, and a few actual program reductions. The fact that most of the spending decreases turned out to be temporary while the tax increases led to a rapid decline in the governor's popularity prevented a further repeat of this compromise. The inability or unwillingness to devise another tax increase and spending cut package created a three-month deadlock the following year. As a result, over the next three years the governor and the legislature turned to a strategy of shifting the responsibility of providing services back to counties and cities and a series of accounting gimmicks in order to close yearly budget deficits. One effect of these actions was to undo the fiscal assistance that the state had provided starting in 1979 following the passage of Proposition 13.

A central question for this chapter is whether the provisions of the California Constitution have created or exacerbated these budgetary failures. And, if so, are there alternative constitutional provisions that would lead to an increase in the state's capacity to budget.

In his 1990 book Allen Schick bemoaned the decline in the national government's capacity to budget (Schick 1990). As evidence he cited:

- "Record deficits (that) have tripled the national debt. . . . "
- "An increasing portion of the budget (being) . . . allocated to mandatory payments. . . . "
- "A breakdown of budgetary procedure. . . . Congress rarely completes its budget on schedule. . . . "
- "Malaise has spread from legislative chambers to executive offices."
- "A general loss of budgetary potency has enfeebled all major participants."
- The basic rules of accounting for budget transactions have broken down. Without actually paring a single dollar from outlays, Congress and the president use bookkeeping tricks to show that spending or the deficit has been cut.

To a remarkable extent these complaints are mirrored by those directed against California's budget process. Specifically:

- Some believe the budgetary process has failed because the state has consistently (and continues to) run General Fund budget deficits.
- The state has allowed an increasing proportion of its General Fund expenditures (up to 88 percent by some counts) to be set by constitutional and/or statutorally mandated formulas rather than through the annual appropriations process. And, to the extent that this is true, some argue that the political process is less and less able to adjust yearly spending to meet unanticipated shocks.
- Over the past decade (including years when the state was not in recession) the legislature has frequently been unable to enact the budget on time. In 1992 it was unable to enact the budget until two months (63 days) after the beginning of the fiscal year. Some would point to this failure to meet deadlines as a failure of the budget process.
- Because of the constitutional requirements of a super majority vote to pass the budget or enact a tax increase, some believe that a minority of legislators will block what they oppose unless they are granted their

personal wish list of policies. To the extent this occurs supermajorities can actually lead to increases in expenditures and the growth of inefficient expenditures and programs.

- Alternatively, even with revenue limitation, expenditure limitations, and supermajority voting requirements in place, some believe that the inherent bias of representative democracy toward ever higher levels of spending and deficits requires further constraints on elected officials.

The fact that the same complaints are directed at a national budget process that is governed by few restrictions (no expenditure, revenue, or deficit limits and simple majority voting) and at a California budget process that is highly constrained by constitutional limits and supermajority voting requirements should restrain those who quickly want to modify the state's budgetary system.

MAJOR CONSTITUTIONAL PROVISIONS AND THEIR EFFECTS ON THE STATE'S BUDGET PROCESSES AND POLICY OUTCOMES

As with many states, California's Constitution reads more like a series of statutes than a document that establishes fundamental jurisdictions and procedures. Many of its provisions limit the discretion of elected officials in small as well as large ways. Thus, retirement benefits for elected and constitutional officers are set out; a minimum public school teacher salary ($2,400/year) is mandated; property tax exemptions are stipulated for such uses as cemeteries, the growing of crops and timber; etc. New restrictions are constantly being added through amendment. Since 1884 California's Constitution has been amended 480 times—placing the state second only to Alabama, which has amended its constitution 538 times (Rosenberg, 1993).

Summary of the California Budget Process

As summarized by Kevin Rosenberg:

> California is one of seven states whose budgetary process is constitutionally mandated (along with Georgia, Maryland, Massachusetts, Missouri, New York and West Virginia). The entire process, which ideally should last eighteen months, begins

when the various agencies within the executive branch develop budgetary figures. (Constitutionally) by January 10th of each year the governor must submit an itemized budget proposal to the legislature for the following fiscal year. . . .

Once the bill has been introduced, (by statute) the Legislative Analyst's Office (LAO) prepares comprehensive evaluations of and recommendations on the governor's budget proposal. During mid-May, again by statute, the governor usually submits an updated version of the budget proposal to the legislature which reflects revisions in budgetary figures. The budget bill should arrive on the floor of the legislature for a vote by the end of May.[1]

The California Constitution requires that the budget bill be passed no later than June 15 by a two thirds vote of each chamber. . . . When both houses pass the bill, it is then presented to the governor for signature. Once the governor signs the bill, it becomes law. Rather than sign the bill, the governor may veto the entire bill or exercise (his Constitutionally provided) line item veto power to reduce or strike individual items of the bill.[2] The legislature may, in turn, override the governor's veto by a two-thirds vote.

Specific Constitutional Provisions

Periodicity

California is one of 31 states that operates on an annual budget cycle. The remaining 19 states operate on a biennial cycle. Although it has been traditionally held that annual budget cycles cause higher levels of expenditures, recent work by Paula Kearns indicates that "biennial states spend more, *ceteris paribus*, than annual budget states spend" (Kearns 1994).

---

[1]After receiving the governor's budget each chamber in effect prepares its own budget. If a conference committee cannot reconcile the differences an informal process occurs during which the governor and the majority and minority leaders of the assembly and senate meet to put together a compromise. During this period there are, in effect, four budgets before the legislature.

[2]The governor has the ability to veto an "item of appropriation."

Deficit Prohibition

Every state but Vermont and Wyoming has a constitutional or statutory provision prohibiting or limiting budget deficits (in most cases deficits in the General Fund). Such prohibitions are of two kinds: some states prohibit deficits between projected revenues and expenditures—that is, they require that the budget that is submitted by the governor, and in some cases passed by the legislature, not be in deficit—while other states require that expenditures not exceed revenues at the end of the fiscal year. California falls in the first category—the constitution requires that the governor submit a budget by January 10th in which estimated appropriated expenditures do not exceed estimated revenues.[3] Of the 47 states that have such provisions, 32 are contained in the state constitution. It should be noted, however, that California is one of only nine states where the legislature does not have to pass and the governor does not have to sign a budget where estimated expenditures are at least equal to estimated revenues. Moreover, California is one of only 14 states that allow actual deficits to be carried over to the next fiscal year. (In the other 36 states actual expenditures—in the General Fund—cannot exceed actual revenues at the end of the fiscal year.) Thus, among the states, next to Vermont and Wyoming which have no constitutional or statutory provisions prohibiting budget deficits, California has the least restrictive of deficit prohibitions.[4]

---

[3]The California Constitution prohibits borrowing for the General Fund in excess of $300,000. The California courts, however, have allowed the state to incur short-term debt to meet General Fund immediate cash flow needs by borrowing against anticipated tax revenues. During periods of multi-year recessions (especially the 1930s and the 1990s)—the state has in effect rolled over its short-term debt (Reforming California's Budget Process 1995).

[4]The exact classifications of budget provisions are open to interpretation. Thus, while we have adopted the Advisory Commission on Intergovernmental Relations (ACIR) classification of California's provisions, in their recent paper on the effects of institutions on the interest rate price set by markets on state debt, Robert C. Lowry and James E. Alt place California among those states that require the budget to be balanced at the end of the fiscal year (see Lowry and Alt 1995).

Line-Item Veto and Ability to Reduce Expenditures Without Legislative Approval

California is one of 41 states where the governor is granted the line-item veto. This veto allows the governor to reduce as well as veto appropriations—but both actions can be overturned by a two-thirds vote in both chambers. But California is one of a minority of 11 states where the governor is not granted power to make expenditure reductions without the approval of the legislature.

Two-Thirds Vote Requirements

The California Constitution requires a two-thirds vote of each chamber for the following types of votes (Rosenberg 1993):

- Approval of General Fund appropriations bills, including the state budget, except for those funding schools.
- Changes in state taxes enacted to increase revenue.
- Overriding the governor's veto of a bill or a budget item (the line-item veto).
- Enactment of an urgency statute—defined as a stature whose fiscal effects will take effect immediately.
- Legislation that submits a constitutional amendment or state obligation bond act to the voters.
- Suspension for one year the constitutionally required minimum funding for school and community college districts (Proposition 98).

California is one of only five states—Arkansas, California, Illinois, Nevada, and South Dakota—that require a supermajority to pass budget bills.[5] (*The Book of the States 1994-95*, followed up by telephone survey.) In addition, California is one of only seven states—Arkansas, California, Delaware, Louisiana, Missouri, Oklahoma, and South Dakota—that require a supermajority to raise revenues. (*The Book of the States 1994-95*, followed up by telephone survey.)

---

[5]In Illinois a supermajority is needed to pass the budget if it has not been enacted by May 30.

Revenue and Expenditure Limits

Revenue Limits: Proposition 13, enacted in 1978, amended the California Constitution to place a limit on the property tax of one percent of the full cash value of the property. Once the property is owned, moreover, its full cash value cannot increase by more than two percent in any year.

Expenditure Limitation: Proposition 4 amended the California Constitution to limit the growth of state and local appropriations to the growth of personal income and the change in the population. California is one of 24 states that have such limitations. In 11 of these states—Alaska, Arizona, California, Hawaii, Louisiana, Michigan, Missouri, Oklahoma, South Carolina, Tennessee, and Texas—the limitation is contained in the state's constitution.

Mandated Spending

In a budgetary world without mandated (or uncontrollable) spending, decision makers are able to respond to unanticipated shocks or changes in public opinion by reducing any program's expenditures for the current or upcoming fiscal year. In practice, however, institutions, processes, and provisions have been established that limit the discretion of policymakers to reduce various programs' expenditures. In short, some mandates are more restrictive than others and to some extent one can rank the order of mandated spending by the degree of difficulty of changing the level of expenditures in the short-run.

Constitutional Mandates: As with many states California mandates spending for various programs through its constitution. California is unique among the states, however, because its constitution mandates a minimum level of funding for the General Fund's biggest program—state aid for elementary and secondary (and community college) education. In 1988 California voters passed Proposition 98, which amended the constitution to guarantee minimum funding for K-14 education (elementary and secondary education and community colleges).[6]

---

[6]As amended by Proposition 111, K-14 education is guaranteed the greater of three tests: (1) the percentage of 1986-1987 General Fund revenues that went to

Other provisions of the constitution as interpreted by the courts have had the effect of limiting the budgetary discretion of elected officials. For example, in *Committee to Defend Reproductive Rights v. Myers* (99 Cal 3rd 252, 20 ALR4th 1118) the State Supreme Court in 1981 held that the California Constitution's privacy and equal protection guarantees prohibited the legislature from barring Medi-Cal funding of abortions. In so doing it declared budgetary actions of the California Budget Acts of 1978, 1979, and 1980 unconstitutional.

In 1994 the voters used the initiative process (Proposition 184) to make sure that the legislature could not modify or revoke the "three-strikes-and-you're-out" sentencing requirements. One effect of this action is to eliminate judicial discretion in a large number of criminal cases. The degree to which this requirement will limit control over the budget will to a great extent depend on the degree to which the appellate courts will limit the ability of trial judges to add discretion to sentencing and the legislature's ability to determine prison conditions.

As will be pointed out below, the California initiative process allows initiatives enacted under a simple majority rule to contain provisions requiring supermajorities for their repeal. Such is the case with the provisions of Proposition 13. The initiative process, in effect, allows voters to significantly limit the discretion of future legislatures.

State Legislative Mandates: The legislature has passed statutes that require spending on many programs, such as Renters' Tax Relief and Youth and Adult Corrections. To set these statutes aside (in order to control spending levels in the short-run) the legislature must enact new (nonbudgetary) legislation. However, for some of these programs incremental funding changes might be possible in the short-run. For

---

K-14 education—about 40 percent); (2) the prior-year level of total funding for K-14 education from state and local sources, adjusted for growth in enrollments and per capita income; or (3) the prior-year total level of funding for K-14 education from state and local sources, adjusted for enrollment growth and for growth in General Fund revenues per capita, plus one-half percent of the prior-year level. These tests can be suspended for one year through an urgency bill (which requires a supermajority for passage in each house) other than the budget bill. The procedure also contains an elaborate formula for a mandatory restoration of K-14 funding to the level it would have attained if the suspension had not occurred (LA0 1992 and Shires, Krop, Rydell, and Carroll 1995).

example, although existing legislation requires that Youth and Adult Correction Facilities be available for offenders, it does not specify how much must be spent for prison guards, beds, food, and other cost components of these facilities. As indicated above, however, the courts (especially the federal courts) have acted in the past to require certain levels of spending for the construction and operations of prisons.

Federal Legislative Mandates: Many policymakers and researchers categorize the state match of a federal program as mandated spending. The two largest programs in this category are the state share of the Medicaid program (called Medi-Cal in California) and the state share of the Aid to Families With Dependent Children (AFDC) program. In the case of the Medicaid program a state can decide whether to participate in the program (for many years Arizona chose not to participate) and can select from a menu of over 30 services that it will fund. The dropping of a service, however, again requires action outside the annual budget process. In the case of AFDC each state is required to establish a minimal standard of living criterion. Once established, a state cannot pay less than 80 percent of the standard unless it receives a waiver from the federal government. This procedure has the effect of locking in the actions of a more "liberal" legislature.

Contracts: The state has little choice (other than default) but to fulfill its many contracts. The most obvious category is the short-term borrowing that is routinely undertaken to balance the General Fund. But the state also is limited in its ability to reduce expenditures for multi-year contracts. A category that few classify as mandated spending are expenditures to fulfill multi-year contracts in nonmandated programs. Often programs that most would classify as nonmandated, such as the Forestry and Parks programs, involve significant yearly expenditures from this type of contracts.

As the above discussion indicates, there is a wide range of opinion as to whether expenditures for various programs are controllable in the short-run. Some analysts have indicated that up to 88 percent of the General Fund's expenditures were mandated to some degree (California Citizens Budget Commission, 1995). To get to this figure one must include corrections expenditures under the mandated rubric (a classification that is more defensible today than at the time). It should be noted, however, that the concept of mandated or uncontrollable spending is attenuated as one adopts a multi-year budgetary perspective. What remains, however, is the fact that some types of spending reductions require larger coalitions and perhaps the agreement of the courts or the federal government than do others. Therefore, the concept of mandated spending becomes another case in which program advocates have been able to insulate their programs from unanticipated shocks—be they economic or political. What makes California unique is not the existence of such barriers but—because of Proposition 98—the extent of their budgetary impact.

The Initiative

Although beyond the scope of this chapter, it is clear that the existence of the initiative has had a dramatic effect on all aspects of the policymaking process in California. Many of the limitations discussed above were put in place by the initiative process. As such, these initiatives clearly reflect the voters' distrust of the legislature and are an attempt to limit the freedom of the legislature on budgetary matters. It should be noted that the initiative process allows voters to appropriate expenditures for programs by a simple majority while the California Constitution requires a supermajority for enacting the budget bill. In addition, the constitution requires that legislatively enacted appropriations must be passed by a two-thirds supermajority while appropriations enacted through an initiative require a simple majority. Also, all appropriations enacted by the legislature are subject to the governor's line-item veto, where the governor can add to or subtract from the legislature's actions. This is not the case for appropriations enacted through the initiative process (Dubois and Feeney 1992). Consequently, some have felt that the initiative process is biased toward higher levels of state spending. It is also the case that while the enacted budget bill for the General Fund must be in balance, the initiative process allows voters to mandate additional spending without specifying the additional revenues (or compensating spending reductions in other programs) needed to maintain the General Fund balance. Moreover, the inability (under the constitution's initiative provisions) of the legislature to amend the provisions of initiatives has the effect of creating a mandated spending program.

A Capital Budget and Special Funds

California is one of eight states that do not have a formal capital budget. Capital expenditures are either approved through individual bond issues or through appropriations (Hush and Peroff 1988).

The various deficit prohibitions of the constitution only apply to the state's General Fund. In the 1995-96 state budget of a total of state expenditures of $56.3 billion, the General Fund accounted for 74 percent, various special funds accounted for 25 percent, and various bond funds accounted for the remaining one percent. Recently an increasing proportion of state expenditures are coming from various special funds. In 1983-84 special funds accounted for about 13 percent of total state expenditures; by 1994-95 this figure rose to 28 percent. In recent years the shift of programs that previously were funded by the General Fund to the counties has been carried out by shifting state tax revenues to a special fund (LAO 1994). Some have argued that faced with limitations on the General Fund the legislature has turned to special fund financing.

Information Asymmetries

Proposition 140, which applied term limits to the state legislature, also contained a constitutional requirement that the legislature reduce its budget by 30 percent. The legislature chose to make the required cuts by reducing its staff. Moreover, it chose to make bigger staff reductions in its analytic than its political staff. To the extent that one believes that information asymmetries matter, the proposition can be argued to have increased the power of the executive branch *vis-à-vis* the legislative branch—particularly in technical policy areas such as budgeting.

Research on the Effects of Constitutional Provisions

The general findings of a wide variety of academic studies of statutory and constitutional restrictions to limit the growth of state expenditures, revenues, and debt are that these institutional and procedural restraints are not very effective in achieving their goals.

Taxation and Expenditure Limitations

- Dale Bails, employing a variety of statistical methods, found that the presence of a tax and/or expenditure limitation had virtually no impact on the growth of statewide expenditures or revenues. In addition, while aggregate state expenditures and revenues exhibited some decline during the tax revolt years, this decline was short-lived and has since been reversed (Bails 1990).
- In an earlier article Bails presented evidence that tax expenditure limitations (as designed in the late 1970s) were relatively ineffective in restraining public-sector growth. He pointed to three factors: First, his historical simulations indicated that neither inflation adjusting limitations nor personal income based tax limitations would have significantly lowered tax burdens in overwhelming number of states. Second, the evidence documented the tendency for these legal maximums to become legal minimums. Finally, the inclusion of emergency escape clauses gave political decision makers a device whereby the limitation could be exceeded with relative ease (Bails 1982).

Deficit Prohibitions and Expenditure Levels

Relying on regression models, Burton Adams and William Dougan found that various constitutional limitations (balanced-budget requirements or constitutional limits on government spending or taxes) did not exert a significant independent effect on aggregate budget decisions. States with these provisions appeared to spend at the same levels as those without the provisions (Adams and Dougan 1986).

Constitutional Prohibitions and Debt Financing

James Clingermayer and B. Dan Wood, employing a pooled time-series analysis of state-level data, have found that constitutional or statutory tax, expenditure, and debt limitations "do not significantly alter growth in debt for state governments. Tax and expenditure limitations may actually increase growth in state debt, as self-interested politicians evade formal constraints through alternative means of financing. Likewise, debt limitation institutions have no effect in reducing the growth in state debt" (Clingermeyer and Wood 1995).

Three recent analyses do find that institutional arrangements matter, however.

- James Alt and Robert Lowry find that, when it comes to state fiscal outcomes, divided government matters, institutions matter, and party control matters. They show that faced with an unanticipated deficit or the inheritance of a deficit, "unified party governments not subject to deficit carryover laws might allow it to grow (if they remained in office) while those subject to such laws eliminate deficits more quickly" (Alt and Lowry 1994).
- In a more recent paper Lowry and Alt find that states that require a balance in the general or operating funds at the end of the fiscal year (that is, states that do not permit the carryover of unanticipated deficits) are charged a lower debt service cost by financial markets, even when economic circumstances compel them to run a deficit, than states that allow unanticipated deficits to be carried over. They posit that strict deficit prohibitions at the end of the fiscal year are effective, "because the operation of bond markets gives politicians an incentive to maintain orderly fiscal policies, namely, lower operating costs of government (and thus more funds to spend on other things) in those cases where unforeseen economic circumstances compel running a deficit in the short term." In short, they posit that such end-of-year deficit prohibitions send a signal to markets that all politicians (whether they are committed to eliminating deficits or not) will more likely act to eliminate unanticipated deficits than would be the case if such prohibitions were not in place (Lowry and Alt 1995).
- James Poterba, using a different data set than Alt and Lowry, also determines that where stronger deficit prohibitions exist governments adjust more quickly to unanticipated deficit shocks. As with Alt and Lowry, Poterba also finds that unified governments adjust more quickly to unanticipated deficit shocks than do divided governments. In addition he finds that unified governments make most of their adjustments with tax changes (rather than spending cuts) (Poterba 1994).

From the above discussion it is clear that the requirement that expenditures not exceed actual revenues at the end of the fiscal year is more likely to limit debt financing than the California requirement that estimated expenditures not exceed estimated revenues.

Annual Versus Biennial Budgeting and Expenditure Growth

As previously indicated, although it has been traditionally held that annual budget cycles will cause higher levels of expenditures, recent work by Paula Kearns indicates that "biennial states spend more, *ceteris paribus*, than annual budget states spend" (Kearns 1994).

Supermajority Vote Requirements

Not much is known empirically about the effects of supermajorities. It stands to reason that such requirements are harder to achieve than simple majorities. It follows that the existence of a supermajority will make passage of budgetary legislation more difficult. At the same time, it is possible that while supermajorities lower the level of activity, they can also increase the inefficiency of how public goods or services are provided (or how revenues are collected). This result could occur if the marginal voter's power under a supermajority rule has increased (over what it would be under a simple majority rule) to such an extent that she can and will demand more inefficient side-payments for her support.

NORMS OF A "GOOD" BUDGET PROCESS

Whether and/or how one would change California's budget process should be driven by one's notion of the norms of an ideal budget process. Or at least, one's recommendations for change should be driven by one's explicit beliefs as to what is wrong with the current budget process.

The Norms of Classical Public Administration

The classical public administration treatment of the budget was first set out by Leon Say in 1885. Say identified four essential qualities of an ideal budget:

1. The budget must have unity.

2. The budget must be annual.
3. The budget must be made in advance.
4. The budget must represent an accounting personality (quoted in Sundelson 1935).

From the work of J. Wilner Sundelson it is evident that by the 1930s students of public administration had expanded the list as follows:

I. As to the relation between the budgetary system and the fiscal activities of the political unit:
   (1) *Comprehensiveness*, or all government expenditures and revenues must be subject to the budgetary mechanism and must enter into the recognized budgetary procedure.
   (2) *Exclusiveness*, or all nonfiscal material should be excluded from the budget. This is a prohibition of adding general legislation—or riders—to the budget.

II. As to treatment by the budgetary mechanism of the factors included in the system:
   (1) *Unity*, or a prohibition of various devices to divide and separate some of the material in the system from the regular or ordinary budget.
   (2) *Specification*. It has two subcategories: qualitative specification and quantitative specification. In the case of qualitative specification appropriations are to be expended solely for the purposes specified in the budget. In the case of quantitative specification expenditures are allowed only when, and to the extent that, funds are provided in the budget.
   (3) *Annuality*, or the notion that every system should have a specified accounting period (not necessarily a year) and the system should adhere to that accounting period.
   (4) *Accuracy*, or the idea that the estimates in the budget should be as accurate (and without bias—particularly intentional bias as in the case of accounting tricks) as possible.

III. As to forms and techniques for presentation of the budget contents:
   (1) *Clarity*, or the notion that no budget system can fulfill any of its functions unless it provides for an understandable presentation and leaves room for no doubt or choice in the minds of those who read or are guided by the budget.

(2) *Publicity*, or the ability of the public to understand and use the budget to hold their representative accountable for fiscal decisions (adapted from Sundelson 1935).

Modern Norms of Budgeting

Many of these budgetary principles or axioms still resonate. The norms of comprehensiveness and unity are mirrored in the desire of economists and policy analysts to be able to compare the marginal dollar for activity X to the marginal dollar for activity Y. The norms of comprehensiveness, unity, and accuracy are still alive with those who worry about end-runs, accounting tricks, and other devices that are used to circumvent institutional rules and limitations. The norm of annuality resonates with those who worry about a budget system not meeting its deadlines. The norms of clarity and publicity are alive and well with those who worry about the failure of the political system to use the budget process as a tool of political accountability.

What is missing from this classical presentation is a notion that a "good" budget process should produce a certain policy outcome. That it should result in no or less deficit financing. That it should result in the limitation of government growth. That it should benefit (or create an incentive for) some types of expenditures and/or revenues as against other types. Listening to the complaints about the failures of the California budget process, one can see both the classical and the policy determinant strains.

WHAT IS WRONG WITH THE CONSTITUTIONAL ASPECTS OF CALIFORNIA'S BUDGET PROCESS AND OPTIONS FOR FIXING THEM

Alternative 1: Nothing is Fundamentally Wrong With the Procedures of the California System

Many commentators believe that the various constitutional restrictions on the California budget process that have been described in this chapter explain why the budget process has failed. Before we turn to the specific failures and possible changes to eliminate them, however, we should consider the possibility that the supposed failures of the process have more to do with the poor performance of the California economy and with the particular partisan divisions of the state than with the specific provisions and political institutions set out in the California Constitution.

As evidence for this hypothesis one could point to the fact that the national budget process—which is not limited by the initiative process, supermajority voting requirements, debt limitations, etc.—seems to be suffering from exactly the same failures as the California process (Schick 1990). The notion that partisan divisions (and the attitude structure of the electorate) have more to do with budgetary outcomes than do various procedural institutions is supported by an examination of the pattern of California state and local expenditures over the past three decades. Before the enactment of Proposition 13 in 1978 California state and local revenues (and expenditures), either on a per capita or per $1,000 of personal income basis, clearly exceeded the national average by up to 30 percent. After the implementation of Proposition 13 California became an average state on these measures—where it has remained to this day. But the pattern of California's capital expenditures gives one pause. Before the Reagan governorship—which occurred before the enactment of Proposition 13—California state and local capital expenditures were also clearly greater than the national average. These expenditures dropped to the national average in 1970—almost a decade before the enactment of Proposition 13—and have remained below the national average since that time. So, it could be that a change in the electorate's preferences led to a policy change and the imposition of Proposition 13's limitations.

One could also take the position that bright politicians and their bright staffs are smart enough to figure a way around the limitations that other bright politicians and their bright staffs have put in place. The academic studies that have found little evidence that revenue, expenditure, and debt limitations have made a difference support this notion.

Alternative 2: The Classical (Norms) Solution—An Unbiased and Transparent Process

This alternative would be chosen by those who believe in the classical norms of budgeting and (perhaps) by their economist allies. It calls for an unbiased and transparent process. It is based on the notion that elected officials are best held accountable through information. As such, if one followed this strategy one would eliminate all provisions that give a comparative advantage to one type of expenditure or revenue over another or limit the activity of elected officials. Specifically, following this strategy one would:

- Ideally, eliminate all supermajorities. Or, alternatively, apply such provisions to all legislation (including the so-called trailer bills that are enacted after the passage of the budget bill to make the necessary modifications in authorizations that are required to achieve the dollar levels of the budget bill.)
- Eliminate revenue, expenditure, and debt limitation provisions.
- Eliminate limitations that have the effect of giving a comparative advantage of one type of expenditure over another. Specifically eliminate the special protection of K-14 funding offered by Proposition 98, as amended.
- Modify the initiative, so that it cannot be used (a) to create mandated spending and/or (b) to appropriate expenditures through a simple majority while other expenditures face supermajority and deficit prohibition rules and procedures.
- Eliminate the Proposition 140 restrictions on the appropriations of the legislature that have had the effect of reducing the number and perhaps quality of analytic staff.

Although the evidence is mixed at best, in all likelihood the implementation of these changes could lead to a larger public sector in California. In practice, therefore, if one is a conservative, one would have to trade-off the comprehensiveness, unity, accuracy, clarity, and publicity of this system for the possibility of more government.

Alternative 3: The Present Limitations Are Not Effective Enough to Bring About the Policy Outcomes Desired by the Voters

If one believes that representative government contains an inherent bias toward a larger public sector and more and larger deficits, one might want to mandate a policy outcome from the budget process. The academic literature offers some evidence for suggestions as to how the present restrictions and limitations that seek to affect the policy outcome can be made stronger.

Specifically:

- It appears that a requirement that actual outlays not exceed actual revenues at the end of the fiscal year is more effective in limiting debt financing than is California's relatively weak requirement that the governor submit a budget in which estimated expenditures cannot exceed estimated revenues. If one thinks that California has been running unnecessary General Fund deficits, creating an end of fiscal year deficit prohibition might make a marginal difference.

- There is a good deal of anecdotal evidence that the California state budget system has responded to the need to reduce expenditures by simply shifting these moneys to various special funds. One answer to this end-run is to place expenditure and revenue limitations on special funds as well as on the General Fund. Alternatively, one could try to create global limitations for total state spending (although this still can be avoided by shifts to the counties and cities).

We should add that we believe that the global cap strategy is futile. Moreover, it comes at the cost of a decrease in the transparency of budgetary decision making and budget documents.

Since most state and local governments do engage in long-term borrowing for large capital projects, it follows that a requirement that actual expenditures not exceed actual outlays should be accompanied with a formal capital budget process. This would allow a global cap on all activities except long-term capital, which could be funded through a sinking fund mechanism. The trick, however, would be to prevent the gradual inclusion of nonlong-term capital projects in the capital budget.

Alternative 4: Decrease the Probability of Budgetary Conflict

Many of the supposed failures of the California budget process result from the state's version of the Madisonian system. Compared to the average state California has a professional legislature. Its long ballot increases the probability of various executive branch officeholders coming from different political parties. One could suggest a range of strategies that would result in what appears to be a 'neater" budget process—one that is more likely, for example, to meet budgetary deadlines.

Alternative 4A: Parliamentary Government

A parliamentary system in which the executive rose out of a majority party in the legislature would sharply reduce conflict within the legislature and between the legislature and the executive. What would not be guaranteed is a particular outcome. Should liberals control the parliament, increased government is more likely than the present system. However, should conservatives control the parliament, a smaller government than the present system is possible.

Alternative 4B: A One-Chamber Legislature

One might hypothesize that moving from a two-house legislature to a one-chamber assembly could reduce the level of conflict, particularly if fewer actors are involved. Party or individual member accountability might also increase.

Alternative 4C: A Weaker Legislature and a Stronger Executive

Turning the California legislature into a nonprofessional citizen legislature might reduce conflict with the executive. Such a strategy would call for a dramatic reduction in legislative staff so as to dramatically increase the information asymmetry between the executive branch and the legislature. Simultaneously the governor's power could be increased by moving from the long to the short ballot.

Alternative 4D: Eliminate Supermajority Voting

One of the side effects of an elimination of supermajority voting is an increase in the ability of legislative leaders to form minimum winning coalitions. Again, the trade-off might be a larger public sector.

Alternative 4E: Eliminate California State Constitutionally Mandated Spending

California is unique in the percentage of its General Fund expenditures that can reasonably be characterized as mandated or uncontrollable in the shortrun. But this unique status results almost totally from two provisions—Proposition 98's K-14 funding mandates and the recently enacted initiative that placed the three-strikes-and-you're-out sentencing requirements in the constitution.

If these two provisions were repealed, up to 60 percent of General Fund expenditures that are currently protected from short-term budgetary changes would again fall within the annual budget process. This would dramatically increase the options open to the legislature (and the governor). As such, it could have the effect of reducing the probability of legislative deadlock (under the assumption that the possibility of compromise increases as the actors have more options to trade).

Alternative 5: Move to a Multi-Year Budget Process

If one is unwilling or unable to roll back the various provisions that mandate General Fund expenditures in the short-run one, can attenuate the negative side effects of such mandates by moving to a multi-year budget process. Budgetary changes that are impossible to carry out in the short-run can become part of a multi-year agenda. It should be noted, for example, that although up to 80 percent of federal budget outlays are relatively uncontrollable by the annual budget process, once a multi-year process is in place the only truly uncontrollable outlays are those for interest on the public debt and other contracts that have been legally entered into by the government (and even here some savings might occur through the cancellation of contracts and the payment of cancellation penalties).

It should be recognized, however, that multi-year budgeting is not a panacea. It requires the adoption of a multi-year baseline, which in turn, is highly dependent on economic and technical assumptions (Muris 1989). Some would argue that it increases the ability of elected officials to "game" the system either by adopting wildly optimistic economic assumptions or by promising to be "good" in the future while maintaining their "bad" behavior in the present.[7]

Alternative 6: Authors' Choice—A Simple Clean Budget Process (That Will Probably Lead to a Larger Public Sector)

No budgetary process is perfect—all are bound to have flaws since we as citizens demand contradictory outcomes. Given our bias in favor of the

---

[7]Some might hold that constitutional spending and taxing mandates, such as Proposition 98 and Renters' Tax Relief, would still be uncontrollable. But from a policy perspective this would not be the case. In a multi-year world one would simply call for a change in the constitutional provisions; realizing, of course, that such a change would be more difficult to bring about than a statutory change.

need for greater public investment and a belief that limitations in the end are bound to be largely avoided or, if successful, create greater distortions than they are worth, we would opt for a classical "clean" system that would include:

1. To the extent possible, everything being on the table so that the marginal dollar of X can be compared to the marginal dollar of Y.
2. The elimination of supermajorities and limitations of all sorts.
3. The simplification of California's governmental structure by modifying the initiative so that its results can be altered by the normal political process and so that it cannot be used to create mandated spending.
4. Increasing the analytic capability that supports the decision-making process.

We have to admit that such a system would probably lead to a larger public sector and would not significantly decrease budgetary conflict. One can even posit a scenario under which conflict would increase.

REFERENCES

Alt, James E., and Robert C. Lowry. 1994. "Divided Government and Budget Deficits: Evidence From The States." *American Political Science Review* 88: 811-28.

Abrams, Burton, and William Dougan. 1986. "The Effects of Constitutional Restraints on Governmental Spending." *Public Choice* 49, no. 2.

Bails, Dale G. 1982. "A Critique on the Effectiveness of Tax-Expenditure Limitations." *Public Choice* 38: 129-38.

_________. 1990. "The Effectiveness of Tax-Expenditure Limitations." *American Journal of Sociology* 49: 223-38.

California Citizens Budget Commission. 1995. *Reforming California's Budget Process: Preliminary Report and Recommendations of the California Citizens Budget Commission.* Los Angeles: Center for Governmental Studies.

Clingermayer, James, and B. Dan Wood. 1995. "Disentangling Patterns of State Debt Financing," *American Political Science Review* 89:108-20.

Constitution of the State of California. 1879. As Last Amended November 3. 1992. and Related Documents 1993-1994. 1993. Sacramento, Calif.: California State Senate.

Council of State Governments, ed. 1994. *The Book of the States, 1994-1995.* Lexington, Kent: Council of State Governments.

Dubois, Philip, and Floyd F. Feeny. 1992. *Improving the California Initiative Process: Options for Change.* Berkeley, Calif.: California Policy Seminar.

Hush, Lawrence W., and Kathleen Peroff. 1988. "State Capital Budgets." *Public Budgeting and Finance* 8: 67-79.

Kearns, Paula S. 1994. "State Budget Periodicity: An Analysis of the Determinants and the Effect on State Spending." *Journal of Policy Analysis and Management* 13: 331-62.

Legislative Analyst's Office. 1992. *The 1992-1993 Budget: Perspectives and Issues.* Sacramento, Legislative Analyst's Office.

__________. 1994. *The 1994-1995 Budget: Perspectives and Issues.* Sacramento: Legislative Analyst's Office.

Lowry, Robert C., and James E. Alt. 1995. "Balanced Budget Laws, Intertemporal Efficiency, and Costly Information," prepared for the annual meeting of the Midwest Political Science Association, Chicago, Illinois, April 6-8.

Muris, Timothy J. 1989. "The Uses and Abuses of Budget Baselines." Stanford: *Hoover Institution Working Papers in Political Science,* no. P-89-3 (January).

Poterba, James M. 1994. "State Responses to Fiscal Crises: The Effects of Budgetary Institutions and Politics." *Journal of Political Economy* 102: 799-821.

Rosenberg, Kevin S. 1993. *Enacting the California State Budget: Two-Thirds is Too Much.* Sacramento, Calif.: McGeorge School of Law.

Schick, Allen. 1990. *The Capacity to Budget.* Washington, D.C.: The Urban Institute Press.

Shires, Michael A., Cathy S. Krop, C. Peter Rydell, and Stephen J. Carroll. 1994. *The Effects of the California Voucher Initiative on Public Expenditures for Education.* Santa Monica, Calif.: The RAND Corporation.

Sundelson, J. Wilner. 1935. "Budgetary Principles." *Political Science Quarterly* 50: 236-63.

Putting the State Back into State Government: The Constitution and the Budget

Mathew D. McCubbins

INTRODUCTION

As we near California's sesquicentennial, we find that the state faces a myriad of social and economic problems, ranging from riots, illegal immigration, and the economic upheaval caused by post Cold War military cutbacks, to the occasional devastating earthquake, droughts, and floods that threaten to plunge us into either chaos, bankruptcy, or both. Californians are placing unprecedented demands upon their government, unfortunately, it does not seem able to accommodate their needs.

Many Californians seem to think that they cannot hold their government accountable. I agree. However, I disagree with those who attribute this lack of accountability to a characteristic venality among the state's political officeholders. Instead, I see both the socio-economic ills of California, *and* the accountability problem as symptoms rather than causes of the way government works. The real causes lie in decades of incremental, piecemeal reforms that were intended to increase government accountability, but have had precisely the opposite effect. That is, measures such as Propositions 13, 4, 98, and 99 have constrained California government to the point where it is nearly impossible to respond to pressing economic, social, and political problems. We are at the point where the current constitution provides state government with almost no flexibility, few resources, and little chance to earn voter trust.

Paper prepared for a Conference on California Constitutional Reform, June 8 - 10, 1995, Berkeley, California. I thank Bruce Cain and Roger Noll for their insightful comments and Robert Schwartz and Mike Thies for their research assistance.

Well meaning but shortsighted reforms have led to a government that is largely incapable of serving the citizens of California. Voters perceive government to be unaccountable, so they pass initiatives[1] to restrict its actions. This constrains government further, and prevents it from responding to the state's pressing demands, which angers voters, and provokes them to press for ever more stringent constraints on the range of government's action. The vicious spiral of government inaction and unaccountability is due to the fundamental inconsistency in California's constitution that separates the legislature from both the statutory and constitutional initiative process, and thus from accountability for state policymaking (Gerber 1995, Cain et al. 1995).

This is the sad irony of California politics. Reforms by the Progressives in the early part of this century, meant to disenfranchise the corrupt power of the political machines, have been captured, and, in turn, corrupted by modern political machines. The reason modern economic powers have been able to turn the process of direct democracy against the general welfare is due to two tragic errors in the reasoning of the Progressives.

The first of these errors is that the current initiative system allows special interests to set the popular agenda by proposing statutory and constitutional initiatives directly to the people. There is no limit to the power of these agenda-setting interest groups, nor is there a check on the authority of "the people" to change the constitution. The Progressives sowed the seeds for the ultimate demise of our constitution by rejecting the basic principle held by the Federalists (the previous generation of American constitutionalists): that all power corrupts, and thus all power must be checked and limited or it will lead to tyranny. We are now living with the results of the basic inconsistencies in the California Progressives' experiment with constitutional design. During the last 150 years, more than 800 constitutional amendments have been proposed and more than half have passed. The cumulative effect of the unchecked use of direct democracy is a 135-page document, full of contradictions and irrelevancies. Perhaps more importantly, it makes adjusting public policy to meet the changing needs of California's people nearly impossible due to innumera-

---

[1]Initiatives can take two forms, statutory and constitutional. Statutory initiatives are direct legislation, while constitutional initiatives are amendments to the constitution itself. Unless otherwise stated, by initiative, I mean both types.

ble constraints on social policy and proactive mandates for earmarked spending.

The second consequence of the Progressives' reliance on direct democracy is that initiatives place statutory and constitutional caps and limits on spending, but leave untouched the incentives of elected representatives to control their own spending. A legislator will always have an incentive to bring the treasury home, but reliance on caps and guidelines gives them an incentive to work around spending limits. If we truly want fiscal responsibility, we need to change the incentive to bring the treasury home, not add more incentives to act irresponsibly. We can and must do better.

The changes I advocate in this paper relate to fiscal policy. The paper proceeds as follows. I begin by analyzing the role of the Federalists and the Progressives in constitutional design, contrast these principles with California's example, then turn to the more specific case of budgetary policymaking. I advocate a new constitutional process that eliminate the causes of California's constitutional contradictions, and in turn eliminate the symptoms that, if left unchecked, threaten to consume the state.

THE FEDERALISTS

The Federalists were concerned with, among other things, protecting the populace from temporary majorities running rampant over the rights of others. The prospect of tyranny of the majority led Mill, Madison, Montesquieu, and others to argue that certain freedoms must be inviolable and that popular sovereignty must be tempered—limited in some way—to protect basic human rights (Mill 1947, Madison 1982, Rawls 1971). They understood that people are self-interested, and if possible, will abuse the institutions of government for their own benefit, "measures are too often decided, not according to the rules of justice and the rights of the minority party, but by the superior force of an interested and overbearing majority" (Madison, *Federalist* 10). They saw that power corrupts and the only way to halt corruption is to limit the power any one branch of government holds. The key was to contrive the internal structure of government so that each branch of government would have the ability and the motive to check the excesses of the other.

The Federalist, however, saw little need for direct appeals to the people. The process to amend the constitution involves state legislatures but does not include the electorate directly. The Federalists were concerned about the ability of majorities to change the constitution and thereby to deprive members of a political minority of their rights or liberties. They also worried about the ability of citizens, who are virtuous but inattentive to politics, to make reasoned, passionate decisions concerning the structure of government and the rights of others, "a pure democracy . . . can admit of no cure for the mischiefs of faction" (Madison, *Federalist* 10). They believed the people need to be protected not only from their own government, but also from each other.

To ensure that those who held office in the U.S. had the incentive to promote the general welfare, the Federalists created a republican form of government. Under the design of this government, officeholders must seek reelection from those whom they serve. To ensure that the limits on government were actually binding (i.e., balanced), so that the legislature was, in fact, unable to abuse its power, the Federalists sought to give each branch of government a separate and different mode of representation, so that, in striving to earn their reelection to office, politicians would have an incentive to serve different constituencies with separate interests. If the personal fate of the individual in office is connected to the fate of the office itself, "ambition" would be made to "counteract ambition," (Madison, *Federalist* 51) and the internal checks on state power would provide the necessary safeguards to ensure that the powerful new central government would indeed be limited by the constitution's design.

The Federalists created a strong, but limited, central government, based upon certain republican principles. The Federalists argued that the diversity of interests in a republic as large as the American nation would be a natural barrier to the concentration of political power, "the variety of sects dispersed over the entire face of [the Confederacy] must secure the national councils against any danger from that source" (Madison, *Federalist* 10). The Federalists were well aware that there could emerge concentrations of economic power. They believed, however, that this concentration could not be so large and pervasive, across the many differing regions of the United States, so as to seize the reigns of government. Perhaps the Federalists overlooked the possibility of logrolling within Congress, where special interests could make bargains with each other, and whereby the few could seize power from the many, but nonetheless, with the benefit of hindsight, we can see that the Federalists were somewhat naive about this belief.

Special interests have been quite successful at using public policy for private gain.

THE PROGRESSIVES

Coming to political prominence in California and elsewhere as the 19th century gave way to the 20th century, the Progressives faced a problem different than the one that animated the Federalists and sought an answer based on different experiences and different beliefs than those held by Hamilton, Jay, and Madison. The Progressives lived in a world in which political power had indeed been captured and perverted by private interests. The concentration of economic power that arose as a result of industrialization led to political dominance by large economic interests. In California it was the Southern Pacific Railroad, whose dominance of state politics led to a revolt by the middle class that culminated in Hiram Johnson's gubernatorial victory in 1910 (Mowry 1976).

The Progressives sought to break the concentration of political power no matter what its source, therefore, "party organizations were deliberately weakened by Progressive reformers during the first decade of the twentieth century on the theory . . . that parties lead naturally to corruption" (Reichley 1985, 178). They believed that the scientific administration of public policy could replace the arbitrary and capricious nature of administration under the political machines of the day. They sought to replace the cronyism and favoritism of machine politics with the truth and fairness of scientific standards (Mowry 1976, 137). The Progressives, therefore, disaggregated government into numerous independent and separately elected offices, forever eliminating the corruption of party machines.

The Progressives believed people to be intelligent, educated, and attentive to politics. They also believed that people are, at least to some extent, other regarding, and that the citizens of the California Republic shared the same core values. Thus, while the Progressives feared and loathed the misuse of power that accompanied machine politics, they saw little to fear from direct democracy. They believed the people have the wisdom and the virtue to control their own destiny directly.

Thus, the Progressives reworked the Federalist's model. The Progressives created a government wherein the people could directly make law and change the constitution. Furthermore, California Progressives, relying on the wisdom and virtue of the educated middle class whose actions are guided by an enlightened view of the general welfare, saw little potential for a tyranny of the majority. The ability of the people to make law and amend the constitution therefore was left unchecked, and the recall and referendums were expanded (Mowry 1976, 142). This reliance on direct democracy, as a panacea for bad public policy, can either be merged with or substituted for republicanism. In the former case, it has lead to an improvement in government, however in the latter case it has been an unparalleled failure.

The failure of the California Progressives began with their rejection of Federalist principles. First, they discounted the fear of a tyranny of the majority, which arose from their lack of understanding the strategy of initiative agenda formation. Initiatives do not bubble up from the desires of millions of individual voters. Rather, special interests, who are capable of writing initiatives and getting them on the ballot, set the agenda for policy formation in the state. The most pernicious aspect of the agenda setting ability of these special interests is that they are responsible to no one. In effect the Progressives substituted "corporate tyranny" for the tyranny of the majority. This takes the form of professional campaign organizations that collect the necessary signatures to put initiatives on the ballot, often without reference to the content of the legislation involved. Thus, the process by which policy is often made in California is neither republican nor democratic, and thus fails to meet the minimum standards of any acceptable democracy.

Sadly, the Progressives did not consider the consequences of unchecked direct democracy in a state dominated by campaign machines rather than the traditional political machines. It is difficult for the electorate to consider a large array of either statutory or constitutional initiatives at any one time. Because of this, it is difficult for the people to explicitly face the trade-offs among policies that arise whenever legislation is passed. As a result, it is extremely difficult for policymaking by initiative to actually promote the general welfare. This is especially true if the people are not as well informed as the Progressives believed them to be. It follows that the failings of direct democracy in the end limit the government's ability to pursue the general welfare. Indeed, this is one of the central concerns of the California Constitution Revision Commission.

Ironically, the California Progressives also failed to realize that, if left unchecked, direct democracy is, itself, self limiting. Ultimately, the choices made at one point restrict not only the government, but also limit choices in the future. Laws are, by nature, self limiting, but initiatives are more restrictive than any other type of legislation for, in the California system, they can be amended or repealed only by another ballot initiative.

Second, the Progressives rejected the Federalists' dependence on the structure of initiatives. The use of caps and limits to control spending has lead to cycles of obfuscation, where the treasury is divided in increasingly imaginative ways. When the voters place a restriction on spending in one area, creative legislators are quick to move to another. The only escape from these cycles is to address the basic legislative incentive to spend as much of the taxpayer's money as possible.

California's radical experiment in direct democracy is flawed in four ways. First, because the use of the initiative is unchecked (Gerber 1995; Cain et al. 1995), the Progressives merely substituted a pernicious variant of the tyranny of the majority for the tyranny of the Southern Pacific Railroad. Second, the end of unchecked direct democracy in a republic is that the accountability of our elected officials is greatly reduced. Third, the separate nonpartisan election of many of California's offices implies that trade-offs among differing policy goals and coordination across policy issues will be difficult or impossible. Fourth, the end of unchecked direct democracy is that California government is now in a position where it can do nothing. The radical California experiment in Progressive government is grinding itself to an end, and it is time that we revise it.

MERGING FEDERALIST AND PROGRESSIVE VISIONS OF GOVERNMENT

In thinking about how to revise the structure of California government, we need to come to grips with what we now believe to be true about human nature and the nature of government. My experience watching politics leads me to believe that the Federalists' premises concerning human nature (that power corrupts) seem more realistic than do the Progressives' (that a citizen has the necessary information to protect his interests from corrupt powers). If this is true, we must limit and check all aspects of policymaking—whether it be a component of republican (Federalist) or democratic (Progressive) government. The Progressives' fantasy that the administration of policy could be made scientific and could thus be divorced from politics, needs to be replaced with a more realistic view of the political forces that surround policymaking. The experience of the

Progressives with the concentration of political and economic power, however, makes the Federalists' argument that power could not be concentrated in a large republic seem a bit naive as well. Having sketched the outline of my beliefs, how do I recommend we redesign our state constitution, and in particular the institutions by which the budget is made?

To be consistent with the Federalists' beliefs, we want to design a form of government that is, in its basic components, republican. We want a republican government that is self limiting, but that is capable of promoting the general welfare and securing the blessings of liberty for its people. If we also believe, as did the Progressives, that concentrated power poses a threat to the people of the state of California, we need to design a form of government that allows the people to check directly the actions of government, and, when necessary, to promote the general welfare themselves. Thus, there is a place for the initiative and referendums in a government consistent with both these sets of beliefs. The proper role of direct democracy in such a government, however, is more limited than has been the case in California.

If we are to return California government to a form of limited republican government consistent with the Federalist's reasoning and premises, we need to undo many of the most radical changes that have made modern California government unaccountable. Accountability is a necessary condition to ensure that republican government produces policies that enhance the general welfare. Only if the representatives of the people share an intimate sympathy with the people will republican government enact policies to advance the public good.

We know that neither the Progressives nor the Federalists effected a perfect government. We can either point to where they went wrong and make recriminations, or we can learn from their mistakes. The Federalists were unable to anticipate the concentration of power in the hands of special interests, and the Progressives were blinded by short-sighted benevolence. If we maintain a commitment to representative government and a system of checks and balances, while at the same time synthesizing the precepts of direct democracy as a check against powerful elites, we can create an effective, responsible, and accountable government. How it is we can accomplish this is the topic to which I now turn.

Mathew D. McCubbins

TOWARDS A NEW ACCOUNTABILITY

Why have Californians believed so fervently and for so long that their government is unaccountable? It is this belief that drove the public to modify the legislative and electoral processes almost 40 times each, and to place restrictions on fiscal policy more than 150 times in the last 115 years. To better design governmental institutions we must first decide what is necessary to make them accountable. Two requirements can be identified: first, the people must be able to identify who is responsible for policymaking, and second, they must have the means to discipline those decision makers who are responsible for the outcomes of government policy. In other words, they must first know who to credit or blame for the policy emanating from the statehouse, and second, the people must have a check on government whether through the courts, the ballot box, or through direct intervention in the policymaking process.

In meeting these two requirements, I maintain that direct lines of accountability are the clearest and easiest for an inattentive public to comprehend. Thus, we need to reform California government so that policymaking authority is centralized. Centralizing policymaking authority, both at the state and local levels, will allow the people to hold their elected officials directly accountable for policy outcomes. I turn now to a discussion of four reforms that would increase government accountability in California.

THE FRAGMENTATION OF ACCOUNTABILITY: THE WHOLE IS LESS THAN THE SUM OF ITS PARTS

A necessary condition for accountability is the existence of a connection between policy emanating from the statehouse and ballots cast in November. By expanding the number of elected offices and by expanding the use of the initiative (both statutory and constitutional), Californians have greatly expanded their ability to intervene directly in the policymaking process. A consequence of this expansion in the avenues of direct voter participation, however, is that the people's ability to identify who is responsible for policymaking has declined commensurately. Well-meaning reforms, intended initially to break the power of local political machines, have had the perverse effect of destroying the accountability of government by making it all but impossible to figure out who is responsible for what aspects of public policy.

There was, of course, a good and earnest reason for separating partisan politics from local offices and decentralizing the state government. The downside of these reforms is that the costs and activities of government are now separated. An important consequence of this separation of powers is that the state legislature and the governor have created programs whose growth rates are determined in a manner divorced from growth rates in general revenues.[2] A second consequence is that local authorities spend money they do not raise, and the state raises money that it cannot spend. Both of these outcomes disrupt the connection between the people and their government officials.[3]

In order to increase both accountability and responsibility in government, we must reduce the number of both elected and appointed government offices. Centralized political authority provides ample incentive for legislators to act in the interest of their constituents by increasing their identifiability and decreasing their opportunity to blame others for their decisions. Since Californians are already protected from despotism by the federal constitution, and since the current system encourages irresponsibil-

---

[2]A related problem, federally mandated programs, and the state's implementation of them, also tend to grow without reference to the ups and downs of the state's tax receipts. There is very little that can be done with respect to this problem by restructuring the state constitution. This is not a new problem; it is not even new to California, nor does it seem likely to go away.

[3]One of the most important contributions of the Progressives was eliminating patronage from state offices. They did this by decentralizing government and making many positions nonpartisan elected offices. While the initial effect was a more responsible government, eliminating party cues from the electoral process has further separated electors from their representatives. Party identification is a simple, clear cue that most people rely on to aid their decisions (Campbell et al. 1980). By eliminating party identification from the electoral process, the Progressives denied voters the only useful information most of them have.

Second, the effect of eliminating party competition from most offices is that there is no collective responsibility for the activities of government. If these offices were partisan, then the parties would have an incentive to monitor and coordinate the activities of these officials. As it is, a smorgasbord of individually elected "free agents" have no incentive to work in the interests of their constituents, to say nothing of working together in that pursuit.

ity and a lack of accountability, centralizing state authority has much to recommend it.

THE DISJUNCTION OF ACCOUNTABILITY AND POLICYMAKING

We must also establish a link between taxation and expenditures. Local governments must either do less or be responsible for more of their revenue. Particularistic spending or revenue-raising authorities should be eliminated. We must make clear the division of labor between the state, city, and county governments. Accountability can only be achieved if the electorate can recognize how, and on what level, decisions are made. Once politicians are held accountable for their actions, the budget problem can be properly addressed.

HUMAN NATURE: THE IMPULSE TO SPEND OTHER PEOPLE'S MONEY

Many of the reforms passed over the course of this century have sought to limit the mischief caused by human nature. Californians realized long ago that people prefer more (of good things) to less, and they prefer to pay later, if at all, to paying now. People are especially profligate when spending someone else's money. This problem is ubiquitous to all human endeavors. When the owners of a firm hire a manager, the manager will be more willful when spending the stockholders' money than when spending his or her own money. The same is true, of course, of our elected representatives. They will be less thrifty when spending the state's money, for their political gain, then they will be if they are spending their own resources. In response to this realization, Californians put into place nearly 150 restrictions on the government's ability to spend, tax, and borrow. At present, there are at least 170 sections in the various articles of the California Constitution that affect government budget policy. Many of these provisions contradict others. Further, few address the real issue: human nature itself.

While it is true that Proposition 4 (codified as Article 13B) sought to limit the mischief of profligacy, it also limited the satisfaction of other democratic ideals. Article 13B established an appropriations limit, based on the 1978-79 budget. Increases in the appropriations limit were to be adjusted for inflation and population growth. Under Article 13B, half of all revenues in excess of this limit were to be returned to the people within two years in the form of lower taxes. Article 13B thus also set a limit on the size of the tax increase that the government may impose in any one year.[4]

The problem with Article 13B is that while it constrains certain potential consequences of profligacy, it does not directly address the causes, for it does little to change legislators' incentives. Presently, this and other constitutional provisions, in concert with constitutionally earmarked spending (such as Proposition 98) and strict constitutional limitations on the types and levels of taxes that may be imposed (such as Proposition 13), limit options and thus make decision making by representatives or by voters more difficult. This in turn creates the downward spiral of government accountability, unchecked spending, and direct constitutional amendments. Legislators need incentives, rather than guidelines, to control their own spending, as caps only lead to cycles of obfuscation (Ellwood and Sprague 1995, Kiewiet 1995), where creative accounting can be used to circumvent spending limits as soon as they are in place. The solution to the basic problem of human nature lies within the structure of these incentives (as I shall argue, by tying outcomes of the budget process directly to the electoral fates of government officials, they will have real incentives to act responsibly).

INCREASING ACCOUNTABILITY

In every republican system of government there is a trade-off between increasing the accountability of elected officials and limiting the ability of these same officials to exercise the powers delegated them by the polity. The more confining the limitations, the less responsible they are for the outcomes of government. Beyond making the lines of accountability as direct as possible, as just discussed, we must also choose the limitations so

---

[4]Proposition 4 was later amended, weakening many of these restrictions, demonstrating how difficult caps and limits are to enforce. There were several other restrictions on the ability of the state government to raise revenue as well. Article 13A (passed as Proposition 13 in 1978) restricts the ability of state and local governments to tax real and personal property. Article 13, Section 3 enshrines in the constitution a long list of tax exemptions—further reducing the choices available.

that they retard if not eliminate those governmental actions we most fear, but at the same time allow the government to do those things that we most desire (as long as these things are not mutually exclusive) and for which we hold our elected leaders responsible.[5]

To bring accountability to California government, the existing bicameral state legislature should be rendered effectively unicameral for the purposes of budgetary policymaking. That is, for most policy, we retain a two house legislature, where legislation sent to the governor must be approved by both houses. For budgetary policy, however, legislation that determines spending for authorized state programs, sets tax rates, or borrows money, the assembly alone would be responsible. Moreover, the governor's line-item veto over budgetary matters should be replaced with a simple package veto.

Unicameral legislative sovereignty on the budget is the norm around the world—even otherwise bicameral legislatures such as the Japanese Diet and the German Bundestag give all budgetary authority to the lower house alone (Cain and Persily 1995; Brady and Gaines 1995). Bicameralism, especially when augmented by divided government, is often associated with higher budget deficits. If a second chamber and a separately elected executive must also agree to any eventual budget, then budgets will be more difficult to pass, prone to logrolling, and less responsive. A package veto will not affect the governor's ability to check the creation of new programs, but it will help shift the balance of legislative accountability to those who actually make the decisions.

At the same time we need to amend the legislative rules by which budgets are passed. Under the current system all revenue and appropriations bills must pass both chambers of the legislature with a two-thirds majority (Article 13A, Section 3). The practical implication of this is that, because a single political party rarely, if ever, controls two-thirds of the seats in both chambers of the legislature, all spending and revenue bills require compromise between the two parties. While it might appear that compromise between the two parties could lead to policies that reflect the will of a larger portion of the populace, it is not a very likely outcome.

---

[5]I will assume for present purposes that there will remain in California an elected, bicameral legislature, and a separately elected governor. Of course, the discussion that follows can be revised easily to work with proposals to eliminate one house of the legislature.

What is most likely is that in some cases, the two parties' stands will be mutually exclusive, and deadlock will prevail. In other cases, such as with the budget, compromise takes the form of bargaining and logrolling, where funding is provided to everyone's favorite programs. Both insidious cases, gridlock and irresponsibility, can be observed much more frequently in California than mature compromise.

We should thus change the legislative process to a simple majority requirement and the budgetary process should run for the legislature's complete tenure in office. The majority party in the assembly will then be responsible for the budget, and can be judged by their performance in the subsequent elections. Finger pointing at the other chamber, intransigent bureaucrats, or the minority party will no longer be credible. One party will control a majority of the only chamber that matters, so it will be relatively simple for voters to attribute credit or blame for budgetary policy at the only time it matters, election day.

Two additional constitutional provisions serve merely to destroy accountability without providing any useful checks on government authority and should thus be eliminated. First, while the current constitution requires that the governor submit a balanced budget, the state need not enact one. The only requirement is that the estimates for spending equal the estimate for revenues. These estimates are highly sensitive. The spending estimates are always underreported while revenue estimates are inflated, and they are easily manipulated by accounting tricks. Last, of course, there is no practical means for enforcing the balanced budget provisions in the constitution. The details of the budget process should be left to legislation.

Second, the provisions of Proposition 140 that limit expenditures for legislative staffs do not serve the cause of democracy or republicanism. Rather they merely increase the legislature's reliance on interest groups and other outside experts. If the general will can be served better by allowing the legislature to determine the size of their staff, the restriction should be removed. Legislatures need information in order to assess the outcomes of their actions. If they cannot provide it themselves, they will be forced to rely on lobbyists and special interests to provide them with information that serves neither the legislature's nor the public's best interests.

These recommendations will enhance the ability of Californians to hold their government accountable for its actions. This will lead to an increased satisfaction among voters with the government and will lead to improved, more responsive policymaking.

Mathew D. McCubbins

THE ROLE OF DIRECT DEMOCRACY[6]

The Referendum

While I have argued that some of the internal checks on representative government should be eliminated, I also believe that external checks, through the referendum process, should be expanded. In a very real sense, the people should be asked to approve their government's decisions directly. Referendums on such matters as bond issues are built into the current California Constitution, and more categories of legislative policymaking should be subject to the veto of the people.

How might this work? The legislature will be asked to enact a budget for every biennium. The legislature will be subject to a variety of constitutional limitations with regard to the contents of the budget. Spending, tax, and borrowing ceilings may be imposed on the budget as passed by the legislature and signed by the governor. The legislature, however, may find it necessary or expedient to propose a budget that violates one or more of these constitutional limitations. The legislature would then be required to take the issue to the people and seek a waiver, through a referendum, for the constitutional violation. The legislature would offer the people a choice between two budgets, one in compliance with all constitutional proscriptions and one that requires a waiver. The referendum can be stated in such a way as to explain the differences between the two budgets and then to ask the people to approve the legislature's work.[7] In this way, the people retain their ability to check legislative action, but, importantly, the legislature is the only player in the budgetary game, other than the negative check offered by the electorate.

While it is true that such limitations will reduce accountability, as with any trade-off there is a corresponding gain. The gain takes four forms. First, the people, through referendums, serve to check the excesses of government. This is common in many places including most states and

---

[6]Direct democracy can take the form of a referendum that is proposed by the legislature or an initiative that is proposed by private citizens.

[7]The people also have an option to reject both budgets, in which case the reversionary policy can be a current services budget, where all necessary programs are funded at the level of the previous balanced budget until the legislature's proposal can meet with the approval of the voters.

several countries. Second, it helps to give the members of the legislature an intimate sympathy with the people of the state. Legislators must keep close to the people to know what sorts of referendums they will accept. Third, the fact that the legislature must go to the people to seek a waiver of a constitutional limitation implies that the people will be better informed with respect to their legislature's activities and will be better able to tie policy outcomes to their electoral decisions. This will work especially well if the referendums are voted on at the same time as legislative elections. It is in this way that incentives to act responsibly can be bound to government officials. Finally, the government, with the consent of the people, would have the flexibility to waive constitutional limitations that, at the time, are doing more harm than good. Such a system would provide the legislature with the flexibility to respond to fiscal crises, as long as a majority of the voters believe the remedy to be better than the disease. Not only does the unicameral nature of the legislative decision make it easy for voters to know who is responsible for the policies being proposed (Brady and Gaines 1995; Cain and Persily 1995), but the referendum requirement allows voters to become informed about the legislature's actions.

In choosing the outlines of these constitutional budgetary proscriptions, it is important to keep in mind what the trade-offs are: each limitation comes with an associated loss of accountability. So which limitations are worth the loss? General limitations on the actions of government in the fiscal arena, such as tax, spending, and debt ceilings are very popular. Without these limitations the legislature could (and we might expect they would) make decisions contrary to the public will, benefiting narrow interests at the expense of the public as a whole.

To make the government more accountable and responsive when we impose budget ceilings (e.g., prohibiting borrowing of any kind, by any office of the state, without voter approval), we must also make sure they are simple, straightforward, and consistent. For example, the tax and spending ceilings could simply be a requirement that growth in revenues and expenditures (from all sources created by the state) are limited to either the rate of inflation or growth in population, whichever is greater. The tax and spending restrictions now in the constitution are so complicated that even the most diligent voter would be unable to master every detail. If we are to make such constraints binding, the people need to quickly understand when these constraints have been violated. We need to allow the state legislature to waive the budget ceilings with explicit voter approval.

Finally, to make the planning of such budget referendums feasible, the process needs to be stretched, creating a two-year fiscal cycle.

The benefits from this system are apparent. No longer will one generation's reforms hamper another generation's growth. Government can and must change as the state changes. No temporary majority should have the power to alter the constitution without regard to the consequences. This system forces the electorate to take responsibility for their own decisions and allows them to assign blame for the decisions of their legislators. The flexibility and responsiveness of a unicameral, biennial budgetary process will restore the accountability that California has lacked for so long.

Several questions are raised by this proposal. First, would this lead to a geometric rise in the number of times voters would have to trek to the ballot box? The answer would appear to be no. In the normal course of events, the legislature would need only to exceed the growth limits imposed by the constitution occasionally, and the biennial budget cycle should further reduce the opportunity for the legislature to ask for more money. Second, would such a system allow a future legislature to effect large changes in the size of government if that was its mandate? Yes, the legislature would simply have to do as it promised in the election, then submit the bottom line of the plan for voter approval. The democratic ideal is well served by allowing people to change their minds.

Third, and most important, would this system solve the conflicts inherent in human nature? I believe it at least addresses these problems directly, and limits the mischief that these problems may bring about. The streamlined (effectively unicameral) legislative process will make decision making more efficient and legislators more accountable by altering their incentives. These features, along with the voter check on budgetary measures, will increase the accountability of government and force decision makers to face the trade-offs engendered by their policy decisions.

THE INITIATIVE

In *Federalist 49*, James Madison argues that "a constitutional road to the decision of the people ought to be marked out and kept open for certain . . . occasions. But there appear to be insuperable objections against the proposed recurrence to the people, as a provision in all cases for keeping the several departments of power within their constitutional limits." In other words, the people should retain some check on representative government other than elections, but that check should not devolve into an ubiquitous use of direct democracy. If we are to take advantage of the efficiency and accountability of a unicameral cabinet government for budgetary policy (Cain and Persily 1995; Brady and Gaines 1995), we should restrict the application of direct popular sovereignty.[8] Further, if we believe that all power corrupts those who exercise it, then we must place checks on the exercise of all power, including the power of the people of the state of California to make policy and to amend the constitution.

California's system of direct democracy is much less restrictive than any other state's in the union, and the consequences of this experiment in unrestricted direct democracy are now painfully evident. Twenty-six states have either the initiative, the referendum, or both (Gerber 1995, Cain et al. 1995), but none allow legislation without the participation of the legislature. The idea behind the initiative in other states is that the people can spur the legislature into action, but they cannot altogether replace republican government with direct democracy. Perhaps a small change is all that is needed.

What limits should be imposed on budgetary policymaking by direct legislation? First, and most important, the legislature should be given the ability to check any budgetary initiative (any statutory or constitutional initiative with a fiscal impact) before it reaches the ballot. I recommend therefore that initiative proposers first submit their drafts to the legislature for approval. The legislator then has the opportunity to either accept the proposal, reject it, or do nothing. If the legislature decides not to consider the proposal, then the initiative's proposers must convince five percent of the state's registered voters to sign a petition to place the measure on the ballot (which is the current system). If the legislature approves of the

---

[8]There is precedent in California for limiting the ability of the voters to add nondiscretionary spending to the state's obligations. Article 16, Section 2—added in 1962—reads:

> *No amendment to this Constitution which provides for the preparation, issuance and sale of bonds of the State of California shall hereafter be submitted to the electors, nor shall any such amendment to the Constitution hereafter submitted to or approved by the electors become effective for any purpose.*

In other words, any bond issues decided upon by referendum may only be statutory, not constitutional.

measure by resolution, then it is placed on the ballot as a legislative initiative.[9] Again, this is feasible under the current system. The real change comes if the legislature rejects the initiative, which would then necessitate the signatures of 15 percent of the state's registered voters to place it on the ballot. While this would limit the ability of initiative machines to manipulate the initiative process, it would not prohibit the people from passing statutory or constitutional initiatives to correct a corrupt legislature. More important, it would put California in line with all other states and foreign governments, where the legislature has the authority to check the excesses of direct democracy, and make a tyranny of the majority, tyranny of initiative organizations, and corporate tyranny less likely.

Some would argue that this proposal puts an insurmountable barrier between the people and the initiative process. Thus, these critics would argue only well-heeled initiative organizations would get their initiatives to the ballot, for only they could afford "buying" the additional signatures needed to place a rejected initiative before the people. Such a criticism is flatly false. It only makes the barrier higher for initiative proposals that the professional policymakers in the legislature feel are unwarranted. It lowers the barrier for both statutory and constitutional initiatives that the legislature approves. The recommendation to put a prior check on the initiative proposals is borrowed from the Federalist premise that all government action should be subject to a system of checks and balances. The internal checks created by the Federalists make it difficult for the average constituent to get their favored policies enacted (if the legislature is accountable to the people, then the interests of the average constituents should be represented by the legislature itself), and thus only the well-heeled can afford to lobby the various divisions of government to have their favored policies become law. In response I would argue that the proposed process is not only better than the current system, unchecked direct democracy, but that the gain in efficiency and responsibility of this system can hurt only the corporate interests that dominate the process today.[10]

---

[9]The approved initiative can, of course, be an amended version of the initiative as originally proposed. In this case the initiative's supporters can ask for a separate resolution approving or disapproving their unamended initiative proposal.

[10]Other checks on the initiative are possible. For instance, many states allow the legislature, with certain limitations, to amend enacted initiatives. The danger

While checking the power of the initiative will go quite far to correcting the defects of our current system, problems will still remain. It is likely, for example, that voters will not face the trade-offs that their decisions involve. They will vote to spend now and pay later. Government spending must eventually be paid for, either through higher taxes or—if the public debt is never paid off—in lower income growth. Once either a constitutional or statutory initiative is passed, these trade-offs are left to state legislators, who must then find ways to pay for all of the spending (or tax cuts) that the voters mandate. Unfortunately, as in California today, the legislature may not be in a constitutional or political position to do so. There may be constitutional rules that make certain necessary decisions impossible. Trade-offs may not be feasible, and certain options may not even be desirable.

Removing restraints on legislators is only half of the solution. Voters must be accountable for their decisions as well. If we are to keep the initiative (as opposed to the referendum), then all direct legislation could be "pay-as-you-go" in regards to budgetary matters. All tax reductions would have to be accompanied by commensurate spending cuts, and all new spending must be accompanied by new revenues.

For statutory and constitutional initiatives concerning fiscal matters, we ought to impose sunset provisions. Each initiative will have a renewal requirement every four years. This will allow voters to examine a decision, once they have seen some of the trade-offs it entails. There is precedent for such "sunset provisions" in the California Constitution—Article 13B, Section 4 allows "the electors" to establish or change appropriations limits for a maximum of four years at a time. In all other states, there are provisions that resemble the sunset provision for legislative amendment of initiatives (Gerber 1995, Cain et al. 1995). Whereas a sunset provision means that an initiative only stands for four years unless the people renew their commitment to it, the temporary restriction against legislative amendment of initiatives means that the initiative stands only for two or four years unless the legislature refrains from changing it.

---

here is that the initiative, then, cannot serve as a check on legislative authority. The initiative serves only to partly set the legislative agenda.

CONCLUSION

The current dilemma in California politics is that the more voters try to restore accountability to their government, the less freedom legislators have. I see the problem as twofold: we must restore accountability to government, and we must ensure that this accountability remains. This is impossible under the current constitutional framework. In order to reach the heart of the inconsistencies engendered by decades of incremental reform, we must recreate the framework. Armed with a new understanding of constitutional principles from the Federalists and the Progressives, we can create a better government.

This government can be limited in any fashion the voters desire, but not beyond the boundaries of reason. The electorate can work as a check against the legislature, and the legislature can act as a check against the electorate. Thus we can benefit from the experience of the Progressives who saw direct democracy as the only method to break the corruption of political machines, along with the wisdom of the Federalists who realized that all civic power must be limited and checked. By taking the lessons of these two groups and directly addressing the dangers of human nature, we can synthesize a new state, an accountable state, a state where legislators act in the best interests of the people, and the people act in their own best interests as well.

REFERENCES

Brady, David W., and Brian J. Gaines. 1995. "A House Discarded? Evaluating the Case for a Unicameral California Legislature." In *Constitutional Reform in California: Making State Government More Effective and Responsive*, ed. Bruce E. Cain and Roger G. Noll. Berkeley, Calif.: Institute of Governmental Studies Press.

Cain, Bruce E., Sara Ferejohn, Margarita Najar, and Mary Walther. 1995. "Constitutional Change: Is It Too Easy to Amend our State Constitution?" In *Constitutional Reform in California: Making State Government More Effective and Responsive*, ed. Bruce E. Cain and Roger G. Noll. Berkeley, Calif.: Institute of Governmental Studies Press.

Cain, Bruce E., and Roger G. Noll. 1995. "Principles of State Constitutional Design." In *Constitutional Reform in California: Making State Government More Effective and Responsive*, ed. Bruce E. Cain and Roger G. Noll. Berkeley, Calif.: Institute of Governmental Studies Press.

Cain, Bruce E., and Nathaniel Persily. 1995. "Creating an Accountable Legislature: The Parliamentary Option for California Government." In *Constitutional Reform in California: Making State Government More Effective and Responsive*, ed. Bruce E. Cain and Roger G. Noll. Berkeley, Calif.: Institute of Governmental Studies Press.

Campbell, Angus, Phillip E. Converse, Warren E. Miller, and Donald E. Stokes. 1980. *The American Voter*. Chicago and London: The University of Chicago Press.

Ellwood, John W., and Mary Sprague. 1995. "Options for Reforming the California Stata Budget Process." In *Constitutional Reform in California: Making State Government More Effective and Responsive*, ed. Bruce E. Cain and Roger G. Noll. Berkeley, Calif.: Institute of Governmental Studies Press.

Gerber, Elisabeth R. 1995. "Reforming the California Initiative: A Proposal to Increase Flexibility and Legislative Accountability." In *Constitutional Reform in California: Making State Government More Effective and Responsive*, ed. Bruce E. Cain and Roger G. Noll. Berkeley, Calif.: Institute of Governmental Studies Press.

Hamilton, Alexander, John Jay and James Madison. 1982. *The Federalist Papers*. Toronto, New York: Bantam Books.

Kiewiet, Roderick D. 1995. "Constitutional Limitations on Indebtedness: The Case of California." In *Constitutional Reform in California: Making State Government More Effective and Responsive*, ed. Bruce E. Cain and Roger G. Noll. Berkeley, Calif.: Institute of Governmental Studies Press.

Mill, John Stuart. 1947. *On Liberty*. Arlington Heights, Ill.: AHM Publishing Company.

Mowry, George Edwin. 1976. *The California Progressives*. Chicago: Quadrangle Books.

Noll, Roger G. 1995. "Executive Organization: Responsiveness vs. Expertise and Flexibility." In *Constitutional Reform in California: Making State Government More Effective and Responsive*, ed. Bruce E. Cain and Roger G. Noll. Berkeley, Calif.: Institute of Governmental Studies Press.

Reichley, A. James. 1985. "The Rise of National Parties." In *The New Direction in American Politics*, ed. John E. Chubb and Paul E. Peterson. Washington, D.C.: Brookings Institution.

Rawls, John. 1971. *A Theory of Justice*, Cambridge, Mass.: Belknap Press of Harvard University Press.

Constitutional Limitations on Indebtedness: The Case of California

D. Roderick Kiewiet

INTRODUCTION

In the heady days following successful completion of the Erie Canal, U.S. states and cities issued unprecedented amounts of debt to finance railroads, turnpikes, and canals (Williamson 1964; Davis and Cull 1992). Dutch and British investors eagerly bought up the American state and local bonds underwritten by Baring Brothers, Huth and Company, and other leading investment houses. Unfortunately, many of the projects funded by these bond issues got underway just as the Depression of 1837 began, and anticipated revenues failed to materialize. Corruption and speculation also took a toll. Nine states and several cities ultimately defaulted on the bonds they had issued.[1] The states eventually resumed payment on these bonds and made at least partial restitution, but it was decades before the confidence of foreign investors was fully restored. For most defaulting states, regaining credit-worthiness required the unpopular expedient of instituting excise and property taxes to raise the necessary revenue (McGrane 1935).

Sobered by these defaults and the undesirable consequences they engendered, the citizens of these and most other states subsequently wrote into their constitutions limitations on the issuance of full faith and credit debt. What is meant by "full faith and credit" is the unconditional promise

---

I would like to thank Bruce Cain, June Fujimoto, Hardy Gumner, Carolyn Lutton, Mat McCubbins, Ellen Moratti, Chuck Nicol, Roger Noll, Peter Schaafsma, Steven Shea, Paul Silva, Kristin Szakaly, Wendy Tam, and David Vasché for their comments. I am especially indebted to Martha Riley for valuable assistance in helping me find out what I needed to know.

[1]The defaulting states were Maryland, Illinois, Indiana, Michigan, Mississippi, Louisiana, Arkansas, Florida, and Pennsylvania (McGrane 1935).

of the state to levy whatever taxes are necessary to meet interest and principal payments. Bonds bearing the full faith and credit pledge are referred to as either general obligation bonds or as "guaranteed" debt. Such debt may in the first instance be funded by designated fees, taxes, or lease revenue (in which case it is called "self-liquidating"), but it is considered guaranteed if the state pledges in the indenture that it will step in with tax revenue if these sources are insufficient.

Most state constitutions have certain idiosyncratic features in their provisions regarding bonded indebtedness, but limitations on general obligation bonds are of four basic types. As shown in Table 1, the most common limitation is the requirement of referendum approval, stipulated in the constitutions of California and 19 other states. Although some states require a referendum to approve any general obligation bond issues, what most constitutions (including California's) actually specify is that voter approval is required to issue guaranteed debt in excess of some small sum, generally ranging from $50,000 to $2 million, that can be applied to short-term, "casual" deficits. As a practical matter, such provisions preclude state authorities from issuing any long-term guaranteed debt until the referendum approval condition is satisfied.[2] The entries in Table 1 indicate that the constitution of California and those of 11 other states also specify that guaranteed debt be approved by a supermajority of the legislature. In California the requirement is two-thirds of the members of both houses, but the required supermajorities vary from 60 percent to three-fourths of the membership.

Fifteen other state constitutions forbid guaranteed debt to exceed a revenue-based ceiling, the most common being fixed percentages of general revenue or of total assessed property valuation. Nine prohibit the issue of guaranteed debt entirely. As in the case of almost all states in the referendum approval category, the states that prohibit guaranteed long-term debt do permit borrowing small sums to cover "casual" deficits, and allow for full faith and credit debt to be issued for "extraordinary purposes" such

---

[2]South Carolina's constitution contains a referendum approval requirement in addition to its revenue-based limit. Prior to 1975 Louisiana's Constitution ostensibly prohibited long-term guaranteed debt. According to Ratchford (1941) and Heins (1963), however, in both cases major loopholes effectively negated these provisions, and they are thus not indicated as present in Table 1.

Table 1. ***State Constitutional Limitations on Guaranteed Long-Term Debt, FY 1990***

State	Referendum Approval	Super-majority	Prohibition	Revenue-based	No Limitation
Alabama			X		
Alaska	X				
Arizona			X		
Arkansas	X				
California	X	X			
Colorado			X		
Connecticut					X
Delaware		X			
Florida	X				
Georgia				X	
Hawaii				X	
Idaho	X				
Illinois	X	X			
Indiana			X		
Iowa	X				
Kansas	X				
Kentucky	X				
Louisiana		X			
Maine	X	X			
Maryland					X
Massachusetts		X			
Michigan	X	X			
Minnesota		X			
Mississippi				X	
Missouri	X				
Montana		X			
Nebraska			X		
Nevada				X	
New Hampshire					X
New Jersey	X				
New Mexico	X			X	
New York	X				

Table 1. ***Continued***

State	Referendum Approval	Super-majority	Prohibition	Revenue-based	No Limitation
North Carolina	X			X	
North Dakota			X		
Ohio			X		
Oklahoma	X				
Oregon				X	
Pennsylvania	X			X	
Rhode Island	X				
South Carolina				X	
South Dakota		X		X	
Tennessee					X
Texas			X		
Utah				X	
Vermont					X
Virginia		X		X	
Washington		X		X	
West Virginia			X		
Wisconsin				X	
Wyoming	X			X	

as repelling invasions or suppressing insurrections. Only five states currently have no constitutional limitations on general obligation bonds, which means that their issue is authorized in the manner of ordinary legislation.

Presumably, constitutional provisions impose constraints on policy-makers because they are difficult to enact and thus difficult to overturn. Certainly this is the article of faith to which backers of the federal Balanced Budget Amendment subscribe. But is this actually the case when it comes to state constitutional debt limitations? Are they effective in holding down debt?

According to Kiewiet and Szakaly (1995), states whose constitutions either prohibit them from issuing guaranteed debt, or, like California, that require referendum approval to issue it, carry substantially less guaranteed debt than other states. Revenue-based limitations and legislative supermajority requirements, in contrast, are not effective in limiting the issuance of general obligation bonds.

Interestingly, Kiewiet and Szakaly's findings indicate that referendum requirements are as effective in limiting the issuance of guaranteed debt as outright prohibitions against doing so. The reason why prohibitions do not entirely prohibit is because approval for general obligation bond issues can be gotten in the form of an amendment to the constitution! It is thus probably more accurate to view debt issuance prohibitions as equivalent to the requirements for adopting constitutional amendments, which in most states consist of obtaining both referendum and legislative supermajority approval. Given that it does not appear to pose much of an obstacle, the imposition of a legislative supermajority requirement on top of a referendum approval requirement would appear to be superfluous.[3] In general, then, Kiewiet and Szakaly's findings support Moak's (1982) contention that "The history of public debt in the United States at all levels tends to show that the electorate is financially more conservative than are its representatives in government" (p. 114).

THE LIMITS OF CONSTITUTIONAL LIMITATION

Although effective in limiting full faith and credit debt, state constitutional debt limitations are readily and routinely circumvented (Ratchford 1941; Heins 1963; Bunch 1991; Nice 1991). The most widely recognized means by which public authorities sidestep these strictures is to issue bonds that are not backed by the taxing power of the state, but rather by a nontax

---

[3]The California Constitution forbids amending the constitution in order to approve general obligation bond issues. This seems moot at best, in that the requirements for obtaining approval for a bond issue are identical to the requirements for amending the constitution. One can only speculate as to what the courts would do if an amendment to the state constitution authorizing a bond issue were in fact approved.

flow of revenue. Because the taxpayers of the state are not directly liable in the case of default on such bonds, the courts have ruled that constitutional limitations on debt do not apply. Debt of this nature is referred to as either revenue bonds or as "nonguaranteed" debt.

Lacking the full faith and credit pledge associated with general obligation bonds, nonguaranteed revenue bonds generally pay higher rates of interest (Forbes, Fischer, and Peterson 1981). Nonetheless, there remain several reasons why a public entity might still prefer to issue revenue bonds, particular when there is a bona fide flow of revenue to back them, e.g., utility bills, tolls, or user fees. In many cases, however, nonguaranteed debt is issued for projects that generate little or no revenue, for the sole purpose of circumventing constitutional limitations on guaranteed debt. Most notably, public authorities issue nonguaranteed "lease-payment" bonds to build facilities, such as prisons, schools, hospitals, and office buildings, that traditionally are funded through general obligation bonds. The authorities then lease the facilities to other state and local government agencies, who pay the rent out of the ongoing appropriations they receive (Bennett and DiLorenzo 1982). Certificates of participation are another form of nonguaranteed debt that is nevertheless financed out of general tax revenue.

A second major reason why state constitutional debt limitations do not constrain debt financing is because of devolution—the displacement of long-term debt issuance from the state level of government to the local level. To be sure, it may not be practical for most local governments to undertake large-scale capital projects, but in most cases anything that can be financed by a state government can be done by either local governments or by special districts as well. Moreover, state governments have broad authority to mandate that local governments provide particular services and facilities that may necessitate debt financing to be put into place (Glendening and Reeves 1984). Several previous studies report strong evidence of devolution (Heins 1963; Nice 1991; Kiewiet and Szakaly 1995).

Although proponents of constitutional debt limitations tend to characterize both circumvention and devolution as subterfuge, there is nothing in these debt "end-runs" that are illegal, conspiratorial, or even disingenuous in nature. These complaints are thus similar to those concerning the existence of loopholes in the federal tax code. On the other hand, one need not have a phobia about debt financing to have some serious concerns about these phenomena. First, shifting from guaranteed debt to nonguaranteed debt (or from debt issued at the state level to the local level) results in significantly higher borrowing costs. In addition to the higher interest rates that must be paid, issuing nonguaranteed debt entails higher administrative, legal, and insurance costs, and typically requires bond "upsizing" to cover reserve fund requirements and carrying charges during project construction. According to Nicol's (1995) calculations, debt service costs on lease-payment bonds are approximately 20 percent higher than for general obligation bonds.

The issuance of large amounts of nonguaranteed state debt or local debt can drive up interest rates on state guaranteed debt as well. This is because only citizens of the state in which state and local bonds are issued can claim the interest they yield to be exempt from state and local taxes. Issuers of all types of municipal bonds (guaranteed or nonguaranteed, state or local) must thus sell to the same pool of in-state investors. As Bahl and Duncombe (1993) put it, all debt issued by public authorities, be it guaranteed or nonguaranteed, state or local, "ultimately is a claim on the resource base of the state"(p. 32).

It is also naive to believe that the taxpayers of a state are insulated from the consequences of default just because a bond is nonguaranteed, or because it was issued by a single city or county. According to Jones (1984), the Washington Public Power Supply System (WPPSS) default of 1983 drove up the state of Washington's cost of credit by a full percentage point. The negative impact of the recent Orange County bankruptcy fiasco upon California bonds in general has also been widely documented.[4]

A final problem arises from the fact that state governments rarely issue nonguaranteed debt directly, but instead establish authorities, boards, agencies, special districts, and commissions to do so. O'Brien (1989) posits that because they shift debt issuance away from elected officials to others

---

[4]In general, the distinction between guaranteed and nonguaranteed debt is blurred by the fact that actions which are possible from a legal standpoint are unthinkable from a practical standpoint. For instance, the state could legally close down a department or agency that is making lease payments to another state entity (in California the lessor is usually the Public Works Board), thus eliminating its budget and necessarily producing a default. The reaction of the credit markets to such a move, however, would be swift and terrible. In all likelihood the state would be unable to borrow any money for any reason until the situation were rectified.

who are far less accountable, constitutional limitations on guaranteed debt may actually *increase* total state debt. Others worry more generally about a loss of accountability, but this need not be the case; several states, including California, require legislative approval of revenue bond issues or place other statutory limitations upon them.

Rather, the problem that inevitably arises from the delegation of debt-issuing authority to large numbers of separate agencies is the diffusion of responsibility and the fragmentation of decision making. Policymakers never directly confront trade-offs among the myriad competing demands for long-term debt financing, and fail to set priorities. In a major report issued by the National Conference of State Legislatures, Yondorf and Puls (1987) identify the failure to prioritize capital projects as one of the major weaknesses in the financial operations of state governments.

THE CASE OF CALIFORNIA

The discussion so far has been based upon the collective experience of state and local governments in general. We turn now to the record of long-term bond issuance by the state of California. Figures 1, 2, and 3 compare the total amounts of outstanding state guaranteed debt, nonguaranteed debt, and total long-term local debt from FY1962 through FY1992. In each case the figures reported are in constant (1994) dollars per capita.

Turning first to Figure 1, we see that by the late 1960s guaranteed debt in California exceeded $1,200 per capita in today's dollars, which was three times greater than the national average. From then on, however, it fell rapidly, and by the end of the 1980s it was substantially lower than the national average. This decline owes to continued rapid population growth as well as to a relatively slow rate of new general obligation bond issues. The sharp increase in per capita guaranteed debt levels that have occurred since then results from the decision of the Department of the Treasury (under then-Secretary Kathleen Brown) to expedite sale of the $11 billion of general obligation bonds the voters had approved over the past several years but that had not been issued. Very little guaranteed debt has been approved in the 1990s, which implies that per capita guaranteed debt levels are likely to begin declining again in the near future.

Given that referendum requirements do constrain guaranteed debt levels while other constitutional limitations do not, the fact that the state of

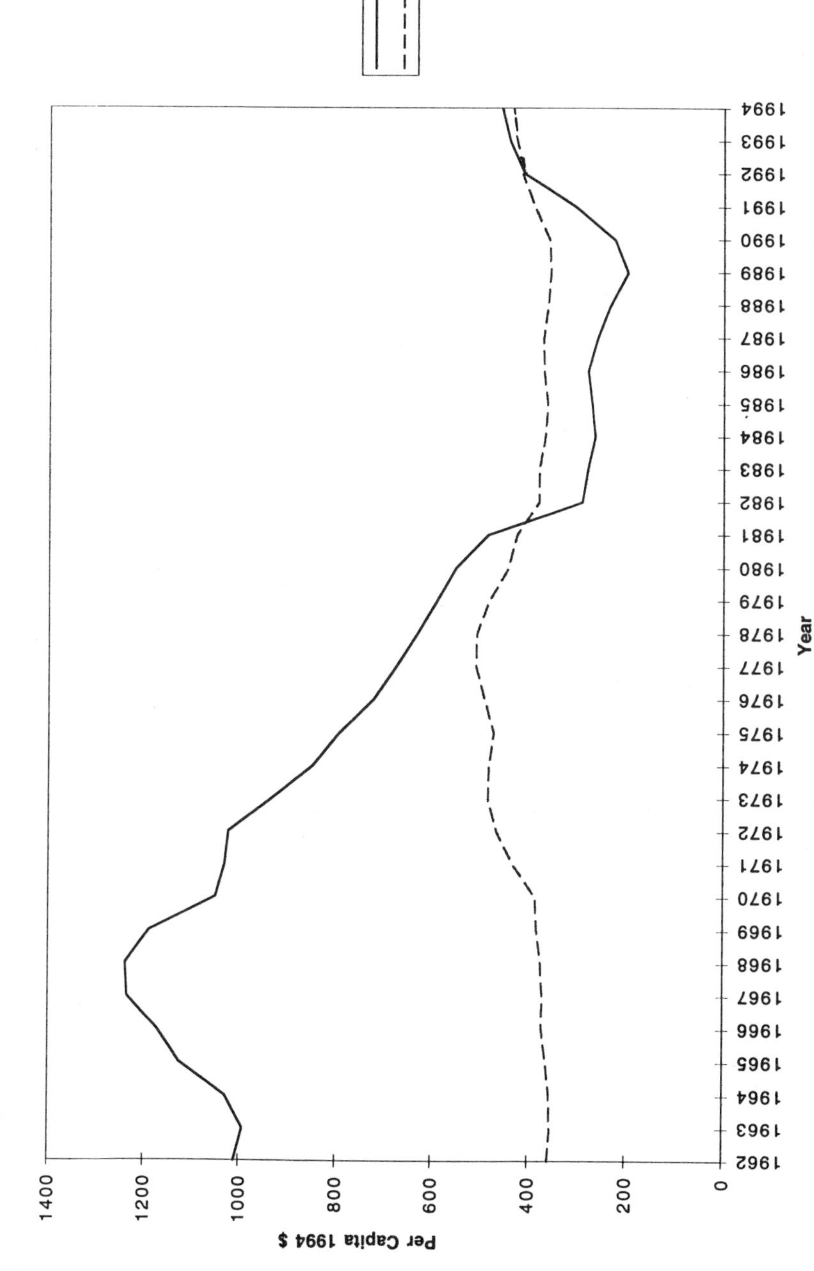

Figure 1. ***State Full Faith and Credit Debt: FY 1962-94***

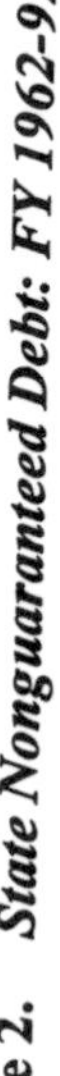

Figure 2. ***State Nonguaranteed Debt: FY 1962-92***

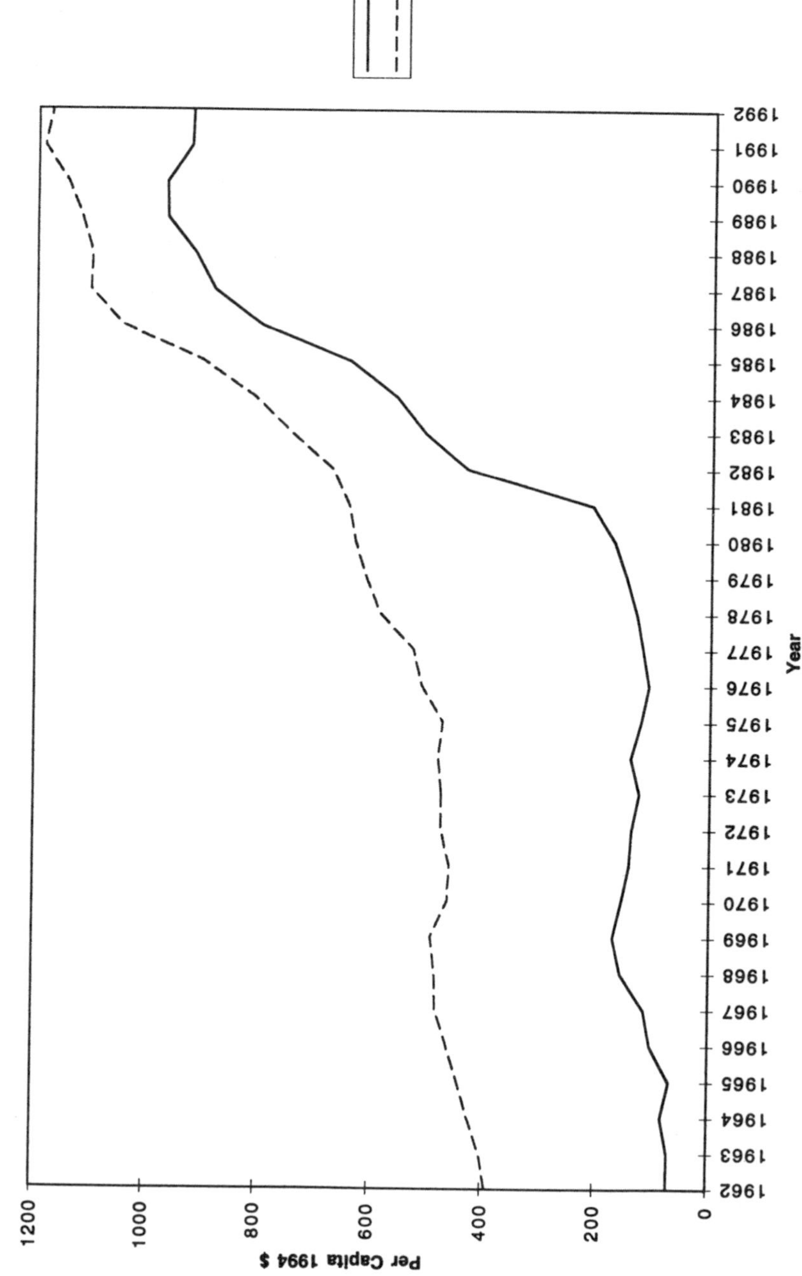

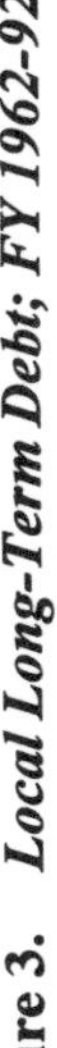

Figure 3. ***Local Long-Term Debt; FY 1962-92***

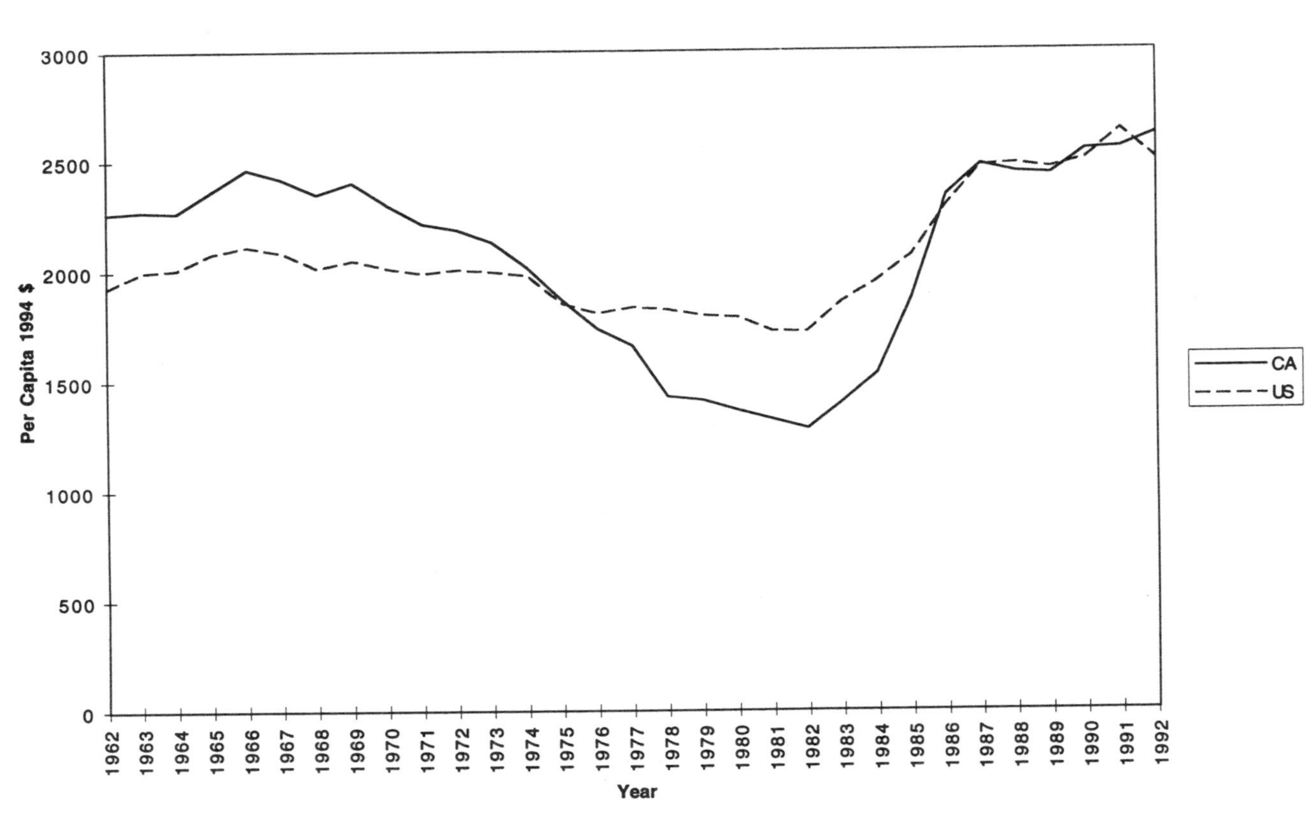

California has managed to issue the volume of general obligation bonds that it has is fairly remarkable. In fact, in the many other states that also have referendum requirements, only in Rhode Island and New Jersey have voters consistently been as willing to take on guaranteed debt (Kiewiet and Szakaly 1995).

In contrast to the guaranteed debt series portrayed in Figure 1, the data on nonguaranteed state debt in California closely track the national average. Nonguaranteed debt levels increased rapidly in California in the 1980s, just as they did in the rest of the country. As many authorities on municipal bonds have noted, this surge largely reflects the proliferation of "public debt for private purposes," or what is referred to in California as "conduit" revenue bonds (Forbes, Fischer, and Peterson 1981; Leonard 1986; Zimmerman 1991). In this form of debt financing, the proceeds of the issue are made available to a private party for activities that are judged to be in the public interest.

The original manifestation of private-purpose debt was the industrial revenue bond. In the mid-1970s, however, state and local governments began issuing such debt for housing developments, mortgage loans, shopping malls, fast food franchises, student loans, and sports stadiums. Ironically, this type of debt financing, which had been creeping upward in volume during the 1960s, accelerated rapidly after Congress ostensibly acted to curtail it (Leonard 1986). Congress ultimately reacted to the burgeoning loss of tax revenue resulting from the proliferation of private-purpose debt by imposing statewide volume caps in the 1986 Tax Reform Act (Kenyon and Zimmerman 1991). The impact of this legislation is evident in Figure 2, which shows the state nonguaranteed debt series flattening out, in California as well as in the country as a whole, in the years following 1986.

Figure 3, which reports real per capita level of long-term debt carried by local governments, also indicates that the experience of California generally tracks that of the country as a whole. In the first half of the series local governments in California carried somewhat more debt than average, and in the FY1977-86 period somewhat less than average, but the differences were never large.

THE PROBLEM OF PUBLIC-LEASE BONDS

There is nothing in the aggregate debt series, then, that is particularly alarming. By the late 1970s the state had managed to substantially reduce the relatively high level of per capita general obligation debt it had amassed in the 1960s and now carries a level of per capita guaranteed debt that is very close to the national average. Nonguaranteed debt has remained at a level that is significantly lower than average, and levels of local debt often lower (and never much higher) than average.

It is when state nonguaranteed debt is decomposed into its constituent parts, however, that a worrisome pattern of circumvention emerges. These data are reported in Table 2 and Figure 4. As the data in Table 2 indicate, much of the nonguaranteed debt issued at the state level in California during the past decade has been in the form of enterprise revenue and conduit revenue bonds—in both cases debt that is backed by a well-defined stream of nontax revenue, and therefore no real cause of concern. What is a matter for concern is the nearly $6 billion in public-lease revenue bonds that are currently outstanding. As indicated earlier, the "lease" payments that back such debt comes primarily from general state tax revenue. As noted by the California Debt Advisory Commission (1990), bond-rating agencies typically include lease-revenue bonds and certificates of participation (along with general obligation bonds) in calculating total state tax-supported debt.

If no additional lease-payment bonds are issued, debt service on those already issued will soon exceed $500 million (Hill 1995). Moreover, all indications are that resort to this type of debt-financing will only continue to increase in the future. The governor's budget for fiscal year 1996 calls for the authorization of $3.3 billion in new lease-payment bonds, primarily for new jails and prisons. According to projections made by the state Department of Finance (1995), in the next decade the state will issue nearly as much in public-lease revenue bonds ($8.7 billion) as in general obligation bonds ($11.6 billion). Presumably, the decision to go with lease-payment financing instead of issuing general obligation bonds is based at least in part upon concern that the voters would balk at approving such a large bond issue. After approving 42 of 43 state bond issues in the 1980s, California voters have rejected almost every proposed issue since then, including two for correctional facilities that appeared on the November 1990 ballot.

Table 2. ***Major Issuers of Long-Term Debt on Behalf of the State of California, 1985-94***

Issuer	General Obligation Bonds	Enterprise Revenue Bonds	Conduit Revenue Bonds	Public Lease Revenue Bonds	Certificates of Participation
State	17,971	340	0	0	0
Regents (UC)	0	1,569	0	95	211
Trustees (CSU)	0	206	9	22	0
Alt. Energy	0	0	149	0	0
Water	0	1,106	0	240	0
Educational	0	0	854	0	0
Health	0	861	4,206	0	2
Housing	0	0	2,786	0	0
Pollution	0	0	3,686	0	0
Public Works	0	105	0	4,388	0
L.A.	0	0	0	952	0
Veteran Affairs	0	0	988	0	0
Schools	0	0	0	77	0
Fairs	0	1	0	0	126
Other	0	12	7	7	0
Total	**17,971**	**4,200**	**12,685**	**5,781**	**339**

*amounts are in $millions

As indicated earlier, lease-payment bonds are a particularly costly way for the state to borrow money. The burgeoning use of lease-payment bonds also threatens to produce levels of tax-supported debt that investors will deem excessive. This will have deleterious consequences for bond ratings, and will necessarily drive up borrowing costs even further.

Even more important, the use of public-lease bonds to circumvent constitutional requirements for issuing general obligation bonds is a mechanism by which policymakers can escape from the demanding and uncomfortable task of prioritizing projects and making trade-offs among

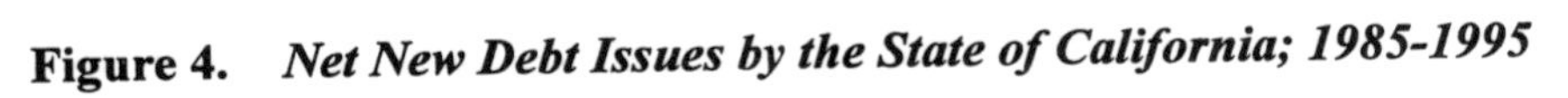

Figure 4. ***Net New Debt Issues by the State of California; 1985-1995***

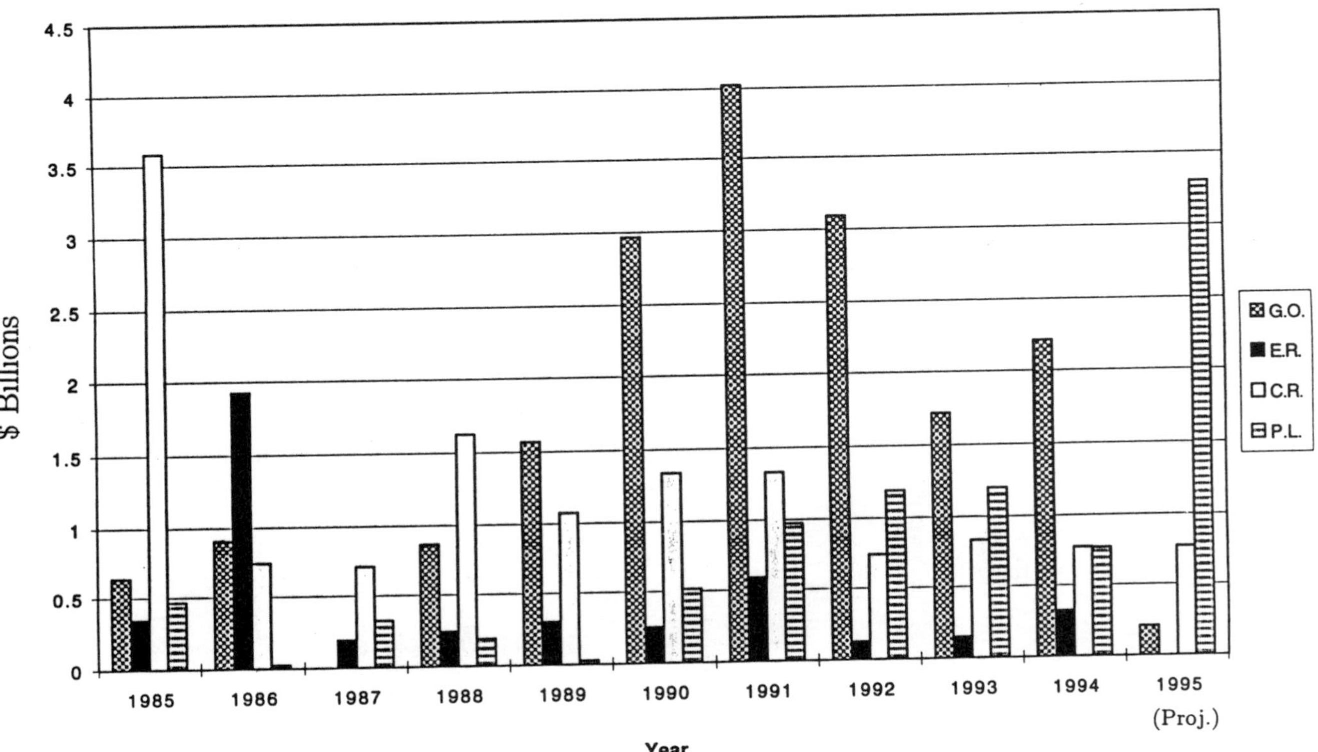

competing demands. This is symptomatic of a larger problem. The state government has established a large number of boards, commissions, and authorities that issue bonds. Although individual boards and authorities prioritize capital outlays within their own domains, there is currently no mechanism for making trade-offs in capital projects across policy domains. The Legislative Analyst's Office has repeatedly called for reform of the way in which the state government makes capital outlay decisions. In a report issued in the halcyon days of a booming state economy and low debt-service costs, the answer to the question, "What is most wrong with the State's Current Process?" was the lack of a multi-year capital outlay plan that prioritized the many competing demands for long-term borrowing (Vasché 1987, 24). This call for reform was repeated again in this year's analysis of the governor's budget:

> If the state is to address its capital outlay investments in a context of limited fiscal resources, the current piecemeal approach to capital outlay decision-making needs to be addressed. The Legislature could make significant strides toward changing this approach and maximizing the state's expenditures for capital outlay by initiating a comprehensive and proactive legislative process for the review and financing of capital programs (Legislative Analyst's Office 1995, I-17).

RECOMMENDATIONS

The people of California are not being well served by the debt limitations that are currently specified in the state constitution. To be sure, the referendum and legislative supermajority approval requirements for issuing general obligation bonds have served the purpose of preventing the state from issuing excessive levels of guaranteed debt. However, this has only led the state to issue more costly debt instruments, most notably lease-payment bonds and certificates of participation, to carry out policies that voters or their representatives presumably support, e.g., more prisons in which to put more criminals. There remains a strong argument that taxpayers ultimately need some constitutional safeguard against excessive debt, and as far as we can tell the requirement of referendum approval is the most reliable. What is necessary, then, is to extend the scope of the referendum approval requirement to cover lease-payment bonds and related methods of debt financing.

Even more significant a problem is the lack of prioritizing that is inherent in the currently fragmented system for issuing bonds. The requirement of referendum approval for general obligation bonds does not enhance and most likely detracts from the ability of state policymakers to set priorities and to make trade-offs among competing demands for scarce fiscal resources.

The major goal of constitutional reform in this area, then, should be to establish an institutional framework for setting capital outlay priorities, to provide the governor and legislature with incentives to adhere to that framework, but to retain the ultimate safeguard of the referendum approval mechanism. Fortunately, such provisions do not need to be invented *de novo*, as they are already present in the constitutions of several states. Adopting these provisions, which are as follows, would lead to significant improvements in the way in which the state of California issues and finances long-term debt:

Recommendation 1:

The governor shall annually submit to the legislature a comprehensive, unified, multi-year capital budget that proposes capital projects for the upcoming fiscal year and establishes a priority order for all such projects across all agencies and departments of the state government. The legislature shall use this budget proposal to adopt an annual Capital Outlay Budget. As the proceeds of bond issues became available, projects shall be undertaken in the priority order established in the Capital Outlay Budget.

This is similar to the chief recommendation made in the report, alluded to earlier, issued by the National Conference on State Legislatures (Yondorf and Puls 1987). Although specific provisions differ widely, over a dozen states currently require their executives to propose and their legislatures to approve capital budgets.

Recommendation 2:

a) Long-term bonds may be issued by the state of California and by its agencies without approval by the voters for capital projects specifically itemized and prioritized in the capital budget, provided that such bonds at the time of issuance would not cause the total amount of principal and interest payable in the current or any future fiscal year, whichever is higher, on such bonds and on all outstanding debt, to exceed a sum equal to 12 percent of the average of the general fund revenues of the state in the three fiscal years immediately preceding such issuance.

b) Any bond issue by or on behalf of the state may exceed the debt limit if it has been approved by a two-thirds vote of all the members elected to each house of the legislature and if, at a general election or primary, it has been submitted to the people and shall have received a majority of all votes cast for and against it at such election. For any issue that would cause the total amount of principal and interest payable in the current or any future fiscal year, whichever is higher, on such bonds and on all outstanding debt, to exceed a sum equal to 18 percent of the average of the general fund revenues of the state in the three fiscal years immediately preceding such issuance, such issue shall have received two-thirds of all votes cast for and against it in a general election or primary.

Part (a) of this recommendation resembles provisions of the constitution of Pennsylvania that was ratified in 1968. The intent here is to allow state policymakers maximal flexibility in setting capital outlay priorities, but retains the requirement that they obtain voter approval for bond issues when debt levels approach a relatively high level. The ceiling recommended here is debt service payments amounting to four percent of general revenue, calculated on a three-year rolling average basis (this type of formula is stipulated in Hawaii's Constitution). Bond-rating agencies tend to regard five percent of general revenue as the threshold at which debt service payments become a matter of serious concern, so this is a little lower than that.

The second part of the recommendation simply increases the requirement of voter approval for new debt issues to a two-thirds supermajority when debt levels rise above an average of six percent of general revenue. This does not make it impossible to issue debt in excess of the six-percent ceiling, but the case for doing so obviously must be quite compelling if the two-thirds referendum approval requirement is to be met.

Recommendation 3:

In calculating the amount of principal and interest payable on all debt, issued and outstanding, totals shall include all general obligation bonds and all other debt financed from lease rentals or other charges payable directly or indirectly from state revenue.

This provision is also drawn from a similar provision in the constitution of Pennsylvania. It stipulates that the debt ceilings specified previously apply to lease-payment bonds, certificates of participation, and other forms of debt, which, although technically nonguaranteed, is not supported by a nontax flow of revenue. Would such a measure make it impossible to circumvent constitutional debt limitations? Probably not, but it would remove a major incentive for issuing higher cost, nonguaranteed debt instead of guaranteed debt. The record of Pennsylvania is also encouraging in this regard, in that it is one of the handfuls of states that was carrying less nonguaranteed state debt per capita in 1990 than in 1960.

REFERENCES

Bahl, Roy, and William Duncombe. 1993. "State and Local Debt Burdens in the 1980s: A Study in Contrasts." *Public Administration Review* 53: 31-40.

Bennett, James, and Thomas DiLorenzo. 1982. "The Limitations of Spending Limitation: Off-Budget Financing and the Illusion of Fiscal Fitness." *Economic Review* 18: 15-17.

Bunch, Beverly. 1991. "The Effect of Constitutional Debt Limitations on State Governments' Use of Public Authorities." *Public Choice* 68: 57-69.

California Debt Advisory Commission. 1990. *California Debt Issuance Primer*. State of California: Sacramento, Calif.

Davis, Lance, and Robert Cull. 1992. "International Capital Movements and American Economic Growth 1820-1914." In *The Cambridge Economic History of the United States*, ed. Stan Engerman and Robert Gallman. New York: Cambridge University Press.

Department of Finance. 1995. "Capital Outlay and Infrastructure Report." State of California: Sacramento, Calif.

Erikson, Robert, Gerald Wright, and John McIver. 1993. *Statehouse Democracy*. New York: Cambridge University Press.

Forbes, Ronald, Philip Fischer, and John Peterson. 1981. "Recent Trends in Municipal Revenue Bond Financing." In *Efficiency in the Municipal Bond Market: The Use of Tax-Exempt Financing for "Private Purposes*, ed. George G. Kaufman. Stanford, Conn.: JAI Press.

Glendening, Parris, and Mavis Reeves. 1984. *Pragmatic Federalism*. Pacific Palisades, Calif.: Palisades Publishers.

Heins, A. James. 1963. *Constitutional Restrictions Against State Debt*. Madison, Wis.: University of Wisconsin Press.

Hill, Elizabeth. 1995 "California's Debt Burden." Legislative Analyst's Office, State of California, Sacramento, Calif.

Jones, L. R. 1984. "The WPPSS Default: Trouble in the Municipal Bond Market." *Public Budgeting and Finance* 4 (Winter): 60-77.

Kenyon, Daphne, and Dennis Zimmerman. 1991. "Private-Activity Bonds and the Volume Cap in 1990." *Intergovernmental Perspective* 17: 35-37.

Kiewiet, D. Roderick, and Kristin Szakaly. 1995. "Constitutional Limitations on Borrowing: An Analysis of State Bonded Indebtedness." California Institute of Technology, Pasadena, Calif.

Legislative Analyst's Office. 1995. *Analysis of the 1995-96 Budget Bill.* State of California: Sacramento, Calif.

Leonard, Herman. 1986. *Checks Unbalanced: The Quiet Side of Public Spending*. New York: Basic Books.

McGrane, Reginald. 1935. *Foreign Bondholders and American State Debts*. New York: The MacMillan Company.

Moak, Lennox. 1982. *Municipal Bonds: Planning, Sale, and Administration*. Municipal Finance Officers Association: Chicago, Ill.

Nice, David C. 1991. "The Impact of State Debt Policies to Limit Debt Financing." *Publius* 21 (Winter): 69-82.

Nicol, Chuck. 1995. "Uses and Costs of Lease-Payment Bonds." Legislative Analyst's Office, State of California, Sacramento, Calif.

O'Brien, Timothy. 1989. "Treasury Performance and Financial Audit." Report of the Colorado State Auditor. Denver, Col.

Peterson, John. 1991. "Innovations in Tax-Exempt Instruments and Transactions." *National Tax Journal* 44: 11-27.

Ratchford, B. U. 1941. *American State Debts*. Durham, N.C.: Duke University Press.

Vasché, Jon David. 1987. "A Perspective on Bond Financing." Office of the Legislative Analyst, State of California, Sacramento, Calif.

Williamson, Jeffrey. 1964. *American Growth and the Balance of Payments, 1820-1913*. Chapel Hill, N.C.: The University of North Carolina Press.

Yondorf, Barbara, and Barbara Puls. 1987. "Capital Budgeting and Finance: The Legislative Role." National Conference on State Legislatures. Denver, Col.

Zimmerman, Dennis. 1991. *The Private Use of Tax-Exempt Bonds*. Washington, D.C.: The Urban Institute Press.

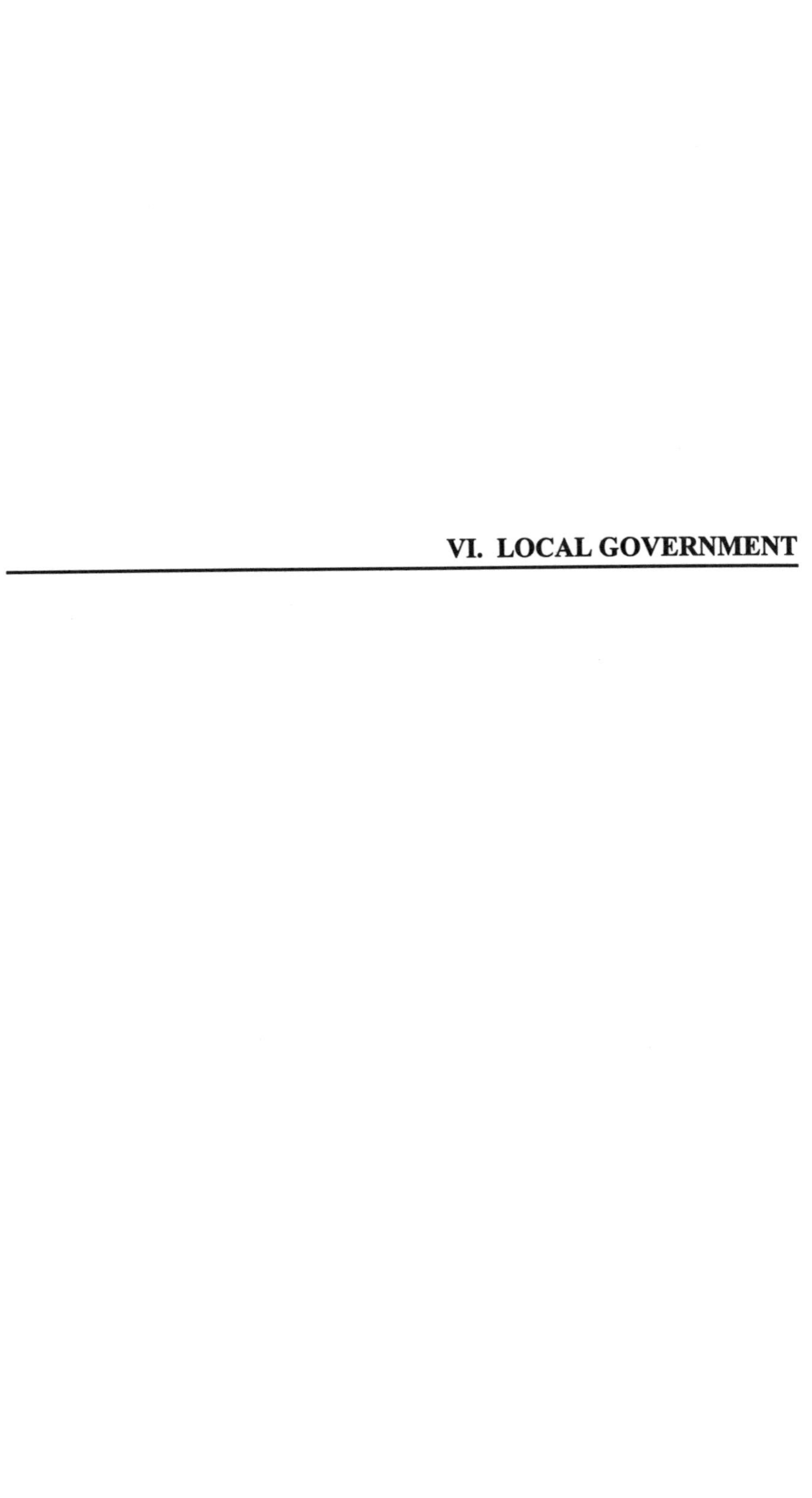

VI. LOCAL GOVERNMENT

State Supremacy, Local Sovereignty: Reconstructing State/Local Relations Under the California Constitution

Daniel B. Rodriguez

The constitutional distribution of state and local power in California essentially follows the principle of state supremacy: local governments are entities subordinate to state authority.[1] Their legal status is much like administrative agencies, and their powers are dependent upon the delegation by the states of legal power through general enabling laws. The structural twist on this state supremacy/local dependency relationship is significant: the establishment of home rule in the California Constitution entitles charter cities and counties to exercise powers without resort to state legislative grant. Home rule municipalities may enact ordinances by the constitutional grant of power in Article XI.[2] The other element of home rule authority is, at least on paper, far more significant as a reallocation of constitutional power between state and home rule municipalities. Under Article XI, Section 5, local governments, "[A]ll charters . . . should be subject to and controlled by general laws *except in the area of municipal affairs*."[3] But for this phrase, charter municipalities would be permitted to act without express legislative grant but would be vulnerable to state laws that *preempt* local ordinances. The "municipal affairs" amendment to the California Constitution reshapes the dimensions of state/local sovereignty;

I thank the convenors of the Conference, Roger Noll and Bruce Cain, for their useful advice and also Preble Stolz of the law school for his comments on this chapter's proposals.

[1]See, e.g., *Hunter v. City of Pittsburgh*, 207 U.S. 161 (1907); Howard Lee McBain, "The Doctrine of an Inherent Right of Local Self-Government," 16 *Colum. L. Rev.* 16 (1916): 190.

[2]Cal. Const. Art. XI.

[3]Cal. Const. Art. XI, Sec. 5.

it indicates that there is a sphere in which local governments are sovereign, that is, in which ordinary state laws cannot preempt local initiatives.[4]

The core question of what constitutes "municipal affairs" has vexed California courts for the century that this phrase has been part of the constitution. The issue, while seemingly involving a narrow question of interpretation of a provision buried in little-noticed Article XI, sheds light on general, fundamental issues concerning the constitutional status of local governments in California and of the structural-legal relationship between the state and localities in an era in which local governments are increasingly vulnerable to fiscal burdens and state encroachment on local prerogatives. In this chapter, I concentrate on Article XI, Section 5 and the proper scope of "municipal affairs" in order to shed some light on these larger issues. The chapter proceeds as follows: in the first part, I spell out some of the details of the legal controversy over the "municipal affairs" clause in Article XI. In order to provide a base for a consideration of some reform proposals, I trace out, in the second part of this chapter, the case for expanded local power through constitutional reconstruction. Next, I describe a few proposals for reconstructing the constitutional relationship between states and home rule charter municipalities.[5]

STATE SUPREMACY, HOME RULE, AND THE "MUNICIPAL AFFAIRS" PUZZLE

Although there is little indication in the debates over the ratification of either the original 1848 constitution or of the constitution of 1879 that the framers gave much thought to the foundations of local government power, to the extent that they expressed their views, they expressed the principle of state supremacy.[6] The central question for the framers of the constitu-

---

[4]Professor Sho Sato describes this as the "protective" function of home rule. Sato, "'Municipal Affairs' in California," *Cal. L. Rev.* 60 (1972): 1055.

[5]While this chapter considers state/local relations in California only in regard to home rule municipalities, it should be noted that while there are various "general law" (and, thus, nonhome rule) cities and counties in the state, the vast majority of the state's citizens live in home rule municipalities.

[6]See the discussion in John Peppin, "Municipal Home Rule in California I," *Cal. L. Rev.* 30 (1941): 1. See also James W. Govert, "California Municipal Corporation Law, 1849-1914: A Preliminary Inquiry" (May 1994 draft on file with

tion (especially in 1878-79) was pragmatic: to what use should municipalities be put? And what is the proper institutional structure in which decisions about the appropriate locus of decision-making authority? On the one hand, the delineation in Article XI of a state/local structure of power that preserved the essential elements of state supremacy indicated that the decisions of which functions municipal governments should perform would properly be made by state political institutions through legislation and by state voters through the initiative and referendum power. On the other hand, the innovation of home rule in the 1878 constitution and, especially, the establishment at the end of the last century of a "municipal affairs" clause reconstituted, at least for cities and counties of a certain size, the legal status of local governments. As far as this dimension of the state/local relationship was concerned, the critical questions of allocation of legal authority would be made by the courts in carrying out their responsibilities to interpret the scope of localities' home rule powers under Article XI, Section 5.

There are precious few clues about how the late 19th-century lawmakers in California thought about the structural changes wrought by constitutional home rule. The apparent concern of the various Progressive Era municipal reform-types who fueled the home rule movement in California, Missouri, Washington, Colorado, and elsewhere was that municipalities lacked a secure basis in state law for the exercise of lawmaking powers.[7] Requiring municipalities to resort to state political processes every time they wished to pass local ordinances was cumbersome and undependable; and states were understandably wary of entitling local governments to use a general "police power."[8] The home rule device was very much a product of the ideas of government reformers who argued that municipalities required more liberal powers in order to carry out essential governmental

---

the author).

[7]See Howard McBain, *The Law and the Practice of Municipal Home Rule* (New York: Columbia University Press, 1916).

[8]Indeed, there were a number of reasons why states were wary of entrusting municipalities with substantial legislative powers. See, e.g., Joan C. Williams, "The Constitutional Vulnerability of American Local Government: The Politics of City Status in American Law," *Wis. L. Rev.* (1986): 83. Gerald Frug, "The City as a Legal Concept," *Harv. L. Rev.* 93 (1980): 1057.

functions.[9] The reasons for this innovation are ably described by 19th century legal scholar Howard McBain:

> [I]t is simply a fact that in the course of time the legislature has, by the enactment of elaborate and ever more elaborate charters and charter amendments, thrust its hands into the very minutiae of city government. It has occupied field after field that was formerly either wholly unoccupied or left to local action. It has regulated detail after detail that never should have been made the subject of charter provision. . . . Bound in the innumerable impediments of complicated charter laws, cities have too little opportunity for constructive self-development. They must eternally appeal to an extraneous superior, the state legislature; and they must often be denied their requests. They must eternally fight against "interference" in their affairs, which is none the less reprehensible because it is legal.[10]

Constitutional home rule did not shatter the dependency relationship of local government and state government. Home rule did not represent the legal secession of municipalities; after all, municipal charters still had to be approved by the state legislature. In a sense, these charters functioned like corporate bylaws, describing the basic architecture of powers that the governing officials of the municipal corporation could exercise.[11] The key change in the constitutional status of localities came with the 1896 addition of the caveat "except in municipal affairs." What this did was to create a shield around home rule municipalities when they acted in the area of "municipal affairs." Was it the intent of the framers of this amendment to create such a shield? Again, the evidence is thin. We can speculate, though, that the impetus of the municipal reform movement that thrived briefly during the Progressive Era was to secure a constitutional foundation

---

[9]See the discussion of city power and progress in Howard McBain, *American City Progress and the Law* (New York: Columbia University Press, 1918); Frank Goodnow, *Municipal Home Rule* (New York and London: Macmillan and Co., 1895).

[10]See McBain, *City Progress*, at 3.

[11]See McBain, *Municipal Home Rule*, at 200-28 (section entitled "The Legal Nature of a Freeholders' Charter").

for local power and, perhaps, a reservoir of inherent authority for local governments.[12] With hindsight, we know that this movement largely failed. Few states actually enacted a "municipal affairs" clause during this era; and none of the many states that adopted home rule during the 1960s created a "municipal affairs" clause that protected localities from state preemption.[13] Thus, California's "municipal affairs" amendment to its home rule provision was not only radical in its reorientation of state/local authority, it was also rare.

So much for the constitutional parchment. The phrase "municipal affairs" cried out for interpretation. Whether Article XI, Section 5 would represent a *volte face* in the historic constitutional relationship between state and local governments would depend upon judicial interpretation. The earliest decisions construed "municipal affairs" rather broadly. In *Ex Parte Braun*,[14] for example, the California Supreme Court considered an ordinance enacted by Los Angeles "providing for licensing and regulating the carrying on of certain professions, trades, callings, and occupations." In construing this ordinance in favor of local power and against the assertions by the state of its sovereign prerogatives, the court opined that municipal affairs "are words of wide import, broad enough to include all powers appropriate for a municipality to possess and actually conferred upon it by the sovereign power."[15] In the next several years, local governments expanded the scope of their regulatory and taxing power; they responded to state attempts at encroachment by invoking this broad judicial

---

[12]See Peppin, *Home Rule*, at 7-41.

[13]The first wave of constitutional home rule amendments came in the late 19th century. These included California, Missouri, Washington, Minnesota, Colorado, Oklahoma, Arizona, Oregon, Michigan, Ohio, Nebraska, and Texas. The second wave came in the 1960s. The impetus for this second wave was the publication of a report entitled "Model Constitutional Provisions for Municipal Home Rule" under the aegis of the National League of Cities. See Kenneth Vanlandingham, "Constitutional Municipal Home Rule Since the AMA (NLC) Model," *Wm. & Mary L. Rev.* 17 (1975): 1.

[14]*Ex parte Braun*, 141 Cal. 204 (1903).

[15]141 Cal. at 210.

reading of "municipal affairs" and, in a number of important decisions, the California courts upheld these invocations.[16]

This expansion of local autonomy under the rubric of Article XI was short-lived, however. In the decades following *Ex Parte Braun*, the California courts decided a number of cases that restricted the scope of the constitutional provision and, thereby, limited severely the domain within which local governments could act without preemption by the state.[17] Courts frequently took the viewpoint of the state and accepted the state legislature's arguments that local regulations would interfere with critical state policies. The sphere in which localities' independent decisions about the scope of their regulatory initiatives were sovereign was whittled to nearly nothing. As a consequence, the "municipal affairs" clause became a legal anachronism, a weak caveat to the essentially plenary authority of the state through its general laws.[18]

Two difficult issues recurred throughout the decided cases. These issues framed rather well the basic dilemmas confronted by courts' attempting to delineate the boundaries of state and local power under Article XI. The first issue was whether the boundaries of "municipal affairs" were exclusive, that is, whether a finding that an issue was a municipal affair meant it could not therefore be a matter of "statewide concern." Courts in other states had held that matters may be both municipal and statewide affairs; to the extent that they were both, the result was that the *state*, and not the *local*, government was authorized to make the choice of whose law governed.[19] Of course, such a resolution meant that the state would choose itself, and therefore the "municipal affairs" determination became just another species of traditional preemption analysis, with the question becoming whether and to what extent there was a *true* conflict between state and local law. By contrast, most of the

---

[16]See, e.g., *Clouse v. City of San Diego*, 159 Cal. 434 (1911); *Popper v. Broderick*, 123 Cal. 456 (1899).

[17]See, e.g., *Strumsky v. San Diego County Employees Retirement Ass'n*, 11 Cal. 3d 28 (1974); *California State Employees' Ass'n v. Flourney*, 32 Cal. App. 3d 219 (1973); *In re Hubbard*, 62 Cal. 2d 119 (1964); *Department of Water & Power v. Inyo Chem. Co.*, 16 Cal. 2d 744 (1940).

[18]See Sato.

[19]See, e.g., *State ex rel. Haynes v. Bonem*, 845 P. 2d 150 (N.M. 1992); *City and County of Denver v. State of Colorado*, 788 P. 2d 764 (Colo. 1990).

California decisions struggled mightily to keep separate the categories "municipal affairs" and "matters of statewide concern."[20] This had the effect of preserving the sovereignty of local governments in their category; it also had the effect, though, of empowering state government.

Courts found with frequency that particular issues implicated a statewide concern. As a result, state power was enhanced at the expense of local prerogative. The courts tended toward a functional analysis of the *effects* of a local regulation.[21] If the regulation had extraterritorial effects or if it implicated issues that the state had become involved in through legislative action, then the courts held that the issue was one of statewide concern. As California grew and the problems with which all levels of government multiplied, the likelihood that either or both of these functional prerequisites would be triggered was enhanced. Beyond looking at the functions and effects of local regulations, the courts frequently rested their judgments concerning the statewide versus local dimensions of municipal laws on the views of state political institutions. This raised the second difficult issue: Is the "statewide concern" determination to be made by the courts apart from whatever judgments reached by the state legislature? In short, does the state legislature get to decide whether a matter is or is not of statewide concern?

The model of home rule adopted by California appears to answer this question "no." And, indeed, this is precisely what the California Supreme Court announced in its 1972 decision of *Bishop v. San Jose*.[22] "[T]he fact," said the court, "standing alone, that the Legislature has attempted to deal with a particular subject on a statewide basis is not determinative of the issue as between state and municipal affairs . . . the Legislature is empowered neither to determine what constitutes a municipal affair nor to change such an affair into a matter of statewide concern." [23] This seems the proper view. After all, entrusting to the state legislature the plenary power to decide whether and to what extent an issue is a matter of statewide concern turns over the responsibility of constitutional interpretation to the legislature. However, the court carefully avoided deciding whether the

---

[20]See, e.g., *In re Hubbard*, 62 Cal. 2d 119 (1964). See generally *Sato, Municipal Affairs*, at 1066-74.

[21]See Sato, *Municipal Affairs*, at 1072-74.

[22]1 Cal. 3d 56 (1969).

[23]1 Cal. 3d at 63, 66.

state legislature's judgment is ever *relevant* to the municipal/statewide determination. Perhaps the state legislature's view is probative, if not outcome-determinative. In any event, California courts have wavered on this question; the result has been a morass of confusing cases and jerry-built analytic approaches.[24]

Two recent decisions of the California Supreme Court have recast somewhat the meaning of "municipal affairs." In *California Federal Savings & Loan v. Los Angeles*,[25] the Supreme Court considered a business license tax imposed by the city of Los Angeles on all corporations doing business in the jurisdiction. This tax conflicted with the state's scheme of taxation for financial institutions. In striking down the local tax, the court described the appropriate analysis for considering "municipal affairs" issues:

> In those cases where the preliminary conditions are satisfied, that is, where the matter implicates a "municipal affair" and poses a genuine conflict with state law, the question of statewide concern is the bedrock inquiry through which the conflict between state and local interests is adjusted. *If the subject of the statute fails to qualify as one of statewide concern, then the conflicting charter city measure is a "municipal affair" and "beyond the reach of legislative enactment."* [citing *Ex Parte Braun*] . . . If, however, the court is persuaded that the subject of the state statute is one of statewide concern and that the statute is reasonably related to its resolution, then the conflicting charter city measure ceases to be a "municipal affair" *pro tanto* and the Legislature is not prohibited by article XI, Section 5(a), from addressing the statewide dimension by its own tailored enactments.[26]

With this decision, the court constructed a more organized analysis; yet, it made little headway in defining with certainty which matters *implicate* municipal affairs and which matters are of statewide concern. What *Cal Fed* accomplished, though, was in establishing what amounts to

---

[24]See generally Sato, *Municipal Affairs*, 1066-75.
[25]54 Cal. 3d 1 (1991).
[26]54 Cal. 3d at 17.

a multifactored test for considering whether a local regulation properly implicates municipal affairs. As with any such test, the critical questions lie in the factors that the courts must consider in moving from step to step in the analysis.

The most recent decision that applies the test of *Cal Fed* is the 1992 decision of *Johnson v. Bradley*.[27] The city of Los Angeles had enacted a campaign reform law called Measure H. Among its many provisions, Measure H established a scheme of public financing for local elections. On its face, this conflicted with Proposition 73's amendment to the Political Reform Act of 1974, which provided that "[n]o public officer shall expend and no candidate shall accept any public moneys for the purpose of seeking elective office."[28] In *Johnson*, the Supreme Court applied the test of *Cal Fed* and concluded that, while this local regulation may well implicate matters of statewide concern, the law was not "reasonably related to the resolution" of the statewide concern that underlay Proposition 73; therefore, the local law was within the scope of Article XI, Section 5 and superseded conflicting state law.[29] Significantly, the Court in *Johnson* added to *Cal Fed's* test the requirement that the state law be "narrowly tailored to limit incursion into legitimate municipal interests."[30] This requirement of "fit" between the articulated state policies and the state's law is, while not relevant to the Court's analysis in *Johnson*, potentially significant as a restriction the state's ability to resort to any means to implement its statewide agenda. The "tailoring" requirement indicates the state must try to avoid unnecessary conflicts with local laws.

Lower court cases decided in the few years since *Cal Fed* and *Johnson* are confusing in a way reminiscent of the dozens of cases construing the "municipal affairs" clause prior to these two Supreme Court decisions.[31] The substitution of a multifactored test for the rather piecemeal, functional approach of pre-*Cal Fed* decisions has contributed little to resolving the confusions of this constitutional provision. Moreover, there does not seem to be any more encouragement for local initiatives and creativity provided by the California courts' recent approaches to construing Article XI,

---

[27]*Johnson v. Bradley*, 4 Cal. 4th 389 (1992).

[28]Gov. Code, Section 85300.

[29]4 Cal. 4th at 411.

[30]4 Cal. 4th at 404.

[31]See, e.g., *Fisher v. County of Alameda*, 20 Cal. App. 4th 120 (1993).

Section 5. Local governments continue to be at the mercy of uncertain judicial tests and of courts reluctant to expand in substantial ways the boundaries of municipal power and of local sovereignty.

THE CASE FOR EXPANDED LOCAL POWER THROUGH CONSTITUTIONAL REVISION

Any effort to carve out distinct boundaries of authority between state and local governments in an unwieldy *polis* like California should proceed with caution. The multiplication of entities each with their own sovereign legal powers can potentially confound efforts at constructing efficient, fair public policy for all citizens of the state. So, given the concerns with this subdelegation of sovereign power, what can be said on behalf of such local power? The task of this section is to trace out, albeit in rather general and speculative terms, the case for expanded local power. There are three dimensions to this brief for augmenting local power through constitutional revision: First, augmenting local power can fuel local creativity in regulation; such creativity can contribute to expanding the range of regulatory options and thereby construct a scheme of competition and comparative advantage that improves the economy of the state and its citizens. Second, such augmentation gives to local governments greater fiscal control, a necessary control in an era of diminishing federal and state support and constrained financial flexibility. Third, expanded home rule power can, when exercised with prudence, offer a greater protection of individual rights at the local level.

Regulatory Competition and Innovation

One idea behind Justice Brandeis' famous description in *New State Ice Co. v. Liebmann*[32] of states as "laboratories of experimentation," was the advantage to be gained from innovation by decentralized political units. From the vantage point of the era in which Brandeis was opining about these governmental "laboratories," states were perhaps the best suited entity to pursue innovative regulatory strategies. In the modern era, as population has risen and as the plausibility of state lines reflecting the

---

[32]285 U.S. 262 (1932).

appropriate boundaries of interest and capacity is questioned, it may be that local governments are the best suited to act as laboratories of experimentation.[33] Indeed, many of the key regulatory innovations of late that have been ascribed to state decision makers, have in fact reflected the choices of local/regional institutions. These innovations have involved such far-flung issues as transportation, crime control, land-use planning, and environmental regulation. To be sure, the issue is seldom "either/or"; municipalities frequently act in partnership with state institutions. Yet, the tendencies toward experimentation and innovation that the devolution of power from state government to local government allows suggests that we look for means of facilitating these salutary strategies.

Regulatory competition among localities can be expected to benefit the economic climate of the state in which these localities exist and in which this competition takes place.[34] This competition could be over such factors as tax rates, regulatory burdens, employment opportunities, and, as well, the mix of public goods that will attract the appropriate collection of businesses and service providers. Not all localities will have the same incentives to compete for business. Some areas may content themselves with living nearby an industrial area in order to reap some of the benefits (access to close jobs) of business without its burdens (noise, crowds). Nor will all localities have the resources available to them for such competition. There are, after all, resource-poor jurisdictions and there are some business/municipality matches that cannot work because of natural or logistical considerations. Yet, in a state as large and diverse as California, the potential for rewards in connection with vigorous regulatory competition are great.[35]

---

[33]See, e.g., Edward L. Rubin and Malcolm Feeley, "Federalism: Some Notes on a National Neurosis," *UCLA L. Rev.* 41(1994): 903 (questioning connection between values of federalism and of decentralization).

[34]See Wallace Oates, *Fiscal Federalism* (1972).

[35]Professor Martti Vihanto describes, from the perspective of Austrian economic theory, another benefit of decentralized, interlocal competition—the facilitation of information that will instruct us about *when* competition produces desirable outcomes and where, by contrast, centralization is called for. See Martti Vihanto, "Competition Between Local Governments as a Discovery Procedure," *J. Inst. & Theor. Econ.* 148 (1992): 411.

The regulatory competition that currently persists in California is constrained by a number of factors. One constraint that is directly relevant to the constitutional issue considered in this chapter, is the fact that localities compete not only among themselves but with the state government. In the *Cal Fed* litigation, the Court considered one element of this regulatory competition—the competition for tax dollars.[36] The state predictably worried that the imposition of local business license taxes would, alongside state taxation, risk overtaxing financial institutions. Permitting local governments to capture tax revenues through their license tax in addition to, or instead of, whatever revenues would be generated by imposing a state income tax, interfered with the state's ability to raise revenues for their own purposes. At a surface level, it would not seem accurate to describe the state as *competing* with local governments; they are, after all, part of the same governmental structure. Yet, to the extent that state and local governments pursue distinct regulatory agendas and to the extent that localities are *expected* to shoulder much of the burden for financing local public goods, there is a substantial competitive dimension to the state/local relationship.

With respect to the regulatory competition among localities, states can confound local government efforts to compete through regulatory initiatives through the imposition by the state of minimum standards. These might be, for example, environmental or health and safety standards. They might also be such standards as restrictions on the ability of local governments to impose fees or taxes, such as the restrictions established in Article XIII of the California Constitution. The effect of these minimum standards is to limit the range of issues over which local governments may compete with one another. On the surface, these minimum standards do not appear to restrict the capacity for regulatory competition since the standards apply equally to all localities. In reality, of course, these standards impact localities differently. Imposing environmental standards on industrially developing areas that must scramble for resource opportunities will restrict their ability to compete with localities that can more effectively adapt to these same standards. Socking rural communities that rely on seasonal, migrant labor with statewide health and safety regulations

---

[36]For a description of the legal and economic context in which this litigation arose, see *Cal Fed*, 54 Cal. 3d at 7-10.

can leave such communities at a comparative disadvantage with respect to other municipalities that rely on a more white collar workforce. To be sure, the case for statewide standards is strong. Indeed, if we take seriously the notion that individuals within a state should not be solely at the mercy of the standards set by the communities in which they live and work and that the state has an obligation to protect its citizens, then we should be wary of completely decentralizing regulatory protections. Moreover, the state has a role in protecting against the so-called race to the bottom; regulatory competition must be regulated to ensure that localities do not drive down to unacceptable levels regulatory protections.[37] But the question still is whether this state responsibility must be carried out in a constitutional environment in which municipalities enjoy limited legal prerogatives. The "municipal affairs" inquiry represents a close scrutiny into the proper domain of state supremacy; this, in turn, requires a studied attention to whether the state can be trusted to exercise sensibly and fairly its responsibilities regulate interlocal competition. However, the incentives for the state to mismanage this responsibility give us reasons for skepticism.

From a cynical vantage point, the state restricts interlocal competition in order to capture its own benefits. State politicians may engage in rent-seeking behavior by curtailing the opportunities of local governments to compete for a fixed sum of dollars. Such restrictions run the risk, of course, of weakening the position of the state *vis-à-vis* other states—states, after all, compete against one another.[38] But this means simply that the state decision makers must make an on-balance judgment about whether state-imposed restrictions on interlocal regulatory competition benefits themselves to an extent that justifies the restrictions. Less cynically, we can see such restrictions as part of efforts at centralizing regulatory control in order to secure a consistent level of state service and regulatory benefits/burdens for the state as a whole. Interlocal competition should not result in their being winners and losers in certain municipalities. This centralization serves an essentially redistributive function; circumscribing regulatory competition that would result in winners and losers redistributes the benefits and burdens of regulatory activity. In this way, centralization

---

[37]For a critique of these race-to-the-bottom rationales, see Richard Revesz, "Rehabilitating Interstate Competition: Rethinking the 'Race-to-the-Bottom' Rationale for Federal Environmental Regulation," *N.Y.U.L. Rev.* 67 (1992): 1210.

[38]See Revesz, *Interstate Competition, supra.*

protects against the race to the bottom, a race that would weaken the safety net of public goods and services.

Although the determination of whether one of these characterizations is more plausible than the other as a description of the purposes of state centralization is ultimately an empirical question, there are reasons to believe that releasing the state's strong grip on interlocal regulatory competition may well be desirable. A reconstructed Article XI, Section 5 would enable local governments to argue that "municipal affairs" includes, especially, those affairs that concern the capacities of local governments to innovate and, thereby, to compete with one another using as currency regulatory benefits and burdens. More to the point, states should not be able to turn all issues into matters of statewide concern by the mere invocation of their intention to centralize regulations at the state level. While statewide policies are often necessary to limit the risks of the race to the bottom, we have reasons to be skeptical of state decisions to centralize. Decisions that pay fidelity to state judgments about the values of statewide regulation accept too uncritically the arguments of state officials with incentives to centralize. Complete fidelity to local judgments would, of course, create distorting incentives in the opposite direction. However, it is important to remember that localities' incentives to engage in rent-seeking behavior are at least checked by the persistence of interlocal competition; in the absence of a coherent constitutional constraint, states face no similar limits from "below," that is, from local governments.

Fiscal Control

Another advantage to be gained from reconstructing the home rule relationship between state and local governments is the increase of local fiscal control. As described in detail elsewhere, Proposition 13 has drastically curtailed the ability of local governments to cope with financial responsibilities.[39] The feared curtailment in the provision of local public goods and services has been forestalled somewhat by uses of various forms of creative financing, including impact fees, debt financing, and user fees.

---

[39]See Daniel Rubinfeld, "California Fiscal Federalism: A School Finance Perspective"; John Ellwood and Mary Sprague, "Options for Reforming the California State Budget Process," both in this volume.

Moreover, state and federal aid has managed to provide the finger in the dike to guard against the collapse of local government economies. But trends indicate that these devices are waning, and that state fiscal crises loom ahead. What this means for the local governments in particular is the severe curtailment of public goods provisions. While not a panacea, returning greater control to the local governments over the generation of revenues through taxation and over the distribution of these revenues throughout their jurisdiction would improve substantially the fiscal viability of municipalities in a Proposition 13 environment.

How would the augmentation of local power through a reconstructed Article XI, Section 5 accomplish this? Local power over taxation is one of the central issues in litigation over the scope of the "municipal affairs" clause.[40] From one perspective, the taxing power would seem to be the quintessential municipal affair. After all, the extraterritorial effects of a tax are, if anything, indirect. Surely it could not be that the fact that a particular local law imposes burdens on individuals and entities such that they have incentives to leave means that this taxation implicates matters of statewide concern. All taxes—indeed all local regulations—impose burdens that are subject to this sort of "incentives-effects" analysis.[41] However, courts have been quite wary about extending a broad net of approval over local tax initiatives. As with issues involving regulatory competition discussed above, the state's interest here seems clearly to be

---

[40]See, e.g., *Weekes v. City of Oakland*, 21 Cal. 3d 386 (1978).

[41]Instead, the extraterritorial effects that are of concern to courts in construing Section 5 must be effects related to the *severity* of the tax. Perhaps taxes that are confiscatory have the sort of extraterritorial effects that justify statewide concern; this standard, though, has been notoriously difficult to define where it comes up elsewhere in state constitutional jurisprudence. See, e.g., *Amador Valley Joint Union High School District v. State Bd. of Equalization*, 583 P.2d 1281 (Cal. 1978). *Cf. City of Pittsburgh v. Alco Parking Corporation*, 417 U.S. 369 (1974). Or perhaps the intent to discriminate against certain businesses—for example, those that cannot easily move to avoid these burdens—implicates statewide concerns. But notice that these approaches all turn on subjective judgments about public policy. It may be local governments will enact stupid tax laws. And it may be that there are strong public policy interests in limiting the reach of localities to raid business and individual treasuries. Yet, the view that local decisions cease to be municipal affairs because state political institutions have an interest in imposing their views of public policy statewide is problematic.

related to capturing a competitive advantage over local governments for the collection of money through taxation. Although sometimes the state steps in to limit local taxation with the stated purpose of removing the financial burden altogether, frequently the state argues against local taxes on the grounds that these taxes interfere with the state's ability to collect its own revenues through a tax. In these latter cases, the case for state control rests on our view about the competence of the state legislature in making its judgment that the *state's* interests in tapping revenue sources outweigh *localities'* interests in this regard. Where the issue is not restricting deleterious interlocal competition but, instead, curtailing local taxation in order to preserve the prerogatives of the state to tax, we have little reason to trust the state legislature to make the appropriate judgment.

The facts of *Cal Fed* are illustrative. California had, since the 1920s, imposed a state income tax on commercial banks and had squarely preempted municipal income taxes on these banks.[42] Municipalities took advantage of a loophole in this act, which left Savings and Loans institutions out; these institutions were subject, then, to municipal taxes. In order to avoid subjecting these institutions to excessive taxation, California provided an offset for taxes paid to municipalities in calculating their net state tax liability.[43] In 1979, California abolished the offset and extended its state income tax laws to all financial institutions.[44] In order to soften the blow to localities, California enacted as part of the 1979 reform, a section that created a Financial Aid to Local Agencies fund.[45] With this fund, made up of a portion of the income tax revenues paid by financial corporations, the state distributed money back to the local governments as a way of making up for the shortfall created by the restriction on local taxation. Significantly, though, the state legislature did not renew this fund after 1982. As a consequence, local governments were faced with losing a substantial revenue source without any compensation by the state. The business license tax was constructed by Los Angeles and several other home rule municipalities to recoup some of the revenues lost through these

---

[42]See generally Roger Traynor, "National Bank Taxation in California," *Cal. L. Rev.* 17 (1929): 83.

[43]See the description in *Cal Fed*, 54 Cal. 3d at 8.

[44]Rev. & Tax. Code Section 23182.

[45]Rev. & Tax. Code Section 26482.

legislative revisions.[46] As this example illustrates, localities simply cannot depend upon the state legislature to look out for their fiscal well-being. Nor can state voters, as Proposition 13 indicates, be entrusted with this task either. Facilitating local fiscal control is especially important in an environment in which localities cannot depend upon state beneficence and support.

As mentioned above, Proposition 13 restricts the domain of local tax power; one critical dimension of this restriction is the requirement of a supermajority to enact nonproperty tax taxes.[47] At the same time, local governments bear the burden of federal and state mandates, many of which are unfunded and therefore represent additional demands on the fiscal capacities of municipalities.[48] In the face of these fiscal burdens, localities seek sources of revenue and, as a predicate, the authority to raise revenue through devices such as local taxes and fees. Vesting in local governments essentially plenary power to impose such taxes would secure to localities a necessary amount of control over their financial responsibilities and activities. This control serves, at base, two critical functions. First, tying service/good provision to local resource bases is, all things equal, a more efficient system of public finance. Second, and relatedly, tethering local expenditure decisions to local revenue-generating decisions in a clearer way, improves the accountability of local officials to their constituents. Such accountability has intrinsic value to the extent that we value local self-determination and government close to the people. Moreover, reducing the agency costs associated with monitoring decisions of local

---

[46]See L.A. Mun. Code, Section 21.00 *et seq*. Los Angeles collected $186 million in 1985-86 from this business license tax, roughly nine percent of the city's total revenues.

[47]Cal. Const. Art. XIII A, Section 4. This section provides as follows: "Cities, Counties and special districts, by a two-thirds vote of the qualified electors of such district, may impose special taxes on such district, except ad valorem taxes on real property or a transaction tax or sales tax on the sale of real property within such City, County or special district."

[48]See Edward A. Zelinsky, "Unfunded Mandates, Hidden Taxation, and the Tenth Amendment: On Public Choice, Public Interest, and Public Services," *Vand. L. Rev.* 46 (1993): 1355.

officials who must act with an eye toward mollifying state decision makers facilitates a more efficient revenue-raising/expenditure process.[49]

Lest we fear that the expansion of local tax power undermines the state's ability to establish sensible fiscal policies and priorities, we should remember that local governments are subject to a myriad of state regulations and restrictions that bear on localities' ability to take advantage of their broad taxing power. Not only are there a series of constitutional restrictions on local taxing decisions—for example, the requirement of uniformity and the procedural rules of Article XIIIA, there are regulatory policies established through state general laws that local governments are obliged to respect. Even if the taxing power of local governments is regarded as within the category of "municipal affairs," courts will continue to face difficult questions of whether the exercise of this constitutionally authorized taxing power conflicts with other constitutional limits on local initiatives and, in addition, whether this power can be authorized consistent with general state policies. What the expansion of local taxing power *does* accomplish, though, is the removal of the convenient argument of the state that its decision to tax indicates that local tax laws implicate matters of statewide concern and, insofar as they pass the other requirements described in *Cal Fed* and *Johnson*, this state decision will govern. If we trust local governments to make decisions to accomplish its fiscal objectives more than we trust state governments to make fiscal decisions *for* local governments, we would welcome this shift in the burden of persuasion.

Municipal Rights

A final part of the case for expanded local power through a reconstructed "municipal affairs" clause concerns the capacity of localities to define and protect the individual rights of its citizens. The framers of the United States Constitution made clear that, in the words of the Ninth Amendment, "[t]he enumeration in the Constitution, of certain rights, shall not be construed to deny or disparage others retained by the people."[50]

---

[49]See Kenneth J. Arrow, "The Economics of Agency," in *Principals and Agents: The Structure of Business*, ed. John W. Pratt and Richard J. Zeckhauser (Boston, Mass.: Harvard Business School Press, 1985), 37-51.

[50]U.S. Const. Amend. IX.

Among the sources of these rights are the state constitutions which, from the beginning of the Republic, contained a variety of rights, some of which went beyond those established in the Bill of Rights to the federal Constitution.[51] It has never been clear, though, whether there is room in the American constitutional tradition for an established system of *municipal* rights. Perhaps such rights are merely hortatory, dependent upon recognition by the state through the constitution or through general laws. The issue of whether and to what extent local governments can create enforceable rights is an important one, however. The creation and preservation of rights is, in one view, constitutive of a community;[52] it is, moreover, a device by which individuals can constrain the powers of government—of *any* government, including municipalities.

The notion that local governments should create and preserve rights against state encroachments is appealing. The diversity of interests of citizens through California are reflected in the variety of policies pursued by localities in the state. Anyone who has spent any time travelling throughout California is struck by the differences among localities and their citizens. This variety is reflected in the pattern of local ordinances; to some extent, it is reflected in the city charters. It would follow that different localities would have interests in constructing different rights. These rights may not, to be sure, retreat at all from the rights of individuals contained in the state and federal Constitution. But it does not follow that local governments may not add to the contents or dimensions of the rights established in the state and federal Constitutions. Indeed, the argument made by Justice William Brennan and others for attention to state constitutions as an independent, and expansive, source of individual rights can be joined with an argument for a similar independence for localities. City charters are designed as essentially constitutions for municipalities. While they are constructed in the shadow of the state constitution, these charters represent a declaration of municipal responsibilities; to the extent

---

[51]See *Protecting Individual Rights: The Role of State Constitutionalism*, Barbara Wolfson (Washington, D.C.: Roscoe Pound Foundation, 1993); William J. Brennan, Jr., "State Constitutions and the Protection of Individual Rights," *Harv. L. Rev.* 90 (1977): 489.

[52]For an excellent recent discussion of liberal constitutionalism as part of classical liberalism, see Steven Holmes, *Passions and Constraints* (Chicago: University of Chicago Press, 1995).

permitted by the federal and state constitutions, they may represent a declaration of municipal *rights* as well.

To understand how the notion of municipal rights created under the rubric of constitutional home rule powers would function, consider a situation (similar to that arising in Colorado recently) in which a city enacts an ordinance that prohibits individuals and businesses, including public entities, from discriminating against gays, lesbians, and bisexuals. Suppose California voters pass an initiative that provides that no state civil rights protection be extended to such individuals. There is a clear conflict between the two laws. Under traditional preemption analysis, the state's policy, embodied in this new state law, would govern and the municipality would not be permitted to protect gays, lesbians, and bisexuals through their discrimination ordinance. Supposing that these individuals would enjoy no federal or state constitutional protection against discrimination, the effect of this preemption is to destroy the capacity of local governments to create and implement their own set of individual rights. What is lost in this legal arrangement is the ability of municipalities to construct their own regime of rights. To be sure, localities are already limited in their ability to *subtract* rights from those established under the state and federal Constitution. The framers of the federal Constitution, though, seemed to contemplate that rights definition would function in a federal system as a collaborative process. If we take seriously the clause in the Ninth Amendment that rights are retained to the people, but regard the project of rights-creation to be a political process, rather than, say, a declaration of "natural" rights, then there is reason to believe that the Constitution contemplated—or, indeed, expected—the creation of rights at a local level. Facilitating the establishment of municipal rights through a fortified Article XI, Section 5 is consistent with the spirit of the Ninth Amendment. What is less certain, though, is whether it is consistent with the spirit of the state supremacy/local dependency model of municipal government.

The purposes for which local governments are formed remain controversial. The range of views extend from Andrew White's 19th-century view that "[t]he questions in a city are not political questions. . . . The work of a city [is] . . . the creation and control of city property"[53] to

---

[53]Quoted in Nancy Burns, *The Formation of American Local Governments* (New York: Oxford University Press, 1994), 109.

Jeffersonian theories of local governments as loci of communitarian, participatory democracy.[54] The augmentation of local power under constitutional home rule for the reasons described in the previous two sections does not require taking a clear position on what conception of local governments should be preferred. By contrast, viewing local governments as right-creators presupposes a model of localities as more than managers of property and, indeed, more than providers of public goods and services. I would suggest, more in order to stimulate further thought than to lay out the essentials of a theory of local self-determination, that local governments be understood as arenas for the development and exercise of rights.

The three issues that form the broad contours of the case for expanded local power under home rule will take different shapes depending upon the circumstances faced by state and local governments at any point in time. For example, the disadvantages of regulatory competition may outweigh the advantages of such competition in certain instances; perhaps California may have an interest in establishing minimum regulatory standards that will circumscribe some aspects of regulatory competition. Surely any reconstituted "municipal affairs" doctrine must take account of state interests in pursuing statewide policies in appropriate cases. In a sense, local sovereignty of the sort traced out above will never be *true* sovereignty. Local power will be evaluated by courts in light of other, translocal concerns. However, the arguments for expanded local power counsel a revision of the current constitutional home rule relationship between state and local governments in California. This proposed revision is described in the next section.

PROPOSALS TO REVISE STATE/LOCAL RELATIONS UNDER HOME RULE IN CALIFORNIA

There are two central structural impediments to the development of a suitable constitutional home rule relationship between state and local governments in California. The first problem lies in the absence of clear delineation of what powers are exclusively local and which are subject to state preemption. Notwithstanding the dozens of cases over the past

---

[54]See, e.g., Frug, *City as a Legal Concept, supra.*

century in which the California courts have struggled to develop a sensible test, we appear to be hardly any closer to a satisfactory delineation of state/local power under Article XI. Although the Supreme Court's formulation in *Cal Fed* and *Johnson* moves us a good deal closer in the direction of a test for distinguishing what is properly local from what is properly a statewide concern, there remains, as the previous discussion suggested, serious ambiguity in the way in which legal doctrine measures state/local relations under California's home rule provision.

A second impediment concerns the political relationship between state and local governments. There is an undercurrent to many of the home rule decisions that seems to express the view that local governments can trust state decision makers to make the appropriate distributions of regulatory and taxing power through legislation. Notwithstanding the California Supreme Court's rejection of the view that localities' home rule powers are entirely dependent on the decisions of state political decision makers, California courts still turn to state judgments in assessing whether and to what extent a particular matter is of statewide concern. In *Cal Fed*, for example, the Court found persuasive the state legislature's decision to reconstruct the system of taxing financial corporations and, in the process, to replace local prerogatives with comprehensive state regulation. The problem, from the standpoint of state/local relations is straightforward: state legislators have incentives to act in the interest of state prerogative and have correspondingly fewer incentives to safeguard local power. As a result, the structure of the system is set up to disadvantage local power. Indeed, the very fact that home rule is expressed as a constitutional power—as a sort of local "right," to be preserved against state encroachment—indicates that state decision makers cannot be entrusted with the exclusive responsibility to protect local power from state encroachment.

It should be noted here that we need not regard state legislatures as especially venal or confiscatory; the point, rather, is that statewide political institutions necessarily have a different structure of incentives and agendas than do local decision makers. Accordingly, the impact of a rejuvenated system of home rule is to provide to local governments a greater degree of insurance against legislation enacted by statewide political institutions that legislation would give undue attention to the concerns, demands, and interests of local governments and their constituencies.

In this section, I discuss three approaches to restructuring this relationship. At the outset, I offer the caveat that these proposals fall short of the sort of clear line-drawing that would make certain the distribution of authority between state and local governments in California. No bright line is possible. As with the state and federal government, there is inevitable tension between governmental units, tension that is not dissolved by the constitution's distribution of powers. The aim of the following proposals, then, is substantially more modest. To the extent that we can improve upon the century of judicial confusion with Article XI, Section 5, we have made progress in reforming the constitutional relationship between state and localities.

First, we should amend Article XI to provide for a clearer delineation of what sort of affairs are exclusively "municipal." The list is a very short one, not because municipalities should have narrow powers, but rather because the denomination of certain powers as exclusively local is a drastic step. Much of the powers exercised by local governments should remain shared; thus, most of the issues involving state/local conflicts that reach the courts should be resolved by resort to preemption analysis.

The most important clarification in the definition of "municipal affairs" is the proposed addition in the text of the California Constitution of the power to tax. States should not be permitted to proscribe local governments from imposing taxes.[55] To be sure, the power to tax will be limited by other provisions of the constitution. However, the addition of the power to tax into the constitution and its connection to exclusive municipal affairs would make clear that charter city's taxing power could not be limited, as it was in *Cal Fed* and in previous cases, by state tax decisions. This proposed revision embodies in a textual form an interpretation of Article XI, Section 5 given by Justice Richardson in his concurring opinion in *Weekes v. City of Oakland*.[56] In *Weekes*, Justice Richardson explained that "the power of municipal corporations operating under a freeholder's charter to impose taxes for revenue purposes is strictly a municipal activity authorized by the state constitution and subject only to those limitations appearing in the constitution or the charter itself."[57] Amending Article XI to reiterate Justice Richardson's view that the taxing power "is strictly a

---

[55]*Compare County of Los Angeles v. Sasaki*, 23 Cal. App. 4th 1442, 1453-54 (1994); *City of Woodlake v. Logan*, 230 Cal. App. 3d 1058 (1991).

[56]21 Cal. 3d 386 (1978).

[57]*Id.* at 405 (quoting *A.B.C. Distributing Co. v. City and County of San Francisco*, 15 Cal. 3d 566 [1975]).

municipal activity" would clarify state/local relations in this area. The result would be to facilitate greater control by the local governments over their fiscal responsibilities. The benefits of this increased control include enhanced efficiency and accountability.

The other important clarifying amendment to Article XI is the addition of the land-use power of local governments as part of "municipal affairs."[58] The land-use/zoning power has long been protected by California courts against state intrusions. More recently, however, the state courts have permitted growing encroachments by the state on quintessentially local land management decisions. As a consequence, what had long been regarded as exclusively municipal affairs has been subjected to what amounts to a local versus statewide affairs balancing test. The advantages that the zoning power creates for interlocal regulatory competition are limited to the extent that states restrict local powers. A recent decision of the California Supreme Court, *DeVita v. County of Napa*,[59] brings these issues into relief.

In *DeVita*, the court considered whether a local government could, through an initiative, amend its general land-use plan. To determine whether the state intended to circumscribe the power of the voters of the county to amend its plan through an initiative, the court considered whether the county's general plan implicated matters of statewide concern. This inquiry entailed an examination of California's zoning and planning legislation. In reaching its conclusion that the state planning law "does not alter this local control over land use matters," the court noted that land-use regulation in California is a product of the state's delegation of a certain amount of its inherent police power in accordance with Article XI, Section 7. As the court had previously explained the distribution of state/local land-use authority, "[t]he legislature has been sensitive to the fact that planning and zoning in the conventional sense have traditionally been deemed municipal affairs. It has thus made no attempt to deprive local governments . . . of their right to manage and control such matters, but rather has attempted to impinge upon local control only to the limited

---

[58]Issues involving land-use policy and the California Constitution are discussed at greater length in Professor Margaret Radin's contribution to this volume. See Margaret Jane Radin and Brendan P. Cullen, "Real Property and Direct Democracy in California."

[59]1995 Cal. Lexis 706 (March 6, 1995).

degree necessary to further legitimate state interests."[60] Yet, the fact that the court resorts to a careful examination of state zoning and planning legislation indicates that this "police power" basis of local control is limited; state prerogatives to regulate are thereby protected. The analysis resembles preemption analysis, albeit with a healthy dose of deference to local control, more than it resembles analysis of whether land-use control is an exclusively municipal affair.

By amending Article XI, Section 5 to include land-use decisions, the California Constitution will preserve to local governments the essential elements of control over zoning, planning, and other land-use decisions. Any efforts by the state legislature to curtail such decisions in the interests of statewide policy must be evaluated in light of the state's constitutional powers to so regulate. The authority of the state legislature to enact, for example, various environmental regulations as well as the state's authority to limit localities' ability to use their land-use powers in a racially discriminatory fashion indicate that such sources of constitutional authority can be found. However, the establishment of clear local control under Article XI, Section 5 best preserves the foundations of state/local relations in this important area of policy.

The second element of my proposed revision to constitutional home rule in Article XI, Section 5 is a procedural one. A critical issue faced continuously by local governments asserting the power to regulate is the real political power that can be mobilized by the state, either through the legislature or through the voters. The power of the voters through the initiative device is especially troubling. Voters statewide have little vested interest in respecting the prerogatives of local governments to regulate. Consider the following simple thought experiment. Suppose a state tax initiative is on the ballot which, if passed, would preempt a local tax ordinance (e.g., the facts of *Cal Fed*). A voter faced with this choice will consider the potential benefits to her from the initiative. Although the marginal benefit to the individual from the revenues generated by this state tax are small, the burdens are probably perceived to be zero and, therefore, she will have an incentive to vote "yes." The voters of the locality whose law is preempted will, of course, have an intense preference against the

---

[60]*Id.* at 12 (quoting *City of Los Angeles v. State of California*, 138 Cal. App. 3d 526 [1982]).

initiative, since they will each benefit much more from the revenues of the tax generated locally than they will from the statewide tax. But their intense preferences are not reflected in the vote. They have the same individual vote as every other voter in the state. So, chances are high that their preferences will be dwarfed by the preferences of the rest of the state and, in a large state like California, this will mean that initiatives of this type will tend to pass.

One way to protect against this outcome is to limit the ability of the state voters to enact preemptive tax measures. The purpose of the "taxation" amendment described above is to accomplish this aim. A different approach would be to require a supermajority vote for state initiatives that preempt local regulatory laws. This supermajority requirement would be especially valuable in the case of initiatives, but it would also function with state legislation as well. Of course, this procedural rule would not completely ensure against state encroachments; the aim is merely to make such encroachments more difficult. Given the comparative weakness of local voters *vis-à-vis* state voters where the issue is state versus local regulatory policies, this supermajority requirement would level the playing field somewhat.[61]

The trigger for this supermajority requirement would be all state laws that potentially preempt local ordinances; thus, in at least this respect, we would not have to define with certainty what are "municipal affairs." We may want to construct a sensible scheme to determine, in advance of the initiative process or the legislative enactment of a potentially preempting law, whether the state law poses: (1) a conflict with a local law in an area that is not an exclusively municipal affair, therefore triggering only the procedural requirement of a supermajority; or (2) a conflict that *is* a municipal affair, thus triggering the substantive protection of local sovereignty. The aim of such a preenactment procedure would be to avoid litigation and, with it, the substantial financial burdens on state and, especially, local governments associated with fighting one another in court. In connection with this state versus local government litigation, I offer a

---

[61]A more radical suggestion along these lines would be a ratification requirement, that is, a requirement that local voters ratify decisions made by the state legislature or state voters before the law would take effect. This ratification requirement would be triggered by a determination (reviewable by courts) that the issue involved is one of exclusively local concern.

final proposal to facilitate the reconstruction of state/local home rule power under Article XI.

The doctrinal confusion in California decisions construing "municipal affairs" has limited the scope of local government power. Not only are state legislators encouraged to pursue state policies without fearing that courts will often strike down their initiatives, but local governments must consider whether, in light of this uncertainty, to proceed with enacting local laws and in defending these laws in court. While the incentives of state and local governments may be similar, the relative resources of these two levels of government will redound to the benefit of the richer state government. Local governments thus face a serious resource-based disincentive to fight the state of California in court. It is surely no accident that the main "municipal affairs" cases that reach the California Supreme Court cases involve cities such as Los Angeles, Oakland, and San Jose, rather than smaller, poorer cities. In light of the relative poverty of municipalities, it is important to construct a weapon that localities can wield against state efforts at encroachment. In this vein, another procedural revision is the enactment of a constitutional provision that would permit localities to recover attorney's fees from the state government where the state court upholds a claim of the locality. Perhaps it would be sensible, as well, to provide for the awarding of fees to local governments in every case in which a plausible, even if unsuccessful claim is made by the local government against the assertion of state control. While only a technical, litigation-oriented suggestion, this would, I believe, help to reconstruct the incentives for local governments to pursue initiatives in the face of state efforts to restrict local power.

Despite these suggestions, it remains clear that the key to unraveling the "municipal affairs" conundrum is to create a more sensible approach to interpreting Article XI, Section 5 where, as will frequently be the case, a precise, textual delineation of state and local powers is impossible. Judicial approaches should build on analyses that are essentially functional and pragmatic. Courts should consider, with the benefit of empirically oriented advocacy and available data, the comparative impact of conflicting state and local laws. This consideration will, to be sure, be called for in only those cases that arise under Article XI, Section 5. And classifying these cases is no easy matter. The starting point, though, is provided by Article XI itself: Home rule charter cities are of a different status under the state constitution. It would be appropriate for courts to consider *any* law enacted by home rule charter cities to be subject to this sort of functional analysis.

Issues that the courts should consider should include whether the local laws have "spillover" effects and, relatedly, whether statewide regulation would redound to the net benefit of citizens without substantially burdening citizens of the locality or—and this part is critical—substantially removing from these local citizens the benefits that would be associated with the local regulations if they were to survive scrutiny. It is important to curtail the state's powers to enact what amount to redistributional policies through their power of statewide regulation. Some redistribution is appropriate, of course; the state, after all, is charged with the responsibility to ensure that local governments should not exploit the public fisc through the enactment of rent-seeking local laws. However, there are limits to how far state legislatures and state voters should be able to go to forestall efforts of voters in municipalities to capture local benefits associated with regulatory and tax initiatives. Rent-seeking behavior by local governments is less problematic than similar behavior by state governments. The reason is the persistence of interlocal competition that restricts the ability of governments to exploit capital resources and individuals without restraint. So long as individuals are permitted to exercise their "voice" and their prerogatives to "exit" there are significant, albeit imperfect, constraints on the abilities of localities to exploit relentlessly resources.[62] At the end, we are left with a choice among institutional frameworks: do we prefer that regulatory and tax decisions be made by local or state institutions?

CONCLUSION

The aim of this chapter is to stimulate further reflection on questions concerning the constitutional reallocation of power between state and local government in California. The central problem with the current distribution is the imprecision of Article XI. While the structure of home rule under the California Constitution promises a degree of local sovereignty, the combination of vague language, erratic court decisions, and distorted

---

[62]See generally Albert O. Hirschman, *Exit, Voice, and Loyalty: Responses to Decline in Firms, Organizations, and States* (Cambridge, Mass.: Harvard University Press, 1970).

incentives of state decision makers, has rendered Article XI, Section 5's distribution of powers a flawed device for the sensible construction of state/local relationships. Perhaps a more thorough revision of the California Constitution's delegation of state/local authority is called for; as it stands, the constitution is rather silent on the critical questions concerning the lines of authority and responsibility among levels of government. While these proposals to improve Article XI, Section 5 do not address systematically the absence of comprehensive constitutional guidance, they aim to correct some of the more serious deficiencies in the structure of state/local relations under the California Constitution.

Moreover, the principles sketched out above concerning the advantages associated with regulatory competition, fiscal control, and municipal rights, can be usefully concerned in the context of *all* units of local government in California, and not merely those designated as "home rule" municipalities. It is crucial, in evaluating the scope of state power generally and the political and legal structure of state/local relations in this state, to understand how we might best distribute power and roles among governmental units. Perhaps the single most important feature of state/local relations is that they are intrinsically dynamic; municipalities are not carved in stone but can—and do—shift and change in light of the needs of a modern, heterogenous state population. Considering the legal relationship between the state government under the California Constitution and the various evolving (or sometimes devolving) local units of government is an essential first step to considering the larger, diffuse question of the appropriate structure of government in the state of California for the next century.

California Fiscal Federalism: A School Finance Perspective

Daniel L. Rubinfeld

INTRODUCTION

California's system of public finance has undergone a radical change over the past 20 years. This change was brought about by the actions of a wide group of interested political actors—by citizens, through the initiative process; by the legislature, through the passage of a variety of fiscal measures; by the executive, through the administration of a California finance system that became more centralized over time; and by the judiciary, through decisions that have substantially restricted the funding options available to local school districts.

This paper provides a critical review of the important actions that have altered California's fiscal federalist system. I begin with a brief review of the constitutional limits that existed in California's federalist system prior to the 1970s. Next, I focus on California school finance; schooling is not only the most important budgetary item for California governments, it has also been affected fundamentally by both the initiative process and the judiciary. The following section extends the discussion beyond school finance to the general fiscal budget. Finally, I comment on the implications of the analysis for California Constitutional federalism.

Robert L. Bridges Professor of Law and Professor of Economics, University of California, Berkeley. The author served as an economic expert for the California Board of Education in *Serrano IV*. He appreciates the helpful comments of John Kirlin, Joseph Remcho, and participants of the California Constitution Reform Commission.

CALIFORNIA FEDERALISM IN PERSPECTIVE

Prior to 1970 the California state constitution provided a relatively clear assignment of spending and taxation functions to the three most important levels of government: local, county, and state. Specifically, the constitution gave to the state the exclusive right to tax franchises, banks, and public utilities. The income tax,[1] retail sales tax,[2] and federal grants,[3] were, and are, the primary sources of state revenues. While the property tax was reserved explicitly as a local source of revenue, local jurisdictions could in principle use any tax instrument that had not been exclusively allocated to the state. The property tax, federal grants, state grants,[4] and service charges were the primary sources of county revenues, while the property tax, state[5] and federal grants, local sales taxes,[6] and service charges provided the bulk of local revenues.

In California as in most states, local governments have the power to control land use, and the authority to provide sanitation, police, and fire services, as well as services relating to community development, transportation, utilities, culture, and recreation. Counties administer state programs, including health and welfare, courts, jails, elections, and property tax collections. They are also responsible for parks, museums, libraries, and roads.

---

[1]The California personal income tax is highly progressive, with rates ranging from 0 to 11 percent. There is also a 9.3 percent tax on corporate net income.

[2]The tax is currently levied at 4.75 percent of value.

[3]For example, the Supplemental Security Income Program is fully funded by the federal government, but administered by the state, along with its own State Supplemental Program. Other major programs include the Community Block Grant program, Aid to Families with Dependent Children, Medi-Cal, Indigent Health Care, and Special Education.

[4]Grant programs from the state include sales tax revenues, highway user fees, vehicle license fees, trial court funding, AFDC, mental health programs, and indigent health care.

[5]State grants include sales tax revenue, highway user fees, vehicle license fees, school aid, special education, desegregation funding, and state mandate reimbursements.

[6]The permanent rate is 1.25 percent for most localities.

During the 1950s and 1960s the California Constitutional restrictions on revenue sources were the only constraints that affected California's hierarchical system of governments. However, as the initiative process evolved during the 1970s and the 1980s, and two constitutional amendments, Proposition 13 and Proposition 4, were passed, all levels of government began to face additional restrictive constraints.

Interestingly, prior to June 1978, the property tax had been the primary funding source for the California public sector generally, and for primary and secondary education in particular. The enactment of Proposition 13 as a California Constitutional amendment on June 6, 1978 drastically changed the fiscal environment of local and state governments.[7] Property tax rates were limited to a maximum of one percent of assessed value, and the property tax base was limited to a maximum increase of two percent per year.[8] Proposition 13 did allow for additional nonproperty tax revenues to be raised, but only by a minimum two-thirds vote of cities, counties, or special districts.

The fiscal effects of Proposition 13 were felt almost immediately. The proposition's limitations on the use of the property tax and on the local taxing authority generally led to a substantial budgetary shortfall—for primary and secondary education alone this amounted to $2.8 billion.[9]

Proposition 4 (the Gann Amendment), which followed on Proposition 13, established an appropriations limit based on the 1978-79 budget. Increases in this limit were restricted to the lower of (a) the rate of inflation as measured by the change in the U.S. Consumer Price Index, or (b) the percentage change in California personal income.[10] The proposition also contained an "unfunded mandates" provision that required the state to reimburse local governments for the costs of new and increasing require-

---

[7]Superior Court of California, Memorandum of Decision, SCHOOL FINANCE CASES, Coordinated Actions, April 28, 1983.

[8]The rates were limited to 1 percent of the full cash value of real property subject to taxation (Cal. Const. Art. 13A. Para. 1).

[9]Because property taxes are deductible on the federal personal income tax, not all of the reduction in taxes benefited California citizens. Moreover, a portion of the lost revenues was eventually replaced by increased sales taxes, which have had limited federal personal income tax deductibility.

[10]Half of all revenues in excess of the limit are to be returned to the taxpayers within two years in the form of lower taxes.

ments imposed by the legislature. Because the Gann limit was the minimum of the two factors, it limited increases in per-capita spending to less than the rate of inflation and less than the growth in nominal per-capita personal income. In effect, Proposition 4 constitutionally guaranteed that education would eventually become an inferior good.[11] As a practical matter, however, Proposition 4 has had relatively little impact on the California fiscal environment to this point. The combination of Proposition 13 and economic recession served as a much more powerful constraint on the growth of government in California.

SCHOOL FINANCE IN CALIFORNIA

In combination, Proposition 13 and the Gann Amendment greatly limited the flexibility of California's system of fiscal federalism. Perhaps more importantly, they encouraged a shift towards centralized state control. This shift was felt particularly strongly in the funding of K-12 public schools, where Proposition 13 and the Gann Amendment were "complemented" by the *Serrano v. Priest*[12] school finance decision and by the passage of Proposition 98. In the section that follows I briefly survey how each of these vital changes in the environment of school funding affected California's school finance federalism.

Before the filing of the *Serrano* case in 1971, California school districts substantially controlled their own finances. Each district's funding came from local property tax revenues that were raised through a local school district property tax levy, with the funds being collected by the counties and distributed to the districts. In part because of taste differences, and in part because of variations in tax base, spending levels differed substantially among school districts. These variations existed despite the fact that the state allocated its K-12 education aid in a manner that was inversely related to per-pupil property wealth (assessed value) in each district.[13] This system amounted to a "foundation plan," in which the state effectively set a minimum per-pupil expenditure level that was guaranteed to every district (provided that the district levied a certain property tax rate).

---

[11]Inferior goods are discussed in Pindyck and Rubinfeld (1995), 98.

[12](1971) 5 Cal. 3d 584 487 P.2d 1241 96 Cal. Rptr. 601.

[13]The state uses ADA, average daily attendance, as the relevant measure of the number of pupils in a school district.

Despite the fact that the foundation plan was somewhat equalizing, substantial variations in property wealth and per-pupil spending remained. This residual variation encouraged the filing of a lawsuit by attorneys representing John Serrano, the parent of a student in a low-wealth school district. *Serrano I*, which was initiated in 1971, claimed that substantial disparities in per-pupil spending denied California children equal protection under the California Constitution.

The state supreme court ruled for the plaintiffs in 1971, declaring the funding to be unconstitutional and requiring the state to revamp its system of finance. In response to this ruling, the state enacted SB 90.[14] This legislation effectively limited the maximum amount of general purpose state and local revenue that each local school district could receive. Under SB 90, if district funds were sufficient to finance the foundation level, the district received only "basic aid" from the state. However, those districts that could not fund the foundation level were given "equalization aid" on the basis of a power equalization scheme.

SB 90 first introduced the concept of revenue limits—limits on per-pupil spending placed by the state on the amount of funds that a school district could raise.[15] The base revenue limit was determined by the amount of general purpose revenues available to the district in 1972, and was adjusted upward annually for inflation.[16] Importantly, SB 90 allowed supplementation; each school district could vote to override revenue limits by a two-thirds approval of their voters, or by legislation of "permissive overrides" for special purposes.[17]

Because the inflation adjustment associated with SB 90 was greater for low-wealth districts than for high-wealth districts, spending differences among school districts would have been gradually equalized over time. However, the California superior court in 1974 ruled that the SB 90 legislation was unsatisfactory—that equalization was not occurring at a

---

[14]Chapter 1406, 1972 as amended by AB 1267 (Ch. 208, 1974).

[15]These revenue limits exclude state and federal categorical funds.

[16]The 1973-74 base revenue limit was equal to the general purpose revenues per ADA (average daily attendance) in 1972-73, adjusted for inflation.

[17]Other adjustments for declining enrollments and contributions to the State Teachers' Retirement System were also allowed.

sufficiently rapid pace.[18] Specifically, in *Serrano II*,[19] the court stated that the system of finance still violated the state's constitution; the court further allowed only an additional six years for the state to bring the system into compliance. The court ruled in particular that "wealth-related disparities in funds should be reduced to insignificant differences, which means amounts considerably less than $100 per pupil" by 1980-81.[20] In effect, the court argued that the school system must be financed in such a way that there was no correlation between the per-pupil wealth of the district and per-pupil expenditures.

This *Serrano* decision moved the state much further towards equality of spending than a number of the original supporters of the *Serrano* litigation had expected.[21] More importantly, it questioned whether local school districts could control their own school finances by using local revenues to supplement state funded spending levels. According to *Serrano II*, any attempt to increase local spending that was "wealth-based" could be seen as inconsistent with the *Serrano* mandate.

In response to the court's ruling in *Serrano II*, the legislature continued to modify and improve its own tax base equalization program. In 1977, AB 65 was passed; it would have expanded the power equalization program associated with SB 90 by putting into effect a guaranteed yield program, and by providing aid to low wealth districts that wanted to spend above their foundation level.

With the passage of Proposition 13, however, property taxes were limited to one percent of assessed value, and AB 65 was superseded.[22] The most obvious means of increasing local school spending—the local property tax—was no longer a viable option, even if some or all of the property tax increases were not wealth-based (as would occur, for example, under a power equalization scheme). Proposition 13, in combination with *Serrano II*, had effectively cut the link between taxing and spending at the

---

[18]The court also ruled that, because education is a fundamental interest and wealth is a highly suspect classification, the state of California was required to devise a valid financing system.

[19]*Serrano v. Priest* (1976) 18 Cal. 3d 728 557 P.2d 929 135 Cal. Rptr. 345.

[20]*Serrano v. Priest*, Judgment, August 30, 1974, at paragraph 3(c).

[21]Coons, Clune, and Sugarman (1970) support tax-base equalization, but not spending equality.

[22]It was to have gone into effect on July 1, 1978.

local school district level. What had once been essentially a locally controlled K-12 public school system with some state financial support, had been transformed in relatively few years into a state controlled and state funded system.[23] Whereas 53.75 percent of public school income in 1977-78 was from local sources, only 24.18 percent was local in 1979-80 immediately following the passage of Proposition 13.[24]

There remains substantial disagreement in the academic community as to the "cause" of Proposition 13. William Oakland (1979) suggests that excess state spending in general, and a large state surplus in particular, was the source, while Geoffrey Brennan and James Buchanan (1979), supported by Thomas Downes (1988), emphasize the inefficiency of a "Leviathan" government. William Fischel (1989), however, puts the blame squarely on the court's prior *Serrano* decisions. He argues that *Serrano* equalization meant that voters could no longer use the property tax as an effective means of increasing their own local spending. As a result, it was much easier to make the next step with Proposition 13—to eliminate local control over property taxes entirely.[25]

Whatever its true cause, it is clear that Proposition 13 created an almost immediate crisis for many public school districts, simply by reducing the available property tax revenues. After the passage of Proposition 13 in 1978, the state legislature introduced SB 154 as a stopgap solution to the short-run funding problem. The bill[26] introduced a system of block grants from the state to the school districts, which effectively transferred state budgetary surplus funds to local districts. Moreover, the bill allowed for some local control, through certain overrides and additional funds for adult education and "emergencies." However, once the state surpluses disappeared and a recession hit in 1982-83, the state was no longer willing or able to fund the inflation adjustment that had been previously available to the local districts.

---

[23]The local property tax remains a source of financial support for schools, but there is no local control over those funds, and they are therefore best seen as state-controlled monies.

[24]Downes (1992), Table 1, p. 407.

[25]None of these authors point to the inability of the legislature and the governor to put forth a more moderate alternative to Proposition 13.

[26]Ch. 292, 1978, as amended by SB 2212 (Ch. 332, 1978).

A further Proposition 13-related change accelerated the movement of control from the local districts to the state. Prior to Proposition 13 and after *Serrano II*, each school district could determine its local property tax revenues by subtracting its allotted state aid from its state-determined base revenue limit (which, apart from grandfathering, was a function of the district's assessed property value per pupil). Because of Proposition 13, however, each district's property tax revenue—a portion of all property taxes raised by the county—was limited. In response to Proposition 13, therefore, each district determined its share of the one percent of property tax revenues first (with the remaining portion allocated to other local and county functions), and state aid was supplied until the district's revenue limit was reached. The result was that the state became the marginal funding source for all school district funds, and the move from local to state control had more or less been completed.

The continuing saga of *Serrano* litigation did not end with the passage of Proposition 13. While *Serrano III* was a post-Proposition 13 appellate decision of relatively little fiscal consequence, *Serrano IV* raised issues concerning the meaning of fiscal equity in school finance that could conceivably have led to a substantial further change in California's school funding arrangements. In fact, however, there was little change. On May 15, 1986,[27] the *Serrano IV* court decided that the appropriate equity standard implicit in *Serrano II* was whether the vast majority of districts fell within a $100 per ADA (average daily attendance) band in real (inflation-adjusted) 1971 dollars. In 1982-83, 93.2 percent of all districts' pupils fell within that band (which had increased to $198 nominal 1982 dollars per ADA).[28] By 1990-91, the equalization process had continued further, with only 4.9 percent of the pupils in districts being outside the allowable range, which had increased nominally to $268 per ADA.[29]

The *Serrano* court also confronted the difficult conceptual question of how to separate the portion of local school spending that is wealth-based from the portion that is not. (Recall that differences in tax-base per ADA that result in differences in the "price" of local education will, other things

---

[27]In the Court of Appeal of the State of California, Second Appellate District, Division Two, School Finance Cases, May 15, 1986.

[28]Had the nominal band been $100 per ADA, a substantial further equalization of spending would have been required.

[29]Goldfinger (1992), 11.

equal, lead to spending differences. But demand differences, even with no difference in tax base per ADA, can also lead to spending differences. The conceptual problem is how to sort out the two.) The court found that no more than 10 to 30 percent of the difference in base revenue limits (the measure of per-pupil spending) was due to property wealth. Had Proposition 13 not been in effect, the court's decision in *Serrano IV* would have effectively re-empowered local school districts with spending authority. However, with Proposition 13, school districts could not levy additional property taxes, even if such levies were consistent with the *Serrano* mandate.

Did *Serrano*, in fact, achieve the desired goals of the court? Downes (1992) provides one answer. He utilized data from unified school districts to estimate that 36.1 percent of the school districts' 1975-76 revenue limits fell within a $100 band centered around the median. At the same time, the correlation between revenue limit funding and assessed valuation per pupil was .78.[30] By 1985-86, substantial equalization, although certainly not complete equality, had occurred. At that time approximately 65 percent of school districts fell within the same $100 per pupil (inflation adjusted) band, and the correlation between revenue limit funds and wealth had fallen to .52.[31] This equalization continued beyond the middle 1980s. By the 1992-93 school year, approximately 92.6 percent of unified school districts were within the $100 per pupil band,[32] and in 1993-94 96.1 percent of all districts were within the band.[33]

While *Serrano* effectively required near spending equality in education, and Proposition 13 limited the use of property tax revenues to fund schools, California was not statutorily limited in the amount of funding from sources other than the property tax that could be allocated to K-12 public

---

[30]Downes (1992), 409.

[31]*Ibid.*, 418 (fn.12) and 410.

[32]The comparable number was smaller for high school districts and elementary school districts. The data are from the California State Department of Education. Note also that the growth of categorical state aid raises additional questions concerning the equalization of school spending. While categorical spending is in many cases equalizing, it is not included in the Court's equalization requirements. Moreover, it is quite possible that substantial categorical assistance can lead to less rather than greater equalization.

[33]California Department of Education.

education. Given the broad array of revenue-raising instruments available to the state of California, it was not surprising that the political war over school funding moved to the state level. An important battle was won by supporters of K-14 public education in 1988, with the passage of Proposition 98, the School Funding and Accountability Initiative, which required that 40 percent of the state's General Fund tax increases go to K-14 education.

Initially Proposition 98 led to additional educational funding at the expense of other state budgetary items (since Proposition 4, the Gann Amendment, was still in effect.) Taxpayers in the state eventually responded by passing Proposition 111 in 1990. Proposition 111 eased to some extent the severe constraint set by Proposition 4—instead of allowing the Gann Appropriations limit to increase at the lower of the rate of increase of the CPI or the growth of personal income, Proposition 111 changed the constraint to be the growth of personal income. This made it less likely that the Gann limit would become a binding constraint on state educational funding, but it did nothing to reintroduce a link between local spending and local control over school district educational spending.[34]

As one looks at California school finance today, K-12 funding is not only state controlled, but is also highly dependent on factors that affect the state's sensitive fiscal environment. In particular, a statewide recession leading to less state revenue will almost certainly lead to less school funding, even with Proposition 98. Further, prior to Proposition 13, mandates from the state that were not fully funded could be paid for by an increased local property tax levy. Today, however, the legislature and the governor must approve additional funding to cover federal or judicial mandates.[35] Finally, local school districts have very little authority or ability to raise additional funds for K-12 schooling. Other than private contributions, such funds have been raised by a small number of school

---

[34]The minimum amount of funding provided to K-14 education is based on three separate tests: the greater of (1) the same share of the General Fund as the 1986-87 base year, or (2) the prior years's funding from state and property taxes adjusted for inflation (measured by the growth in per capita personal income) and enrollment increases. Further (3), in low growth years, inflation in test (2) will be measured by the growth in per capita General Fund revenues plus ½ percent. The shortfall will be restored in years of higher revenue growth. See EdSource (1992).

[35]If not, the funds must come from reductions in other programs.

districts through a two-thirds vote in support of a parcel tax, which is exempt from the Proposition 13 limitation because it is not an *ad valorem* property tax.[36]

While centrally financed schools are not unusual outside the U.S., California's state-dominated educational system is quite distinctive within the U.S. fiscal federal system. In 1991, for example, 66.4 percent of all California school district revenues came from the state, whereas the comparable national average was only 47.7 percent.[37] Such a state-dominated system has the potential to be highly sensitive to the whims of the state budgetary process generally, and to the business cycle in particular.

Moreover, *Serrano* and Proposition 13 effectively separated the taxing and spending decisions of local school districts. The result is that individual households have little incentive to participate in the local political process as it relates to school funding, and local school officials have less reason to be accountable to individual households in performing their management activities. It is not surprising, therefore, that the overall effect of limitations on financing and the removal of state control was to reduce public support for school funding. During the time period under study, California school funding fell substantially in its relative ranking among states. As Table 1 shows, while California had been 19th in spending per ADA in 1971-72, it had fallen to 36th by 1991-92.

Perhaps more troubling is the fact that California's support for K-12 schools lies substantially below the support levels of most other relatively high income, industrialized states. Table 2 shows that California's spending was 88 percent of the national average in 1990-91, while the spending of New York, Pennsylvania, and Massachusetts were 162 percent, 124 percent, and 121 percent of average, respectively.

While spending per ADA in California has fallen substantially in relative terms, teacher salaries have declined only slightly. In 1991-92, California's average salary was $40,192 compared to the national average of $34,148.[38] It should not be surprising therefore, that when one focuses

---

[36]The first parcel tax election was held in 1983. By June 1992, 97 school districts had voted in a referendum on parcel taxes and 41 had passed at least one. Thirty-three of these 41 districts are in the Bay Area. See Jones (1994).

[37]ACIR (1991). See Musso and Quigley (1993), Table 17.

[38]EdSource (1992), 7.

Table 1. ***California vs. U.S. School Spending—Current Nominal Expenses per ADA***

Year	California	U.S. Average	Calif. Rank
71-72	$ 955	$ 970	19
73-74	1,171	1,147	16
75-76	1,457	1,441	18
77-78	1,680	1,755	23
79-80	2,273	2,267	22
81-82	2,675	2,721	26
83-84	3,023	3,183	26
85-86	3,531	3,785	27
87-88	3,868	4,279	27
89-90	4,460	4,975	33
90-91	4,644	5,261	33
91-92	4,686	5,466	36

Source: National Education Association, "Rankings of the States, 1992"; and California Department of Education, from Goldfinger (1992), Table 1-1.

on the most important determinant of educational output (other than the students' abilities), the picture looks particularly gloomy. California ranks second highest nationally in the number of pupils enrolled per teacher (23.1). Only Utah, with 24.8, ranks higher, while the national average is only 17.3.[39]

This decline in relative spending and increase in absolute class size is, in my view, directly related to the overall trend toward equalization within California. Prior to *Serrano* and Proposition 13, there was substantial variation in per-pupil spending. Yet, by the early 1990s, spending had been

[39]*Ibid.*

Table 2. ***School Spending: California vs. Other States—Current Expenses per ADA***

State	*Expense/ADA*	*% of U.S. Average*
New York	$8,500	161.6%
Pennsylvania	6,534	124.2
Massachusetts	6,351	120.7
Ohio	5,639	107.2
Michigan	5,257	99.9
Illinois	5,062	96.2
Washington	5,045	95.9
California	4,644	88.3
Texas	4,238	80.6
Alabama	3,648	69.3
Utah	2,993	56.9

Source: National Education Association, "Rankings of the States, 1992"; and California Department of Education, from Goldfinger (1992), Table 1-1.

substantially equalized, to the point where California may be the state with the most equalized spending, other than Hawaii, whose system is not directly comparable, because it is entirely state run.

PUBLIC FINANCE IN CALIFORNIA

Many of the changes that affected public schools affected other components of the state and local system of finance as well. In this section, I broaden the analysis by commenting about California government finance generally.

First, while Propositions 13, 4, and 98 are perhaps the best known of the California fiscal initiatives, they represent only a small portion of all initiatives that have been enacted since 1978 and which directly affect the taxing and spending powers of the State of California. Each of the following additional initiatives has to one extent or another constrained the choices that California governments face in making their fiscal decisions:[40]

- Propositions 5 and 6 (1982)—state gift and inheritance taxes were abolished
- Proposition 7 (1982)—the state income tax was indexed for inflation
  Proposition 37 (1984)—34 percent of state lottery revenues were earmarked for education
- Proposition 46 (1986)—two-thirds vote was required to increase the property tax to finance bonds
- Proposition 62 (1986)—two-thirds governing board approval and majority voter approval was required for any measure that increases local taxes
- Proposition 163 (1992)—the state sales tax on snacks and bottled water was repealed

The dynamics of California fiscal federalism have been shaped by external forces (federal grants) as well as internal ones (state propositions). Federal grants to California actually peaked in 1977 in real dollars, declined until 1980, and remained relatively constant thereafter.[41] Partly as a replacement for lost federal aid, and partly as a response to various state propositions, state aid to local governments increased substantially over the same period.

Table 3 provides a brief summary of the relevant information.[42] Over the period from 1974 to 1988, there was a slight decline in the portion of state and local government expenditures funded by the federal government. A more notable change, however, was the substantial increase in the fraction of expenditures funded by the state—from 39 percent to 48 percent. As we have seen specifically in the case of education, the passage of Propositions 13 and 4 was responsible for much of this change.

---

[40]Two initiatives, Proposition 37 (lotteries) and Proposition 99 (cigarette tax), actually increased the revenue options of the state of California.

[41]Federal grants to the states actually increased somewhat (through programs such as AFDC and Medi-Cal), while federal payments to counties and cities declined.

[42]The Bureau of Census data do not accurately account for specific revenue items such as the revenues of county transportation commissions. However, accounting for these and other differences would not change the broad generalizations made in this paper. For further details, see Kirlin, et al. (1994).

Table 3. ***The Changing Role of State and Local Funding in California***

Year	*Federal*	*State*	*Local*
1974	19%	39%	42%
1977	20	41	39
1980	22	47	32
1983	19	47	36
1986	17	49	34
1988	17	48	36

Source: U.S. Department of Commerce, Bureau of the Census, Government Finances.

The gradual decline in federal support for the state of California shows up when we look in Table 4 at how the revenue mix has varied over time. Not only did federal grants fall in importance from 22 percent of revenue to 18 percent, but retail sales taxes declined as well. Despite the decline in federal support, however, real revenues for the state nearly doubled from 18.801 billion 1974 dollars in 1974 to 36.181 billion real dollars in 1989. County governments have been especially affected by both the reduction in grants and by the initiative process. The net result has been a reduction in grants from 22 percent to 16 percent of revenues that has more or less coincided with a reduction in property tax revenues (following Proposition 13). As Table 5 illustrates, counties have, of necessity, become more dependent on both state grants and on various user charges. Despite the mandated funding requirement of Proposition 4, counties have been and will continue to be in a highly sensitive fiscal situation, squeezed on one side by the mandates of the state and the federal government to provide health and social service programs, and restricted on the other side by the California Constitution in their ability to raise revenues. As an example, counties have had to pay an increased share of the costs of state-required programs, because the costs of these programs have increased more rapidly than has state funding. Further, because the programs are inherently redistributive, the counties cannot fund such programs through a system of user charges. The problems of counties have been further exacerbated by

Table 4. ***The Revenue Mix of California State Government***

Year	*Federal Grants*	*Income Taxes*	*Sales Taxes*	*Other Taxes*	*Pension Contributions*
1974	22%	20%	26	15	17%
1977	20	23	23	14	19
1980	20	25	24	14	17
1983	20	25	22	14	20
1987	17	24	20	16	22
1989	18	25	19	16	22

Source: U.S. Department of Commerce, Bureau of the Census, Government Finances, and State Government Finances.

Table 5. ***The Revenue Mix of County Governments***

Year	*Federal Grants*	*State Grants*	*Property Taxes*	*Service Charges*	*Other*
1974	22%	24%	34%	12%	9%
1977	25	23	32	12	7
1980	23	29	18	20	11
1983	19	30	20	22	9
1986	16	31	20	23	10
1989	16	33	21	20	10

Source: U.S. Department of Commerce, Bureau of the Census. Government Finances, and State Government Finances.

the stricter criminal sanctions of Governors Deukmejian and Wilson, and the California legislature, which led to a substantial growth in the California prison population.

Table 6 completes the picture. It shows an expected decline in both the use of the property tax and in state aid. As explained previously, localities have responded by increasing their use of whatever alternative sources of finance may be constitutionally appropriate and politically feasible.

IMPLICATIONS FOR CALIFORNIA CONSTITUTIONAL FEDERALISM

My brief review of California federalism has highlighted a number of fundamental changes in the way California governments are financed. Perhaps the most remarkable have been those changes affecting K-12 public school funding. In brief, the following represent the significant changes in California fiscal federalism.

School Finance

1. Proposition 13 has substantially limited the ability of local and county governments to make independent fiscal choices. These limitations were especially severe with respect to K-12 school funding, where the California Supreme Court had effectively turned a decentralized local school system into a centralized state system. While the school system has become more equalized, it has also become less flexible. Further, because this lack of local control reduced local political support for public schools, it may be a major cause of the substantial decline in per-pupil school spending. This is particularly troubling in light of the fact that public opinion polls continually show strong citizen support for K-12 public education.
2. By separating the taxing and spending decisions of local school districts, *Serrano* and Proposition 13 together have weakened incentives for political and economic accountability on the part of local school officials. In the current environment, those who benefit from K-12 state school support—school districts and the parents of public school children—are not directly accountable for the costs involved in the educational program.

Table 6. ***The Revenue Mix of Local Governments***

Year	*Grants*	*Property Taxes*	*Sales Taxes*	*Charges*	*Other*
1974	20%	17%	13%	35%	15%
1977	25	15	12	34	14
1980	19	9	13	41	18
1983	13	9	12	38	27
1986	12	9	12	38	28
1989	10	9	11	38	31

Source: U.S. Department of Commerce, Bureau of the Census, Government Finances and State Government Finances.

3. While Proposition 98 has benefited K-12 schools, it has created additional fiscal problems for other state and local governments. In recessionary periods such as 1993, the state has been unable to meet its Proposition 98 requirement. The state's response—shifting $2.6 billion in property tax revenues from counties and cities to the public schools—temporarily resolved the state's fiscal problem, but put even further pressure on the counties.[43]

City and County Finances

4. Along with the counties, California cities have also felt the increased fiscal pressure created in part by the state. For example, cities lost approximately $300 million with the property tax reallocation from other spending items to public school funding that was needed to support schools in light of Proposition 98. Further, cities are severely constrained in their revenue choices because of Proposition 13. Only

[43]The state did remove some county statutory responsibilities and earmarked a temporary one-half cent sales tax for public safety programs.

in rare cases have localities been able to get the political and constitutional support to raise additional revenues.

5. Initiatives in California have substantially limited the ability of all California governments to raise revenues and to provide goods and services. Proposition 13 has been particularly constraining.
6. The growth in entitlement programs and other spending demands has greatly increased the pressure on the state to fund its activities while balancing the budget. The state has responded occasionally by raising revenues (e.g., a one-half cent sales tax increase in 1991), and in part by shifting additional program responsibilities to the counties. The net effect has been to squeeze California counties severely.
7. Proposition 4 served as a binding constraint on selected local governments only in 1987, but it could severely limit the future options of at least a minority of California's local jurisdictions. It is not surprising, therefore, that without the traditional source of local funding, the property and sales tax, localities have resorted to user fees (service charges) and to other more esoteric revenue sources, such as the parcel tax.
8. Despite the historical precedent in California, there appears to be little conceptual support for counties taking primary responsibility for health and welfare programs. Such programs have typically been seen as under the purview of the state.

While the fiscal changes in California federalism made governmental units less accountable and reduced policy flexibility, I believe these results were largely unintended. But, whether they were intended or not, these changes have proven contrary to the interests of the California electorate. I believe, therefore, that constitutional reform should be directed towards making the same political entity responsible for both spending and taxing decisions.

While this could, in theory, be resolved by further centralization of the system, I believe that the benefits of decentralization, which include the added flexibility given to local school districts, are substantial.[44] The following policy suggestions are consistent with this latter view.

---

[44]Under one version of a centralized system, the state would support a "voucher" program. The state would license schools and allocate payments on a per-ADA basis, while parents and students could choose to attend the school of their choice.

1. Proposition 13 should be repealed or amended. One of its original goals—to limit the size of state and local governments—is explicitly accounted for by Proposition 4. Another major goal, to reduce the level of residential property taxation can be achieved through other means.
   a. If local governments are allowed to levy additional property taxes to finance education, the link between local taxation and spending will be reattached. This, in itself, should increase local support for public schools, which could lead to a substantial improvement in K-12 funding.
   b. Requiring a 50 percent majority vote to increase funding for public schools is inherently more democratic than is a two-thirds requirement. The latter allows a substantial minority to oppose fundamental positive changes in the educational system.
   c. On equity grounds, the property tax should be preferred as a source of public school funding to many of the sources of finance that have replaced it. To the extent that the tax is applied broadly across all jurisdictions, it is in substantial part a tax on capital, which is progressive. The parcel tax, however, is somewhat regressive, since all units, whether rental or owner-occupied, are taxed the same amount.[45]
   d. If additional property tax revenues are to be raised, while maintaining a cap on residential property taxes, the introduction of a split role whereby businesses are assessed on a market value basis, while residential assessments continue to be limited as directed by Proposition 13, should be seriously considered.[46]
2. The California Constitution should be amended to require that disparities in the provision of education not be wealth-based, consistent with the *Serrano I* decision. However,

---

[45]The volume of parcel tax revenue has been sufficiently small so as to have little effect on the overall distribution of tax burdens in California.

[46]Alternatively, all current assessments could be grandfathered, with future assessment increases (for residential, commercial, and industrial property) indexed to market values. If a split role approach is used, the state will need to consider the broader question of whether businesses ought otherwise to be compensated for the increased cost of operating in the state of California.

   a. The amendment should make it clear that equality of per-pupil spending is not required. As a result, attention can be moved away from the question of whether each local district's spending per ADA lies within the *Serrano*-equalization band, and towards more fundamental educational finance reform.
   b. This amendment would pave the way for the legislature to put into effect a percentage equalization reform plan with a substantial minimum revenue limit per ADA. There would, however, be no upper limit on spending, since renewed parental choice would broaden the political support for public funding of K-12 schools.
3. The fiscal squeeze faced by counties and other local governments must be ameliorated. This can be accomplished by requiring that the state provide sufficient funding to support the health and welfare programs that they mandate.

REFERENCES

Brennan, Geoffrey, and James Buchanan. 1979. "The Logic of Tax Limits: Alternative Constitutional Constraints on the Power to Tax." *National Tax Journal* 32 (June supp.): 11-22.

Coons, John E., William H. Clune, and Steven D. Sugarman. 1970. *Private Wealth and Public Education*. Cambridge: Belknap Press of Harvard University Press.

Downes, Thomas A. 1988. "The Implications of the *Serrano* Decision and Proposition 13 for Local Public Choice." Ph.D. dissertation, Stanford University.

_________. 1992. "Evaluating the Impact of School Finance Reform on the Provision of Public Education: The California Case." *National Tax Journal* 45 (December): 405-19.

EdSource. 1992. "School Finance 1992-93." (October): 1-8.

Fischel, William A. 1989. "Did Serrano Cause Proposition 13?" *National Tax Journal* 42 (December): 465-73.

Goldfinger, Paul M. 1992. "Revenues and Limits." *A Guide to School Finance in California*, 1992 edition, School Services of California, Inc.

Jones, Martha. 1994. "Voting for Local School Taxes in California: How Much Do Demographic Variables Matter?" Draft, February 28.

Kirlin, John J., Jeffrey I. Chapman, Peter Asmus, and Roy Thompson. 1994. "Fiscal Reform in California." Prepared for the Task Force on Fiscal Reform, California Business Higher Education Forum, Feb. 17.

Musso, Juliet A., and John M. Quigley. 1995. "Intergovernmental Fiscal Relations in California: A Critical Evaluation." Working Paper #216, Graduate School of Public Policy (January).

_________, and John Quigley. In press. "Public Investment in California." In *Regional Finance and Economic Development in the Pacific Rim*, ed. John Quigley. New York: Cambridge University Press.

Oakland, William. 1979. "Proposition 13: Genesis and Consequences." *National Tax Journal* 32 (June supp.): 387-409.

Picus, L. O. 1991. "Cadillacs or Chevrolets?: The Evolution of State Control over School Finance in California." *Journal of Education Finance* 17: 33-59.

Pindyck, Robert S. and Daniel L. Rubinfeld. 1995. *Microeconomics*, 3d ed. Englewood Cliffs, N.J.: Prentice-Hall.

Silva, Fabio, and Jon Sonstelie. 1995. "Did Serrano Cause a Decline in School Spending?" *National Tax Journal* 48 (June): 199-215.

VII. RESOURCE MANAGEMENT

Real Property and Direct Democracy in California

Margaret Jane Radin
Brendan P. Cullen

INTRODUCTION

Initiative and referendum, the processes of direct democracy, are an important aspect of California politics. In an initiative, the voters create a new statute or constitutional amendment. In a referendum, they approve or disapprove of a statute enacted by their representatives.[1] Article II of the California Constitution broadly enables these processes. The initiative and referendum power is available to voters not only for statewide matters, but at the local level as well. Article II, Section 11 provides: "Initiative and referendum powers may be exercised by the electors of each city or county under procedures that the Legislature shall provide."[2]

In this chapter, our topic is real property and direct democracy, that is, the use of direct democracy to regulate the use of real property. This process is called "ballot box zoning." The broad power to use initiative and referendum at the local level to enact or repeal land-use measures renders landowners' property rights insecure. It also underwrites exclusion of new residents in ways that may be inefficient or unwise.

---

[1]The instruments of ballot box zoning examined here are measures arising from petitions among a sufficient number of citizens to place on the ballot either a new zoning measure written by the petitioners (an initiative) or a zoning measure that has been adopted by a local government that the petitioners seek to repeal (a referendum). This chapter does not deal with measures placed on the ballot by local governments.

[2]Provisions of the Elections Code govern initiatives and referendums. See Cal. Elec. Code §§ 4002 - 4061 (West Supp. 1994). Groups wishing to submit measures to popular vote must get a percentage of voters (10 percent for a referendum, 15 percent for an initiative) to sign petitions to place them on the ballot.

Ballot box zoning accounts for a small fraction of zoning changes, but its frequency of use does not indicate its significance. If use of referendum or initiative is a credible threat, then when local government officials make any zoning decision they must take into account the possibility that the power of direct democracy will be used to rewrite it. Indeed, if the goals of all interested parties who could mount initiative campaigns, as well as the ultimate outcome an initiative would achieve, are known to public officials, then all zoning decisions will be influenced by groups who pose a credible threat to place a zoning measure on the ballot even if they do not actually do so. The initiative or referendum will never actually need to be used because the interests that threaten to use it will not have to go through with their campaign in order to win their objectives. Both the local zoning officials and the interest group that is able to pose the credible threat of mounting a ballot measure can avoid the cost of the initiative process by simply compromising their disagreement.

These compromises, which will not be made explicit, represent the effect of the availability of direct democracy on the entire process of zoning decision making. As a result, the availability of direct democracy for land-use issues creates uncertainty about the nature and security of the property rights enjoyed by all property owners. Furthermore, the threat of exclusionary ballot measures that would benefit certain groups of voters at the expense of would-be newcomers who do not vote in the jurisdiction may deter local governments as well as owners of undeveloped land from providing housing that would serve those would-be newcomers.

The core problem created by ballot box zoning is that there are many situations where the availability of direct democracy does pose a credible threat to the land-use decision-making process. An interest group with a very large stake in a particular zoning decision (for example, owners of existing homes) can underwrite the cost of an initiative that has the effect of transferring a great deal of wealth to that interest group from a small minority of property-owning voters (for example, owners of vacant land), or from nonvoters. If the transfer can be made to look like something that will enjoy widespread popular support, such as an action that transfers wealth from a few to the majority, or if it can be packaged with another zoning issue that will do this, then the use of the initiative becomes a credible threat to local officials. In practice, it would be difficult or impossible for local officials to act in a way that avoids responding to such threats.

Thus, the existence of the broad power of direct democracy affects property rights and exclusion whether or not it is exercised very often, as long as it is a credible threat. All California real property owners must take into account the fact that a popular vote may change the scope of their property rights, and all people belonging to groups historically subject to exclusion must understand that local electoral units have the power to exclude them by popular vote.

This chapter suggests that Article II, Section 11 could be amended to ameliorate (though not eliminate) the potential of ballot box zoning for abuse of direct democracy at the local level. The potential for abuse may be greatest when a majority has the power to exploit one or a few real property owners through individual zoning decisions. Our tentative proposal will be to add to Article II, Section 11 a provision having the effect of limiting ballot box zoning to measures that are sufficiently general to lessen this potential for exploitation.

SPECIAL CHARACTERISTICS OF LAND-USE REGULATION

California's constitutional provisions for direct democracy do not make any distinction between land-use regulations and other kinds of enactments. Zoning (and rezoning) is technically a legislative act, because zoning is done by ordinance enacted by the city council. Zoning (and other kinds of land-use regulation like landmarking or historial districting) differs markedly, however, from the generic picture that the idea of legislation may conjure up. These differences have some bearing on how we should view land-use decisions by local direct democracy, and might justify a constitutional provision that separates land-use decisions from other kinds of legislation.

In this section we review four characteristics of typical local zoning decisions that are relevant to their suitability as subjects of direct democracy: (1) the need for coordination, (2) the potential to single out particular owners for adverse economic impact, (3) close involvement with the private sector, and (4) lack of generality of individual decisions. These considerations are relevant to the appropriateness of decision making by direct democracy, but they do not all point in one direction on the issue.

(1) *Individual zoning decisions cannot provide coherent structure for a community unless they are coordinated in some way. They are counter-productive if they are arbitrary and piecemeal.*

Euclid v. Ambler Realty Co.,[3] the U.S. Supreme Court case that validated zoning against constitutional attack in the 1920s, rested partly on the rationale that zoning regulations are analogous to traffic regulations. The Standard State Zoning Enabling Act, which many states enacted in the 1920s, required that zoning be in accordance with a comprehensive plan. This requirement was thought to be necessitated by constitutional requirements of fairness and rationality. Over the years comprehensive planning, an administrative rather than a legislative function, has grown ever more important. At this point complex provisions of state law require zoning to be in accordance with the local jurisdiction's adopted plans (although no coordinated statewide enforcement mechanism enforces compliance). The requirements of consistency and coordination are supposed to work to protect the security and stability of property owners' interests against arbitrary or inconsistent land-use regulations.

Ballot box zoning can be criticized because it does not consider the proposed zoning action in the context of the entire plan. A number of other state courts have been responsive to this objection and have placed severe limits on ballot box zoning because of the way it plays havoc with statewide planning mandates. California courts, however, have by and large been unmoved by this objection.

(2) *Individual zoning decisions have a particular potential to single out one or a small class of owners, as well as a small class of neighbors, for adverse economic impact.*

Perhaps because of its potential for adverse economic impact, state law makes zoning invalid absent a panoply of procedures for public hearing and debate, a form of due process not considered necessary for other kinds of legislative acts. A number of other state courts have considered ballot box zoning to deny procedural due process to owners and developers who cannot argue their case rationally and in detail to the public at large. Moreover, nonresidents who want to protest exclusionary zoning by initiative and referendum have no forum in which to do so. California courts, however, have by and large been unresponsive to the due process objection as well.

(3) *Individual zoning decisions are enmeshed with the private sector more directly than other legislation.*

---

[3]272 U.S. 365 (1926).

Zoning amendments are "applied for" in a way regular statutes are not. Negotiations between affected parties and administrative officials (planning boards) and elected officials (city council members) are explicit. In general legislatures are not allowed to make contracts that bargain away their police power. Developer agreements are an exception, however, in which state law now permits a municipality explicitly to bind itself not to change zoning after a developer commits to a project.[4]

Developer agreements seem problematic because land-use regulations are particularly vulnerable to being bought by individual permit-seekers who need only pay off the individual council member from their district. Thus, in situations where a single land-use decision that voters disapprove of might not be sufficient to throw their representatives out of office at the next election, direct democracy might serve as a check on representatives who bargain away their power to their supporters. Indeed, among other safeguards, the California statute explicitly provides that developer agreements are subject to referendum.

(4) *Individual zoning decisions, unlike other legislation, lack generality. They are case-specific. They are not readily distinguishable from other classes of case-specific governmental acts that the courts have held to be administrative or adjudicative, not subject to legislative power.*

In certain contexts official actions denominated zoning amendments are quite similar in form and scope to official actions denominated variances, use permits, and subdivision approvals. Those actions have been denominated administrative or adjudicative by California courts. One reason they are so characterized is that they involve case-by-case decisions about a particular parcel of land (but so can a rezoning). Another reason they are so characterized is that the potential for arbitrariness and corruption in the process of granting and denying such permits calls for detailed judicial review for evenhandedness, which is accepted when actions are "judicial" but not when they are "legislative." (But the same arguments may apply to rezoning.)

Thus ballot box zoning seems to be available only for a subset of regulations affecting land, those regulations that are deemed legislative in nature, rather than administrative or adjudicative. This is not a rational

---

[4]See Cal. Govt. Code §§ 65864 et seq. (West. Supp. 1995).

basis upon which to build a distinction between those land-use regulations that are subject to direct democracy and those that are not.

MARKET POWER AND THE ISSUE OF EXCLUSION

Economists have been puzzled by the issue of externalities in respect to land-use decisions—what to do about owners who impose costs on their neighbors instead of keeping them to themselves. Noneconomists have been puzzled by the same problem described in terms of harm-causing or nuisance-like activities.

How do these theoretical problems arise in practice? When an owner proposes to develop vacant land a certain way in order to make a profit, owners of already-developed land object. They want the parcel zoned open space! Their objections could reflect either of two nonoptimal scenarios.

(1) Scenario 1: Existing owners of developed land could be objecting because the new development will harm them. It will cause pollution and congestion and engender a need for more infrastructure that they will have to pay for as local taxpayers. In economic terms this harm would amount to a wealth transfer from old owners to the new developer—higher taxes for one, higher profit for the other.

This wealth transfer could be neutralized by a well-calibrated exaction from the developer in return for permission to develop. That is, in scenario 1, it seems appropriate for the local government to make the developer pay a fee before it will grant the requested zoning change or building permit.

(2) Scenario 2: On the other hand, owners of developed land could be objecting to the new development because they want to keep their own property values artificially high. They want to restrict the local supply of housing, which keeps the market prices of already developed property high, and they want value-enhancing open space surrounding their property. In economic terms, they want to force the would-be developer to confer upon them the external benefit of open space. This would amount to a wealth transfer from the would-be new developer to the old owners.

This wealth transfer to owners of developed land from owners of undeveloped land could be neutralized by a well-calibrated compensation payment to the owner of vacant land. Thus, in scenario 2, a court should find that the local government's denial of development authorization is a "taking" of property rights in violation of the constitution.

In addition, scenario 2 is the typical case of exclusionary zoning. People who want to move into the community cannot do so because the community will not allow housing for them to be built. Often the situation takes on discriminatory overtones if the excluded outsiders differ in respects deemed socially significant (e.g., class or race).

Subdivision exactions, and other transfer payments from developers to the municipality such as annexation fees, could represent compensation to the municipality (i.e., to existing owners who are taxpayers) for the harm caused (if scenario 1 rightly describes the circumstances) or could represent extortion by a monopoly, and appropriation of the developer's expected profit (if scenario 2 rightly describes the circumstances). Compensation to owners whose development expectations are frustrated by restrictive land-use regulations could represent appropriate payment to prevent a windfall loss (if scenario 2 rightly describes the circumstances) or could represent a windfall gain to an owner whose expectations included the unjustified desire to inflict externalities on others (if scenario 1 rightly describes the circumstances). Unfortunately, economists, lawyers, and policymakers have not figured out a way to know which scenario we are playing out in any given land-use decision.

A number of years ago Robert C. Ellickson made an interesting suggestion in this regard.[5] He describes the politics of growth control as capable of being explained by either of two models, which he calls the "majoritarian model" and the "influence model" of political community.[6]

Ellickson's "majoritarian model" describes a small, elite suburb in which the rate of homeownership is high, in which relatively few issues are before the legislative body, and in which there are relatively few voters. In such a community, land-use is often the only issue before the legislative body that voters really care about. In the majoritarian model, the homeowners have a common interest in exclusion. They will take advantage of their voting majority to force officials to adopt exclusionary land-use practices like open space designations, large subdivision exactions, quotas on the number of units permitted to be built, moratoria on development,

---

[5]See Robert C. Ellickson, Suburban Growth Controls: An Economic and Legal Analysis, 86 *Yale L. J.* 385 (1977).

[6]Ellickson noted that few communities followed either model exactly and that many communities demonstrated some aspects of both models. *Id.* at 409.

etc.[7] Ellickson suggests, in a nutshell, that small, socially homogeneous residential suburbs are likely to be playing scenario 2.

In the majoritarian model the interest-group model of politics does not apply, because one interest group has the political process monopolized. In the "influence model," on the other hand, the interest-group model of politics does apply. In communities in which the interest-group model applies, the "strength of an interest group is purely a function of its ability to contribute money, manpower, or other political assets to election campaigns."[8] What community characteristics make the interest-group model more apt? The need for their governments to confront a great number of more complex issues. This need in turn is engendered by a larger and less socially homogeneous population and a diverse mixture of land uses. Because of the complexity and variety of issues, organizing a majority to support one side of any one issue becomes difficult, and logrolling and bargaining among organized minorities are more likely to determine outcomes.

Ellickson theorizes that one of the minorities that can be expected to flourish under the influence model is the development interest. Through a course of strategic campaign contributions to carefully selected local politicians, developers can gain approval of individual development projects. They will not be plagued with the free-rider problems associated with programs that disperse their benefits throughout the industry, which make it more difficult to obtain prodevelopment legislation at the state or regional level. Further, because of the number and variety of issues in play in the political process, developers can expect to achieve development-specific gains without strong public interference. Officials will not be voted out of office because of one land-use decision. Ellickson suggests, in a nutshell, that larger and more politically diverse communities are likely to be playing scenario 1. These communities may have to put up with more pollution and congestion, but new residents will have housing. Depending on market circumstances, developers will have to pass on the extracted rents to their customers, in which case new residents have a windfall gain at the expense of old, or developers will keep them as profit.

---

[7]*Id.* at 405-7.

[8]*Id.* at 407.

Ellickson suggests that judges should be aggressive in striking down local governmental acts under the majoritarian model. His suggestion elicits strong responses questioning the extent to which local government restrains competition in the way he asserts. It is possible that communities will compete with one another for the efficient level of development (or nondevelopment), thus preventing the monopolistic results of scenario 2. Vicki Been, for example, argues that aggressive judicial review may be unnecessary (and indeed a windfall for developers) because competition among municipalities in the market for development may well constrain to the right level the exactions that local governments extract from developers.[9]

Ellickson's anticompetitive majoritarian model could perhaps be refined to take more fully into account the arguments drawn from the idea of competition among suburbs by making a distinction between small, socially homogeneous residential suburbs that possess unique characteristics and those that are rather interchangeable.[10] The cookie-cutter suburbs may be price-takers in a competitive market, while the unique suburbs have the market power to behave monopolistically. This would at least mean that cookie-cutter suburbs would not be able to charge large subdivision exactions (enriching local taxpayers at the developer's expense) because the developer would go to some other cookie-cutter suburb that would charge less.

This still may leave the individual owner of vacant land holding the bag, however, in a suburb that deliberately prices itself out of the market for development. Perhaps it can be argued that in a market in which the supply of land does not increase but the number of housing demanders does, over a period of time a developer will be willing to pay a higher price to the municipality. It might be argued as well that over a period of time as the existing housing stock gets older the land value of existing owners will decline unless new development finances new infrastructure and supports new enterprises.

Accepting provisionally that municipalities can be roughly identified as belonging to the majoritarian model or the influence model by their size

---

[9]Vicki Been, "Exit" as a Constraint on Land Use Exactions: Rethinking the Unconstitutional Conditions Doctrine, 91 *Colum. L. Rev.* 473 (1991).

[10]See Stewart E. Sterk, Competition Among Municipalities as a Constraint on Land Use Exactions, 45 *Vand. L. Rev.* 831 (1992).

and heterogeneity, what are the characteristics of direct democracy in each model? In the majoritarian model, officials hold office under threat of ouster at the next election if they make land-use decisions that undermine the cartel-like exclusionary preferences of the majority of voters—i.e., if they fail to play out scenario 2.

In this situation, referendum allows a quicker and more finely tuned disciplinary mechanism. Officials who make one "wrong" (i.e., pro-development) decision need not be recalled or voted out at the next election; instead they can be countermanded and warned. Initiative allows a bypass of the public hearing review process, if the majority thinks the council is likely to cave in to a vocal minority. In short, it seems that the availability of ballot box zoning can make scenario 2 easier to implement in at least some cases, while in no cases making it harder to implement (always assuming a stable majority with cartel-like motives). Facilitating scenario 2 is obviously not in the public interest, and leads us to question the wisdom of permitting ballot box zoning.

On the other hand, referendum and initiative could serve the public interest in an influence model community. Where the size of the electorate and the number and complexity of issues before the legislative body allows officials to feel relatively free of the possibility that one "wrong" land-use move will result in losing the next election, these officials may readily grant permission for externality-causing developments that will benefit their friends and campaign contributors at the expense of the community at large. In other words, elected officials will try to implement scenario 1.

If, however, the land-use decisions in such a community are subject to voter approval, it may be more likely that the developments that are allowed to proceed will be ones that do not take more from a community (in the way of externalities created) than they give (in the way of exactions received in return for approval of the development, or other net positive contributions to the community). The potential for direct democracy decision making on any given development, even if it remains unused, may create an incentive for elected officials to proceed with caution when considering the requests of any developer for favors in the way of land-use decisions, no matter how enticing the *quid pro quo*. The threat of direct democracy may undermine the viability of scenario 1, which would be in the public interest as long as it does not facilitate scenario 2 instead (see below).

Thus direct democracy might be a salutary check on developer wealth-grabbing in communities described by Ellickson's influence model. Certain factors render this supposition less than clear, however. In a large, heterogeneous community aptly described by the influence model, there is no reason to assume that a majority of voters will be predisposed to vote antidevelopment rather than prodevelopment. The greater the number of land-use decisions that are subject to voter approval, the less likely each is to be considered on its own merits, and the less likely that anything meaningful can be said about whether direct democracy is acting as an appropriate check on developer overreaching, as a rubber stamp of developer overreaching, or as an indiscriminate antidevelopment hammer. Further, there is the possibility that the money formerly spent on convincing elected officials to go along with a wealth-grabbing development plan will now be diverted into wasteful campaigns designed to persuade voters to approve the plan.

Perhaps more importantly, direct democracy may help a community described by the influence model behave more like a community described by the majoritarian model. That is, direct democracy may facilitate monopolistic behavior in communities that otherwise would find it difficult to orchestrate. Some communities described by the influence model for purposes of election of representatives may nevertheless have a strong antidevelopment interest group consisting of homeowners wishing to maintain higher than competitive value for their property. In such a community, even though the issues before the legislative body may be too multifarious to promise effective control over any one official by antidevelopment interests, when land-use issues appear on the ballot, voters need not decide how to vote based on review of a candidate and the bundle of attributes that candidate offers, but instead are free to express their monopolistic, antidevelopment preferences in voting down any proposed development.

This is particularly troubling in circumstances where this process facilitates exclusion based on race or class. In social circumstances where racism or classism is endemic to the culture, buyers and sellers will share these prejudices. Then the prospect of diverse people moving into a community will lower the demand for the already existing housing and will lower property values. In these circumstances, when antidevelopment forces politically prevail they not only realize economic gains at the expense of developers and their potential customers, they also maintain a pattern of discrimination that at least has the appearance of injustice. Courts that rely on analysis of motive in order to decide whether a practice is discriminatory have immunized exclusionary practices in which the existing property owners can truthfully say they were merely trying to maintain their own property values.[11]

Even if direct democracy facilitates cartelization and exclusion in some communities, that does not mean it should be abolished, for the cure may be worse than the disease. Next we will examine reform strategies.

WHAT (IF ANY) REFORM IS APPROPRIATE?

A state without a constitutional reservation of the power of initiative and referendum might simply enact a statute prohibiting direct democracy in the field of land-use regulation. A New Jersey statute reads, "No zoning ordinance and no amendment or revision to any zoning ordinance shall be submitted to or adopted by initiative or referendum."[12] Such a statute would, of course, be invalid in California because of the current constitutional provisions enabling initiative and referendum without any exception for land-use regulations.

] Some might argue that the problems with ballot box zoning can be alleviated by means of appropriate judicial review. Nothing theoretically prevents California courts from adopting an approach severely restricting ballot box zoning because of the way it plays havoc with comprehensive planning and involves the potential for arbitrariness and abuse. Such an approach has been taken by judges in other states. Yet it appears that California courts are unwilling to chart a new course in light of the solidity of their precedent granting expansive scope to direct democracy.

Ellickson argues that activist judicial review of land-use decisions might reduce the power of majoritarian-model communities to extract rents from owners of developable land. He argues that state court judges should take an activist stance in reviewing land-use schemes that are apparently monopolistic or exclusionary.[13] Ellickson and a few other commentators argue as well that activist review of land-use decisions under the just

---

[11]See *Arlington Heights v. Metropolitan Housing Development Corp.*, 429 U.S. 252 (1977).

[12]N.J. Stat. § 40:55D-62(b) (1993).

[13]Ellickson, *supra* note 5 at 473.

compensation ("takings") clause of the federal Constitution is in order, an approach to which several members of the U.S. Supreme Court are now sympathetic.[14] Under this approach zoning measures that would alter the property interests of existing owners would require just compensation for doing so. Of course, compensation would be perverse in a situation where the landowner and would-be developer are already able to play on scenario 1.

California state courts may or may not follow the U.S. Supreme Court's lead in according more credence to takings claims against certain land-use regulations.[15] In any case, the prospect for arbitrary and inconsistent behavior on the part of judges makes judicial activism not a very promising solution for perceived problems of direct democracy. Judicial activism would embrace all land-use decisions, not just those enacted by initiative or repealed by referendum. And to try to escape the perceived evils of populism by substituting the evils of judicial nonpopulism seems ill-advised.

That brings us to consideration of constitutional amendment. An amendment abolishing the powers of initiative and referendum in toto is beyond the purview of consideration here and no doubt politically untenable in any case. Adding land use to the constitutional exemptions already listed in the constitution (e.g., tax levies) could be considered. (This would be like constitutionalizing New Jersey's statutory approach.) A consideration against this, apart from the strength of the political opposition it would confront, is that ballot box zoning has the potential to act as a check on corruption of local officials in communities described by Ellickson's influence model.

---

[14]See especially the opinions of Justice Scalia, in *Nollan v. California Coastal Comm.*, 483 U.S. 825 (1987), and *Lucas v. S. Car. Coastal Council*, 112 S.Ct. 2886 (1992), and the opinion of Justice Rehnquist in *Dolan v. City of Tigard*, 114 S.Ct. 2309 (1994). For commentary on the possible emerging tendency to subject certain regulatory takings claims to stronger judicial review, see M. J. Radin, *Reinterpreting Property* (Chicago: University of Chicago Press, 1993), chapters 4 and 6.

[15]So far the Supreme Court's cases indicate that heightened scrutiny may be limited to cases in which actual dedication of land to the public is required (Nollan, Dolan), and cases in which land is required to be left in its natural state (Lucas). See *id.*

We might consider attempting to translate the insights of the Ellickson analysis into a more finely tuned constitutional scheme. This attempt would presuppose our possessing certain kinds of empirical evidence we do not possess, about what kinds of communities are likely to possess economic market power (and exclusionary power), and what kinds of actions by those communities are most likely to be implementations of inefficient or unjust exclusion. The majoritarian model posits a small, socially homogeneous residential community. Perhaps an index could be composed that would take into account the number of voters, the percentage of land that is devoted to single-family housing, and the median household income.

Trying to limit ballot box zoning to communities that score a certain way on such an index seems constitutionally unworkable, however. Even a community that scores high on such a homogeneity index need pose no dangers of market power if it is fungible with other suburbs. Without a firmer factual basis for defending its rationality than we can currently envision, such a scoring mechanism would invite equal protection challenge under the federal Constitution.

Rather than distinguishing between types of communities for which land-use regulation by direct democracy will or will not be permitted, it seems preferable to focus on the type of land-use regulation in question. It is possible that a large portion of the exclusionary effects leads us to regard direct democracy as a mixed blessing result from measures aimed at individual plots of land or land owned by just a few, rather than more general measures. Real property owners whose particular development plans are singled out by the majority are perhaps in the most danger of exploitation by the majority. In these cases members of the majority can protect their own property value at the expense of one or a few owners, while maintaining the option to sell out to a developer themselves later if the price is right. The situation is perhaps different when owners of already-developed property use direct democracy to enact more general measures that can be expected to bind everyone. This suggests that it would be worthwhile to try to limit direct democracy to measures that are general and do not single out particular owners or parcels.

Attempting to limit direct democracy to measures that are sufficiently general in scope does not seem constitutionally unworkable. The argument that *ad hoc* rezoning of single parcels or small areas is not appropriately considered legislative in character has been accepted in other states and is a significant minority rationale where it has not been accepted. The lingering due process concerns that surround California's characterization of all zoning as legislative in character attest to the worry about exploitation of isolated real property owners, and there does not seem to be any reason of constitutional dimension why individual rezoning decisions should be considered legislative while decisions about use permits and variances are clearly not.

All things considered, after due deliberation it may well turn out that, in spite of the perceived problems with direct democracy, when it comes to decisions affecting real property, it is best to stick with the present scheme. A reform with the effect of limiting direct democracy to decisions that are sufficiently general in scope might preclude some opportunities for voters to curtail favoritism on the part of their elected representatives and would do nothing about measures that are general but seem exclusionary. Nevertheless, of all the plausible possibilities for constitutional reform of ballot box zoning, it seems to us that this one is the most worthy of serious consideration. This form of limitation on ballot box zoning would carry the important symbolic message that direct democracy measures shall not be used to disrupt individuals' legitimate property-based expectations nor to implement exclusionary measures against those who wish to move into a community.

PROPOSAL

Accordingly, for purposes of discussion, we propose that Article II, Section 11 of the California Constitution be amended to read:

> Initiative and referendum powers may be exercised by the electors of each city or county under procedures that the Legislature shall provide. Land-use regulations are legislative acts within the initiative and referendum powers only if they affect more than [a relative small number, like 100] acres of land, or affect the land of more than [a relatively small number, like three] owners, or affect more than [a relatively small number, like one] percent of the land area of the city or county.

Environmental Policy and the State Constitution: The Role for Substantive Policy Guidance

Barton H. Thompson, Jr.

INTRODUCTION

The federal Constitution focuses largely on shaping the *process* of government. As befits a government of limited powers, the federal Constitution specifies the general substantive areas in which Congress can act. Yet the Constitution gives virtually no directives on what substantive policies Congress should pursue in these areas. Even constitutional provisions that embody substantive individual rights are frequently aimed at improving process: the First Amendment's free speech clause, for example, ensures a more informed electorate and open debate.

A handful of state constitutions similarly are concerned mainly with process. Yet most contain a myriad of substantive policy provisions, setting forth edicts for such issues as (in roughly the order of how often they are found in state constitutions) tax policy, education, corporations, the environment and natural resources, employment, and public utilities. Sometimes these provisions set out broad principles to guide particular substantive policies. More often, the typical state constitution is riddled with superlegislation identical in detail and character to statutory law.

When should a state constitution set out substantive policy? The answer depends on the perceived purposes of a state constitution. If the principal purpose is to set out and ensure an optimum system of representative democracy, the constitution might leave virtually all policy decisions up to that system and include few substantive provisions. If one views constitutions as also helping to solidify and educate the polity, the constitution might include a wide array of general policy statements.

Political expediency, unfortunately, has generated a large number of the existing substantive provisions. The relative ease of amending constitutions in states like California has led many interests to use the state constitution as a substitute for both the legislative and initiative processes, evading legislative obstacles and protecting current majoritarian views against shifting future coalitions. Given these goals, such politically driven provisions tend often to be quite detailed. One result is that state governments frequently find it difficult to change policies to meet shifting conditions and needs. Another consequence is a cluttered constitution that alienates and confuses the average reader.

This chapter considers the proper role and character of substantive provisions in the context of environmental and natural resource policy. California's Constitution contains a number of environmental provisions. As a package, the provisions could be dramatically improved: many are outdated and overly narrow; others are far too detailed and constrictive of legislative flexibility. Depending on the particular model of constitutionalism adopted, moreover, the list of environmental issues addressed in the California Constitution could be valuably expanded.

CURRENT CONSTITUTIONAL PROVISIONS

As shown in Table 1, all but 18 state constitutions contain one or more provisions specifying environmental or natural resource policies; most include multiple provisions. The provisions generally fall into three broad categories. Some of the oldest guarantee or protect public access to navigable waterways, tidelands, or other property of historic public importance. A much newer set of provisions provide in varying degrees for the general protection of the environment. Finally, the constitutions of western states, and other states with significant mineral deposits, fisheries, or other valuable natural resources, often provide for state ownership, protection, or regulation of the resources.

The California Constitution contains a number of environmental or resource provisions. All but one, however, predate World War II, giving the California Constitution an archaic, 19th or early-20th century air. The current constitution emphasizes maximum public use of the state's resources: public navigation and fishing, for example, are both protected; water is to be used "to the fullest extent" possible. More modern environmental and preservation needs are left virtually unaddressed.

Table 1. ***Major Environmental Provisions***

Type of Provision	Number of State Constitutions
Public Access	19
Environmental Policy	18
Natural Resource	15
No Provision	18

Note: Numbers total more than 50 because some states include multiple types of provisions.

Public Access and Use Provisions

Over a third of all state constitutions guarantee the public access to and use of various waterways or state-held lands. These provisions are generally among the oldest of the environmental provisions found in state constitutions, often dating back to the 19th century. The earliest provisions ensured public access to navigable waters, reflecting public rights of navigation dating back as far as the Roman Institutes of Justinian. As shown in Table 2, more recent public access provisions often apply to a broader set of uses and lands including hunting and forests.

The principal California public access provisions focus on older navigation interests. Since the 1878-79 state constitutional convention, the California Constitution has prohibited the owners of "frontage or tidal lands" from excluding access to navigable waters "for any public purpose" or from obstructing "the free navigation of such water."[1] Courts have used this provision not only to prevent private property owners from interfering with navigation and access to navigable waterways, but also to strike down local ordinances limiting public use of navigable waters. A separate provision of the California Constitution strictly limits sales to private interests of tidelands "within two miles of any incorporated city, county,

[1]Cal. Const., art. X, § 4.

Table 2. ***Public Access Provisions (19 States)***

Type of Access Provided	Number of State Constitutions
Navigation	7
Tidelands	6
Legislatively Designated Lands	5
Fishing and Hunting	4
Forest Preserves	1
Oyster Beds	1

Note: Numbers total more than 19 because some states include multiple types of public access provisions.

or town . . . and fronting on the water of any harbor, estuary, bay, or inlet used for the purposes of navigation."[2] Although this provision is virtually absolute on its face, state courts have recognized that such sales can actually promote the public interest in some situations and have read a number of exceptions into its ban.

In 1910, voters supplemented these provisions with a constitutional amendment declaring a public right to "fish upon and from the public lands of the State and in the waters thereof," although the legislature is authorized to regulate fishing seasons and conditions.[3] The latter proviso, along with recognition that unregulated fishing could quickly deplete fish stocks, robbed the constitutional fishing right of much of its force during the first 60 years of its existence. Until the late 1970s, California courts uniformly deferred to legislative and administrative restrictions on fishing, subject only to an antidiscrimination principle. As demand for recreational facilities has grown in recent years, however, courts have occasionally taken a harder look at various governmental restrictions and overruled governmental decisions to close some properties to fishing.

[2]Cal. Const., art. X, § 3.
[3]Cal. Const., art. I, § 25.

Environmental Policy Provisions

The California Constitution does not explicitly specify any general environmental rights or policies, focusing instead on the public access provisions just discussed and on a small number of specific resource provisions examined below. All state constitutions written since 1959, by contrast, include environmental provisions addressing, to varying degrees, more modern concerns of pollution and preservation. Half a dozen states with pre-1960 constitutions have also amended their constitutions to address broader environmental concerns. In total, over a third of all state constitutions contain general environmental policy provisions.

As shown in Table 3, these provisions vary enormously across a number of dimensions. The most important variation is in functional purpose. At the spectrum's weak end, two states simply authorize their legislature to protect the environment—an authorization with little practical significance given that state governments enjoy inherent power to regulate the environment. Other state constitutions encourage legislative action either by specifying policy goals or instructing the legislature to provide various environmental amenities. At the strong end of the spectrum, a handful of state constitutions create explicit environmental rights or impose environmental obligations or duties on their citizens.

Environmental policy provisions also vary in what, if any, means are provided for judicial enforcement of their content. Of the five provisions that create express rights or duties, two explicitly authorize judicial enforcement and one orders the legislature to provide for judicial review. Other types of environmental policy provisions, by contrast, are generally silent regarding judicial enforcement.

Environmental policy provisions also differ in the environmental issues addressed. Most focus broadly on the importance of a "clean" or "healthful" environment, the protection of scenic beauty and natural resources, or both. A few set out explicit lists of environmental policies, directives, or rights that vary considerably from state to state. Specific goals found in various state constitutions include clean air and water, noise abatement, wildlife preservation, protection and conservation of other specific natural resources, and maintenance of historic buildings and sites.

A final distinction among provisions lies in the degree to which they recognize competing values. Three general variations are found. Most state

Table 3. *Environmental Policy Provisions (18 States)*

	Goal
Type	Number of State Constitutions
Legislative Authority	2
State Policy	4
Legislative Mandate	7
Constitutional Right	3
Constitutional Duty	2
	Enforcement
Provision	
Judicial Enforcement Available	2
Legislature to Establish	1
Available with Court's Consent	1
Silent Regarding Enforcement	14
	Recognition of Competing Values
Provision	
Explicit Balance	5
Implicit Balance	2
No Discussion	11

constitutions encourage the pursuit of environment goals with no apparent recognition of potential trade-offs. Some state constitutions, such as Hawaii's, implicitly recognize the need for trade-offs by emphasizing both the need to protect natural resources and the environment and, either in the same or a related section, the need to "promote the development and utilization of these resources in a manner consistent with their conservation and in furtherance of the self-sufficiency of the State."[4] A few constitutions place explicit limits on environmental goals. The Louisiana Constitution, for example, mandates a "healthful" environment only "insofar as possible and consistent with the health, safety, and welfare of the people."[5]

Natural Resource Provisions

Many general environmental policy provisions, as just noted, promote both environmental quality and the conservation and protection of natural resources. As outlined in Table 4, almost a third of state constitutions also include special provisions setting out policies for particular resources. The California Constitution, like that of most western states, reserves its most extensive treatment for water—which enjoys its own separate article, Article X. The critical provision is Section 2, which calls for putting California's waters "to beneficial use to the fullest extent of which they are capable" and bans the "waste or unreasonable use or unreasonable method of use of water."

The most recent environmental amendment to the California Constitution represents the type of superlegislation that seems oddly misplaced in a constitution generally concerned with broad issues of governmental process and individual rights. In 1990, California voters approved a lengthy new constitutional article devoted almost entirely to banning the use of gill and trammel nets, which can entangle and injure or kill sea-lions, porpoises, and other noncommercial marine life.[6] Appropriately named the Marine Resources Protection *Act* of 1990, Article X-B sets out in exacting detail how the ban should be implemented, what penalties and fines should be imposed, and what reports should be prepared.

A REPRESENTATIVE DEMOCRACY MODEL

The substantive environmental provisions that should be in a state constitution depends on the intended purpose of the constitution. Under a

---

[4]Haw. Const., art, 11, § 1.
[5]La. Const., art. IX, § 1.
[6]Cal. Const., art. X-B.

Table 4. ***Natural Resource Provisions (15 States)***

Type of Provision	Number of State Constitutions
General Natural Resource Regulation	2
Water Policy	11
Mining and Mineral Policy	2
Forest Policy	2
Fish and Game Policy	2
Reclamation Policy	2

Note: Numbers total more than 15 because some states include multiple types of natural resource provisions.

"Representative Democracy Model," constitutions are the means by which the polity agrees to a *system* of representative democracy by which they will determine policy and govern their interactions. The purpose of the constitution in this case is not to make substantive policy judgments, but to design an optimal system of representative democracy for making those judgments. As noted in the Introduction, the federal Constitution and a handful of state constitutions lean toward this model.

Substantive provisions have a role under the Representative Democracy Model, but the role is limited. First, the constitution might specify substantive rules or constraints where unavoidable imperfections in the constitution's system of representative government could bias decision-making on a particular issue to an unacceptable degree. Second, the constitution might dictate substantive policy where an issue is judged too fundamental or principle-driven to be delegated at all to democratic discretion.

As illustrated below, the latter exception is difficult to apply in practice. What appears to some a matter of fundamental principle will often appear to others a mere policy preference. How then can one determine what substantive policies are sufficiently fundamental to include in a constitution? Seizing on the fact that constitutions purport to speak for "the People" as a whole, one possibility is to see whether there is broad societal *consensus* that a particular substantive policy is too fundamental to leave to shifting political winds. An alternative approach is to ask whether a broad consensus would exist if people were able to remove themselves from immediate political influences. Would people agree to a particular principle, in short, if they were placed behind a "veil of ignorance" concerning what policies would best promote their current interests?

To further complicate matters, whether process concerns or fundamental principles call for a constitutional response represents only part of the relevant inquiry. The ability and willingness of courts to enforce the response is also relevant. Although the political wings of government might voluntarily comply with a substantive provision, they are likely at some point to ignore or challenge any prescription that runs contrary to their political goals. Absent effective judicial relief, the legislature will successfully flaunt the substantive provision—leaving the original justification for the constitutional provision unmet and damaging the general constitutional structure.

Public Access

To see the difficult and detailed calls often required under a Representative Democracy Model, consider how the three general types of environmental provisions found in state constitutions would fare under the model. Both process concerns and principle drove the original inclusion of navigation and fishing provisions in the California Constitution. At the time of the 1878-79 Constitutional Convention, development interests dominated both the California legislature and state land agencies, and effectively pushed, often through surreptitious means, for the transfer of large segments of California's tidelands and other foreshore into private hands. The public interest in maintaining access to waterways for navigation and fishing was largely ignored. Doubtful of the ability of California's two political wings to make unbiased land decisions, the 1879 constitution stripped the government of the authority to alienate tidelands in areas close to harbors and bays and imposed a public access servitude on all tidelands. Many members of the 1879 Constitutional Convention also believed that access across California's tidelands should not be left entirely to democratic discretion. Prior to modern modes of transportation, oceans and navigable waterways were the best and often only means of commerce.

Sustenance required the ability to either hunt or fish, and fishing required access to waterways.

Both justifications seem outdated today. Considering process concerns first, state legislative and administrative processes are far more transparent than a hundred years ago, making it difficult to abdicate public interests in the state's waterways and shoreline. A number of environmental and conservation organizations also police state actions and help educate and mobilize public opinion. Legislation now outpaces the constitution—banning the sale of all tidelands and, through state commissions, both promoting public access to the state's foreshore and carefully controlling and overseeing disposition of alienable state land. Turning to substantive justifications, open access to waterways is no longer fundamental for either commerce or sustenance. When asked whether the public should have open access to tidelands, few today would immediately think of commerce or sustenance needs. The focus instead is likely to be on recreation and aesthetics.

The Importance of Access

Although California's public access provisions have outlived their original justifications, other principles and process concerns argue today for even broader public access provisions. Turning to principle first, a minimum quantity of *common property* seems essential to a modern democracy governed primarily by private property principles. An effective democracy depends on the existence of commons where all citizenry can "commonly" mingle and interact both with each other and with their shared physical environment. Commons provide an opportunity for people to understand each other and to learn how better to socialize and live together. Commons also contribute to shared values and, where the commons is a natural environment, to a reflective peace of mind valuable to democratic decision making. Finally, commons can help reduce the tensions that otherwise grow out of and potentially undermine a highly uneven distribution of private property. For all these reasons, the preservation of significant commons arguably is essential to the effective maintenance of the State.

The strong democratic argument for public commons suggests that the current public access provisions in the California Constitution are too narrow rather than unnecessary. Shaped by late 19th century concerns, the provisions are too narrow in both their purpose and geographic focus to meet democratic needs. As described above, the current provisions ensure access to and use of California's waterways for navigational and fishing purposes. An effective democracy built on private property, however, requires that the public be able to use commons for recreation and aesthetic enjoyment, as well as navigation and fishing. Current provisions also focus narrowly on waterways and foreshore, even though public park land, forests, undeveloped foothills, and other open spaces also provide important commons today.

The value of common property to both an effective democracy and private property suggest the need for a broad "commons trust" protecting public access to all state-owned lands of unique importance to public communion and encouraging the acquisition and protection of similar privately held lands. A handful of state constitutions already provide potential models for a California Commons Trust. Alabama, Maine, New York, and North Carolina have all amended their constitutions in the last 30 years to provide for broad land preserves or trusts.

These existing provisions highlight several defining issues in creating a commons trust. First, what lands should be included? Given the difficulties of specifying which lands now or in the future will be of importance to the public, existing constitutional trusts generally leave the choice of most lands to legislative discretion. The California Constitution could safely include all public trust lands currently held by the state, including tidelands and the navigable foreshore, given their historic importance as a public commons. For other lands, however, the best approach would be simply to specify the criteria by which the legislature should determine what lands to acquire and include: presumably the value of the land for common recreational or aesthetic use by a broad segment of the general public.

Second, what types of rights should the public enjoy in the protected lands? Constitutional provisions in other states focus on protecting the lands from sale and are silent on the public's rights to use the lands. Common public use of the lands, however, is the very basis for creating a new constitutional trust. A California Commons Trust thus should provide for open public use of the land, except to the degree that the legislature determines that use should be regulated either to protect the land itself from injury or to maximize common benefits by restricting overcrowding or inconsistent uses.

Finally, under what, if any, circumstances should lands be removable from the trust and its protections? The constitution's current restrictions on tideland sales illustrate the dangers of placing inflexible limits on the alienation of particular land. The strict prohibition on sales of tidelands within two miles of any incorporated area and bordering on "any harbor, estuary, bay, or inlet used for the purposes of navigation" was responsive to the 19th century interest in protecting navigation. Given the rigidity of the prohibition, however, courts have been forced to develop a number of exceptions to the restriction over the last century to account for the need to alienate some of these tidelands—for harbor development, in exchange for other lands designed to rationalize current land holdings or eliminate title uncertainties, or for other legitimate public goals. As the public interest has evolved to focus on other interests, moreover, the narrow protection of premium navigation sites has grown increasingly marginal.

Lingering concerns that future legislatures might inappropriately discount the value of protected lands, or act precipitously in removing lands from the trust, could be addressed better through procedural rules than rigid prohibitions. Requirements that land removals be approved by two separate legislative sessions, as the New York Constitution requires, could help ensure full consideration of the potential ramifications. Supermajoritarian requirements, as imposed by both Maine and North Carolina, could help protect against legislative tendencies to discount diffuse public values. Both procedural approaches would permit land decisions to evolve with changing conditions, information, and needs.

Protecting against local discrimination. Although state management of public lands no longer raises process concerns, recent court cases suggest that the narrow political focus of local governments can lead them to constrict access to public lands and resources without giving full consideration to the statewide interest in commons. Local governments, for example, sometimes ban all use of a valuable commons because of purely local and redressable concerns such as noise or littering. Even more troubling, local governments sometimes limit use of local parks and other publicly supported open spaces to local residents. Far from promoting the goals of public commons, such local parochialism unnecessarily threatens to segment the state's citizenry.

California courts have been able to use current constitutional provisions to prevent local governments from limiting public use of navigable waterways or alienating tidelands falling within the narrow protection of the constitution. Yet courts lack a general means of addressing the problem. Although courts outside California have sometimes resorted to novel applications of the "public trust doctrine" and other judge-made rules to require local governments to open their lands to all state citizens, a direct constitutional remedy is preferable to the vagaries of judicial entrepreneurship. Because local governments might have legitimate reasons in some cases to limit use of public lands or waters within their jurisdiction, a process approach, such as requiring state legislative authorization of any local restrictions, is again preferable to a specific substantive constraint.

General Environmental Policy Provisions

Slightly before the first Earth Day, the California Assembly Select Committee on Environmental Quality recommended that an "Environmental Bill of Rights" provision be added to the California Constitution declaring a state policy in favor of "clean air, pure water, freedom from excessive noise, and enjoyment of scenic, historic, natural, and aesthetic values." Although nothing ultimately came of the proposal, similar suggestions have continued to surface every few years.

Justifications for a broad environmental policy provision under a Representative Democracy Model are relatively weak. Some supporters have argued that, absent special constitutional provisions, legislatures might slight the public's significant, yet diffuse interest in environmental protection in favor of the focused opposition of the regulated community. A simple interest group model of the political process suggests that diffuse interests will tend to be underrepresented. Faced with concentrated opposition by industry and business, moreover, few state legislatures were willing to undertake significant environmental action prior to 1970.

The rise of environmental interest groups over the last quarter century, however, has helped change the legislative dynamic. While individual citizens might not have enough at stake to follow and evaluate the actions of their legislators or state agencies on environmental issues, environmental groups like the California League of Conservation Voters both track state actions and help to mobilize public response. Environmental groups therefore carry considerable political clout, particularly in states like California where environmental issues have historically been relatively high on voters' agendas. Industrial opposition to environmental measures, moreover, is not always as cohesive as sometimes assumed.

Empirical studies of environmental policymaking in the United States provide no basis for the feared process concerns. Recent empirical studies of state decision making have found that environmental group strength correlates positively with stronger environmental laws while polluting industry strength does not generally correlate with weaker regulation. Somewhat surprisingly, in fact, stronger industries often correlates with stronger regulations.

Proponents of environmental policy provisions have also argued that the environment is a unique subject for constitutional redress because a "healthful environment" should not be open to democratic derogation. Many of the earliest proposals for environmental policy provisions would have held environmental rights to be "inalienable." Indeed, many proponents have unabashedly compared the need for environmental protection to civil rights, freedom of religion, and the right against cruel and unusual punishment.

Inalienability arguments for general environmental policy provisions highlight the difficulty of determining what policy goals are sufficiently fundamental to include in a constitution under a Representative Democracy Model. Philosophers have constructed often elegant and appealing arguments for various environmental policies based on a human "right" to be free from external harm or on broader biocentric or ecocentric principles. To others, however, environmental policy is best viewed as a balance of risk and benefit. Despite early legislation calling for the elimination of all pollution within a matter of decades, no consensus exists today for eliminating pollution at any cost. Nor would things change if society were placed behind a veil of ignorance: environmental issues would still remain a troublesome trade-off among a variety of objectively important policy goals. Perhaps tellingly, only one of the environmental policy provisions found in state constitutions includes the term "inalienable"; most do not even employ the term "right."

Searching instead for some minimal and fundamental environmental goal is an attractive, but ultimately futile, endeavor. The proposition that no one should be forced to endure any injurious level of pollution, for example, might sound relatively innocuous, but in fact would call for the elimination of virtually all major forms of air pollution. Air quality standards even substantially higher than those employed today would protect most people, but still leave sensitive subpopulations open to illness or injury. Every effort to date to define a minimum standard upon which all can agree has floundered on the inevitableness of trade-offs.

Assuming a legitimate basis for including a general environmental policy provision in the state constitution, could such a provision effectively protect the public interest in a healthful environment? Proponents of environmental policy provisions have anticipated that the provisions would permit environmental advocates to actively influence state environmental policy through the courts. As one proponent of constitutional rights provisions has put it, "An informed, courageous judiciary is needed to help stem the tide of political and economic consequences which have resulted in the current, perhaps irreversible levels of environmental pollution."[7] Courts, however, have been extremely reluctant to wield environmental policy provisions where available, and there is no reason to assume that California courts would behave differently.

Where a legislature has failed to enact strong environmental policies, courts have seen few practical responses. Although courts have occasionally ordered legislatures to take affirmative actions to comply with constitutional mandates in some areas (e.g., equal educational opportunity), courts have generally shied away from requiring state legislatures to develop new policy programs or enact new legislation. The rationale is partly constitutional: the legislature, not the courts, is empowered to legislate. Courts also fear the potential practical consequences of ordering the legislature to appropriate money or institute significant new programs. Majority-driven legislatures will not always comply. Although courts have found some ways around legislative refusals, they have also had to watch embarrassed as many orders have gone ignored. For these reasons, courts have never ordered a state legislature to adopt a particular environmental policy or program based on an environmental policy provision, even in those states where the constitution appears to mandate legislative action.

The only alternative is for courts to develop their own judicial environmental program—enjoining private and public actions that threaten the court's view of a "healthful" environment. Yet here again courts have refrained from taking an active role. Courts have occasionally interceded

---

[7]Robert A. McLaren, "Environmental Protection Based on State Constitutional Law: A Call for Reinterpretation," *University of Hawaii Law Review*, vol. 12 (1990): 123.

where state agencies, without any consideration of possible environmental harms, have granted permits or pursued projects that posed an environmental threat. For this reason, environmental policy provisions were often of some value in the 1970s before environmental considerations were integrated into most state programs. Courts, however, have refused to use environmental policy provisions more generally to regulate the environmental actions of private or public entities. As a result, environmental policy provisions have played an increasingly marginal role in those states where they are found.

Courts have turned to diverse legal arguments to avoid wielding environmental policy provisions. Most often, courts have held that environmental policy provisions are not self enforcing (but require legislative implementation). Whatever the legal justification for not acting, courts have again been troubled by a number of practical concerns. First, the administrative burden of creating a judicial system of environmental rights and obligations could be immense. Absent legislative assistance, courts would need to develop a system for monitoring and regulating the environmental behavior of hundreds or thousands of individual entities.

To turn the bare bones of environmental policy provisions into specific commands, courts would also need to decide a number of fundamental policy issues with little constitutional guidance. What criteria, for example, should courts use in setting environmental standards? Should courts employ health criteria (as parts of the federal Clean Air Act do), technological criteria (as much of the federal Clean Water Act does), some form of cost-benefit analysis (as various toxic-control statutes do), economic feasibility (as again a number of federal and state bills do), or other criteria? Once a general criterion is selected, courts would then need to further refine that criterion. If they chose to pursue health goals, for example, should they adopt a "no injury" rule (much like the infamous Delaney Clauses in the Federal Food, Drug, and Cosmetics Act) or a less protective criterion?

Although courts frequently make difficult policy determinations in implementing other broad constitutional rights such as freedom of speech, courts are more troubled by environmental policy provisions for several reasons. First, there is far less societal consensus on the general goals of a "healthful environment" than of existing constitutional rights such as free speech. Courts might find it difficult to apply speech precedents to a particular setting, but they at least perceive societal consensus on the overarching goals. In the case of longstanding constitutional rights, moreover, decades of precedent have examined and developed a substantive jurisprudence, while environmental policy provisions would require the courts to confront and generate a totally new framework in a complex field.

Because of judicial reluctance to intervene, environmental policy provisions have had virtually no noticeable effect on state law. Table 5 ranks each state's environmental policies. The states with environmental policy provisions, shown in bold face, have an average rank of 24, only marginally higher than those states without such provisions. California, which has no environmental policy provision, ranks first. Even if justified by process concerns or fundamental principles, in summary, the addition of an environmental policy provision to the California Constitution is likely to have no direct impact on the state's environmental laws and so disappoint its proponents.

Natural Resource Provisions

Natural resource issues can be divided usefully into several categories. First are issues that directly concern the environment. These would include questions of whether to permit petroleum drilling in coastal waters, allow the destruction of important species habitat, or sanction the clear cutting of timber. The analysis of general environmental policy provisions applies equally to these issues.

A second category of natural resource issues focuses on allocation of resources among the current population. These would include how to allocate current water supplies, petroleum drilling rights, or fishing and hunting licenses among competing users or developers once appropriate environmental protections have been adopted. The Representative Democracy Model does not call for constitutional intervention into these issues. No fundamental rights will be implicated. Nor is there any reason to distrust the political process with these decisions any more than with other decisions dealing with the distribution of societal wealth.

A final category of resource issues—allocation of resources among generations—raises new concerns regarding both process and fundamental rights. Intergenerational issues would include whether to permit the mining of existing groundwater aquifers, whether and how to limit commercial fisheries, and whether to cap the production of oil, gas, minerals, or other

Table 5. *State Environmental Rankings*

State	Environmental Policy Ranking	State	Environmental Policy Ranking
Alabama	**48**	**Montana**	**32**
Alaska	**46**	Nebraska	28
Arizona	38	Nevada	44
Arkansas	50	New Hampshire	21
California	1	New Jersey	3
Colorado	26	**New Mexico**	**37**
Connecticut	4	**New York**	**8**
Delaware	25	**North Carolina**	**16**
Florida	**11**	North Dakota	39
Georgia	**30**	**Ohio**	**19**
Hawaii	**24**	Oklahoma	42
Idaho	36	Oregon	2
Illinois	**18**	**Pennsylvania**	**20**
Indiana	27	**Rhode Island**	**10**
Iowa	17	**South Carolina**	**31**
Kansas	29	South Dakota	49
Kentucky	34	Tennessee	41
Louisiana	**33**	Texas	35
Maine	6	Utah	40
Maryland	15	Vermont	14
Massachusetts	**9**	**Virginia**	**22**
Michigan	**12**	Washington	13
Minnesota	7	West Virginia	47
Mississippi	45	Wisconsin	5
Missouri	23	Wyoming	43

Average ranking for states with environmental policy provisions **24**

Bold indicates states with environmental policy provisions.

Source: Ranking of environmental policy initiatives, based on 73 separate policy areas, in *1991-92 Green Index: A State-by-State Guide to the Nation's Environmental Health*, by Bob Hall and Mary Lee Kerr (Island Press, 1991).

exhaustible resources. The need for constitutional input stems from the failure of the traditional political process to account fully for the interests or "rights" of future generations in these decisions.

Any discussion of intergenerational equity must begin with John Rawl's *A Theory of Justice*.[8] Under Rawl's now classic approach to determining justice, intergenerational equity is determined behind a "veil of ignorance" in which individuals do not know in which generation they will live. In this setting, Rawls argues that society would agree that each generation has an obligation to save enough resources to permit future generations to enjoy "just institutions," in which members can develop their individual proficiencies and not fight over a deficiency of resources or opportunities.

The current generation, however, does not live, act, or vote behind a veil of ignorance. Although the current generation will often save resources out of love for future generations, moral conviction, or even long-term profit potential, the current generation will have an inevitable bias toward present consumption. The notion that one generation should be concerned about the fate and lives of future generations, indeed, is a relatively recent and primarily western perspective, and even when we act to protect future generations, our attention seldom extends beyond our children and grandchildren. Political tenures and rewards further strengthen the bias toward current consumption of resources. Because politicians have only limited terms in office and future generations cannot vote yet, the political process is likely to favor demands for current consumption over conflicting interests of future generations.

The need to protect future generations in natural resource policy unfortunately does not necessarily yield a clear constitutional solution. Identifying the philosophical basis for protecting future generations, moreover, is different from determining exactly what resource policies intergenerational equity requires. Lacking a clear first-order solution, a state constitution could still take two steps. First, it could provide generally that state and local governments should consider the interests of future generations in setting natural resource policy. Second, it could enshrine specific minimum protections of future generations.

---

[8]John Rawls, *A Theory of Justice* (Cambridge, Mass.: Belknap Press of Harvard University Press, 1971), 284-93.

The most commonly suggested protection is a "sustainability" criterion under which renewable resources would be managed on a "sustainable basis." Even this minimum standard, however, is exceptionally vague and open-ended. Resources can be "sustainable," for example, at various stock levels. Sustainability could involve just yield levels or, more logically, also quality. Even the concept of a "renewable resource" is open to interpretation, depending on the time frame involved.

Here again courts are unlikely to actively embrace any constitutional provisions. Because deficiencies in state policy are more likely to stem from failures to regulate extraction than direct governmental exploitation, courts interested in a more active role would need either to order the legislature to adopt new programs or actively regulate resource use itself—neither an attractive judicial option. Courts, moreover, are likely to feel quite uncomfortable determining without guidance what terms such as "sustainable" mean. Although the Alaskan constitution mandates that all "replenishable resources belonging to the State shall be utilized, developed, and maintained on the sustained yield principle," Alaskan courts have never used the provision to modify the state's natural resource policy.[9]

A COMMUNITY VALUE MODEL

The Representative Democracy Model contemplates only a very limited role for substantive policy provisions. An alternative "Community Values Model" foresees a broader role for substantive provisions and may come closer to reflecting the philosophy of many state constitutions. Constitutions under this model embody and promote general policy views of the polity with several goals in mind. First, inclusion of substantive guidance permits the population to engage in a direct dialogue with all wings of its government concerning what type of policies it wants pursued. Unlike the detailed lawmaking of the initiative process, the guidance here is quite general and leaves definition up to the legislature. Whether the courts are willing and able to intervene is also less relevant here than under the Representative Democracy Model. The constitution becomes a means

---

[9]See Alaska Const., art. VIII, § 4.

of high-level communication between people and government, rather than protection of underrepresented interests or fundamental rights.

At least in theory, incorporation of general values into the state constitution could also help define and promote community identity and understanding within the state. Historically, this was one of the central purposes of state constitutions. In today's California, however, both the meaningfulness and effectiveness of using the constitution to construct and encourage community is open to question. California may simply be too big, and too geographically and socially stratified to treat as a unitary community with shared value. In the constitution's current cluttered form, moreover, few residents are even likely to read and appreciate its substantive provisions. The latter barrier can be removed, but only through a thorough stripping and reworking of the constitution.

Public Access Provisions

The Community Values Model, not surprisingly, would call for a longer list of environmental provisions than the Representative Democracy Model justified. The Community Values Model would again call for expanded public access provisions. California has long been identified by its considerable natural amenities—its beaches, redwood forests, parks, deserts, rivers, and lakes. The attraction of these amenities for immigrants and longtime residents alike stems in part from the public's relative ease of access. A large number of Californians chose this state for their residence primarily because of the communal recreational opportunities available within a short distance of every portion of the state. Central to the values of the state, in short, is public access not only to navigable waterways, tidelands, and the remaining foreshore, but to numerous other communal amenities.

Environmental Policy Provisions

A much stronger case can be made for an environmental policy provision under a Community Values Model. Befitting a state whose greatest asset is its natural setting, California has long espoused and maintained a strong environmental policy. California adopted significant air and water quality laws prior to the 1970s and has continued to lead other states in its environmental policies.

Absent an environmental policy provision, moreover, the current constitution suffers from a misleading prodevelopment bias. The California Constitution, for example, currently accords special importance to private property: "acquiring, possessing, and protecting property" is an inalienable right,[10] and private property cannot be "taken" without the payment of just compensation.[11] The constitution encourages public use of waterways and foreshore, as well as fishing, without considering potentially conflicting environmental interests in preservation. Article X encourages the state to put its water resources "to beneficial use to the fullest extent of which they are capable," without noting environmental interests in instream flows. The absence of an environmental policy provision leaves these provisions without a counterbalance and with the potential implication that when there is a conflict, private property rights and use interests should win out over the environment.

Courts' unwillingness to actively wield environmental policy provisions to shape a state's overall environmental policy, moreover, does not pose the same concern here as under a Representative Democracy Model. First, courts can use lawsuits as an opportunity to promote community values through a dialogue with the legislative or executive branches even though the courts might ultimately uphold the challenged state actions. Decisions refusing to force the government to take particular environmental actions have often been laden with dicta discussing the importance of environmental policy provisions and warning of potential future judicial intervention. Second, even where courts play a totally inactive role, the constitution also speaks directly to the legislature and can help influence and shape legislative debate. In proposing an "Environmental Bill of Rights" in 1970, the California Assembly Select Committee on Environmental Quality urged that such an amendment would "give the voters an opportunity to indicate their views regarding the environment and . . . provide a sense of direction and purpose for California's leaders."[12]

The value of an environmental policy provision should not be overstated. As earlier shown in Table 5, California already has among the strongest environmental laws of the nation and the addition at this stage of

---

[10]Cal. Const., art. I, § 1.

[11]*Id.*, art. I, § 19.

[12]California Assembly Select Committee on Environmental Quality, Environmental Bill of Rights, (March 1990).

an environmental policy provision is unlikely to affect legislative direction to any significant degree. During the inevitable periods when environmental regulation comes under assault, however, the existence of an environmental policy provision might help emphasize the importance of environmental protection to the public.

Natural Resources Provisions

The Community Values Model also strengthens the case for including intergenerational equity provisions in the California Constitution. State policy already claims to incorporate a "sustainable" development value in several contexts. California statutes managing fisheries, wildlife, and timber, for example, all include "findings" or "declarations of public interest" providing for sustained production or development—although the statutes often do not actually ensure sustained yield.[13]

The difficulty of specifying intergenerational rights in implementable terms, which undercut the argument for including intergenerational provisions under a Representative Democracy Model, is again of less concern here. Judicial enforceability is less important than signaling the importance to the polity of intergenerational concerns and opening the way for a dialogue among the various branches of government and the citizenry concerning the role that intergenerational considerations should play. Rather than shying away from policy ambiguities, the Community Values Model views the constitution as a forum for helping to examine and define the specifics of general community values.

PROBLEMS OF OVERSPECIFICITY

Whatever model is used to evaluate the role for substantive guidance in the California Constitution, many current provisions are unjustified. Other provisions demonstrate the problems of including overly detailed and inflexible guidance in the constitution. Some provisions are both unjustified or overly detailed. The gill net embodied in Article X-B constitute an

---

[13]See, e.g., Cal. Fish & Game Code §§ 450 (maintenance of deer populations) & 1700 ("sustained harvest" in fisheries); Cal. Public Resource Code § 4513 ("maximum sustained production of high quality timber products").

extreme but instructional example. Written originally as a statute, Article X-B was introduced as a constitutional amendment only because the requirements for constitutional initiatives are not much tougher than those for a statutory initiative. Article X-B was largely indistinguishable from statutory initiatives on the same ballot, and few voters recognized that they were voting to amend the state constitution.

A narrow ban on the use of gill and trammel nets is misplaced and unjustified in the California Constitution. Any process concerns or values that would justify such a ban also would apply to a broader set of issues and, if addressed in the constitution, should do so in greater breadth. Even if a narrow ban were constitutionally sensible, Article X-B dictates implementation and enforcement at far too detailed a level. In over five pages of text, Article X-B locks into place such details as penalty and fee levels, reporting requirements, and the number and size of ocean-based ecological reserves. Because these details are embedded in the constitution, the legislature is helpless to change them in response to evolving conditions and needs other than by seeking an amendment to the constitution.

APPENDIX

The Scope and Specificity of Several State Constitutions

Subject	California	Illinois	Michigan	New York	Ohio	Texas
Bonds						
authorization	X	X	X		X	X
liability	X			X	X	
method of adoption	X	X			X	X
purpose	X	X	X	X	X	X
restrictions		X		X	X	X
Business/ Commerce						
charters	X	X		X	X	X
restriction of private corps.	X				X	X
restriction of public corps.	X			X	X	
restriction of public support	X	X	X	X	X	X
Civil Rights						
assembly	X	X	X	X	X	X
bear arms		X	X	X	X	X
death penalty	X		X			
due process	X	X	X	X	X	X
eminent domain	X	X	X	X	X	
equal protection	X	X	X	X		X
inalienable	X	X			X	X
involuntary servitude	X		X	X	X	
military	X	X	X		X	X
noncitizen	X		X			
petition	X	X	X	X	X	X
privileges and immunities	X	X			X	X

Subject	California	Illinois	Michigan	New York	Ohio	Texas
property	X	X	X		X	X
religion	X	X	X	X	X	X
speech/press	X	X	X	X	X	
suits vs. state	X		X		X	
treason	X		X			X
victims' rights	X	X	X			X
voting/ officeholding	X			X	X	X
Civil Service						
appointments	X		X	X	X	X
compensation	X		X	X		X
duties	X	X		X		X
eligibility	X	X	X			X
organization	X			X		X
promotions	X		X	X		
Constitutional Convention						
delegates	X	X	X	X	X	X
duties		X	X	X		X
mandatory calling		X	X	X	X	
method of calling	X	X	X	X	X	
Constitutional Revision						
convention	X	X	X	X	X	X
initiative	X	X	X		X	
legislative	X	X	X	X	X	X
ratification	X	X	X	X	X	X
Criminal Behavior						
definitions	X		X			X
punishments			X			

Subject	California	Illinois	Michigan	New York	Ohio	Texas
Education						
funding	X	X	X	X	X	X
goals	X	X	X	X		X
restrictions	X	X	X	X	X	X
supervisory boards	X	X	X	X	X	X
Elections						
method	X		X	X	X	X
nonpartisan	X					X
tallying		X		X		X
voting qualifications	X	X	X	X	X	X
when	X	X	X	X	X	
Environmental Protection						
administrative boards	X					
infrastructure	X					
regulation	X	X		X	X	
Federal Issues						
primary of laws	X					
term limits on federal officials	X		X			
Gambling						
authorized	X		X	X	X	X
regulated	X			X	X	X
Housing						
finance	X			X	X	
qualification of residents	X			X	X	

Subject	California	Illinois	Michigan	New York	Ohio	Texas
Indebtedness						
circumstances allowing	X			X	X	X
limitations	X		X	X	X	
local	X		X	X	X	
payment	X		X	X	X	
Infrastructure						
financing		X		X	X	X
liabilities		X		X	X	X
maintenance			X	X	X	X
ownership	X	X	X	X	X	X
regulation	X					X
supervisory (mgt) boards	X				X	X
use/lease			X	X	X	X
Initiative						
authorization	X	X	X		X	
constitutional revision	X	X	X		X	
limit on use					X	
method	X	X	X		X	
Judiciary						
administration	X	X	X	X	X	X
appointments	X	X		X	X	X
compensation	X	X	X	X	X	X
duties/powers	X	X	X	X	X	X
elections	X	X	X		X	X
eligibility	X	X	X	X	X	X
establishment of courts	X	X		X	X	X
jurisdiction	X	X	X	X	X	X
process	X	X	X	X	X	X
terms	X	X	X	X	X	X
vacancies	X	X	X	X	X	X

Subject	California	Illinois	Michigan	New York	Ohio	Texas
Labor						
hours	X			X	X	
minimum wage	X			X	X	
workman's compensation	X			X	X	
Law Enforcement						
officers	X	X	X	X		X
organization						
prison labor	X			X	X	
Liquor						
administration of regulation	X		X			X
licensing	X					
prohibition						
sale	X					X
Local/County Government						
charters/ formation/ boundaries	X	X	X	X	X	X
duties	X	X	X		X	X
fiscal issues	X	X	X	X	X	X
laws	X	X		X	X	X
organization (personnel)	X	X	X	X	X	X
powers	X	X	X	X	X	X
Militia						
limitations		X	X			
organization	X	X			X	
powers		X	X	X	X	

Subject	California	Illinois	Michigan	New York	Ohio	Texas
Natural Resources						
preservation	X	X	X	X	X	X
recreation			X			
regulation	X	X		X	X	X
supervisory boards/districts	X					X
use	X	X		X	X	X
Recall						
authorization	X		X		X	
liability for expenses	X					
method	X		X			
who is subject	X		X			
Referendum						
authorization	X	X	X		X	
limit on use			X		X	
method	X	X	X		X	
Revenues						
investment of funds	X		X			X
sources other than tax	X				X	X
Social Health and Welfare						
administration				X	X	X
appropriations	X			X	X	X
regulation	X	X		X	X	X
type	X	X	X	X		X

Subject	California	Illinois	Michigan	New York	Ohio	Texas
State Executive						
compensation	X	X	X	X	X	X
duties	X	X	X	X	X	X
eligibility	X	X	X	X	X	X
ethics	X	X				X
jurisdiction	X	X				X
organization	X	X	X	X	X	X
powers	X	X	X	X	X	X
succession	X	X	X	X	X	X
terms	X	X	X	X	X	X
State Expenditure						
appropriations (required)	X	X	X			X
limitations	X	X	X	X	X	X
preparation of bill	X	X	X	X		
rules for passage	X		X	X		
Statehood						
boundaries	X					
language	X					
oath	X	X	X	X	X	X
precedence of laws	X					X
seat	X		X		X	X
symbols	X	X	X			X
State Legislature						
committees	X		X			
compensation	X	X	X	X	X	X
duties	X	X	X	X	X	X
eligibility	X	X	X	X	X	X
ethics	X		X		X	X
impeachment	X	X			X	X
jurisdiction	X	X				X

Subject	California	Illinois	Michigan	New York	Ohio	Texas
number of legislators	X	X	X	X	X	X
organization		X	X	X	X	X
powers	X	X	X	X	X	X
privileges	X	X	X	X	X	X
reapportionment	X	X	X	X	X	X
restrictions	X	X		X	X	X
sessions	X	X	X	X	X	X
terms	X	X	X	X	X	X
vacancies	X	X	X		X	X
Statues						
effective date	X	X	X		X	X
jurisdiction	X					
method of consideration	X	X	X	X	X	X
method of passage	X	X	X	X	X	X
single subject rule	X	X	X	X	X	
subject matter-special treatment	X	X		X		X
Taxation						
assessment/ equalization/ management boards	X					
corporations	X			X	X	X
exemptions	X	X	X	X	X	X
income	X	X		X	X	X
insurance companies	X					
restrictions on jurisdiction of tax	X					X

Subject	California	Illinois	Michigan	New York	Ohio	Texas
limits	X	X	X		X	X
property	X	X	X	X	X	X
rates	X	X			X	X
sales	X	X	X			
special taxes (limited time)	X					X
use/purpose	X	X	X		X	X
value assessment	X	X	X	X	X	X
Usury						
authorization	X		X	X	X	X
guarantees	X					
rates	X					X
Veterans						
care						
exemptions	X					
housing	X					
pensions				X	X	

Note: X indicates a provision in the state's constitution on that subject.

ABOUT THE AUTHORS

Michael Asimow received his B.A. from UCLA in 1961 and his J.D. from Boalt Hall School of Law in 1964. He teaches administrative law, tax, contracts, and business associations at UCLA School of Law. He is the author of numerous books and articles on administrative law including *State and Federal Administrative Law* (1989) and "The Scope of Judicial Review of Decisions of California Administrative Agencies" (*UCLA Law Review*, 1995).

Kathleen Bawn is Assistant Professor of Political Science at UCLA. She received a B.A. from the University of Chicago and a Ph.D. from Stanford University. Her research interests include electoral systems, legislative institutions, and the relationship between legislative and executive branches.

David W. Brady is the Bowen H. and Janice Arthur McCoy Professor of Political Science, Business and the Changing Environment, and Ethics at Stanford University's Graduate School of Business. He received his Ph.D. from the University of Iowa, and he has published widely. His book *Critical Election and Congressional Policy Making* won the Fenno Prize in 1989. Currently he is writing books on the development of careerism in the nineteenth century U.S. Congress and on the problem of policy gridlock in the modern-day Congress.

Bruce E. Cain, Robson Professor of Political Science, UC Berkeley, and Associate Director of the Institute of Governmental Studies, came to IGS and the Department of Political Science in 1989, from California Institute of Technology, where he taught from 1976 to 1989 in the fields of California politics, political theory, and comparative government. A *summa cum laude* graduate of Bowdoin College (1970), he studied as a Rhodes Scholar (1970-72) at Trinity College, Oxford. In 1976 he received his Ph.D. in political science from Harvard University. His writings include *The Reapportionment Puzzle* (1984), *The Personal Vote* (1987), written with John Ferejohn and Morris Fiorina, and *Congressional Redistricting* (1991), with David Butler. He has also edited two books, *Developments in American Politics, Volumes I and 2*, with Gillian Peele. Cain has served as polling consultant for state senate races to Fairbank, Canapary and Maulin

(1985-86); redistricting consultant to the Los Angeles City Council (1986) and the Attorney General of the State of Massachusetts (1987-88); consultant to the *Los Angeles Times* (1986- 1989); and commentator for numerous radio and television stations in Los Angeles and the Bay Area.

Linda R. Cohen is Professor of Economics at the University of California, Irvine. She holds a bachelor's degree in mathematics from UC Berkeley (1974) and a Ph.D. in social sciences from California Institute of Technology (1979). Prior to coming to UCI, Cohen was a Research Associate at The Brookings Institution. Her research falls in the intersection of economics, political science, and law. She is the co-author (with Matthew Spitzer) of "Term Limits" (*Georgetown Law Journal*, 1992) and "Judicial Deference to Administrative Agencies" (*Southern California Law Journal*, 1996).

Brendan P. Cullen received his J.D. from Stanford Law School in 1995, where he was selected for Order of the Coif. He has been selected to clerk for Judge Silverman of the U.S. Court of Appeals, D.C. Circuit in 1995-96 and for Justice Thomas of the United States Supreme Court in 1996-97.

John W. Ellwood is Professor of Public Policy at the University of California, Berkeley's Graduate School of Public Policy. After receiving his A.B. from Franklin and Marshall College he was awarded a Ph.D. in political science from The Johns Hopkins University. He has written extensively on the politics of public budgeting. In addition to his academic appointments, he served as a staff member of the Senate Budget Committee of the U.S. Congress and as a staff member of the Congressional Budget Office.

John Ferejohn is Carolyn S. G. Munro Professor of Political Science and a Senior Fellow at the Hoover Institution at Stanford University and is a Visiting Professor of Law at New York University. He received his B.A. from San Fernando Valley State College and his Ph.D. from Stanford University. Ferejohn has written extensively and is the author or editor of *The Personal Vote: Constituency Service and Electoral Independence*, with Bruce Cain and Morris Fiorina (1987); *Information and Democratic Processes*, edited with James Kuklinski (1990); and "The Elastic Commerce Clause: A Political Theory of American Federalism," with William

Eskridge, *Vanderbilt Law Review* (1994). His research interests include political institutions, political behavior, the theory of social choice and formal theories of politics.

Sara Ferejohn is a senior in the Department of Political Science at the University of California, Berkeley, and an undergraduate research assistant at the Institute of Governmental Studies. Ferejohn serves as the publicity director of the Cal Band.

Brian J. Gaines is Assistant Professor of Political Science at the University of Illinois at Urbana-Champaign. He received his Ph.D. from Stanford University in 1995. His research focuses on elections and legislative behavior in the Anglo-Atlantic democracies.

Elisabeth R. Gerber is Assistant Professor of Political Science at the University of California, San Diego. She received her doctorate in political science from the University of Michigan in 1991 and spent three years on the faculty at California Institute of Technology before joining the UCSD faculty in July of 1994. Gerber's research is concerned with the representational consequences of various electoral laws and political institutions. She has written numerous papers on the policy consequences of direct legislation in California and other states and is currently completing a book on the subject. She has also studied differences in electoral laws in the American states and their effects on election outcomes and representation. Gerber's work has been published in the *American Political Science Review*, the *American Journal of Political Science*, *Political Research Quarterly*, and *Political Behavior*.

Joseph R. Grodin graduated from UC Berkeley and then obtained his J.D. degree from Yale Law School and a Ph.D. in labor law and labor relations from London School of Economics and Political Science. He has practiced law (1955-72), taught law (1972-79 and 1987-present), served as a member of the California Agricultural Labor Relations Board (1975-76), as an Associate Justice and Presiding Justice of the California Court of Appeal (1979-82), and as an Associate Justice of the California Supreme Court (1982-87). After leaving that court he rejoined the faculty at Hastings Law School, where he is a Distinguished Professor, teaching constitutional law, labor and employment law, and other courses. Currently he is on leave as a visiting professor at Stanford Law School. Grodin has written widely in the areas of labor and employment law, state constitutional law, and judicial process. He is co-author of a book on the California Constitution.

D. Roderick Kiewiet is Professor of Political Science and Dean of Students at California Institute of Technology. He received his Ph.D. from Yale University and has been at CalTech since 1979. He is the author of *Macroeconomics and Micropolitics* (1983) and co-author of *The Logic of Delegation* (1991). He has authored or co-authored numerous articles on subjects including the effects of economic conditions upon voting behavior, legislative organization, Russian politics, electoral strategy, and ethnic politics. Kiewiet's current research interests include legislative politics, direct democracy at the state and local level, and state government finance. He has served on the editorial boards of the *American Journal of Political Science*, *Social Science Quarterly*, and *Political Research Quarterly*.

Mathew D. McCubbins, Professor of Political Science, received his Ph.D. from California Institute of Technology in 1983. He was a fellow at the Center for Advanced Studies in the Behavioral Sciences for 1994-95 and is currently the coordinator of the newly established Law and the Behavioral Sciences Project and an editor for JLEO. His principle works include *The Logic of Delegation: Congressional Parties and the Appropriations Process* (1991); *Under the Watchful Eye: Managing Presidential Campaigns in the Television Era* (1992); and *Structure and Policy in Japan and the United States* (1995). He is the author of numerous journal articles and specializes in political economy.

Margarita Najar graduated with honors from the Department of Political Science, University of California, Berkeley, in 1994. Najar's honor's thesis on Christine de Pisan was completed under the guidance of her advisor, Professor Hanna Pitkin. Najar is a management consultant for Anderson Consulting.

Roger G. Noll is the Morris M. Doyle Professor of Public Policy in the Department of Economics at Stanford University. At Stanford, he is also the director of the Public Policy Program and the Program in Regulatory Policy in the Center for Economic Policy Research, and a professor by courtesy in the Graduate School of Business and the Department of

Political Science. Noll received his undergraduate degree in mathematics from California Institute of Technology and his doctorate in economics from Harvard University. The author of seven books and more than 100 articles, Noll's research interests include government regulation of business, public policies regarding research and development, the business of professional sports, applications of the economic theory of politics to the study of legal rules and institutions, and the economic implications of political decision-making processes. Noll's most recent book, written in collaboration with Linda R. Cohen, is *The Technology of Pork Barrel* (1991). He is currently undertaking research on federal programs to promote research joint ventures, the policy consequences of the admission of the westerns states, the role of federalism in regulatory policy, the politics and economic consequences of state constitutions, and international comparative studies of the performance of regulatory institutions and infrastructural industries.

Nathaniel Persily is a graduate student in the Department of Political Science at UC Berkeley and a law student at Stanford University. He received a joint bachelor's and master's degree in political science from Yale University in 1992 and spent the following year at the Hebrew University of Jerusalem as a Raoul Wallenberg and Rotary Foundation Scholar. Since entering Berkeley in 1993, Persily has held Jacob Javits and Edith Pence Scholarships and worked as a graduate student researcher at the Institute of Governmental Studies. His research interests deal with issues of comparative constitutionalism, federalism, and American constitutional law.

Robert C. Post is Professor of Law at Boalt Hall School of Law. He received his B.A. and Ph.D. from Harvard University and his J.D. from Yale University. After clerking for Chief Judge David L. Bazelon of the U.S. Court of Appeals for the D.C. Circuit and for Justice William Brennan, Jr., of the U.S. Supreme Court, Post was a litigator with the Washington, D.C., law firm of Williams and Connolly. He joined the Boalt faculty in 1983. A specialist in the area of First Amendment theory and constitutional jurisprudence, Post is the editor of *Law and the Order of Culture* (1991). He is currently writing Volume X of the Oliver Wendell Holmes Devise History of the United States Supreme Court, 1921-30. Post is on the board of editors of *Representations*, and he is currently the chair of the board of governors of the University of California Humanities Research Institute at Irvine. Recent publications include "Managing Deliberation: The Quandary of Democratic Dialogue," *Ethics* (1993); "Between Democracy and Community: The Legal Constitution of Social Form," *NOMOS XXXV* (1993); and "Racist Speech, Democracy, and the First Amendment," *William and Mary Law Review* (1990).

Margaret Jane Radin is Professor of Law at Stanford University. She received her A.B. from Stanford University in 1963, where she majored in music, her M.F.A. in music history from Brandeis University in 1965 as a Woodrow Wilson Fellow, and became a Ph.D. candidate in music at Berkeley in 1968. Radin received her J.D. from the University of Southern California in 1976. Prior to joining the Stanford law faculty in 1990, she was Carolyn Craig Franklin Professor of Law at USC. Radin has taught at UCLA and Harvard as a visiting professor of law.

Daniel B. Rodriguez is Professor of Law at Boalt School of Law. He received his B.A. from California State University, Long Beach, and his J.D. from Harvard University. Upon graduation from law school, he clerked for Judge Alex Kozinski of the U.S. Court of Appeals for the 9th Circuit. He joined the Boalt faculty in 1988. His research interests include the political economy of administrative law, public law theory, and local government law. Rodriguez was a visiting professor at the Free University of Amsterdam in 1992, was a John M. Olin Fellow of Law and Economics at the University of Virginia in 1993, and was a visiting scholar at the Hoover Institution in 1993.

Daniel L. Rubinfeld is Robert L. Bridges Professor of Law and Professor of Economics at the University of California, Berkeley. He received a B.A. in mathematics from Princeton University in 1967 and a Ph.D. in economics from the Massachusetts Institute of Technology in 1972. He is the author of numerous articles in public finance and law and economics, and two textbooks, *Microeconomics* and *Econometric Models and Economic Forecasts* (both with Robert S. Pindyck). Rubinfeld has been a fellow at the National Bureau of Economic Research, the Center for Advanced Studies in the Behavioral Sciences, and the Guggenheim Foundation. His major research fields are public economics, the economics of the legal process, and law and statistics.

Charles Ruhlin is a graduate student in economics and jurisprudence and social policy at UC Berkeley and a research associate at the Center for the Study of Law and Society. He has a masters degree in public administration from Harvard's Kennedy School of Government and has consulted to the Mexican government on antitrust policy. In addition to comparative analysis of dispute resolution institutions, his research interests include international finance and banking regulation, and generational aspects of fiscal federalism and organization.

Harry N. Scheiber is Stefan Riesenfan Professor of Law and History at Boalt Hall School of Law, UC Berkeley. He teaches in Boalt's Jurisprudence and Social Policy doctoral program and was chair of the Berkeley Faculty Senate (1994-95). Scheiber is a graduate of Columbia College (1955) and holds the doctorate in history from Cornell University (1961). He has twice been a Guggenheim Fellow, twice a Fellow at the Center for Advanced Study in the Behavioral Sciences, and held fellowships or research appointments from the Rockefeller Foundation, the National Endowment for the Humanities, and the Social Science Research Council. His major writings are in American legal and constitutional history and in American economic history. Some of the books he has authored or co-authored include *Ohio Canal Era: A Case Study of Government and the Economy, 1820-1861* (1968); *American Law and the Constitutional Order* (1978); and *Federalism and the Judicial Mind* (1992).

Mary Sprague holds a masters in public policy analysis from the Graduate School of Public Policy at the University of California, Berkeley. She received her A.B. in public policy from Stanford University. Currently a Javitz Fellow, she will be spending the next two years as a staff member of the United States Senate.

Barton H. Thompson, Jr., is Professor of Law at Stanford University, where he heads the law school's Environmental and Natural Resources Law Program. A 1976 graduate of both Stanford Law School and Stanford's Graduate School of Business, Thompson clerked for Chief Justice William H. Rehnquist of the United States Supreme Court. His research and writing focus principally on water resource policy, the impact of constitutional law on environmental regulation, and environmental enforcement.

Mary Walther received her B.A. in political science with honors from the University of California, Berkeley, in 1994. As a 1994 John Gardner Fellow, Walther joined the staff of Congressman Vic Fazio, where she served as his staff specialist for health care, welfare, and education. She is currently permanent staff member in Congressman Fazio's office. Walther is the author of "Marjorie Margolies-Mezvinsky: A Longshot Winner" in *Campaigning for Congress: Politicians at Home and in Washington* (1995).